EUROPEAN SOCIETY
OF INTERNATIONAL LAW SERIES

How International Law Works in Times of Crisis

EUROPEAN SOCIETY OF INTERNATIONAL LAW SERIES

The ESIL Book Series publishes high-quality volumes on the themes of ESIL Annual Conferences and ESIL joint events primarily. The volumes include chapters that are based on selected papers presented at ESIL events, revised to fit the theme and focus of the volume, and complemented by additional chapters that address topics that were not fully explored at the events, but that are essential for a full coverage of the theme.

How International Law Works in Times of Crisis

Edited by

GEORGE ULRICH
and
INETA ZIEMELE

OXFORD
UNIVERSITY PRESS

OXFORD
UNIVERSITY PRESS

Great Clarendon Street, Oxford, OX2 6DP,
United Kingdom

Oxford University Press is a department of the University of Oxford.
It furthers the University's objective of excellence in research, scholarship,
and education by publishing worldwide. Oxford is a registered trade mark of
Oxford University Press in the UK and in certain other countries

First Edition published in 2019

Published in the United States of America by Oxford University Press
198 Madison Avenue, New York, NY 10016, United States of America

British Library Cataloguing in Publication Data
Data available

Library of Congress Control Number: 2019941490

ISBN 978–0–19–884966–7

How International Law Works in Times of Crisis.
George Ulrich and Ineta Ziemele, Oxford University Press (2019).
© The several contributors.
DOI: 10.1093/oso/9780198849667.001.0001

Contents

How International Law Works in Times of Crisis. George Ulrich and Ineta Ziemele, Oxford University Press (2019).
DOI: 10.1093/oso/9780198849667.001.0001

PART II IMMUNITIES THEMES

PART III SUSTAINABLE DEVELOPMENT THEMES

PART IV PHILOSOPHICAL PERSPECTIVES: PROBING KEY CONCEPTS AND PREMISES IN INTERNATIONAL LAW

PART V DOMESTIC ENGAGEMENT WITH INTERNATIONAL LAW

PART VI EPILOGUE

Table of Cases

NATIONAL COURTS

How International Law Works in Times of Crisis. George Ulrich and Ineta Ziemele, Oxford University Press (2019).

DOI: 10.1093/oso/9780198849667.001.0001

Germany

Hong Kong

Italy

Netherlands

Portugal

Romania

Russia

Slovenia

Spain

Switzerland

United Kingdom

United States

INTERNATIONAL COURTS AND TRIBUNALS

Arbitration Institute of the Stockholm Chamber of Commerce (SCC)

Court of Justice of the European Union

European Court of Human Rights

Inter-American Court/Commission of Human Rights

International Centre for Settlement of Investment Disputes (ICSID)

International Court of Justice

Iran-United States Claims Tribunal (IUSCT)

Nuremberg Military Tribunals

Permanent Court of Arbitration

Permanent Court of International Justice

Special Court for Sierra Leone

United Nations Commission on International Trade Law

Table of Legislation

How International Law Works in Times of Crisis. George Ulrich and Ineta Ziemele, Oxford University Press (2019).
DOI: 10.1093/oso/9780198849667.001.0001

Decisions

Directives

Regulations

INTERNATIONAL TREATIES, CONVENTIONS AND INSTRUMENTS

United Nations Resolutions

List of Contributors

Carlos Espaliú Berdud, Dr., Associate Professor of Public International Law and European Law, Universitat Internacional de Catalunya, Barcelona

Marion Blondel, Postdoctoral researcher, Université Saint-Louis, Brussels

Stephen Bouwhuis, Assistant Secretary, Attorney General's Department, Commonwealth of Australia

James Crawford, Judge of the International Court of Justice

Stefano Dominelli, Junior Researcher in International law, University of Genoa

Ilze Dubava, Lawyer, State Chancellery of the Republic of Latvia

Patrycja Grzebyk, Associate Professor at the University of Warsaw, vice-director of the Network on Humanitarian Action at the University of Warsaw

Kushtrim Istrefi, Assistant Professor of Public International Law and Human Rights at Utrecht University

Zeynep Kıvılcım, Associate Professor, Einstein Fellow, Faculty of Humanities and Social Sciences, Humboldt-Universität zu Berlin

David Kosař, Director of the Judicial Studies Institute (JUSTIN) at the Law Faculty of Masaryk University, Brno

Sandra Krähenmann, Thematic Legal Adviser, Geneva Call

Irena Nesterova, Researcher at the Institute of Legal Science, Faculty of Law, University of Latvia

Jan Petrov, Researcher at the Judicial Studies Institute (JUSTIN) at the Law Faculty of Masaryk University

Ignacio de la Rasilla, Han Depei Chair Professor of International Law and One Thousand Talents Plan Professor, Wuhan University Institute of International Law

Ilze Ruse, Associate Professor, Riga Graduate School of Law

Jean-Marc Sauvé, Vice-president of the French Conseil d'État

Annalisa Savaresi, Lecturer in Environmental Law, University of Stirling

Fernando Dias Simões, Associate Professor, Faculty of Law of the Chinese University of Hong Kong

How International Law Works in Times of Crisis. George Ulrich and Ineta Ziemele, Oxford University Press (2019).
DOI: 10.1093/oso/9780198849667.001.0001

Pavel Šturma, Professor of International Law, Charles University Faculty of Law (Prague), Member of the UN International Law Commission (Geneva)

Ozlem Ulgen, Senior Lecturer in Law, School of Law, Birmingham City University

George Ulrich, Professor of Human Rights at the Riga Graduate School of Law

Ineta Ziemele, Professor of International Law and Human Rights at the Riga Graduate School of Law.

Introduction

International Law and Crisis: Dialectical Relationship

George Ulrich and Ineta Ziemele

The 12th Annual Conference of the European Society of International Law (ESIL) took place in Riga, Latvia, on 8–10 September 2016. The Society organized the conference together with the Riga Graduate School of Law and the Constitutional Court of the Republic of Latvia. The overall purpose of the conference was to address the theme: How International Law Works in Times of Crisis. This was a conference characterized by several firsts. It was the first time that the Annual Conference had moved to Eastern Europe. It took place in a country with a wealth of relevant history for international law. It was also the first time that among the organizers we could count a highest national court. The conference gathered one of the highest numbers of participants, that is, 420 from 43 countries representing different parts of the world. The general theme of the conference reflected on both past times and current developments and on both regional and global challenges implicating international law.

At the time of the conference, the word 'crisis' had become part of government and media rhetoric with renewed force following the Russian occupation of Crimea and the Mediterranean migration crisis. Europe was facing serious challenges to its integration project. The Society and the organizers in Riga decided to address several questions about the role of international law and that of international lawyers. It identified two levels of consideration. One has to do with specific contemporary challenges to the international legal order. Are these qualitatively different from what has been faced previously and is international law up to the task of dealing with the given challenges? Against this background, the conference addressed the question whether international law itself should be considered to be in crisis.

It should be recognized, as a point of departure, that crises are not new to the discipline of international law. Arguably, a sense of crisis is in fact integral to the discipline. The role, relevance, and institutions of international law have always been challenged, especially in times of rapid societal and technological change, open conflict, and large-scale dislocation of people—just to mention a few of the triggering factors. By the same token, however, moments of crisis may offer new

George Ulrich and Ineta Ziemele, *International Law and Crisis: Dialectical Relationship* In: *How International Law Works in Times of Crisis*. Edited by: George Ulrich and Ineta Ziemele, Oxford University Press (2019).
DOI: 10.1093/oso/9780198849667.003.0001

possibilities. Historically, such moments have led to innovative solutions in the world community, including new institutional configurations and normative developments. International lawyers should therefore from time to time confront and address the sense of crisis embedded in their discipline. It is precisely this that the speakers and chairs of the fora and agora, indeed all participants of the annual conference in Riga, attempted to do.

Among the many areas where international law and international lawyers face serious challenges the following were selected and included in the conference programme: new forms of warfare and armed conflict; European human rights architecture; minority rights and security considerations; state immunity; territorial disputes; economic and financial crises; migration and refugee flows; cyber security; terrorism; sustainable development; gender; climate change; enforcement of international law; and global and European governance. The question that ran like a thread through discussions in the various panels was whether current crises and pressing challenges can be accommodated within the dominant legal framework in the related areas of law? Should we consider that certain challenges and developments in the current era are showing the established legal regime as longer sufficient to deal with those challenges?

The present publication conveys a rich, albeit partial, representation of the debates in Riga in September 2016. The most salient themes have to do with challenges to the international legal order in relation, first, to security, diplomatic relations, and, in particular, immunities; second, to promotion of sustainable development including in response to climate change; third, to certain fundamental conceptual ambiguities and critical perspectives on the premises underlying the international legal architecture; and fourth to the application of international law at the domestic level. The chapters included in the present volume have been grouped under these main headings.

The conference opened with two plenary debates. First, the then Vice President of ESIL, Professor Anne van Aaken, moderated a debate between Judge James Crawford of the International Court of Justice and Professor Lauri Malksoo of Tartu University (Estonia). The opening words of Judge Crawford in 'Reflections on Crises in International Law' make for a suitable foreword to this volume. Each reader will retain different aspects of Judge Crawford's reflections. The editors would emphasize the following. 'International law exists because crises occur, and crises occur, in a way, because international law exists, because the absence of any constitutional order, other than constitutional order of states, is still the dominant fact of our world.' Moreover, in Crawford's view there is nothing to prevent us from reversing existing international law. Yet, 'international law is principled in a sense that there are certain basic values incorporated, which are systemically spread throughout it'. The chapters presented in this volume show how each time new challenges bring out the same questions of the nature and function of international law and how the solutions adopted settle for reinforcing the existing and the known. Second, Pauls Raudseps, a journalist from the Latvian weekly *Ir* interviewed HE Edgars Rinkevičs, the Minister of Foreign Affairs of Latvia. The debate with the Latvian Minister of Foreign Affairs confirmed the importance of a legal framework for political solutions to pressing geopolitical challenges. It also showed the need for a more evident presence of the voices of international lawyers when decision-makers deal with crises.

Most of the chapters, while addressing a wide variety of subjects and spelling out the challenges that legal regimes face, come to rather similar conclusions; that is, they look at the way forward and identify solutions within dominant legal regimes and existing structures. In other words, the possible scenario which Crawford brought up concerning the reversal of rules has not been evidenced so far. Given the challenges we are facing today, it is no surprise that many of the articles selected for inclusion in this volume could be grouped under security themes. The pivotal importance of security considerations in the world and in Europe is confirmed by the fact that the European Union (EU) which, according to Ilze Rūse in her chapter, 'Multiple Actors in Framing EU External Policy: The Case of the EU Global Security Strategy', for years has not been able to agree on an updated strategy for its coordination of foreign affairs and external defence, finally adopted a Global Strategy for EU Foreign and Security Policy in 2016. This shows that even in the security area so typically guarded as part of state sovereignty, better coordination has emerged as the way to deal with security challenges regionally and globally. In 'Activating the Mutual Assistance Clause of the Treaty on the European Union and the Right of Self-defence', Carlos Espaliu Berdud also discusses the response by the EU and its implications for international law. His analysis and reflections deal with Article 42(7) of the Treaty on European Union (TEU) which embodies a mutual assistance clause in case of armed attack on the territory of one member of the EU. This clause was activated after the Paris terrorist attacks in 2015. Based on state practice, especially the response by the EU to the these attacks, Berdud argues that a new customary rule is about to emerge accepting that the right to self-defence as embodied in Article 51 of the United Nations (UN) Charter also applies in responding to terrorist attacks. On the contrary, in her chapter, 'Authorizing Attacks in Response to Terrorist Attacks: A Dark Side of the Law of Armed Conflicts', Patrycja Grzebyk questions the attempt by states to expand the boundaries of applicable legal regimes and to conflate *ius in bello* and *ius ad bellum* when faced with the challenge of the war on terror. She points out the evident difficulties faced by states when dealing with terrorist groups which do not respect any legal regime within international law. Nevertheless, after the analysis she concludes that in the long run, a combination of the two regimes will have far-reaching negative results. The author notes that a recognition thus emerges that respecting the original distinction between the two legal regimes allows for more appropriate legal guidance, including human rights, during armed conflict with Al-Qaeda or 'Islamic State'/ Daesh. Another aspect of the new kind of armed conflict is the unprecedented number of so-called foreign fighters who join terrorist groups. Due to the large numbers, argues Sandra Krähenmann in her chapter, 'The Challenge of "Foreign Fighters" to the Liberal International Legal Order', foreign fighters are considered a particular security threat both abroad and at home. However, she argues that this phenomenon does not just pose a security threat but also challenges fundamental elements of the international order based on the rules that embody liberal values. The author sums up four aspects of this challenge and examines the response to the phenomenon of 'foreign fighters', qualifying it as somewhat extraordinary. UN Security Council resolution 2178 imposes sweeping obligations on states, including by creating a new offence in criminal law: travel for terrorist purposes. Krähenmann examines two counterterrorism measures in particular: limitations on freedom of expression extending to digital space and deprivation of citizenship. Her conclusion is that the effectiveness and thus the necessity of these two counterterrorism measures are doubtful. In this context, chapters about the implications of human rights law are unavoidable. Kushtrim Istrefi in 'The Policy Effects of the Decisions of European Courts on Targeted Sanctions: Whither Human Rights?', and Irena Nesterova in 'The Crisis of Privacy and Sacrifice of Personal Data in the Name of National Security: CJEU Rulings Strengthening EU Data Protection Standards', each deal with different aspects of human rights law that are engaged when states resort to various measures aimed at preventing or countering terrorism. Istrefi discusses the approach of the European Court of Human Rights (ECtHR) in '*Al-Dulimi v Switzerland*' which dealt with the fair trial guarantees at the domestic level for persons who are placed by the UN Security Council on the sanctions lists and are thereby deprived of access to their bank accounts. *Al-Dulimi* is considered to continue setting the European approach to UN Security Council measures and follow in the footsteps of the *Kadi* case law of the Court of Justice of the European Union (CJEU). Istrefi points out that the approach of the ECtHR is to be preferred to that of the CJEU as a more balanced one. He especially points out the usefulness in the long-term of the arbitrariness test developed by the ECtHR. Irina Nesterova tackles the problem of mass digital surveillance in relation to the right to privacy and data protection. Arguably in this context, the CJEU has been an important guarantee for the right to privacy and data protection. The author examines the Court's approach in the *Digital Rights Ireland* and *Schrems* judgments. She points out that responses to security challenges such as mass collection of data and creation of large-scale databases as well as data exchanges with third countries pose serious questions in the light of the CJEU case law. The Court requires a link between the data retained and a threat to public security that cannot be established if the data of unsuspicious persons are retained in bulk. Nesterova shows how in a short period the Court's position has affected policy and legislative decisions in the EU. The chapter highlights an area which clearly faces numerous challenges beyond security issues and where the responses found indicate future solutions while upholding existing legal principles of the right to privacy and data protection. Overall, the section on security themes amply shows that the modern digital era has opened up new possibilities and encouraged new social phenomena. The situation is one that the current law has not been developed to address in many instances but the authors also show that, at least to some extent, the law is adjusting to be capable of embracing the new phenomena. Given that a different legal path can be taken, the chapters also highlight the dangers that some options might entail. Certainly, unilateral approaches and those that move away from some basic values that have been protected in the past should be carefully evaluated. The authors have noted in this new context the need for a strengthened cooperative attitude among decision-makers at an international level and confirmed that solutions could be found within existing legal regimes which stand their ground.

The section on law of immunities advances the current debate in this field where the law itself could be said to be in crisis. The law on immunities has been central to the legal order that was born with the 1648 Treaty of Westphalia though, while remaining central to the current international legal order, it faces challenges from rules which have emerged since 1945 embodying liberal values such as human rights rules. This section contains contributions by two authors, Stefano Dominelli and Pavel Šturma. In 'Recent Opposing Trends in the Conceptualisation of the Law of Immunities: Some Reflections', Dominelli sums up the challenge to the very foundation of state immunity by exploring Italian jurisprudence, asking what—if *jus cogens* were to become a widely accepted limit to immunity—would remain of state sovereignty itself? He takes the view that Italy, through its domestic practice in the area of state immunity, is in violation of international law but acknowledges that other domestic courts may follow. His conclusion is that while the law on state immunity has not reached a state of crisis, it is subjected to various tensions. Pavel Šturma continues in his chapter, 'How to Limit Immunity of State Officials from Foreign Criminal Jurisdiction', with the question whether international law on immunities is in crisis by focusing on immunity of state officials from foreign criminal jurisdictions. In view of the developments following the Second World War in the field of international criminal law, as well as the growing rejection of impunity for most serious crimes, important arguments are raised against immunity of state officials. Šturma explores the debate starting with the *Arrest Warrant* case and draws a distinction between immunity *ratione personae* and immunity *ratione materiae*, making the point that if the latter is accepted the very purpose of international criminal law would be undermined. He proposes a solution for various legal developments which, among others, contain exceptions to immunity rules, even though he shares the view of the International Court of Justice (ICJ) with regard to the difference between *jus cogens* rules and the rules on immunity as procedural rules. The possible conflict of norms, says the author, is to be resolved by means of systemic interpretation of international law. He proposes to consider as *lex specialis* those conventions that place obligations on states to prosecute perpetrators of serious crimes. The author is convinced that international law as a coherent legal system cannot at the same time provide for obligations and prevent compliance with those obligations.

A prominent theme in numerous conference debates relates to sustainable development, both in response to widening income gaps and access to public and private goods and services and in relation to large-scale global issues, such as climate change, which in various ways challenge the international law framework. In 'The Future We Want: Sustainable Development as an Inherent Aim of Foreign Investment Protection', Ilze Dubava invokes a latent crisis of international investment law, which in an era of triumphant neoliberalism is not immediately apparent. She cautions that unchecked investment regimes are potentially self-defeating as they prevail at the expense of wider policy concerns. This has been a point of contention in recent investor–state disputes before international arbitration tribunals and in the drafting of international trade and investment agreements. In response to this predicament, Dubava proposes a systemic rethinking of the international investment regime *from within* in the form of a reconceptualization of economic development within the wider framework of sustainable development. As a new paradigm of international law, this provides a principle to integrate investment protection concerns and general public interests. Such a reconceptualization, Dubava argues, will ensure that states retain their sovereign policy space while still forging an attractive investment environment. Turning to international climate law, Annalisa Savaresi proceeds from the premise that climate change should not be thought of as a stand-alone challenge or crisis; rather, it is a 'risk multiplier' that exacerbates virtually all crises facing humanity in the current era. In 'The Paris Agreement and the Future of the Climate Regime: Reflections on an International Law Odyssey', Savaresi identifies several promising features of the then newly adopted Paris Agreement, including a shift in policy orientation from 'targets and timetables' to a 'pledge and review' approach; the institution of a unitary system for reviewing implementation; focusing attention on collective long-term goals; and the involvement of a broad cross-section of parties—including non-state actors—in tackling climate change. However, crucial challenges remain in relation to ensuring effective monitoring and reporting and in developing a common standard for emissions trading.

In 'How International Law Works in Investment Law and Renewable Energy: Green Expectations in Grey Times', Fernando Dias Simões examines the emerging practice of arbitration tribunals in cases where governments, ostensibly in the public interest and typically in response to a financial crisis, change the existing legal provisions regulating investment in renewable energy. 'The crux of the question', in the words of the author, 'is whether investors can seek compensation under international investment treaties when governments encourage investments via economic support schemes but decide to reduce or eliminate them after investment costs are already sunk.' To determine this, tribunals must 'strike a balance between foreign investors' reliance on the regulations that underpin their long-term investments and the host state's right to adapt regulations to new circumstances'. A detailed review of nine recent arbitration disputes reveals that respondent states prevailed in five cases whereas investors were successful in four. On that basis, Simões provisionally concludes that economic support mechanisms are susceptible to regulatory change and that the precise application of investment protection standards in such cases is far from well established. They tend rather to be determined on a case-by-case basis in view of the underlying national regulatory frameworks. Even so, certain basic principles such as transparency, stability, non-discrimination, due process, and investors' legitimate expectations are emerging as core elements of the applicable investment law. This is essential from a climate policy point of view, as the predictability of arbitration outcomes will have important consequences for future investments in renewable energy.

In the cluster of philosophy-oriented chapters, concepts and underlying presuppositions of international law are critically examined from different perspectives. In 'Vulnerability as a Virtue: An Attempt to Transpose the Care Ethic in International Law', Marion Blondel undertakes a feminist-inspired review of international law from the point of view of an ethics of care. She views the prominence of the concept of vulnerability in contemporary international law as a symptom of crisis, as it is intrinsically linked with exposure to risk and insecurity in modern society. However, consistent with the overall conference theme, the author seizes this implicit crisis as an opportunity to rethink notions of individuation and human fulfilment, recognition, autonomy, relatedness, and responsibility. These various analytical strands converge in an anthropological underpinning of international law which acknowledges emotion and interdependence as primary features of the human condition, thus enabling us to recognize vulnerability as a virtue and the vulnerable subject as agent. The chapter by Ignacio de la Rasilla, 'Playing Hide and Seek with "*Vergangenheit, die nicht vergehenwill*" ("a Past that Will Not Pass") in the History of International Law', examines the role of international law in confronting dark chapters of history. The Spanish Historical Memory Act of 2007 is presented as a test case illustrating complexities in the legal review of crimes committed under Francoism from 1936 until 1952, during and after the Civil War. The author identifies obstacles to a candid confrontation with atrocities in the past at four levels: a general neglect of history in international law; an only very recent interest in the 'darker legacies' of international law; the weight of a national pact of forgetfulness (reinforced by amnesties enacted in the name of national reconciliation); and what the author identifies as 'national identity myths'. He calls for a heightened readiness of the discipline of international law to confront its own complicity in legitimating repressive regimes and argues that the capacity to confront blind spots in historical memory may contribute to avoiding recurrence.

Ozlem Ulgen, in her chapter on 'Human Dignity in an Age of Autonomous Weapons: Are We in Danger of Losing an "Elementary Consideration of Humanity"?' looks to Immanuel Kant for a conceptual framework to analyse the challenges posed to the international legal order by a rapid proliferation of autonomous weapons. Ulgen argues that weapon technologies that preclude interaction and interrelatedness between warring parties are fundamentally at odds with human dignity, both with regard to the underlying presumption that all humans possess equal moral value and with regard to fundamental principles of respectful human treatment, including in situations of armed conflict. Ulgen further argues that the use of robotic killing machines confounds basic premises of the theory of just war and runs counter to the categorical imperative that moral precepts must be made universal—which a rule that permits mistreatment and death by autonomous weapons clearly cannot be. Moreover, the complete separation between combatants and human targets generates a dangerous human accountability and responsibility gap and threatens to perpetuate a 'cycle of irrationality'. These are profound challenges that international law in the current era needs to confront squarely. Zeynep Kıvılcım, in 'La Démocratie Radicale dans les Discours Légaux Contemporains au Rojava au Cœur de la "Crise" Syrienne: Une Analyse Genrée', draws attention to the pursuit of radical democracy and gender equality in Rojava, Northern Syria, in the wake of the Syrian civil war. This has been widely overlooked in the general confusion and sense of crisis generated by multiple interwoven conflicts. Kıvılcım argues that the case is significant not only due to its immediate local and regional implications but also because the Kurdish women's movement is spearheading an original feminist theory, 'jineology', which is adapted to the context of the Middle East. The movement's reconceptualization of the principle of self-determination without the state under the banner of democratic confederalism is potentially instructive for international relations and international law theory, precisely at the intersection of crisis and new opportunities. As observed by the author, 'this war, in which serious violations of human rights and humanitarian law are committed by different parties to the armed conflict, is also a very important site of resistance where the women of the Middle East, the peripheral subjects of international law, reconceptualize democracy, politics, sovereignty, and law through their daily practices'.

A final cluster of topics addresses issues related to the interface of national judiciaries and administrative bodies with international law mechanisms. This is seen as integral to the effectiveness of international law and its ability to rise to challenges facing the international community. In their joint chapter, 'The Domestic Judiciary in the Architecture of the Strasbourg System of Human Rights', David Kosař and Jan Petrov examine the role of domestic judiciaries in the functioning of the ECtHR. They concur with the widely accepted emphasis on the crucial role of domestic judiciaries in diffusing and filtering judgments of the Strasbourg Court but caution that the matter is more complex than apparent at first sight, as the domestic layer of the convention system involves a plurality of actors (many of which are non-judicial) with divergent, sometimes conflicting attitudes to Strasbourg judgments and diverse powers and willingness to make these operational. Based on this observation, the authors call for and delineate a more detailed and precise analysis of the interface between domestic and international judicial actors and bodies, which in turn may yield insights into how to enhance the effectiveness of the latter. In 'The Chilcot Report: International Law and Decision-Making in Times of Crisis', Stephen Bouwhuis undertakes a detailed examination of the inquiry by the United Kingdom into its decision to intervene in Iraq, commonly referred to as the 'Chilcot Report'. Disputes about the legality of the intervention notwithstanding, Bouwhuis argues that the inquiry demonstrates that the responsible UK decision-makers in fact did treat favourable legal advice concerning the legality of the intervention under international law as a requirement for the intervention to proceed. While not necessarily indicative of the conduct of other governments in analogous predicaments, the case provides a positive indication of the importance of international law to government decision-making, and in this light it is argued that more should be done to alert key decision-makers to the finely balanced nature of legal advice.

As an epilogue to the volume, Jean-Marc Sauvé, Vice-President of the State Council of France at the time, provides 'Reflections on How International Law Functions in Times of Crisis'. It contains reflections by the author on the theory of crises and future prospects, especially at the European level. Sauvé observes that 'the solutions to contemporary crises will be primarily political, but law can make a contribution and the legal community has a role to play in this respect'. This marks a point where the Latvian Foreign Minister and the Vice-President of the State Council, even though intervening at different times during the conference, echoed one another on a fundamental issue of substance. Sauvé formulated three priorities. The first of these is the need to recall and strengthen the benefits of international cooperation and of European integration. This can be done through enhanced organization of international society based on a didactic approach which counters discourses and strategies founded on isolation and autarchy. Secondly, fundamental rights must be defended without compromise. Finally, 'in the contemporary framework of legal pluralism, national identities and sovereignties must be re-linked with the European enterprise'.

This underlying sense of optimism about the contemporary relevance of international law may be regarded as a somewhat unexpected outcome of the ESIL 2016 conference papers. As explained at the outset, the very idea of the conference was to discuss the crisis of and in international law. The debate and papers selected for this book show under different themes the processes and new phenomena that international law has to face and address, but the authors confirm that legal regimes and mechanisms are able to address them. We believe that the way forward, as indeed several authors have noted, is the view taken on the nature of the international legal system. It is only by considering that it is a coherent and comprehensive legal system based on some shared values that appropriate solutions to conflicts, tensions, and new challenges can be found.

Reflections on Crises and International Law

James Crawford

If there were no international crises, many of us would not be international lawyers. We go around crying 'crisis', at the same time trying to find one and seeing one sometimes when it is not there. We validate calling ourselves international lawyers by reference to some international crisis which touched us in one way or another.

Certainly this is true of me. I would not be an international lawyer but for an international crisis, but the crisis was a long time ago, in 1962—the Cuban missile crisis. At that point of time I was thirteen and recall walking around the school playground; I had a premonition, which turned out to be true, that there was an imminent prospect of nuclear conflict, if not an outright thermonuclear war, at least the first use of nuclear weapons since the end of the Second World War. I felt that there needed to be something that people could do, even from a place as remote as Adelaide, to influence events of that sort which could affect so many. I do not disparage Adelaide for being remote; everywhere is remote from somewhere and the people who live there do not regard it as remote, but my brother, who lives in Hong Kong, says that Adelaide is a good place to have come from, and he has a point. So that was my case.

I was struck later when I realized I was teaching international law to students who had not been born at the time of the Cuban missile crisis and had never heard of it. Of course, for students the past is not a continuum, it is a given; and their view of the past is rather that the Cuban missile crisis was coeval with the fall of Constantinople, Attila the Hun, and possibly other, even more remote events. So we define ourselves by reference to our own crises, the crises of our time.

As a judge of the International Court with its general remit, I can hardly talk about modern crises or recent events. Given that every generation has its crises and defines itself in terms of the crises that it has had, it would be possible to have a lengthy discussion on the crises of the period of 1814–1815, for example: the status of Napoleon on Elba, the status of Napoleon during the 100 days, his position vis-à-vis his captors after Waterloo, and so on. It turns out, if we look at them carefully, that they were crises which were resolved in part through the use of then-current legal language; some of it being used, no doubt, for the first time. Part of the fascination and difficulty with our subject is that it tries to deal with events that may have

James Crawford, *Reflections on Crises and International Law* In: *How International Law Works in Times of Crisis*. Edited by: George Ulrich and Ineta Ziemele, Oxford University Press (2019).
DOI: 10.1093/oso/9780198849667.003.0002

occurred for the first time, using language which is sanctified by time. That is a tension in the field of international law, but it is part of its attraction.

Isabel Hull has looked carefully at the crises of the First World War and argues that there was much more legal about them than more recent scholars have been prepared to concede.[1] I believe that was true of the crises of the 1920s, the Locarno Pact, the crises of the 1930s, the 1940s, and so on, until we become conscious that we too have our own crises and can talk about them with the authority of someone who was there at the time.

I suppose the crises in which international law played no role occurred where international law provided no language over which to disagree. Someone once said that a treaty is a disagreement reduced to writing. A crisis is a key conflict of interests reduced to the language of disagreement, and the language of many disagreements is a language we are used to using when talking about international relations. International relations scholars who profess to despise international law nonetheless use normative language drawn from international law all the time. But we should get worried when we have an international crisis in which the language of international law is not used; it is something, even if it is used in contentious, non-opposable, possibly counterproductive ways. In dealing with the problems of the world, we first have to reduce them to writing or to a sort of writing; we have to reduce them to a sort of dialogue, and the dialogue operates across time to produce outcomes which may or may not have been predictable at the time, may or may not have been influenced strongly or at all by international law, but nonetheless international law was part of the fabric of those crises.

Can we say anything useful about how international law works in relation to crises? The first thing, which is obvious and which international lawyers have to confront, is that each of those crises is a crisis because of a conflict of power and a conflict of pretensions by leading states or the leaders of leading states. Any analysis which ignores the element of power and power rivalry will obviously miss the point. At the same time international lawyers would say, 'I've got to use words when I talk to you, I've got to use words when I disagree with you', and international law provides as a minimum the vocabulary, the words that are used in such cases, whether it is the vocabulary of collective self-defence, of pre-emptive action, or of quarantine. The thesis of Abram Chayes' book on the Cuban missile crisis is that given a President and an Attorney General who were deeply conscious of the risks they were running, international law provided (not necessary lawfully) a median solution, a way out, which could be adopted and which would not be thought to conflict with the major security aims of both parties.[2] When we discovered later (what I had intuited in that Adelaide school playground) that the Soviet naval

[1] I. Hull, *A Scrap of Paper. Breaking and Making International Law during the Great War* (Cornell University Press 2014).

[2] A. Chayes, *The Cuban Missile Crisis: International Crisis and the Role of Law* (OUP 1974).

commander in the Caribbean had the authority to use nuclear weapons without recourse to Moscow, we realized that that mattered.

Likewise, when we find out later that it was an international lawyer who suggested a hotline between Washington and Moscow, we should be grateful for our profession. It cannot necessarily solve crises but it can sometimes provide the means for their solution. So, part of the language of international law is the language of communication and compromise, and one of the problems we have with modern international law is that so much of its language does not seem to allow for compromise but tends to force disputants to state their positions in zero-sum ways. Part of the difficulty of trying to cope with, for example, the aftermath of cases of state responsibility is to realize that 'law rules, OK?', but only with a question mark.

There is another category of crisis which seems to me to create difficulties for international law in a way in which (in retrospect, at least) the crises I have been talking about did not, which is where people in dealing with these situations deliberately abandon international law for other means. There would have been an international law of the Third Reich;[3] there would have been an international law of the Vienna Award.[4] It would not have been an attractive international law, but who said we went into the subject because it was attractive? We went into it because it is a way of being a part of and conceivably influencing crises.

1 On Power Structures and Power Interests and their Channelling in a Certain Way via International Law

International law works at a given moment if it works at another given moment in the future. The problem is we do not know at the first given moment what is going to happen; we do not know whether our efforts will be successful. We bring to situations certain professional techniques—the capacity to draft, to write things down, the capacity to learn from what has been written down before, and the capacity, I hope, to be honest about our ability to learn. You can trace the decline to the point of virtual collapse of international law during the 1930s by tracking the treaties of alliance that were concluded in the 1920s and 1930s. You realize the decline in normativity—notwithstanding the award to Austen Chamberlain and Gustav Streseman of the Nobel Prize for Peace—when you realize that the Locarno Pacts, which brought Germany into the League of Nations, only guaranteed the boundaries of Western Europe, not the boundaries of Eastern Europe. Subsequently, each failure led to further failure to the point where the whole

[3] D. Vagts, 'International Law in the Third Reich' (1990) 84 *American Journal of International Law* 661.

[4] Award relating to the Territory ceded by Romania to Hungary (Second Vienna Award), 30 August 1940, 28 RIAA 407.

system was discredited. So, after the failure of the League of Nations under British and French leadership to stop the invasion of Ethiopia or to reverse it, a group of states, including the Scandinavian states, proposed a resolution which in effect amended Article 8 of the Covenant to be non-binding; that is to say, the core of the Covenant mechanism was eviscerated because of reaction to that failure. That was an example of system failure in operation and you can trace it accurately by looking at successive texts. But, and this is the interesting 'but', I have got to use words when I speak to you, and international law of a sort continued to be used. The seminal event in terms of the collapse of international law in the 1930s was the Molotov–Ribbentrop Pact. There is a photograph showing Molotov and Ribbentrop at the moment of signature of the Pact. Stalin is walking up and down behind them with a big smile on his face. We know that was acting because he was extremely worried, but the person who was putting the Pact in front of Ribbentrop, whose signature eventually condemned him to death under international law, was the German legal adviser. International lawyers were there for bad as well as for good. At a certain point you have to realize that the techniques and capacities that you have as a result of what is, hopefully, increasingly good training is only half the picture, and the other half is your determination, which does not come from law, that you use these in a way which is constructive or which you deem to be constructive as a way out of whatever crisis it is you happen to have the fortune to own at a time.

2 On Whether International Law Might Work Differently

I agree that there is not much point in having very bad international law; if you are convinced of its badness, it is better to go and do other things, like development economics or history of art. Yet, if you look carefully behind the scenes and not just at the headlines, you see that there is a process going on. It is a serious mistake to identify the process of international law with the process of adjudication. There is very little adjudication of crises in international law; there just isn't time. The Permanent Court of International Justice was counted as having been generally successful; for example, it established a modality of operation of multimember courts which did not exist in international law before that time. But Hans Morgenthau made the point that the one case which was clearly a failure was the *Customs Union* case, which was the one crisis case the Permanent Court faced. He worked on the assumption, which I agree with, that the actual decision was wrong, but, as I said, very little of the resolution of crisis is done in terms of adjudication. What adjudicators do is to move in later and help tidy up the mess. They are a bit like curators of an assembly hall: after the assembly is gone they clean up the mess and get ready for the next performance. We must be honest about our role in those respects, but we also, I think, can conceive the possibility that at least someone is cleaning up the mess, and that these issues remain on the table (or the floor) because, *inter alia*, there is no closure of them in terms of international law.

One of international law's strengths (it has many weaknesses) is its capacity to keep issues on agendas for decades, and that was true of the Baltic States. In my Hague lectures I compared the Melian dialogue with the position of East Timor and Indonesian 'annexation'. About one-third and possibly more of the pre-1975 population of East Timor died during that conflict. The death rate was higher than the worst death rate of any country in the Second World War, yet international law, as against Indonesia and also against Australia, two of the more powerful states in the region, kept that dispute from being closed. It was not very much, but it was facing something which was for the East Timorese people an existential crisis. Thus, Timor-Leste remained on the agenda, became independent, and is re-litigating some of the consequences, some of the aspects of the dispute.[5] It is an object lesson in the capacity of international law to keep things on agendas, which is a valuable capacity, even if it is not the capacity to tell the most powerful entities in the world what they must do. For the moment, the opportunity to be part of a linguistic community which addresses such issues is something. It may not be very much, but we have not been offered very much.

3 On Three Wishes for International Law to Work Better in Times of Crises

It is difficult to wish without being cast in fairy-tale mode, which is not very comfortable. An easy answer would be not to have any wishes for international law at all. All my wishes are personal. International law is what happens to you when your preferred candidate does not get elected or when the United Kingdom decides to leave the European Union, or whatever crisis might unfold. If everything went well, we would not be needed, except perhaps as a subspecies of aviation law or some other speciality. International law exists because crises occur, and crises occur, in a way, because international law exists, because the absence of any constitutional order, other than constitutional order of states, is still the dominant fact of our world.

If I had a wish, I suppose I would have the same wish three times; it might make it a more powerful wish. I wish that we would come to more stable methods of collaboration than we have had. This is one of the reasons I regret the outcome of the Brexit referendum; it reduces the options open for the development of new

[5] J. Crawford, *Chance, Order, Change. The Course of International Law* ((AIL-Pocket 2014) 49–54.

methods of doing international law. Over the coming years we will see just how much multilateralism, internationalism, regionalism, and international law the world can stand.

The fundamental difficulty is that our allegiances are essentially national. I have met a few people whose primary allegiance was to the European Union, but a high proportion of them derived their income, or much of it, from the European Union. I doubt there are many ordinary Dutch or British people whose main allegiance is to the Union. That is true more fundamentally about the international system. As international lawyers we may have some allegiance to international law, but that is simply a *sine que non* of the system; it is not particularly a strength. A strength would be lots of people who are not international lawyers having a primary allegiance to it, and, as far as I know, such people do not exist. People have their primary allegiance to their own state, and international law is useful if it helps their state to address the problems that it has. As professional international lawyers we are used to living in a system in which international law prevails over national law, but national sentiment prevails over international sentiment, and it is that combination which gives character to international law. If you read real international lawyers of the eighteenth century or even the seventeenth century grappling with problems and not talking about general theory, as they were too prone to do, you find that they're dealing with issues which we are dealing with, even in much the same way. So, there is a continuity of technique, and my wish is effectively that that continuity of technique would be put in operation in systems more resilient than the ones we currently have.

4 On Whether International Law Might be Sliding into a Crisis of its Own

International law exists in some basic way. It is a predicate of the system in which there is no constitutional arrangement between the units of power, but how much there should be is a completely contingent question, and there is no rule in international law that says you cannot have a reversal of rules. Things can go backwards as well as forwards, which is true of trains and cars as well, and is quite a good design feature in trains or cars. It may be a necessary design feature for international law as well that it would be able to go backwards, keeping reserved capacity for new creation, visible when international law reached its lowest point in 1940. At the same time, and with increasing determination, those who were involved in the post-war period were trying to work out how much international law the world could afford, and, concretely, what should be done to avoid the failures of the League of Nations. I think that the 1945 settlement, despite the many criticisms of it, was basically a positive one. It illustrated the capacity of the bureaucratic systems of the world to absorb lessons, in particular those of 1919, and I hope we do not throw it away. We can reduce as well as increase the scope and influence of the World Trade Organization (WTO), but the WTO itself was part of the 1945 settlement; the International Criminal Court was part of the 1945 settlement, though even longer deferred. I still support the International Criminal Court despite all the problems that it has had because I think there are situations when we have to get individuals out of circulation in accordance with due process, and I am not keen on targeted killings. I hope this is not utopian, although it is optimistic.

5 On International Law as Servant of Compromise or as Fuel for Crisis because it has become Principled

International law is principled in the sense that there are certain basic values incorporated, which are systemically spread throughout it, so the value of the autonomy of states and near-state entities is spread through the law of nationality, for example, and spread throughout aviation law, and that is why international law is a system. Not for any grand constitutional purpose, which we might wish to have, but because it is the way we regulate a decentralized system, nothing more or less than that.

The principles are principles in the sense of *Brownlie's Principles*. They are almost descriptive principles, principles required if you have a society of this general character. Take Article 53 of the Vienna Convention on the Law of Treaties on peremptory norms: there is quite a series of statements by writers pontificating about peremptory norms and saying 'therefore, it follows that ...'. It often turns out that some rather absurd conclusion 'must be' peremptory. International law does not work that way, not even the international law of peremptory norms. If you want to make it work that way you'd be living in a world of your own; a coherent world, a happy world because you'd get along with all the other participants in that world, but not one that bears much relationship to reality. My eighteen-month-old son has his own language; it is a quite elaborate language, wonderful in fact, except no-one else speaks it. We do not want an international law that no-one else speaks; there are problems enough already.

6 On E.H. Carr's *Twenty Year's Crisis* and Parallels between the Interwar Period and Modern Disillusionment with International Law

I was influenced by E.H. Carr's work; *The Twenty Years' Crisis* was a splendid polemic. If you look at the world now, there are about 200 more or less functioning entities at the state level. In E.H. Carr's time there were less than fifty, mostly Western, and some had large empires. I think the situation we are in, in 2016, is better than the situation E.H. Carr envisioned we would be in, and international law is part of the functioning of that system. There are economic problems, but they are greatly exaggerated. There is a rise of protectionism, but the rise and fall of protectionism is a long-term process, largely uninfluenced by law. Then there are the problems we all know about—radicalism and terrorism, large-scale migration. International law is an arsenal of devices for dealing with situations, and one of the situations it deals with is the reduction of violent inter-state conflict. Of course, there has always been violent inter-state conflict, but there is a lot less than there used to be; most of the victims of war in the last fifty years have been victims of civil war. Where international war breaks out there are usually pressures to contain it (the Security Council, etc.). It is much more difficult to contain civil war, and that is because we lack the various devices international law uses to contain international conflicts, which is its primary concern.

PART I
SECURITY THEMES

Authorizing Attacks in Response to Terrorist Attacks

A Dark Side of the Law of Armed Conflicts

*Patrycja Grzebyk**

1 Introduction

The armed conflict against Al-Qaeda, the Taliban, and associated forces continues to this day.[1] This includes armed operations against 'Islamic State'/Da'esh and other splinter groups.[2] Even if hostilities take place in the territory of various states, these are treated as elements of the same conflict which would probably never end.[3]

* The project was financed from the means of the Polish National Center of Science based on the Decision No. DEC-2013/11/D/HS5/01413.

[1] See, e.g., speech by Harold Hongju Koh, Legal Adviser, US Department of State, Annual Meeting of the American Society of International Law, Washington, DC, 25 March 2010 (available at <http://www.state.gov/s/l/releases/remarks/139119.htm>) in which he stated: 'the United States is in an armed conflict with al-Qaeda, as well as the Taliban and associated forces, in response to the horrific 9/11 attacks, and may use force consistent with its inherent right to self-defense under international law'. See also Harold Hongju Koh, 'The Trump Administration and International Law' (2017), 56 *Washburn Law Journal* 413, 454; as well as the speech by Stephen W. Preston, 'The Legal Framework for the United States' Use of Military Force Since 9/11', Annual Meeting of the American Society of International Law, Washington, DC, 10 April 2015 (available at <http://www.defense.gov/News/Speeches/Speech-View/Article/606662/the-legal-framework-for-the-united-states-use-of-military-force-since-911>).

[2] See, e.g., S/RES/2214 of 27 March 2015. Cf. also, e.g., S/RES/2253 of 17 December 2015 or S/RES/2396 of 21 December 2017 where the Security Council in the context of foreign terrorist fighters referred to: 'entities such as (ISIL), the Al-Nusrah Front (ANF) and other cells, affiliates, splinter groups or derivatives of ISIL, Al-Qaida or other terrorist groups'.

[3] The White House, 'Report on the Legal and Policy Frameworks Guiding the United States' Use of Military Force and Related National Security Operations' (December 2016) 12: 'Progress has been made in disrupting and degrading al-Qa'ida's core and senior leadership, and in disrupting and degrading ISIL. But these groups still pose a real and profound threat to U.S. national security. As a result, the United States remains in a state of armed conflict against these groups as a matter of international law, and the 2001 AUMF continues to provide the President with domestic legal authority to defend against these ongoing threats.' Cf. also State of Israel, *The 2014 Gaza Conflict (7 July–26 August 2014): Factual and Legal Aspects*, May 2015, para. 4: 'The 2014 Gaza Conflict was another peak of hostilities in the ongoing armed conflict that has been waged against Israel for well over a decade by terrorist organisations operating from the Gaza Strip.' (available at <http://mfa.gov.il/ProtectiveEdge/Documents/2014GazaConflictFullReport.pdf>). See also Christopher Greenwood, 'The Relationship between ius ad bellum and ius in bello' (1983) 9 *Review of International Studies* 221, 224 ff.

Patrycja Grzebyk, *Authorizing Attacks in Response to Terrorist Attacks: A Dark Side of the Law of Armed Conflicts* In: *How International Law Works in Times of Crisis*. Edited by: George Ulrich and Ineta Ziemele, Oxford University Press (2019).
DOI: 10.1093/oso/9780198849667.003.0003

States engaged in this conflict struggle with legal constraints derived from human rights law (HRL) and the law on the use of force (*ius contra bellum*/*ius ad bellum*) concerning use of lethal force against specific persons who remain in the territory of a third state.

At the same time, the terrorist groups involved in this conflict openly disregard legal constraints, even though technically both the law of armed conflicts (LOAC) and HRL are binding on them.[4] Moreover, the terrorist groups pay no heed to the sovereignty of states and the inviolability of their territory. In consequence, they have greater flexibility in conducting armed operations in comparison to states.

Not surprisingly, states have been looking for a solution to overcome legal obstacles to their actions. The United States (US) has been a leader in these efforts and therefore the focus in this chapter is on US practice. Winning the 'war on terror' has been perceived as a priority,[5] but proper justification of the legality of actions undertaken against terrorist armed groups is important for both internal and international policy reasons.

The intermingling of norms of the LOAC and of the law on the use of force seemed to be extremely useful in justifying particular instances of the use of force. While the LOAC puts 'inconvenient' restraints upon warfare, as a regime it is still far more permissive concerning the use of lethal force against persons and objects in comparison to HRL.

In addition, on the one side, the provisions of the LOAC can be used to justify violations of the norms of the law on the use of force or to stretch them to the extreme taking into account authorization of attacks on military objectives which can be derived from the LOAC. On the other hand, interpretation of the norms of self-defence can be used to justify the broadening of the material and geographic scope of the LOAC. Overall, this means that problems with the absence of consent of third states for military intervention on their territory, or difficulties with

[4] On the question of how the LOAC or the HRL bind armed groups, see Special Tribunal for Sierra Leone, Decision, *Prosecutor v Sam Hinga Norman*, SCSL-2004-14-AR72(E), 31 May 2004, para. 22; International Court of Justice, Judgment, Military and Paramilitary Activities In and Against Nicaragua (*Nicaragua v United States*) Merits, 27 June 1986 (ICJ Reports 1986, p. 14) paras 218–19; Jann K. Kleffner, 'The Applicability of International Humanitarian Law to Organized Armed Groups' (2011) 93(882) *International Review of the Red Cross* 443 ff; Robin Geiss, 'Humanitarian Law Obligations of Organized Armed Groups' in Marco Odello and Gian Luca Beruto (eds), *Non-State Actors and International Humanitarian Law. Organized Armed Groups a Challenge for the 21st Century. 32nd Round Table on Current Issues of International Humanitarian Law Sanremo, 11–13 September 2009* (Franco Angeli 2010) 93 ff; Daragh Murray, 'How International Humanitarian Law Treaties Bind Non-State Armed Groups' (2015) 20(1) *Journal of Conflict and Security Law* 101; Marco Sassòli, 'Taking Armed Groups Seriously: Ways to Improve their Compliance with International Humanitarian Law' (2010) 1 *Journal of International Humanitarian Legal Studies* 5, 13; Jean d'Aspremont and Jérôme de Hemptinne, *Droit international humanitaire* (Editions A. Pedone 2012) 95 ff; Andrew Clapham, 'Human Rights Obligations of Non-state Actors in Conflict Situations' (2006) 88(863) *International Review of the Red Cross* 491 ff.

[5] See, e.g., National Security Strategy of the United States (December 2017) 10–11; available at: <https://www.whitehouse.gov/wp-content/uploads/2017/12/NSS-Final-12-18-2017-0905.pdf>.

application of HRL's restrictive approach to the use of lethal force, are to some extent overcome by 'blurring of the boundaries of the applicable framework'.[6]

The objective of this chapter is to demonstrate how the provisions of two theoretically separate regimes, the LOAC and the law on the use of force, are abused in order to justify attacks in various regions of the world, often below the threshold of an armed conflict. This tendency is more visible in times of crisis. Then, states are still interested in having legal justification for their actions but they tend to see the role of law differently: the law is expected to serve the authorities, rather than to guide them, when the state's fundamental interest—its security—is under threat.

The chapter argues that a reinterpretation of the norms of these two regimes has opened the way for violating both other states' sovereignty and the rights of particular persons. The chapter stresses that political and strategic decisions are undertaken after considering legal arguments, and thus the recent trend of abusive interpretation of the LOAC and the law on the use of force could encourage decision-makers to resort to military measures instead of using less intrusive instruments, such as criminal cooperation. The chapter also includes a discussion of whether the distinction between *ius in bello* and *ius contra bellum* remains valid, and contemplates whether it might be falling into desuetude despite the protests of legal scholars.

The first part of the chapter describes how the LOAC is treated as a source of authorization for attacks and why states today tend to use it rather than HRL as a legal basis for their actions in the area of counterterrorism. The second part demonstrates how the modern interpretation of the LOAC in fact encourages states to execute military actions in third states and broadens the scope of exceptions from the prohibition on the use of force enshrined in Article 2(4) of the UN Charter of 1945.[7] The third part discusses the validity of the traditional approach to the complete separation of the LOAC and the law on the use of force, in light of recent practice. It addresses the impact of the mix of arguments based in both regimes on observance of their respective principles.

2 Does the Law on Armed Conflicts Limit or Authorize?

One of the main purposes of the fundamental treaties of the LOAC, that is, the Geneva Conventions Relative to the Protection of War Victims of 1949[8] (GCs) and their Additional Protocols of 1977[9] (APs), was to constrain hostilities in order to

[6] A/HRC/14/24/Add.6, 28 May 2010, para. 3, Philip Alston, 'Report of the Special Rapporteur on extrajudicial, summary or arbitrary executions, Addendum, Study on targeted killings'.

[7] 1 UNTS XVI.

[8] 75 UNTS 31.

[9] 1125 UNTS 3.

avoid losses among those not taking part in them and to protect property whose destruction is not necessary in terms of military requirements.

Both the GCs and the APs excluded persons with a particular status (combatants)[10] or those who engaged in some conduct (direct participation in hostilities)[11] from protection against attacks. Nonetheless, treaties and customary law limit the means and methods of attacking even persons in these categories.[12] Two questions arise in this light. Does the LOAC authorize attacks against specific categories of persons? If so, does this authorization prevail over limitations derived from other regimes, such as the law on the use of force?

On the one hand, nowhere in the treaty is there an obligation or encouragement to kill any categories of persons, such as combatants. The so-called Martens clause stresses that 'populations and belligerents remain under the protection and empire of the principles of international law, as they result from the usages established between civilized nations, from the laws of humanity and the requirements of the public conscience'.[13] Thus, even those who are fighting are not totally deprived of the protection of law, since belligerents have no full freedom of decision about their life and death. In addition, the letter of the Martens Clause emphasizes that the absence of an explicit prohibition of something under treaty law does not mean that it is automatically permitted according to the LOAC.[14] It could be argued that it is actually perverse to use the provisions of the LOAC as a source of legitimization of killing and destroying, that is, providing a legal basis for hostilities while its original role was to limit them.[15]

On the other hand, it can also be argued that the absence of an explicit prohibition of attacks on persons with a specific status results in the absence of a necessity to prove the existence of a permissive rule to kill them.[16] The purpose of

[10] Arts 43 (2), 48, 50 AP I; cf. Art. 4 GC III.

[11] Arts 51 (3) AP I, 13 (3) AP II, 3 GC.

[12] See Art. 35 AP I and rule 70 of Customary International Humanitarian Law (available at: <https://www.icrc.org/customary-ihl/eng/docs/v2_rul>). Customary rules of the LOAC were identified in Jean-Marie Henckaerts and Louise Doswald-Beck, *Customary International Humanitarian Law*, Vol. I (ICRC, CUP 2005).

[13] The Martens Clause appeared in the preamble to the 1899 Hague Convention (II) with respect to the laws and customs of war on land. It was also restated in the Geneva Conventions of 1949 (Art. 63 GC I, Art. 62 GC II, Art. 142 GC III, Art. 158 GC IV) and in the two Additional Protocols of 1977 (Art. 1(2) AP I, Preamble of the AP II). For more about the Martens Clause see Rupert Ticehurst, 'The Martens Clause and the Laws of Armed Conflict' (1997) 317 *International Review of the Red Cross* 125. See also Michael Schmitt, 'Military Necessity and Humanity in International Humanitarian Law: Preserving the Delicate Balance' (2010) 50(4) *Virginia Journal of International Law* 796, 800.

[14] See, e.g., Yves Sandoz, Christophe Swinarski, and Bruno Zimmermann (eds), *Commentary on the Additional Protocols of 8 June 1977 to the Geneva Conventions of 12 August 1949* (International Committee of the Red Cross, Martinus Nijhoff 1987) 39.

[15] Richard R. Baxter and Hamilton De Saussure, 'Comments' in Peter D. Trooboff (ed.), *Law and Responsibility in Warfare. The Vietnam Experience* (The University of North Carolina Press 1975) 63 ff.

[16] See Permanent Court of International Justice, Judgment, *The Case of the S.S. 'Lotus'* Publications of the PCIJ, Ser. A, No. 10, at 19–20; but cf. Judge Simma, Declaration on the International Court of Justice, Advisory Opinion, Accordance with International Law of the Unilateral Declaration of Independence in Respect of Kosovo, 22 July 2010 (ICJ Reports 2010, p. 403) para. 2.

the Martens clause is only to stress that the main principles of the LOAC must always be respected, even if the legal status of persons and objects is unclear. The LOAC limits hostilities but it is a result of compromise between the principles of humanity and of military necessity. The original purpose of the LOAC was not to eliminate hostilities altogether, and so there must be some categories of persons against whom lethal force can be used because it is required by military necessity. If the LOAC describes who and what is protected mainly by negative definitions (as according to Article 50 AP I civilians in international armed conflicts are those who are not combatants and civilian objects are those which are not military objectives under Article 52 AP I), it must at the same time indicate who and what is a military objective whose destruction is allowed as necessary in light of the LOAC. Limitation and authorization are two sides of the same coin.[17] If the possibility of attacks is limited but hostilities as such are not outlawed, the mentioned limitations indicate who and what can be attacked.[18]

Greater doubts arise with regard to non-international armed conflict (NIAC). On the one hand, Article 3 of the GCs and AP II do not establish combatant status. Thus, these treaties do not provide anyone with combatant privileges, including the right to take part in hostilities, that is, to attack specific persons and objects. Therefore, the Law of NIAC cannot be treated as a source of authorization to use lethal force. Authorization must be found in other regimes instead, for example in national law.[19] This logic works perfectly for states when they deal with traditional non-international armed conflict taking place on their territory. Yet when the conflict spreads to the territory of other states, the legal situation becomes far more complicated as it is impossible to refer to authorization derived from a national law to attack particular persons (categories of persons) on the territory of a third state to which obviously a different national law applies.

On the other hand, Article 3 of the GCs and Article 4 of the AP II indicate that only those who are not taking an active part in hostilities enjoy protection. This

[17] Cf. Jens D. Ohlin, 'The Duty to Capture' (2013) 97(4) *Minnesota Law Review* 1268, 1304; Geoffrey Corn and Chris Jenks, 'Two Sides of the Combatant Coin: Untangling Direct Participation in Hostilities from Belligerent Status in Non-international Armed Conflicts' (2011–2012) 33 *University of Pennsylvania Journal of International Law* 313, 330.

[18] Another issue is to decide whether military necessity must always be taken into account, even in the case of attacks on lawful targets, or if it is already incorporated into existing provisions concerning the principle of distinction, thus there is no need to assess the usefulness of attacking military objectives.

[19] The present article deals with the so-called Hague Law, i.e., conduct of hostilities. However, it is worth noting that the question of authorization in non-international armed conflicts was also discussed in the context of the 'Geneva Law', i.e., detention of civilians/fighters; see, e.g., Ryan Goodman, 'The Detention of Civilians in Armed Conflict' (2009) 103 *American Journal of International Law* 48 and debate on *EJIL Talk!* including posts by Lawrence Hill-Cawthorne, Dapo Akande, 'Does IHL Provide a Legal Basis for Detention in Non-International Armed Conflicts?' (7 May 2014) and 'Locating the Legal Basis for Detention in Non-International Armed Conflicts: A Rejoinder to Aurel Sari' (2 June 2014); Aurel Sari, 'Sorry Sir, We're All Non-State Actors Now: A Reply to Hill-Cawthorne and Akande on the Authority to Kill and Detain in NIAC' (9 May 2014); Kubo Mačák, 'No Legal Basis under IHL for Detention in Non-International Armed Conflicts? A Comment on Serdar Mohammed v. Ministry of Defence' (3 May 2014).

in turn implicitly results in the legal possibility of attacking those who are taking direct part in hostilities. The Law of NIAC does not prohibit prosecution of members of a non-state party for taking part in hostilities (Article 6 AP II), but at the same time it does not establish a basis for such prosecution. Therefore, there is a possible inequality concerning the treatment of states and non-state actors in that authorization for members of a non-state armed group to take part in hostilities which could be possibly derived from the LOAC can be lifted by national law.

The dark (that is, permissive, authorizing) side of the LOAC is clearly visible when we compare its approach to the use of lethal force to the approach promoted by HRL.[20] The LOAC does not outlaw killing certain categories of persons, such as combatants in international armed conflicts (Article 43 AP I) or fighters in non-international armed conflicts,[21] only because of their status, that is, membership in armed forces or in armed groups (with some exceptions concerning medical personnel and chaplains).[22] In addition to status-based attacks, the LOAC accepts conduct-based targeting of persons directly engaged in hostilities in every kind of conflict (Article 51 (3) AP I and Article 13 (3) AP II). As the LOAC establishes combatant privileges (at least in IACs), including the right to attack, that is for example, to kill certain persons, thus the state of armed conflict and the related application of the LOAC 'lays a blanket of immunity' over conduct normally regarded as criminal.[23]

In turn, HRL prohibits any arbitrary deprivation of life.[24] Arbitrariness is understood as the use of lethal force for reasons other than protection of

[20] See more Gloria Gaggioli, *L'influence mutuelle entre les droits de l'homme et le droit international humanitaire à la lumière du droit à la vie* (Editions Pedone 2013) 243 ff.

[21] Arts 3 AP I or AP II do not use the term 'fighter' or 'combatant'. The notion of 'fighter' was introduced in para. 1.1.2 of the *San Remo Manual relating to Non-International Armed Conflicts* as a separate category of persons which are not protected against attacks in NIAC. Moreover, according to Rule 1 of Customary IHL (<https://ihl-databases.icrc.org/customary-ihl/eng/docs/v1_rul_rule1>) parties to the conflict should distinguish between 'civilians' and 'combatants' also in non-international armed conflicts. There are also publications in which authors use the term combatant to describe the situation of fighters in NIAC (see, e.g., Gérard Avio, *Le statut de combattant dans les conflits armés non internationaux* (Bruylant 2013) *passim*; Lorenzo Redalié, *La conduite des hostilités dans les conflits armés asymétriques: un défi au droit humanitaire* (La Librairie *générale de droit et de jurisprudence* 2013) 100.

[22] In the case of non-international armed conflicts, no provision similar to Art. 50 AP I is applied in international armed conflicts which would limit the possible status of persons to two—namely, civilian and combatant. Therefore, in theory it is possible to distinguish many different statuses in NIACs. That is why—based on propositions by the International Committee of the Red Cross concerning definitions of civilian in NIAC and excluding from this category members of non-state armed groups with a combat function (see Nils Melzer, *Interpretive Guidance on the Notion of Direct Participation in Hostilities under International Humanitarian Law* (ICRC 2009) 27)—it is possible to distinguish the separate status of a fighter, i.e., a member of an armed group; see, e.g., Michael Schmitt, 'Deconstructing Direct Participation in Hostilities: The Constitutive Elements' (2010) 42 *International Law and Policy* 697, 704; Geoffrey Corn and Chris Jenks, 'Two Sides of the Combatant Coin: Untangling Direct Participation in Hostilities from Belligerent Status in Non-international Armed Conflicts' (2011–2012) 33 *University of Pennsylvania Journal of International Law* 313, 337.

[23] Chris A. Anderson, 'Assassination, Lawful Homicide, and the Butcher of Baghdad' (1992) 13 *Hamline Journal of Public Law & Policy* 291, 300.

[24] See, e.g., Art. 6 International Covenant on Civil and Political Rights, 19 December 1966, 999 UNTS 171.

life[25] and, apart from exceptional instances, 'for the prevention of crime or in effecting or assisting in the lawful arrest of offenders or suspected offenders'.[26] In consequence, according to HRL, there is no room for a status-based authorization to kill anyone. Consequently, it cannot be planned in advance that some categories of persons can be killed; other measures must always be taken into account and the whole operation must be planned in such a way as to minimize the risk of death or injury.[27] Yet judicial or quasi-judicial organs do not undermine the legal possibility of killing combatants/fighters in situations of armed conflict.[28]

The differences in the approach to the use of lethal force explain why it is much more convenient to apply the LOAC instead of HRL when there is a perception that certain persons must be eliminated for the sake of security.[29] The LOAC does not require risking the life of state agents to arrest a person threatening security of the state. It accepts application of the shoot-to-kill policy resulting—in theory—in permanent elimination of the threat.[30]

In consequence, it is not surprising that despite various judgments of different international institutions,[31] the US and Israeli authorities stubbornly stress in their official statements that first, HRL is not applied to hostilities in armed conflicts,

[25] See para. 9 of the Basic Principles on the Use of Force and Firearms by Law Enforcement Officials of 1990, adopted by the Eighth United Nations Congress on the Prevention of Crime and the Treatment of Offenders, Havana, Cuba, 27 August–7 September 1990 (available at <http://www.ohchr.org/EN/ProfessionalInterest/Pages/UseOfForceAndFirearms.aspx>), which stresses that 'intentional lethal use of firearms may only be made when strictly unavoidable in order to protect life'.

[26] See Commentary to Art. 3 of The Code of Conduct for Law Enforcement Officials adopted by General Assembly resolution 34/169 of 17 December 1979 (available with commentary at <http://www.ohchr.org/EN/ProfessionalInterest/Pages/LawEnforcementOfficials.aspx>).

[27] Cordula Droege, 'The Interplay between International Humanitarian Law and International Human Rights Law in Situations of Armed Conflict' (2007) 40(2) *Israel Law Review* 310, 344–5.

[28] See, e.g., European Court of Human Rights, Former First Section Judgment, Case of *Isayeva v Russia* (App No 57950/00), 24 February 2005, para. 180, European Court of Human Rights, Former First Section Judgment, Case of *Isayeva, Yusupova and Bazayeva v Russia* (App Nos 57947/00, 57948/00, and 57949/00), 24 February 2005, para. 178. See also Marco Sassòli and Laura M. Olson, 'The Relationship between International Humanitarian and Human Rights Law: Where it Matters: Admissible Killing and Internment of Fighters in Non-international Armed Conflicts' (2008) 90(871) *International Review of the Red Cross* 599, 612. See also on the lawfulness of killing conscripts in Karima Bennoune, 'Toward a Human Rights Approach to Armed Conflict: Iraq 2003' (2004–2005) 11 *University of California Davis Journal of International Law and Policy* 171, 186–7, 193, 205.

[29] It is also worth noting that the LOAC was invoked by states before the Inter-American Court/Commission of Human Rights not only to justify particular use of lethal force (see, e.g., IACHR, *Juan Carlos Abella v Argentina*, Judgment, 18 November 1997, § 73, 147–8, 161) but also to undermine the Court's competence to assess alleged violations of the LOAC, see, e.g., IACtHR, *Las Palmeras v Colombia*, Judgment on Preliminary Objections, 4 February 2000, § 28, 32–34 and Judgment (Merits), 6 December 2001, § 37; cf. IACtHR, *Bámaca-Velásquez v Guatemala*, Judgment (Merits), 25 November 2000, § 207–9.

[30] On doubts concerning the legality of applying a 'shoot to kill' policy during armed conflicts, see Ryan Goodman, 'The Power to Kill or Capture Enemy Combatants' (2013) 24(3) *European Journal of International Law* 819.

[31] See, e.g., International Court of Justice, Armed Activities on the Territory of the Congo (*Democratic Republic of the Congo v Uganda*), ICJ Rep 2005, 168, para. 216; European Court of Human Rights, Grand Chamber Judgment, *Hassan v UK*, App No 29750/09, 16 September 2014 (HUDOC), para. 77; European Court of Human Rights, Grand Chamber Judgment, *Cyprus v Turkey*, App No 15318/89, 18 December 1996, para. 52.

and second, they are not obliged to apply HRL extraterritorially in the case of armed operations conducted in the territory of a third state (as it is not under their jurisdiction).[32] They often describe the LOAC as *lex specialis*—a term once used and then abandoned by the International Court of Justice[33]—in order to guarantee that assessing the legality of depriving someone of life (for example in so-called targeted killings) will be done only from the perspective of the LOAC.

In light of the above, it is worth noticing how the attitude to the applicable legal framework of counterterrorism operations has drastically changed. Upon ratification of the GC of 1949 and of the AP of 1977, it seemed clear that LOAC should not be applicable in the case of terrorist attacks. Those attacks are considered criminal and subject to law enforcement measures.[34] As a side note, this does not affect the prohibition on spreading terror among civilian populations, which is sometimes undertaken by armed groups (or state forces) which were (are) parties to armed conflict.[35] In consequence, the LOAC could clearly be used, in the framework of an armed conflict, as a legal basis to assess the lawfulness of attacks against 'terrorists' qualified as combatants/fighters or civilians taking part in hostilities. Yet in this scenario, application of the LOAC was triggered not by the use of terror but by the existence of an armed conflict.

In principle, terrorism was considered as an internal problem, a type of criminal activity.[36] Therefore, even during an armed conflict, terrorists who were not members of the armed forces of a party to the conflict should be countered through law-enforcement measures. If a terrorist group undertook transnational operations,

[32] CCPR/C/USA/CO/4; 23 April 2014, para. 4; CCPR/C/USA/CO/3/Rev.1, 18 December 2006, para. 10; A/50/40, 3 October 1995, para. 284; CCPR/C/ISR/CO/4, 21 November 2014, para. 5; CCPR/C/SR.1675, 21 July 1998, paras 23, 25; CCPR/CO/ISR/3, 3 September2010, para. 5; CCPR/CO/78/ISR, 21 August 2003, para. 11; CCPR/C/79/Add.93, 18 August 1998, para. 10; CCPR/C/ISR/2001/2, 4 December 2001, para. 8. See also Michael Dennis, 'Non-application of Civil and Political Rights Treaties Extraterritorially during Times of International Armed Conflict' (2007) 40 *Israel Law Review* 453, 457 ff; Yoram Dinstein, *War, Aggression and Self-Defence, 4th edn* (CUP 2005) 248 (the author speaks of so-called extra-territorial law enforcement operations to which the HRL is not applied).

[33] Description of the LOAC as *lex specialis* was used by the International Court of Justice in *Advisory Opinion on the Legality of the Threat or Use of Nuclear Weapons*, 8 July 1996 (ICJ Rep 1996, at 226), para. 25. However, in subsequent judgments, the ICJ avoided reference to *lex specialis* as it was much criticized for its previous usage, see Droege (2007) *supra* note 28, at 335.

[34] See, e.g., UK Declaration of 2 July 2002 to AP I: '(d) Re: ARTICLE 1, paragraph 4 and ARTICLE 96, paragraph 3. It is the understanding of the United Kingdom that the term "armed conflict" of itself and in its context denotes a situation of a kind which is not constituted by the commission of ordinary crimes including acts of terrorism whether concerted or in isolation.' Cf. also Nils Melzer, *Interpretive Guidance on the Notion of Direct Participation in Hostilities under International Humanitarian Law* (ICRC 2009) 24: 'Lastly, it should be pointed out that organized armed violence failing to qualify as an international or non-international armed conflict remains an issue of law enforcement, whether the perpetrators are viewed as rioters, terrorists, pirates, gangsters, hostage-takers or other organized criminals.'

[35] See Art. 33 GC IV, Art. 51 sec. 2 AP I, Art. 4 sec. 2 (d) and Rule 2 of Customary IHL.

[36] William Bradford, 'Barbarians at the Gates: A Post September 11th Proposal to Rationalize the Laws of War' (2004) 73 *Mississippi Law Journal* 639, 669; Thomas J. Bogar, 'Unlawful Combatant or Innocent Civilian? A Call to Change the Current Means for Determining Status of Prisoners in the Global War on Terror' (2009) 21(1) *Florida Journal of International Law* 29, at 68.

states were forced to enhance interstate cooperation on criminal matters still rooted in law enforcement measures and not in the LOAC.[37] There were no claims about the possibility of targeting terrorists on the territory of other states without the consent of those states (although there were instances of state-sponsored assassination).[38] If there was consent from a third state, it was quite clear that anti-terrorist actions must be undertaken according to the HRL and not the LOAC as there was no armed conflict. This meant that lethal force could be used only if it was absolutely necessary. A person could not be killed without a trial, and even if that person was the head of a terrorist group, it did not justify extrajudicial decapitation. The aim of the operation would be to capture and try the terrorist. Killing would not be an option but might happen accidentally or as a solution of last resort when no other means were available. In other words, in the law-enforcement framework, a terrorist could not be treated as a target who can be killed no matter what (s)he is doing at a given time.

This approach changed after 2001, when some states—primarily the United States— (re)discovered the lethal virtues of the LOAC. This legal framework has allowed for greater flexibility and effectiveness in eliminating terrorists without risking the life of a state's own troops and without engaging in long negotiations with third states.[39] The Americans started to refer to both self-defence and the LOAC to justify attacks against terrorists legally.[40] Qualifying a terrorist group as a party to an armed conflict has allowed the argument that the members of this group (at least those with a combat function) can be targeted (i.e., killed) at any time with the blessing of the LOAC and in consequence, HRL restrictions can be disregarded.

3 How to Trigger a Regime in a Non-triggerable Situation?

The conflict with Al-Qaeda and associated forces, including Da'esh, is qualified as non-international: on the one side there is (are) state(s), and on the other armed

[37] Christian J. Tams and James G. Devaney, '*Ius ad bellum*: Crossing Borders to Wage War Against Individuals' in Steven Barela (ed.), *Legitimacy and Drones. Investigating the Legality, Morality and Efficacy of UCAVs* (Ashgate 2015) 29.

[38] Anderson, *supra* note 24, at 291.

[39] See more in Laurie R. Blank, 'Targeted Strikes: The Consequences of Blurring the Armed Conflict and Self-Defense Justifications' (2012) 38(5) *William Mitchell Law Review* 1655, 1657 ff.

[40] Speech by Harold Hongju Koh, *supra* note 2: 'Thus, in this ongoing armed conflict, the United States has the authority under international law, and the responsibility to its citizens, to use force, including lethal force, to defend itself, including by targeting persons such as high-level al-Qaeda leaders who are planning attacks.' Also: 'But a state that is engaged in an armed conflict or in legitimate self-defense is not required to provide targets with legal process before the state may use lethal force.' Similar argumentation is presented in the American doctrine, e.g., Amos Guiora, *Legitimate Target: A Criteria-Based Approach to Targeted Killing* (OUP 2013) *passim*.

groups described as terrorists.[41] However, in order to qualify a situation as a non-international armed conflict, as opposed to an international armed conflict (which starts from the first shot between states' armed forces[42]), the appropriate threshold of hostilities must be achieved. Isolated terrorist attacks against an embassy, a ship, or even the tallest building cannot trigger the Law of NIAC as such.

Similarly, an appropriate threshold is necessary according to the law on the use of force in order to trigger a state's right to self-defence, as use of force in self-defence can be invoked only in response to an armed attack (Article 51 of the United Nations Charter). Terrorist attacks rarely achieve this threshold.[43]

Yet, in 2001 the international community allegedly agreed that the United States with its allies could invoke self-defence and commence an armed conflict on the territory of Afghanistan.[44] In consequence, Al-Qaeda's attacks on the World Trade Center and the Pentagon triggered the self-defence regime as well as application of the LOAC—both of international armed conflicts (against Taliban forces) and non-international armed conflicts (against Al-Qaeda), taking into account the scale of military response by the United States to the 11 September attack.[45]

In their fight against terrorism, the United States and other states have not stopped at mere response to the 'armed attack' which took place in 2001. They want to prevent any possibility of such attacks from those groups. However, Article 51 of the UN Charter excludes preventive strikes. That is why the idea of a worldwide smouldering conflict issuing from one incident over a decade ago (a

[41] See, e.g., Supreme Court of the United States, *Hamdan v Rumsfeld*, Secretary of Defense et al., 29 June 2006.

[42] Marco Sassòli and Antoine A. Bouvier, *How Does Law Protect in War? Cases, Documents and Teaching Materials on Contemporary Practice in International Humanitarian Law, Volume I, 2nd edn* (International Committee of the Red Cross 2006) 116; Robert Kolb and Richard Hyde, *An Introduction to the International Law of Armed Conflicts* (Hart Publishing 2008) 101.

[43] Cf., e.g., International Court of Justice Judgment of 27 June 1986, Case Concerning Military and Paramilitary Activities in and against Nicaragua (*Nicaragua v United States of America*), Merits, (ICJ Reports 1986, 14) para. 191; International Court of Justice, Judgment of 6 November 2003, Case Concerning Oil Platforms (*Islamic Republic of Iran v United States of America*) (ICJ Reports 2003, 161), para. 64.

[44] See letter of the Permanent Representative of the United States to the President of the UN Security Council or the invocation by NATO of Art. 5 of the North Atlantic Treaty, which pertains to self-defence. For more information about the reactions of the international community to the 9/11 attacks, see more in George K. Walker, 'The Lawfulness of Operation Enduring Freedom's Self-defense Responses' (2002–2003) 37(2) *Valparaiso University Law Review* 489, 499; Simone Preiser, '"Operation Enduring Freedom" and the UN Charter: The Terrorist Attacks of 11 September 2001 and the Subsequent Military Response' (2004) 8 *International Peacekeeping* 213, 223–5. It should be well noted that the Security Council in resolutions 1368 and 1373 (both of 2001) did not state that a strike by a non-state actor amounts to an armed attack; it only declared that terrorist acts are a threat to peace which, in any case, the Council had also done before S/RES/405 and S/RES/419 (1977).

[45] On the classification of the conflict in Afghanistan, see, e.g., Jordan Paust, 'NIAC Nonsense, the Afghan War, And Combatant Immunity' 44 *Georgia Journal of International and Comparative Law* 555; Francoise Hampson, 'Afghanistan 2001–2010' in Elisabeth Wilmshurst (ed.), *International Law and the Classification of Conflicts* (OUP 2012) 242 ff; Marko Milanovic, 'The Applicability of the Conventions to "Transnational" and "Mixed" Conflicts' in Anthony Clapham, Paola Gaeta, and Marco Sassòli (eds), *The 1949 Geneva Conventions. A Commentary* (OUP 2015) 29.

modern version of the state of war doctrine) is so useful.[46] It eliminates the necessity to check each time whether the threshold of armed conflict is achieved and to verify whether the conditions for using self-defence under Article 51 of the UN Charter are fulfilled in each case of terrorist activity by a non-state armed group.[47] According to the extreme American view, a spillover of the Afghan conflict affects the whole world (the so-called global war on terror concept[48]).

Certainly, the concept of spillover of an armed conflict fails to solve the problem completely of violation of other states' sovereignty (territorial integrity), a value protected by the law on the use of force. However, a state can refer to the qualification of the conflict in light of the LOAC, which treats hostilities between a state's armed forces and non-state armed groups as a non-international armed conflict no matter on which state's territory it currently takes place. This creates the impression that the sovereignty of another state is not violated, especially if there is no public condemnation on behalf of that state.[49] In other words, the fact that a third state intervenes on the territory of another state to combat a non-state armed group does not internationalize the conflict.[50] Therefore, we are arguably dealing with a non-international armed conflict and the sovereignty of the state is not endangered as hostilities are not aimed at state bodies. However, it should be noted that this argument disregards the fact that in the past, the UN Security Council condemned unilateral attacks on individuals on the territory of a third state without its consent.[51]

The concept of a worldwide spillover of an armed conflict derived from the LOAC is also needed because the scope of self-defence (even broadened in line

[46] Linking the conflict against ISIL with the one against Al-Qaeda is necessary in order to refer to the authorization for use of military force obtained in 2001, see 115 Stat. 224, Public Law 107–40, 18 September 2001; The White House, *Report on the Legal and Policy Frameworks Guiding the United States' Use of Military Force and Related National Security Operations* (December 2016) 4.

[47] See Remarks of Brian J. Egan, Legal Adviser, American Society of International Law (ASIL), Washington, DC, 1 April 2016, International Law, Legal Diplomacy, and the Counter-ISIL Campaign (available at: <https://2009-2017.state.gov/s/l/releases/remarks/255493.htm>): 'it is not necessary as a matter of international law to reassess whether an armed attack is imminent prior to every subsequent action taken against that group, provided that hostilities have not ended.'

[48] See the National Security Strategy of the United States of America of September 2002, available at: <http://www.state.gov/documents/organization/63562.pdf>: 'The United States of America is fighting a war against terrorists of global reach.' On the concept of a global armed conflict, see, e.g., Noam Lubell and Nathan Derejko, 'A Global Battlefield? Drones and the Geographical Scope of Armed Conflict' (2013) 11 *Journal of International Criminal Justice* 65 ff.

[49] See Remarks by Brian J. Egan, Legal Adviser, American Society of International Law (ASIL), Washington, DC, 1 April 2016, International Law, Legal Diplomacy, and the Counter-ISIL Campaign, where Egan put much emphasis on qualifying the conflict with Al-Qaeda as non-international ('This is true of our operations against ISIL as it has been true in our non-international armed conflict against al Qa'ida and associated forces.'; 'Because we are engaged in an armed conflict against a non-State actor, our war against ISIL is a non-international armed conflict, or NIAC.').

[50] Cf. T. Ferraro and L. Cameron, 'Article 2 Application of the Convention', *Commentary on the First Geneva Convention. Convention (I) for the Amelioration of the Condition of the Wounded and Sick in Armed Forces in the Field* (ICRC, CUP 2017) para. 224, where the authors claim that intervention by a third state triggers the law of international armed conflict in the context of protection of civilians.

[51] See, e.g., S/Res/527 (1982); S/Res/573 (1985).

with the US-promoted concept of legality of intervention in the case of a state that is 'unwilling or unable' to combat terrorist groups on its territory[52]) is too narrow to encompass preventive operations. Therefore, the norms of the Law on Use of Force are not sufficient to justify attacks against leaders of terrorist group cells in order to prevent a terrorist attack when there is only the threat of an attack which could not be qualified as imminent and serious in order to move from illegal prevention to allegedly legal (in light of customary law) pre-emption.[53] However, according to the LOAC applied in non-international armed conflict, those who have a combatant function can be attacked at any time (it is not necessary to check whether there was an imminent threat from that person against the security of the state), despite the fact that particular persons could have not had a chance to actually take part in hostilities. Under the LOAC, according to which it is completely legal to kill combatants (understood broadly as all those taking part in combat no matter whether they enjoy belligerent privileges), states could claim that they have killed legitimate targets in Somalia, Yemen, Pakistan, Syria, Iraq, and so on in the framework of the same continuing armed conflict.[54] States cannot stop attacking terrorists, that is, military objectives, the moment they cross a state border as this would

[52] See, e.g., Remarks by Egan, *supra* note 48: 'It is with respect to this "where" question that international law requires that States must either determine that they have the relevant government's consent or, if they must rely on self-defense to use force against a non-State actor on another State's territory, determine that the territorial State is "unable or unwilling" to address the threat posed by the non-State actor on its territory.' Cf. The White House, *Report on the Legal and Policy Frameworks Guiding the United States' Use of Military Force and Related National Security Operations* (December 2016) 10 which states: 'The unable or unwilling standard is not a license to wage war globally or to disregard the borders and territorial integrity of other States. Indeed, this legal standard does not dispense with the importance of respecting the sovereignty of other States.'

[53] See Remarks by John O. Brennan (Assistant to the President for Homeland Security and Counterterrorism Program on Law and Security), 'Strengthening our Security by Adhering to our Values and Laws', Harvard Law School, Cambridge, Massachusetts, 16 September 2011 (available at: <https://www.whitehouse.gov/the-press-office/2011/09/16/remarks-john-o-brennan-strengthening-our-security-adhering-our-values-an>): 'Of course, whether a particular individual will be targeted in a particular location will depend upon considerations specific to each case, including those related to the imminence of the threat, the sovereignty of the other states involved, and the willingness and ability of those states to suppress the threat the target poses. In particular, this Administration has carefully reviewed the rules governing targeting operations to ensure that these operations are conducted consistently with law of war principles.'

[54] See remarks by President Barack Obama at the National Defense University, Fort McNair, Washington, DC, 23 May 2013 (available at: < https://obamawhitehouse.archives.gov/the-press-office/2013/05/23/remarks-president-national-defense-university>): 'That begins with understanding the current threat that we face. Instead, what we've seen is the emergence of various al Qaeda affiliates. From Yemen to Iraq, from Somalia to North Africa, the threat today is more diffuse, with Al Qaeda's affiliates in the Arabian Peninsula—AQAP—the most active in plotting against our homeland. And while none of AQAP's efforts approach the scale of 9/11, they have continued to plot acts of terror, like the attempt to blow up an airplane on Christmas Day in 2009.' See also US National Security Strategy, May 2010 (available at: <http://nssarchive.us/NSSR/2010.pdf>): 'The United States is waging a global campaign against al-Qa'ida and its terrorist affiliates.' Cf. The White House, *Report on the Legal and Policy Frameworks Guiding the United States' Use of Military Force and Related National Security Operations* (December 2016) 11. Concerning practice by other states, the incident of the killing of Omar Ibn al Khattab in Chechnya in April 2002 by Russian armed forces or of Mahmoud al-Mahbouh in Dubai in January 2010 by Mossad agents can be mentioned, see more in Nils Melzer, *Targeted Killing in International Law* (OUP 2008).

be against the requirements of military necessity which allows states, 'subject to the laws of war, to apply any amount and kind of force to compel the complete submission of the enemy, with the least possible expenditure of time, life and money'.[55]

Necessity (albeit differently understood) is also a condition that triggers self-defence. However, this is not the only condition that must be met to use force lawfully in interstate relations. Therefore, the fact that a person can potentially threaten or actually threatens the security of a state's citizens is not enough to jump from criminal law cooperation to use of military force without the consent of the third state. However, references to the LOAC help to overcome (or rather blur) this legal constraint.

The same pattern is observable with reference to proportionality. This has a different meaning in the LOAC (assessment of civilian losses to military advantage) and in the Law on Use of Force (limitation of military action to the purpose, that is, repelling armed conflict).[56] However, it is easier to convince public opinion that civilian losses were justified taking into account the higher purpose, such as protection of security, even if this has nothing in common with AP requirements of assessment of incidental civilian losses in relation to the anticipated concrete and direct military advantage (Article 51 (5) AP I). Similarly, absence of civilian losses can be raised as further justification for attacks against military targets on the territory of third states.[57] If civilians are protected, violation of sovereignty does not seem to be so serious—at least, not so serious as to be qualified as an armed attack.

Taking into account the arguments mentioned earlier, it is not surprising that, for example, the United States combines the LOAC and the law on the use of force arguments in its justification of specific strikes. This approach has allowed more flexibility in the use of lethal force against persons (as *lex specialis*, LOAC supposedly prevails over HRL), including on the territory of third states in the situation of absence of explicit consent for a military operation (although usually permission of the state, the right to self-defence, or authorization on behalf of the

[55] *United States v List* (*The Hostage Case*), 19 February 1948 reprinted in *Trials of War Criminals before the Nuernberg Military Tribunals*, Vol XI (United States Government Printing Office 1950) 1230. Cf. also US National Strategy, 2015 (available at: <https://obamawhitehouse.archives.gov/sites/default/files/docs/2015_national_security_strategy_2.pdf>): 'Outside of areas of active hostilities, we endeavor to detain, interrogate, and prosecute terrorists through law enforcement. However, when there is a continuing, imminent threat, and when capture or other actions to disrupt the threat are not feasible, we will not hesitate to take decisive action. We will always do so legally, discriminately, proportionally, and bound by strict accountability and strong oversight. The United States—not our adversaries—will define the nature and scope of this struggle, lest it define us.' On the interpretation of military necessity as a pretext to relaxation of the legal framework, see David Luban, 'Military Necessity and the Cultures of Military Law' (2013) 26 *Leiden Journal of International Law* 315, 322.

[56] On the differences in understanding the principles of proportionality and necessity in the law of armed conflict and Law on Use of Force, see Judith Gardam, *Necessity, Proportionality and the Use of Force by States* (CUP 2004).

[57] See Laurie Blank, '"After top gun": How Drone Strikes Impact the Law of War' (2011–2012) 33 *University of Pennsylvania Journal of International Law* 675, 657 ff.

Security Council are also raised).[58] It is hard to estimate to what extent this mixture of arguments taken from different branches of international law influenced *opinio iuris* on the lawfulness of attacks against terrorists on the territory of a third state without any attempt to obtain its consent, which was not the case before 2001.[59]

However, it must be stressed that the fact that there is a war with Al-Qaeda in the sense of *ius contra bellum* does not mean that there is an armed conflict in the sense of *ius in bello*, and the fact that the LOAC is applied does not mean that the state has fulfilled all conditions for using force in international relations, at least if we take into account that *ius in bello* and *ius contra bellum* are completely distinct regimes. However, it seems that joint references to action in self-defence and to the LOAC have as their purpose dual reinforcement of the shaky justification for achieving/preserving the threshold for lawful use of armed force in alleged self-defence and to argue the existence of an armed conflict.

4 Has the Distinction between *Ius in Bello* and *Ius contra Bellum* Fallen into Desuetude?

Treaty law,[60] jurisprudence,[61] and legal doctrine[62] stress the distinction between *ius in bello* and *ius contra bellum*. Usually this separation is taken to mean that application of the LOAC does not affect the status of parties according to the law on the use of force (and therefore the fact that a state applies the LOAC does not

[58] See The White House, *Report on the Legal and Policy Frameworks Guiding the United States' Use of Military Force and Related National Security Operations* (December 2016) 9 ff.

[59] As an example, American attacks on Libya in 1986 were condemned, see resolution No. A/RES/41/38, as were attacks against targets in Afghanistan and Sudan in 1998 (as a response to the bombing of US embassies in Tanzania and Kenya). For more on the change in the assessment of lawfulness of attacks against non-state actors on a third state's territory, see Raphael L. Van Steenberghe, 'Self-defence in Response to Attacks by Non-state Actors in the Light of Recent State Practice: A Step Forward?' (2010) 23 *Leiden Journal of International Law* 183, 206 ff.

[60] See preamble to the AP I: 'Reaffirming further that the provisions of the Geneva Conventions of 12 August 1949 and of this Protocol must be fully applied in all circumstances to all persons who are protected by those instruments, without any adverse distinction based on the nature or origin of the armed conflict or on the causes espoused by or attributed to the Parties to the conflict'; Art. 1 of the GC ('in all circumstances'); Art. 2 of the GC ('in all cases').

[61] *United States v List* (*The Hostage Case*), 19 February 1948 reprinted in *Trials of War Criminals before the Nuernberg Military Tribunals*, Vol. XI (United States Government Printing Office 1950) 1247. See, however, Final Report to the Prosecutor by the Committee Established to Review the NATO Bombing Campaign Against the Federal Republic of Yugoslavia: 'The precise linkage between jus ad bellum and jus in bello is not completely resolved.' (para. 32). Report available at: <http://www.icty.org/en/press/final-report-prosecutor-committee-established-review-nato-bombing-campaign-against-federal#IVA4b>.

[62] See, e.g., Sassòli, Bouvier *supra* note 43, at 102; François Bugnion, 'Just Wars, Wars of Aggression and International Humanitarian Law' (2002) 847 *International Review of the Red Cross* 3 ff; Elżbieta Mikos-Skuza, 'Autonomia iuris in bello względem ius ad bellum—współczesne wyzwania' in Bronisław Sitek, Tadeusz Jasudowicz, and Martyna Seroka (eds), *Fides et bellum. Księga poświęcona Pamięci Księdza Biskupa, Profesora, Generała śp. Tadeusza Płoskiego* (Wydawnictwo Uniwersytetu Warmińsko-Mazurskiego 2012) 391 ff.

legitimize a non-state party in any way). It also means that assessment of the use of force in light of the Law on Use of Force cannot affect application of the LOAC. Therefore, no matter whether a state is engaged in armed conflict as a result of self-defence or of aggression, it is obliged to apply the LOAC.

Scholars stress the necessity of equal obligations of states parties because it is impossible to separate rights from obligations.[63] However, questions have been raised in reference to the war on terror (in principle, a non-international armed conflict) whether states must apply the LOAC when terrorist groups have no respect for it at all. Notably, the International Court of Justice has justified violations of the LOAC 'in an extreme circumstance of self-defence, in which its very survival would be at stake'.[64]

Less attention has been devoted to the question of the possibility of using terms and principles from one regime in order to trigger application of the other, or to prevail over its limitations. As mentioned earlier, some states are intermingling terms from both regimes, but in legal writings too, scholars can sometimes borrow concepts from other regimes, despite their formal separation.[65]

Undoubtedly, states have abandoned the triggering system of the LOACs based on the law on the use of force, given that a declaration of war plays no role according to the GCs (Article 2). But does it work in reverse?

It is, for example, observable that violations of the LOAC (war crimes) are nowadays used as a reason for intervention under the law on the use of force (*vide* the notion of humanitarian intervention or use of military force in the framework of the Responsibility to Protect doctrine).[66] The notion of occupation, which is so intrinsically a part of the LOAC, is used to state commission of aggression.[67] Therefore, what is stopping us from going further? Perhaps the nature of the conflict with terrorist groups such as Al-Qaeda or Da'esh proves that the strict division between the LOAC and the law on the use of force is untenable and the possibility of applying the LOAC should result in disregarding *ius contra bellum*. In addition, perhaps action in self-defence (including preventive operations) should justify triggering the more lethal regime (which the LOAC assuredly is, in comparison to HRL).

[63] Bugnion (2002) *supra* note 63, at 8.

[64] See International Court of Justice, Advisory Opinion on the Legality of the Threat or Use of Nuclear Weapons, 8 July 1996 (ICJ Reports 1996, 226), para. 97. See also the interesting declaration by France of 11 April 2001 to the AP I in which it states: 'Ni porter préjudice aux autres règles du droit international applicables à d'autres activités, nécessaires à l'exercise par la France de son droit naturel de légitime defense.' Cf. also ICJ, *Advisory Opinion on the Legal Consequences of the Construction of a Wall in the Occupied Palestinian Territory*, 9 July 2004 (ICJ Reports 2004, p. 136), para. 139.

[65] Erika de Wet, 'The Modern Practice of Intervention by Invitation in Africa and Its Implications for the Prohibition of the Use of Force' (2015) 26(4) *European Journal of International Law* 979 ff; Dino Kritsiotis, 'Interrogations of Consent: A Reply to Erika de Wet' *ibid.*, 999.

[66] See documents related with the concept 'Responsibility to Protect' collected at: <http://www.responsibilitytoprotect.org/index.php/about-rtop/core-rtop-documents>.

[67] See resolution of the GA No. 3314 (1974).

Some precedents exist in treaty law for linking both branches of international law; application of AP I is dependent on assessment of the aims of an armed group (being precise in light of Article 1 (4) AP I: of the people 'fighting against colonial domination and alien occupation and against racist regimes in the exercise of their right of self-determination'), that is, on a *ius contra bellum* question.

If we consider the LOAC as a branch of law that is more authorizing than constraining (so that military necessity prevails over humanity), arguably the scope of armed conflict must be as broad as required by necessity. The possibility of applying the LOAC to targets on the territory of third states (excluding clashes with the other state's armed forces) gives states greater flexibility in the fight against terrorism. However, no norm of the LOAC or its expanding interpretation can be treated as justification for violating a *ius cogens* norm.[68]

The prohibition of aggression, or even (according to some scholars) a general prohibition of the use of force enshrined in Article 2(4) of the UN Charter definitely belongs to this category.[69] In consequence, the law on the use of force could be considered as the greatest legal obstacle in combating terrorism: it mandates respect for sovereignty of other states and requires that their consent must be sought to permit military operations on their territory.[70] Consequently, authorization of attacks against military objectives derived from the LOAC does not derogate from norms prohibiting use of force against another state (every attack on the territory of a third state violates its territorial integrity and political independence and thus violates Article 2(4) of the UN Charter). Moreover, the UN Security Council has often stressed that the struggle with terrorism must be conducted by member states in accordance with 'all their obligations under international law, in particular international human rights law, international refugee law, and international humanitarian law', and at the same time the Security Council reaffirmed 'its commitment to sovereignty, territorial integrity and political independence of all States in accordance with the Charter of the United Nations'.[71]

When lines are blurred between the LOAC and the law on the use of force, both regimes suffer. If we admit that the LOAC has broadened the possibility of using force, it means that the right to self-defence, so broadly understood, has vastly diminished the principle of territorial integrity and prohibition on using force or even threatening to do so (Article 2(4) of the UN Charter). In the report of the Secretary General prepared for the World Humanitarian Summit in 2016 'One humanity: shared responsibility', it was rightly stressed that: 'When

[68] See Art. 53 of the Vienna Convention on the Law of Treaties 1155 UNTS 331; Arts 40 and 41 of the Articles on Responsibility of States for Internationally Wrongful Acts, A/56/83 (2001); Art. 41 and 42 of the Articles on Responsibility of International Organizations, 2011, A/RES/66/100 (2011).

[69] See, e.g., Cezary Mik, 'Jus Cogens in Contemporary International Law' (2013) 33 *Polish Yearbook of International Law* 27, 56. Cf. André de Hoogh, 'Ius Cogens and the Use of Armed Force' in Marc Weller (ed.), *The Oxford Handbook of the Use of Force in International Law* (OUP 2015) 1162 ff.

[70] Anderson, *supra* n 24, at 317.

[71] See, e.g., S/RES/2249 (2015) or S/RES/2396 (2017).

States disrespect or undermine international humanitarian and human rights law, including through expansive interpretations, other States and non-State actors regard it as an invitation to do the same.'[72] Acceptance of strikes in Pakistan related to hostilities taking place in Afghanistan can result in claims as to the legality of bombing Molenbeek (a municipality in Brussels), because Belgium was unable to destroy a terrorist group to which we would like to apply the LOAC standard of use of lethal force. This seems to be too far-reaching a conclusion, but perhaps we should ask why with some states criminal law cooperation prevails, and with others we are more willing to sanction bombings or targeted killings. The answer is found not in law but in politics;[73] law cannot be different when applied to states that are equally sovereign according to the UN Charter.

Moreover, the tendency to broaden the scope of the LOAC as allegedly required for the defence of security of a state should not be viewed as positive in the perspective of the purposes of this law, which aims primarily to limit hostilities but not to broaden them. Recent eagerness to apply the LOAC because of its more lenient standards of use of lethal force emphasizes only one side of it, that is, the aspect of military necessity. However, it was not without reason that the LOAC has been renamed international humanitarian law. This is in order to stress its humanitarian aspect.[74] Stressing its authorizing character goes against the grain of its philosophy. By referring to self-defence, states have been trying to justify relaxation of the LOAC's prohibitive nature.[75] Yet, if the LOAC today is perceived as a source of authorization, then certainly this branch of law should not be applied in all cases of use of military force. This would not be in the best interest of humanity, which nowadays seems to be better protected by HRL.[76]

Those who have used the combination of the LOAC and the law on the use of force in order to justify particular uses of force on the territory of third states have felt this approach backfire. That is why Brian Egan, US State Legal Adviser, stressed that it 'does not mean we can use military force whenever we want, wherever we want. International legal principles, including respect for a state's sovereignty and the laws of war, impose important constraints on our ability to act

[72] A/70/709, 2 February 2016, para. 48.

[73] Cf. Harold Hongju Koh, 'The Emerging Law of 21st Century War' (2017) 66 *Emory Law Journal* 487, 491–2 where the author claims that the choice between law enforcement or law of armed conflict approach is based on the stage of stability within a state where the counterterrorism operation is undertaken.

[74] Amanda Alexander, 'A Short History of International Humanitarian Law' (2015) 26(1) *European Journal of International Law* 109, 114. On humanization of the LOAC, see also Theodor Meron, 'The Humanization of the Law of War (Marek Nowicki Memorial Lecture)' in Theodor Meron (ed.), *The Making of International Criminal Justice: The View from the Bench: Selected Speeches* (OUP 2011) 42.

[75] Jasmine Moussa, 'Can Jus ad Bellum Override Jus in bello? Reaffirming the Separation of the Two Bodies of Law' (2008) 90(872) *International Review of the Red Cross* 963, 988.

[76] See more Patrycja Grzebyk, 'Taming the Way of Conducting Hostilities in Times of Global Conflict' in Ekaterina Yahyaoui Krivenko (ed.), *Human Rights and Power in Times of Globalisation* (Brill Nijhoff 2018) 109 ff.

unilaterally—and on the way in which we can use force—in foreign territories.'[77] These words show that even in times of crisis, when the law is often subjugated to the alleged highest interests of states, sooner rather than later states realize that the value of law lies in the purity of its principles and not in its grey areas that are open to abuse. The same norms we are blurring on purpose today can be used against us in the near future.

5 Conclusions

The LOAC can be treated as a regime that is not only prohibiting but also authorizing in terms of use of lethal force. In comparison to HRL, it undoubtedly gives states greater flexibility in the elimination of terrorists. That is why states, if they must apply a legal regime, generally prefer to apply the LOAC to their extraterritorial interventions against terrorists. In light of the declarations submitted by states when ratifying the fundamental LOAC treaties, this contradicts the original views of states on the possibility of its application.

States (mainly the United States and Israel with the tacit acceptance of other states) mix arguments from the LOAC and the law on the use of force in order to strengthen their official legal justifications if their operations raise doubts in light of one of those regimes. In consequence, *ius in bello* is (ab)used to reinterpret *ius contra bellum*, and vice versa. States invoke the right to self-defence against terrorists and the existence of a permanent armed conflict to justify constant application of the LOAC, which is supposed to justify the use of force on the territory of third states (on the reasoning that members of armed groups can be lawfully attacked). In consequence, the provisions of the LOAC have facilitated decisions on the use of force when particular instances of the use of force appeared to be completely legal. In consequence, respect for other states' sovereignty was diminished. The LOAC was used not to protect, but to deprive particular persons of protection based on HRL.

The tradition of separating *ius in bello* and *ius contra bellum* is especially endangered in times of crisis when the fight against terrorism is a priority. It is undermined by the claim that states should be absolved from applying the LOAC as the other side completely disregards international law, but also by using norms from one regime to trigger application of the other. The purpose of this new trigger mechanism is to undermine deeply rooted principles of those regimes: the

[77] See Remarks by Brian J. Egan, Legal Adviser, American Society of International Law (ASIL), Washington, DC, 1 April 2016, International Law, Legal Diplomacy, and the Counter-ISIL Campaign. Cf. also Obama 2013 speech, *supra* note 55: 'times when putting U.S. boots on the ground may trigger a major international crisis. And even then, the cost to our relationship with Pakistan—and the backlash among the Pakistani public over encroachment on their territory—was so severe that we are just now beginning to rebuild this important partnership.'

principles of humanity and respect for sovereignty. This may have far-reaching negative results, both legal and political. Therefore, even the most zealous proponents of combining the two regimes see the appeal of returning to the old rules. The LOACs and the law on the use of force should be treated as separate legal regimes. In consequence, this would mean accepting HRL as a possible regime to apply to the fight against terrorism, which was confirmed by several Security Council resolutions stressing the obligation to obey both the LOAC and HRL.

The Challenge of 'Foreign Fighters' to the Liberal International Legal Order

*Sandra Krähenmann**

1 Context

So-called foreign fighters are not a new phenomenon,[1] but the current mobilization of 'foreign fighters'[2] for Iraq and Syria stands out due to the unprecedentedly high numbers of people travelling abroad, the geographic breadth of their countries of origin, and, more generally, the diversity of those travelling, ranging from teenagers to middle-aged men and, for the first time, significant numbers of women and even entire families.[3] Due to the association of 'foreign fighters' with international terrorism, their large-scale mobilization is a major security threat not only to their country of destination, but also their country of origin. On the one hand, returning 'foreign fighters' risk becoming involved in terrorism.[4] On the other, it is frequently argued that 'foreign fighters' may inspire others to become involved in terrorism.[5] Finally, evidence suggests that 'foreign

* This chapter is written by the author in her personal capacity and may not be interpreted as reflecting the position or policies of Geneva Call in any way.

[1] David Malet, *Foreign Fighters. Transnational Identity in Civil Conflicts* (OUP 2013); Thomas Hegghammer, 'The Rise of Muslim Foreign Fighters. Islam and the Globalization of Jihad' (2010/2011) 35(3) *International Security* 53.

[2] The term 'foreign fighter' is put in quotation marks because, as this chapter illustrates, the term itself is problematic. 'Fighter' conveys the idea that these are individuals who join armed groups and actively participate in fighting, but the current usage of the term covers various forms of assistance, support for, or association with armed groups. These fighters are 'foreign' because they travel from abroad to join those groups. Yet it also asserts their foreignness in relation to their state of origin. Such 'othering' in discourse is translated into legal measures that 'others' them quite literally, namely revocation of citizenship.

[3] The Soufan Group, *Foreign Fighters. An Updated Assessment of the Flow of Foreign Fighters into Syria and Iraq* (2015) 4.

[4] While the majority of 'foreign fighters' never become involved in acts of terrorism outside the armed conflict zone, at least for Western 'foreign fighters', foreign fighting experience is 'one of the strongest predictors of individual involvement in domestic operations that we know'; see Thomas Hegghammer, 'Should I Stay or Should I Go? Explaining Variation in Western Jihadists' Choice between Domestic and Foreign Fighting' (February 2013) 107(1) *American Political Science Review* 1, 10.

[5] UNSC 'Report of the Secretary-General on the Threat Posed by ISIL (Da'esh) to international peace and security and the range of United Nations efforts in support of Member States in countering the threat' (31 May 2016) UN Doc S/2016/501, paras 4–6.

Sandra Krähenmann, *The Challenge of 'Foreign Fighters' to the Liberal International Legal Order* In: *How International Law Works in Times of Crisis*. Edited by: George Ulrich and Ineta Ziemele, Oxford University Press (2019).
DOI: 10.1093/oso/9780198849667.003.0004

fighters' tend to contribute to a radicalization of both tactics and ideology adopted by armed groups and the fragmentation of insurgencies, which, in turn, prolongs conflicts and renders them more intractable.[6] Yet, 'foreign fighters' do not just pose a security threat but also challenge fundamental elements of the international order, an order set up in the aftermath of the Second World War and based on international legal rules that embody liberal values such as individual human rights, the rule of law, democracy, and free markets. First, most—although not all[7]—'foreign fighters' in Syria and Iraq join groups such as the Al-Qaeda splinter group that calls itself Islamic State and other groups associated with Al-Qaeda. These groups reject the liberal international legal order and the values it embodies, in particular human rights and democracy. Second, many of these 'foreign fighters' come from Western states that are among the architects of the liberal international legal order. While most 'foreign fighters' come from Middle Eastern and North African countries, it is estimated that the conflicts in Syria and Iraq have attracted more Western 'foreign fighters' than all conflicts during the last twenty years combined.[8] Third, they challenge one of the most fundamental norms, the monopoly of sovereign States to use force across borders, not just within states' territories.[9] Finally, similarly to the conventional wisdom that democracies are vulnerable to international terrorism because of their adherence to civil liberties,[10] the international legal order may be seen as providing a permissive environment for the unprecedented scale and breadth of the mobilization of 'foreign fighters', amongst others, by enhancing mobility and the ability to connect and communicate across the globe. The string of terrorist attacks since 2014 where the perpetrators were linked in one way or the other to the so-called Islamic State shows the seriousness of this threat. In response, states

[6] UNHRC 'Report of the Working Group on the use of mercenaries as a means of violating human rights and impeding the exercise of the right of peoples to self-determination' (19 August 2015) UN Doc A/70/330, paras 22–24; Kristin M. Bakke, 'Help Wanted? The Mixed Record of Foreign Fighters in Domestic Insurgencies' (2014) 38(4) *International Security* 150; Ben Rich and Dara Conduit, 'The Impact of Jihadist Foreign Fighters on Indigenous Secular-Nationalist Causes. Contrasting Chechnya and Syria' (2014) 38(2) *Studies in Conflict & Terrorism* 138.

[7] In Syria and Iraq, 'foreign fighters' have also joined Kurdish and Shia militias, see Daniel Byman, 'Syria's Other Foreign Fighters' (*Lawfare*, 12 January 2014) <https://www.lawfareblog.com/foreign-policy-essay-syrias-other-foreign-fighters> accessed 28 April 2019.

[8] Adam Taylor, 'Could Syria's Islamist Fighters Hit Europe?' *The Washington Post* (Washington DC, 24 July 2014) <https://www.washingtonpost.com/news/worldviews/wp/2014/07/24/could-syrias-islamist-fighters-hit-europe/?utm_term=.0e88c612ba10 /> accessed 28 April 2019.

[9] Darryl Li, 'A Universal Enemy? Legal Regimes of Exclusion and Exemption Under the "Global War on Terrorism"' (Winter 2010) 41(2) *Columbia Human Rights Law Review* 355, 364.

[10] Celestine Bohlen, 'Why Do Terrorists Target Democracies?' *The New York Times* (New York, 15 September 2015) <https://www.nytimes.com/2015/09/15/world/why-do-terrorists-target-democracies.html> accessed 28 April 2019. Yet, while intuitive and logically appealing, this approach lacks empirical support; see James M. Lutz and Brenda J. Lutz, 'Democracy and Terrorism' (2010) 4(1) *Perspectives on Terrorism* 63; E. Chenoweth, 'Terrorism and Democracy' (2013) 16 *Annual Review of Political Science* 355, 361.

have expanded their counterterrorism laws and policies, resulting in the largest wave of new counterterrorism laws since 9/11.[11]

Rather than providing an overview of the various national and international measures and policies,[12] this chapter proposes an analysis of Security Council resolution 2178 (2014)[13] as an illustration of how states have used the institutional structure set up by the liberal international legal order in order to provide a common legal basis for their response and to coordinate their efforts. Adopted in September 2014, resolution 2178 (2014) sets out a comprehensive framework for addressing the mobilization and recruitment of 'foreign terrorist fighters'. In the second part, two particularly emblematic policies tailored towards addressing 'foreign fighter' mobilization will be analysed. First, against the background of the 'foreign fighter' phenomenon, initiatives to prevent violent extremism and radicalization have gained traction,[14] with the Security Council recognizing the importance of countering violent extremism to prevent 'radicalization, recruitment and mobilization of individuals into terrorist groups and becoming foreign terrorist fighters' in resolution 2178 (2014).[15] In addition, abuse of modern information and communication technology to incite support for terrorism[16] and spread violent extremism is highlighted.[17] Legitimized by resolution 2178 (2014),[18] states have been taking measures to ban, remove, or otherwise render inaccessible 'violent extremist' or 'terrorist' content online, including by pressurizing private information

[11] Letta Tayler, 'Foreign Terrorist Fighter Laws: Human Rights Rollbacks under UN Security Council Resolution 2178' (2016) 18 *International Community Law Review* 455.

[12] For such an overview, see, e.g., various contributions in Andrea de Guttry, Francesca Capone, and Christophe Paulussen (eds), *Foreign Fighters under International Law and Beyond* (Springer 2016); Sandra Krähenmann, 'Foreign Fighters under International Law' (2014) *Geneva Academy Briefing No 7*.

[13] UNSC Res 2178 (24 September 2014) UN Doc S/RES/2178.

[14] UNHRC 'Report of the Special Rapporteur on the Promotion and Protection of Human Rights and Fundamental Freedoms while Countering Terrorism' (22 February 2016) UN Doc A/HRC/31/65, para. 9.

[15] UNSC Res 2178, *supra* note 13, para. 15.

[16] *Ibid.*, para. 17. The president of the Security Council reiterated these concerns in two presidential statements, see Statement by the President of the Security Council (19 November 2014) UN Doc S/PRST/2014/23, 3-4 and Statement by the President of the Security Council (29 May 2015) UN Doc S/PRST/2015/11, 4–5.

[17] UNGA 'Plan of Action to Prevent Violent Extremism. Report of the Secretary-General' (24 December 2015) UN Doc A/70/674, para. 55ff.

[18] Moreover, both the Security Council Counter Terrorism Committee and the Al-Qaida Sanctions Committee have addressed the need to counter violent extremism with a particular focus on the role played by modern information and communication technology; see CTC 'Preliminary analysis of the principal gaps in Member States' capacities to implement Security Council resolutions 1373 (2001) and 1624 (2005) that may hinder their abilities to stem the flow of foreign terrorist fighters pursuant to Security Council resolution 2178 (2014)' (12 November 2014) UN Doc S/2014/807, para 17ff; CTC 'Implementation of Security Council Resolution 2178 (2014) by States affected by Foreign Terrorist Fighters' (14 May 2015), UN Doc S/2015/338, paras 60–63; ISIL (Da'esh) and Al-Qaida Sanctions Committee 'Analysis and Recommendations with Regard to the Global Threat from Foreign Terrorist Fighters' (19 May 2015) UN Doc S/2015/358, para. 46 and paras 52–53; CTC 'Implementation of Security Council Resolution 2178 (2014) by States Affected by Foreign Terrorist Fighters' (2 September 2015) UN Doc S/2015/683, paras 8–15.

and communication technology companies to take action.[19] Second, against the background of the phenomenon of 'foreign fighters', states increasingly resort[20] to revocation of citizenship[21] as a part of their counterterrorism arsenal.[22] Resolution 2178 (2014) defines 'foreign terrorist fighters' as 'individuals who travel to a state other than their states of residence or nationality'[23] for the purposes of involvement in terrorist acts. Even before the adoption of resolution 2178 (2014), the figure of the 'foreign fighter' played a dominant role in the discourse constructing the contemporary terrorism threat posed by the group that calls itself Islamic State. The term 'foreign terrorist fighter' in resolution 2178 (2014) forms part of this discourse. The terms 'foreign terrorist fighter' in resolution 2178 (2014) or 'foreign fighter' asserts their foreignness not only relation to the state of destination but also their state of nationality, which, in turn, contributes to their 'othering', a process well-known in counterterrorism discourse,[24] and measures that tend to focus on foreigners.[25] On the one hand, resort to revocation of citizenship illustrates that such 'othering' takes place not only on a discursive level but is translated into legal measures which quite literally transform 'foreign fighters' into foreigners in their country of origin. On the other, stripping 'foreign fighters' of their citizenship while they are abroad[26] serves national security purposes by trying to prevent their return. Hence, although resort to the Security Council and adoption of resolution 2178 (2014) suggest at first glance that states focus on cooperative[27] and multilateral approaches to address the phenomenon of 'foreign fighters', increasing resort to citizenship deprivation illustrates that many states also prioritize their own security interests.[28] In addition, in a historical perspective, in times of war or national

[19] UNHRC 'Report of the Special Rapporteur on the Promotion and Protection of Human Rights and Fundamental Freedoms while Countering Terrorism', *supra* note 14, para. 38 ff.

[20] Tayler, *supra* note 11, 468ff.

[21] Revocation of citizenship is different from suspension or confiscation of passports and other travel documents to prevent suspected outgoing foreign fighters from leaving, see S. Krähenmann, *supra* note 12, at 59, see also Tayler, *supra* note 11, at 466.

[22] Less commonly, involvement in terrorist activities or being a threat to national security has also been included as an obstacle to acquisition of nationality, e.g., the June 2015 amendment to Organic Law 8/2015 to the Portuguese Nationality Act, see Ana Rita Gil, 'Portugal includes anti-terrorism measures in Nationality Act' (*Global Citizenship Observatory*, 22 June 2015) <http://globalcit.eu/portugal-includes-anti-terrorist-measures-in-nationality-act/>.

[23] UN SC Res 2178, *supra* note 133, preambular para. 8.

[24] Kathryn Marie Fisher, 'Spatial and Temporal Imaginaries in the Securitisation of Terrorism' in Lee Jarvis and Michael Lister (eds), *Critical Perspectives on Counter-Terrorism* (Routledge 2015) 56.

[25] Clive Walker, 'The Treatment of Foreign Terror Suspects' (2007) 70 *Modern Law Review* 427.

[26] Clive Walker 'Foreign Terrorist Fighters and UK Counterterrorism Law' in David Anderson QC, Independent Reviewer of Terrorism Legislation, The Terrorism Acts in 2015 (December 2016) 121.

[27] UN SC Res 2178, *supra* note 13 para. 4 expressly 'calls upon all Member States, in accordance with their obligations under international law, to cooperate in efforts to address the threat posed by foreign terrorist fighters, including by preventing the radicalization to terrorism and recruitment of foreign terrorist fighters, including children, preventing foreign terrorist fighters from crossing their borders, disrupting and preventing financial support to foreign terrorist fighters, and developing and implementing prosecution, rehabilitation and reintegration strategies for returning foreign terrorist fighters'.

[28] Indeed, an argument can be made that deprivation of citizenship and similar measures, e.g., temporary exclusion orders, that aim to prevent the return of suspected 'foreign fighters' run counter to

crises, states and their societies tend to view individuals with a foreign background as suspicious and lacking loyalty, which can lead in the most extreme cases to deprivation of citizenship of those individuals.[29]

2 Security Council Resolution 2178 (2014): A Framework to Combat 'Foreign Terrorist Fighters'

On 24 September 2014, at a high-level summit chaired by US President Barack Obama, the Security Council adopted Resolution 2178 under Chapter VII. Resolution 2178 provides for a general regulatory framework to combat the phenomenon of so-called foreign terrorist fighters, that is, individuals who 'travel to a State other than their States of residence or nationality for the purpose of perpetration, planning, or preparation of, or participation in, terrorist acts or the providing or receiving of terrorist training, including in connection with armed conflict'.[30] In accordance with their obligations under international human rights law , international refugee law, and international humanitarian law, states are required to suppress and prevent the recruitment, organization, transport, and equipment of such 'foreign terrorist fighters,' including by preventing their departure, entry, and transit. To do so, the Security Council requests states to have the necessary legislation to prosecute individuals who travel or attempt to travel to a state other than their states of residence or nationality for terrorist purposes, including to provide or to receive terrorist training; who finance such travel; or who organize or otherwise facilitate such travel, including by recruitment.[31]

This is not the first time that the Security Council has adopted a resolution of a legislative character with sweeping obligations against the background of the fight against terrorism, including the obligation to enact criminal legislation. After the 9/11 attacks, the Security Council adopted resolution 1373 (2001), which required states to criminalize, prosecute, and punish the financing of terrorism.[32] Yet, while resolution 1373 relied on the 1999 Convention for the suppression of

resolution 2178 (2014), see Guy Goodwin-Gill, '"Temporary Exclusion Orders" and their Implications for the United Kingdom's International Legal Obligations, Part II' (*EJIL Talk!* 9 December 2014) <https://www.ejiltalk.org/temporary-exclusion-orders-and-their-implications-for-the-united-kingdoms-international-legal-obligations-part-ii/> accessed 28 April 2019; Sandra Krähenmann, 'The Obligations under International Law of the Foreign Fighter's State of Nationality or Habitual Residence, State of Transit and State of Destination', in de Guttry et al., *supra* note 12, 248ff.

[29] Sandra Mantu, *Contingent Citizenship. The Law and Practice of Citizenship Deprivation in International, European and National Perspectives* (Brill Nijhoff 2015) 339ff.

[30] UNSC Res 2178, *supra* note 13, preambular para. 8.

[31] *Ibid.*, paras 6(a) –(c).

[32] Luis Miguel Hinojosa-Martínez, 'A Critical Assessment of United Nations Security Council Resolution 1373' in Ben Saul (ed.), *Research Handbook on International Law and Terrorism* (Elgar 2014) 626.

financing of terrorism, resolution 2178 requires the criminalization of acts that were previously undefined under international law, namely (attempted) travel for terrorist purposes, including for training,[33] and financing or otherwise organizing such travel. The conduct to be criminalized is preparatory or ancillary, indeed far removed from an actual act of terrorism. The resolution thus endorses the use of broad preventive criminal offences in the fight against terrorism, an approach already used in the EU framework for combating terrorism and many domestic jurisdictions,[34] and extended against the background of the 'foreign fighter' phenomenon.[35]

While providing for sweeping obligations, the scope of resolution 2178 is undefined as it is not clear who is covered by the various elements of the term 'foreign terrorist fighter'.[36] First, resolution 2178 does not define terrorism or limit its reach to international terrorism.[37] Consequently, the resolution, and the obligations enshrined therein, will depend on states' individual definitions of terrorism,[38] an approach that carries a significant risk of abuse.[39] In particular, 'foreign terrorist fighters' are described as people who travel abroad, a routine activity for many people, but with 'terrorist' intent. Yet, it is unclear how to distinguish a person who travels abroad for legitimate purposes from a person who travels abroad with an as yet non-manifest terrorist purpose.[40] The implementation of Security Council resolution 2178 may lead to a de facto prohibition on travel to certain countries or areas known for 'terrorist' activities and their neighbours.[41]

[33] The EU Framework Decision on Combating Terrorism includes provision of training for terrorist purposes, but not receiving such training, see EU Framework Decision 2008/919/JHA on Combating Terrorism art 3(1)(c).

[34] See, e.g., Thomas Weigend, 'The Universal Terrorist. The International Community Grappling with a Definition' 2006 4(5) *Journal of International Criminal Justice* 912, 931; Maria Kaiafa-Gbandi, 'Terrorismusbekämpfung in der Europäischen Union und das vor-präventive Strafrecht: Neue Vorgaben für strafbare Taten nach dem Rahmenbeschluss 2008/919/JI' in Ulfrid Neumann and Felix Herzog (eds), *Festschrift für Winfried Hassemer* (C.F. Müller Verlag 2010) 1161.

[35] For example, in December 2012 France amended its counterterrorism legislation to extend its extraterritorial reach to citizens and individuals who normally reside in France, see Law No. 2012-1432 of 21 December 2012, new Art. 131-13. The British Serious Crime Act 2015 extended the offence of preparation of terrorist acts to conduct abroad, see Serious Crime Act 2015 s. 81.

[36] This part is based on Krähenmann, *supra* note 28, 229.

[37] Martin Scheinin, 'A Comment on Security Council Resolution 2178 (Foreign Terrorist Fighters) as a "Form" of Global Governance' (*Just Security*, 6 October 2014) <https://www.justsecurity.org/15989/comment-security-council-res-2178-foreign-fighters-form-global-governance/> accessed 28 April 2019.

[38] Kai Ambos, 'Our Terrorists, your Terrorists? The United Nations Security Council Urges States to Combat "foreign terrorist Fighters", but Does not Define "Terrorism"' (*EJIL Talk!* 2 October 2014). <http://www.ejiltalk.org/our-terrorists-your-terrorists-the-united-nations-security-council-urges-states-to-combat-foreign-terrorist-fighters-but-does-not-define-terrorism> accessed 28 April 2019.

[39] *Ibid.*

[40] Ambos, *supra* note 38.

[41] *Ibid.* This is indeed the approach taken by the Australian 'foreign fighter' bill, which criminalizes travel to an area where a terrorist organization is engaged in hostile activity, unless the person is in that area for a legitimate purpose, see Counter-Terrorism Legislation Amendment (Foreign Fighter) Act 2014, No. 116, s. 119.2–119.3.

Second, the intended effect[42] of the resolution is to criminalize travel abroad to join armed groups that are considered 'terrorist' or attempts to do so. At least when fighting with certain groups, the resolution thus presumes that engaging in acts of violence during an armed conflict abroad amounts to a 'terrorist offense,'[43] an unreflective extension of 'terrorism' to situations of armed conflict[44] without considering the fundamental differences between terrorism and armed conflict.[45] The problematic linkage between armed conflict and terrorism is also reflected in the usage of the term 'foreign terrorist fighter', with 'fighter' being normally used in the context of armed conflicts. The term 'fighter' conveys the idea that these are individuals who join armed groups and actively participate in fighting. However, the current usage of the term is broader and covers various forms of assistance, support, or association with armed groups and is not limited to individuals who are directly participating in hostilities as this term is understood under international humanitarian law.[46] In particular, persons who assume exclusively non-combat functions, such as administrative, political, or propaganda functions, do not directly participate in hostilities under international humanitarian law.[47] Moreover, gendered interpretations of the term 'fighter'[48] may lead to the assumption that men are 'foreign terrorist fighters' to be prosecuted and punished whereas women would be exempt from this category. However, resolution 2178 does not limit the term to the context of an armed conflict. Instead, the definition of 'foreign terrorist fighter' refers to acts of terrorism 'including in connection with armed conflict', implying that there may be 'foreign terrorist fighters' without a connection to an armed conflict. The description of the conduct to be prevented and suppressed in the operative paragraphs does not contain any elements that would purport to limit their scope of application to an armed conflict context or to individuals trying to join an armed group. The rhetorical usage of the term 'fighter' outside an armed conflict context is problematic as it may serve to extend the application of international humanitarian law—in particular the rules on detention and targeting—to non-conflict zones, a phenomenon that has been a marked feature of the so-called war on terror.

Third, the term 'foreign terrorist fighters' conveys the idea that these fighters are 'foreign'[49] because they travel abroad to a state other than their state of nationality

[42] 'U.N. Security Council Plans to Suppress Foreign Extremist Fighters' *Reuters* (9 September 2014) <http://www.reuters.com/article/2014/09/09/us-iraq-crisis-un-idUSKBN0H408E20140909> accessed 28 April 2019.

[43] Martin Scheinin, 'The Council of Europe's Draft Protocol on Foreign Terrorist Fighter' is Fundamentally Flawed' (*Just Security* 18 March 2015) <http://justsecurity.org/21207/council-europe-draft-protocol-foreign-terrorist-fighters-fundamentally-flawed/> accessed 28 April 2019.

[44] *Ibid.*

[45] See, e.g., Jelena Pejic, 'Terrorist Acts and Groups: A Role for International Law?' (2004) 74 *British Yearbook of International Law* 76.

[46] See UNHRC 'Report of the Working Group on the Use of Mercenaries' *supra* note 6, paras 22–24.

[47] See the 2009 ICRC Interpretative Guidance on the Notion of Direct Participation in Hostilities.

[48] Susan F. Hirsch, 'Civilians under the Law: Inequality, Intersectionality and Irony' in Daniel Rothbart et al. (eds), *Civilians and Modern War. Armed Conflict and the Ideology of Violence* (Routledge 2012) 251.

[49] For an overview of various approaches to defining 'foreign fighters,' including whether co-ethnic fighters are included, see Krähenmann, *supra* note 28, 5–7.

or residence. The concept of state of residence remains undefined and may have different meanings in different jurisdictions. In addition, the interplay between 'State of nationality' and 'State of residency' remains unclear, in particular when considering the situation of members of a diaspora and dual citizenship.[50]

In addition to adopting the term 'foreign terrorist fighter' and requiring the criminalization of (attempted) travel abroad for terrorist purposes, Security Council resolution 2178 also identifies violent extremism as a condition conducive to terrorism and highlights the link between extremist ideology and acts of terrorism.[51] Acknowledging for the first time the importance of countering violent extremism, the Security Council points towards the abuse of modern information and communication technology to radicalize, recruit, and incite to terrorism.[52] While in principle countering or preventing violent extremism[53] is to be welcomed as a new conceptual framework that departs from traditional military and law enforcement-based counterterrorism measures to focus on conditions conducive to terrorism,[54] resorting to elusive, ill-defined, and contested concepts such as violent extremism and radicalization also presents certain dangers.[55] Policy frameworks to prevent radicalization and violent extremism may negatively impact a range of human rights and often have a pronounced gender dimension, including by instrumentalizing women's engagement for security purposes.[56] As the following section illustrates, particular attention should be paid to freedom of expression as the framework for preventing radicalization and violent extremism addresses the ideological basis of violence or terrorism, including the purported role of speech and speakers.

3 Curtailing Freedom of Expression to Prevent 'Radicalization' and 'Violent Extremism'

Freedom of expression is not an absolute right, but limitations provided by law are possible if necessary for a legitimate aim,[57] such as national security.[58] In particular, any restriction must be justified by relevant and sufficient reasons and must

[50] UNHRC 'Report of the Working Group on the Use of Mercenaries', *supra* note 6, para. 62. In preambular para. 20 of resolution 2178, the Security Council highlights 'the situation of individuals of more than one nationality who travel to their states of nationality' for the purpose of terrorist acts, and urges states to take action, yet it does not provide any guidance on how dual nationals fit with the concept of 'foreign terrorist fighter'.

[51] UNSC Res 2178, *supra* note 13, preambular paras 2 and 13; paras 15–16 and 18.

[52] *Ibid.*, paras 11 and 17.

[53] The UN prefers the use of the term 'preventing violent extremism'; see UNGA Report of the Secretary-General 'Plan of Action to Prevent Violent Extremism', *supra* note 17.

[54] *Ibid.*, para. 4.

[55] UNHRC 'Report of the Special Rapporteur on the Promotion and Protection of Human Rights and Fundamental Freedoms while Countering Terrorism', *supra* note 14.

[56] *Ibid.*, §§52–53. See also Naureen Chowdhury Fink, Sara Zeiger, and Rafia Bhulai (eds), *A Man's World? Exploring the Roles of Women in Counter-Terrorism and Violent Extremism* (Hedayah and the Global Center on Cooperative Security 2016).

[57] See, e.g., ICCPR Art. 19 (3) and ECHR Art. 10(2).

[58] *Ibid.*

be proportionate to the legitimate aim pursued.[59] Moreover, freedom of expression also protects ideas that 'offend, shock or disturb the State or any sector of the population'.[60] Prohibiting incitement to violence,[61] including to terrorist violence, may clearly be a permissible restriction. In particular after 9/11, criminalization of incitement to terrorism became more widespread.[62] States justified criminalizing incitement of terrorism and other speech-related terrorist offences as a necessary early preventive tool for contemporary manifestations of terrorism that are based on horizontal and decentralized structures and that rely on mass dissemination of an extremist ideology calling for acts of violence.[63] While it is obviously difficult to properly delimit incitement to terrorism and similar offences such as glorification of terrorism,[64] the 'foreign fighter' phenomenon and the online presence of the so-called Islamic State group accelerated resort to speech-related terrorist offences.[65] Moreover, such measures attained a new qualitative dimension as they are increasingly framed not in terms of protecting national security or prohibiting incitement to terrorism but more broadly in order to prevent radicalization and violent extremism.[66] Content as opposed to context, the intent of the speaker, and a reasonable degree of probability to incite an act of terrorism, has become the overriding factor to justify limitations, including by criminal prohibitions.[67]

Limiting speech in order to prevent violent extremism offers an exemplary illustration of some of the conceptual difficulties that plague the framework for

[59] ECtHR *Handyside v United Kingdom* (1976) Series A No. 24, paras 49–50.

[60] *Ibid.*, para. 49.

[61] In addition, some restrictions are required, namely 'advocacy of national, racial or religious hatred that constitutes incitement to discrimination, hostility or violence', see Art. 20(2) ICCPR. For guidance on the interpretation of what constitutes such incitement, see the Rabat Plan of Action, annexed to UNHRC, 'Report of the United Nations High Commissioner for Human Rights on the Expert Workshops on the Prohibition of Incitement to National, Racial or Religious Hatred (11 January 2013) UN Doc A/HRC/22/17/Add.4.

[62] On the international level, the Security Council called upon states 'to prohibit incitement to terrorist acts', see UNSC Res 1624 (14 September 2005) UN Doc S/RES/1624, para 1. Similarly, the 2005 Council of Europe Convention on the Prevention of Terrorism requires states to prohibit 'Public Provocation to Commit a Terrorist Offence', see Art. 5.

[63] Yaël Ronen, 'Terrorism and Freedom of Expression in International Law' in Ben Saul (ed.), *Research Handbook on International Law and Terrorism* (Edward Elgar 2014) 437, 443.

[64] For example, see *Leroy v France* App No 36109/03 (ECtHR, 20 October 2004). For a brief overview of case law relating to incitement to terrorism, see Louise Doswald-Beck, *Human Rights in Times of Conflict and Terrorism* (OUP 2011) 415–19.

[65] UNHRC 'Report of the Special Rapporteur on the Promotion and Protection of Human Rights and Fundamental Freedoms while Countering Terrorism', *supra* note 14, para. 39. For example, rarely used before, France started to implement prohibition of incitement and glorification of terrorism, which had been moved from the Press Law to the Criminal Code with adoption of Act No. 2014-1353 of 13 November 2014. See Agnès Callamard, 'Religion, Terrorism and Speech in a "Post-Charlie Hebdo" World' (2015) 10 *Religion and Human Rights*, 218.

[66] See, e.g., the section on 'Challenging Extremist and Terrorist Ideology', in *CONTEST. The United Kingdom's Strategy for Considering Terrorism: Annual Report 2015*, paras 2.32–2.33 or the French plan to combat terrorism, which includes new possibilities to block websites: 'Lutte contre la radicalisation violente et les filières terroristes' (24 July 2014) <http://www.interieur.gouv.fr/Actualites/L-actu-du-Ministere/Lutte-contre-la-radicalisation-violente-et-les-filieres-terroristes> accessed 28 April 2019.

[67] Callamard, *supra* note 65, at 218.

countering or preventing violent extremism. First, the distinction between violent extremism and terrorism remains unclear as the two are most often addressed simultaneously.[68] There are open questions whether fundamental differences exist in terms of the behaviour addressed,[69] the actors involved,[70] and their objectives.[71] Second, violent extremism is a contested concept. International initiatives frequently abstain from defining violent extremism,[72] while national definitions tend to be broad.[73] In particular it remains unclear whether the qualifier 'violent' refers to violent conduct, advocating violence, or endorsing—including refusal to condemn—violence. Without the qualifier 'violent', extremism captures virtually everything that deviates from the norm, including national values.[74] Extremism is defined by what is accepted by or acceptable to the majority, which, in turn, is subject to changes over time and in different contexts. Simplistic radicalization theories that portray a linear progression from adoption of extremist views and aspirations to the use of violence as a method for societal change continue to inform policy responses.[75] Suggesting the possibility to detect and intervene against 'radicalization' long before any steps are taken towards resort to violence, such theories tend to overemphasize the role played by ideology or religion,[76] although there is

[68] UNGA 'Plan of Action to Prevent Violent Extremism', *supra* note 17.

[69] The UN Secretary-General argues that the concept of violent extremism is broader, *ibid.* para. 4.

[70] It is often argued that countering-violent extremism is civilian-led, as opposed to military-based, counterterrorism measures, and embraces a holistic approach that includes civil society. Yet at the same time efforts countering violent extremism are often a complement to military efforts and state-led, including by the involvement of law-enforcement agencies. See, e.g., Sarah Sewall, Under Secretary for Civilian Security, Democracy, and Human Rights, 'Mobilizing Against a Preeminent Challenge of the 21st Century: Countering Violent Extremism' (US Department of State, 20 November 2015) < https://2009-2017.state.gov/j/remarks/249839.htm > accessed 4 July 2019.

[71] Indeed, one of the key objectives of countering violent extremism is to prevent terrorism; see references to violent extremism as conducive to terrorism in SC Res 2178, *supra* note 133, para. 15 or the OSCE approach that focuses on violent extremism and radicalization that lead to terrorism, see, e.g., OSCE 'Violent Extremism and Radicalization that Lead to Terrorism (VERLT) <http://www.osce.org/secretariat/107807> accessed 28 April 2019.

[72] The UN Plan of Action to Prevent Violent Extremism, *supra* note 17, abstains from defining violent extremism and simply notes that: 'Definition of "terrorism" and "violent extremism" are the prerogative of Member States and must be consistent with their obligations under international law ... This Plan of Action pursues a practical approach to preventing violent extremism, without venturing to address questions of definition.' (para. 5).

[73] See, e.g., the British definition of violent extremism: 'Violent extremism consists in promoting, supporting or committing acts which may lead to terrorism and which are aimed at defending an ideology, advocating racial, national, ethnic or religious supremacy and opposing core-democratic principles.' Prevent Strategy, Cm 88092 (June 2011), Annex A.

[74] Such as the British definition of extremism: 'Extremism is vocal or active opposition to fundamental British values, including democracy, the rule of law, individual liberty and mutual respect and tolerance of different faiths and beliefs. We also include in our definition of extremism calls for the death of members of our armed forces, whether in this country or overseas.' Prevent Strategy, CM 8092, June 2011, Annex A.

[75] UNHRC 'Report of the Special Rapporteur on the Promotion and Protection of Human Rights and Fundamental Freedoms while Countering Terrorism', *supra* note 14, para. 15.

[76] *Ibid.*

no empirical causal link between adoption of extremist views or exposure thereto and resort to violence.[77]

In the context of freedom of expression, the necessity and proportionality of measures taken to counter violent extremism, short of incitement to terrorism, appear questionable and may infringe freedom of expression.[78] Without providing a thorough analysis,[79] measures taken to limit online-based modes of expression illustrate the difficulties that arise for protecting freedom of expression in the context of countering violent extremism. Against the background of the so-called Islamic State's use of digital information and communication technology and its online presence, states are pressurizing information and technology companies to remove 'terrorist' content from their platforms by taking down entire websites or deleting specific websites, blogs, posts, videos, or articles, in addition to traditional law-enforcement measures. In many instances, such requests are not official removal requests or based upon a court order[80] but are based on violations of the terms of use established by such companies.[81] Yet the same principles governing freedom of expression continue to apply in the online environment.[82] These principles are still evolving, taking into account the specificities of online-based means of expression. Hence, any restriction must be provided by law, but the legal basis for removals based on terms-of-use violations notified by governments remains unclear. Normal safeguards against excessive government interference, including the right to a remedy, are undermined.[83] Moreover, terms of use tend to allow for broader restrictions than

[77] H.J. Giessmann, 'Fundamentalism, Extremism, Terrorism. Commonalities, Differences and Policy Implications of "Blacklisting"' in B.A. Arrigo and H.Y. Bersot (eds), *The Routledge Handbook of International Crime and Justice Studies* (Routledge 2014) 523. Similarly, Thomas Hegghammer notes the lack of data to establish why some returning foreign fighters become engaged in terrorism, while the majority do not; see Hegghammer, *supra* note 4, at 10.

[78] For example, the UN Special Rapporteur on Freedom of expression highlighted in a statement that countering violent extremism 'can be used to restrict a wide range of lawful expression', Statement of the Special Rapporteur on Freedom of Opinion and Expression, 'Countering Violent Extremism, a "Perfect" Excuse to Restrict Free Speech and Control the Media' (3 May 2016) <http://www.ohchr.org/EN/NewsEvents/Pages/DisplayNews.aspx?NewsID=19916&LangID=E> accessed 28 April 2019; see also UNHRC 'Report of the Special Rapporteur on the Promotion and Protection of Human Rights and Fundamental Freedoms while Countering Terrorism', *supra* note 14, paras 39 and 40.

[79] For such an analysis, see Callamard, *supra* note 65.

[80] Although states are also taking such measures, including by expanding their legal frameworks. For example, France adopted a new law that provides for the blocking of websites that incite to or glorify terrorism, see Loi No. 2014-1353, 13 November 2014. For an overview of legal frameworks governing not only removal of content, but also blocking and filtering in Council of Europe states, see Swiss Institute of Comparative Law, *Comparative Study on Blocking, Filtering and Take-Down of Illegal Internet Content* (2015), available at <http://www.coe.int/en/web/freedom-expression/study-filtering-blocking-and-take-down-of-illegal-content-on-the-internet> accessed 28 April 2019.

[81] Scott Craig and Emma Llansó 'Pressuring Platforms to Censor Content is Wrong Approach to Combating Terrorism' (CDT, 5 November 2015) <https://cdt.org/blog/pressuring-platforms-to-censor-content-is-wrong-approach-to-combatting-terrorism/> accessed 28 April 2019.

[82] *Ashby Donald and Others v France* App No 36769/08 (ECtHR, 10 January 2013), para. 34; UNHRC, 'Report of the Special Rapporteur on the Promotion and Protection of the Right to Freedom of Opinion and Expression' (16 May 2011) UN Doc A/HRC/17/27, para. 24.

[83] Craig and Llansó, *supra* note 81; UNHRC 'Report of the Special Rapporteur on the Promotion and Protection of Human Rights and Fundamental Freedoms while Countering Terrorism', *supra* note 14, para. 40.

national law.[84] While the terms of use for online platforms and services are accessible to their users, their actual implementation lacks transparency and seems to lack consistency,[85] which in turn raises questions whether relevant and sufficient reasons are provided to justify limitations. Amongst the characteristics of the internet, it not only has the potential to enhance public access to seek and to disseminate information[86] but also enables individuals to exercise their freedom of expression,[87] including by providing a platform to persons and groups that are traditionally marginalized in public debates, which in turn enhances the exercise of a range of other human rights.[88] At the same time, it also allows for the widespread dissemination of unlawful speech, such as incitement to violence, and risks infringing the rights of others.[89] In the context of countering violent extremism, the content targeted is overwhelmingly user-generated content on various online platforms based on the argument that such widely available content fosters radicalization and mobilization of foreign fighters. However, the necessity to limit 'extremist speech' falling short of incitement to violence, including terrorist violence, is questionable in light of the lack of an empirical basis of radicalization theories that tend to overestimate the role played by ideology and the link between extremists' views and resort to violence.[90] Similarly, a recent social network analysis of German 'foreign fighters' in Syria and Iraq concluded that online mobilization on 'social media was not a significant mobilization factor independent of actual peer-to-peer networks'.[91] Finally, the focus on user-generated content in online platforms brings to the forefront the question whether and to what extent such online platforms have duties and responsibilities. In *Delfi*, the European Court of Human Rights held that holding a newspaper online portal liable for offensive comments by users was not disproportionate interference with the company's freedom of expression,[92] but stressed that 'the case concerned a large, professionally managed internet news portal run on a commercial basis which

[84] Craig and Llansó, *supra* note 81.

[85] For example, Facebook's internal guidelines for the moderation of content only became public recently following an investigation by *The Guardian*. The same investigation indicates that Facebook will not block content that denies the Holocaust in all countries where this is unlawful, but focuses on countries where the authorities are likely to contact Facebook. See N. Hopkins, 'Revealed: Facebook's Internal Rulebook on Sex, Terrorism and Violence' (*The Guardian*, 21 May 2017) <https://www.theguardian.com/news/2017/may/21/revealed-facebook-internal-rulebook-sex-terrorism-violence> accessed 28 April 2019; 'How Facebook Handles Holocaust Denial' (*The Guardian*, 24 May 2017) <https://www.theguardian.com/news/gallery/2017/may/24/how-facebook-handles-holocaust-denial> accessed 28 April 2019.

[86] *Delfi AS v Estonia* App No 64569/09 (ECtHR, Grand Chamber, 16 June 2015), para. 132.

[87] *Ibid.*, para. 110.

[88] UNHRC, 'Report of the Special Rapporteur on the Promotion and Protection of the Right to Freedom of Opinion and Expression', *supra* note 82, paras 19–22.

[89] *Delfi AS v Estonia, supra* note 86, para. 110.

[90] UNHRC 'Report of the Special Rapporteur on the Promotion and Protection of Human Rights and Fundamental Freedoms while Countering Terrorism', *supra* note 14, para. 40.

[91] Sean C. Reynolds and Mohammed M. Hafez, 'Social Network Analysis of German Foreign Fighters in Syria and Iraq' *Terrorism and Political Violence* (14 February 2017) <http://dx.doi.org/10.1080/09546553.2016.1272456> 20 accessed 28 April 2019.

[92] *Delfi AS v Estonia, supra* note 86, para. 162.

published news articles of its own and invited its readers to comment on them',[93] not 'other fora on the internet where third-party comments can be disseminated'.[94] Yet, regardless of questions of intermediary liability, modern information and communication technologies providers are under pressure to do more to limit misuse of the services they provide, in particular against the background of countering violent extremism.[95] However, when private companies restrict online content, the delicate exercise of delimiting freedom of speech becomes increasingly privatized.[96]

4 Revocation of Citizenship

Against the background of the phenomenon of 'foreign fighters', a remarkable number of states resort to revocation of citizenship as a part of their counter-terrorism arsenal.[97] Most states' nationality laws include grounds for loss or revocation of citizenship, for example absence, fraud, serious criminal offences,[98] but also grounds that are related to public order and national security, such as acts prejudicial to the vital interests of the state or serving a foreign government or army.[99] The latter grounds, reminiscent of banishment or exile for 'undesirable' citizens,[100] were rarely used, but have resurged against the background of the 'foreign fighter' phenomenon. For example, the Swiss Secretariat for Migration initiated the procedure to revoke the citizenship of a suspected Swiss 'foreign fighter' in Syria on the basis of Article 48 of the 1952 Citizenship Act that allows revocation in the case of 'conduct seriously detrimental to the interests or reputation' of Switzerland; an article that has never been used before.[101] Similarly, powers to revoke citizenship had not been used in the United Kingdom since 1973. Yet, after an amendment to

[93] *Ibid.*, para. 115.

[94] *Ibid.*, para. 116. However, others generally reject the imposition of intermediary liability, see, e.g., *Delfi AS v Estonia, supra* note 86, para. 43.

[95] See, e.g., Andrew Sparro and Alex Hern, 'Internet Firms Must do More to Tackle Online Extremism, says No 10' (*The Guardian*, 24 March 2017) <https://www.theguardian.com/media/2017/mar/24/internet-firms-must-do-more-to-tackle-online-extremism-no-10> accessed 28 April 2019.

[96] Freedom House, *Privatizing Censorship, Eroding Privacy. Freedom on the Net 2015*, October 2015.

[97] Tayler, *supra* note 11, 468ff.

[98] Recently, some countries expanded the list of crimes for revocation of nationality to include terrorist offences or extended the terrorist offences covered, such as the 2014 Strengthening Canada Citizenship Act, Section 10 (2) or Art. 7 of the 2015 Belgian Loi visant à renforcer la lutter contre le terrorism.

[99] Report of the Secretary General, 'Human Rights and Arbitrary Deprivation of Nationality' (2013) UN Doc A/HRC/25/28, paras 7–21.

[100] Audrey Macklin, 'Citizenship Revocation, the Privilege to Have Rights and the Production of the Alien' (2014) 40(1) *Queen's Law Journal*, 5.

[101] 1952 Bundesgesetz über Erwerb und Verlust des Schweizer Bürgerrechts, Art. 48. A legal opinion concluded that Art. 48 is not a sufficiently clear legal basis for such a withdrawal; see Alberto Achermann, 'Kurzgutachten zum Entzug des Bürgerrechtes nach Artikel 49 BüG' (2015) <http://static.nzz.ch/files/0/7/0/Kurzgutachten+Achermann_Entzug+B%C3%BCrgerrecht+%282%29_1.18775070.pdf> accessed 28 April 2019.

the British Nationality Act in March 2006 to empower the Home Secretary to revoke the citizenship of dual nationals 'if conducive to the public good,'[102] a broader standard than the previous 'seriously prejudicial to the vital interests of the UK standard,[103] twenty-seven persons were deprived of their citizenship between 2006 and 2014, many allegedly while they were abroad.[104] In 2014, in response to the case of Mr al-Jedda, a suspected British 'foreign fighter' who had returned to Iraq in 2004, the British government pushed through an amendment that allowed the Home Secretary to remove the citizenship of naturalized mono-nationals if the Home Secretary 'has reasonable grounds for believing'[105] that the person may acquire the citizenship of another country. Although not used so far, the amendment remains controversial as it allows revocation of citizenship even when a person is rendered stateless as a result.[106] Other states followed the British example with legislation that specifically targets the 'foreign fighter' phenomenon. The 2014 Strengthening Canadian Citizenship Act provided for revocation of citizenship if a citizen joins an armed group engaged in an armed conflict with Canada, but this was repealed in June 2017.[107] Austria amended its citizenship act in 2014 to provide for revocation of citizenship if a citizen joins an armed group in an armed conflict abroad.[108] The 2015 Australian Citizenship amendment (Allegiance to Australia) Act provides three additional grounds for how dual citizens, whether by birth or naturalization, lose their citizenship: first, for service in the armed forces of an enemy country or a declared terrorist organization;[109] second, for conviction of terrorist offences;[110] and finally, for 'renunciation by conduct', which includes engaging in terrorist activities, providing or receiving training, recruitment, or financing of terrorism.[111]

[102] 1981 British Nationality Act s. 40 (2).

[103] For an in-depth analysis of changes in UK legislation, see Mantu, *supra* note 29, 179 ff.

[104] Walker, *supra* note 25, at 440. For national security reasons, the UK government refuses to disclose the number of people who were deprived of their citizenship while abroad, see David Anderson QC 'Citizenship Removal Resulting in Statelessness', (April 2016) First Report of the Independent Reviewer on the Operation of the Power to Remove Citizenship Obtained by Naturalisation From Persons Who Have No Other Citizenship, §2.16.

[105] 2014 Immigration Act s. 66.

[106] Guy S. Goodwin-Gill, 'Mr Al-Jedda, Deprivation of Citizenship, and International Law' (2014) Information Paper submitted to the UK Parliament <https://www.parliament.uk/documents/joint-committees/human-rights/GSGG-DeprivationCitizenshipRevDft.pdf> accessed 28 April 2019. See also Mantu, *supra* note 29, 199ff.

[107] 2014 Strengthening Canada Citizenship Act, Section 10 (2). For an analysis, see Macklin, *supra* note 100. In June 2017, the Act to amend the Citizenship Act and Make Consequential Amendments to Another Act repealed the 2014 amendment to revoke citizenship for joining an armed group in an armed conflict abroad.

[108] 1985 Staatsbürgerschaftsgesetz para. 32, see also Ralph Janik 'Gesetzesverschärfung in Österreich: Dschihad und Staatsbürgerschaft (*Verfassungsblog* 17 July 2014) <http://verfassungsblog.de/gesetzesverschaerfung-in-oesterreich-dschihad-und-staatsbuergerschaft/> accessed 28 April 2019.

[109] Australian Citizenship Amendment (Allegiance to Australia) Act 2015 Section 35.

[110] *Ibid.*, Section 35A.

[111] *Ibid.*, Section 33AA.

In principle, each state determines the rules regulating acquisition and deprivation of nationality.[112] However, international law limits states' discretion in this respect. First, international law regulates the opposability of such a decision.[113] Second, under human rights law, individuals are entitled to a nationality,[114] although there is no right to a particular nationality.[115] Yet, even without such a right, arbitrary, or discriminatory refusal to grant citizenship may raise human rights issues, in particular under the right to private and family life.[116] In respect of deprivation of citizenship, international law prohibits arbitrary deprivation of nationality, which implies the right to retain a nationality.[117] Moreover, if the result of deprivation of citizenship is that the individual concerned is expelled or unable to return, the right to family and private life may be negatively affected.[118]

Deprivation of citizenship against the background of the 'foreign fighter' phenomenon combines both punitive and preventative elements.[119] On the one hand, revocation of citizenship punishes breach of the bond of allegiance between citizens and the state. However, such punishment is not the outcome of a criminal conviction. On the other hand, deprivation of citizenship serves national security purposes by preventing purportedly dangerous individuals from returning or by

[112] *Nottebohm Case (second phase)*, Judgment of 6 April 1955, ICJ Report 1955 4, 20. In international law, the term 'nationality' rather than 'citizenship' is used because the latter is traditionally conceived as regulating the consequences of nationality within the domestic legal system. In contrast, nationality concerns the relationship between a state and an individual for international purposes; see Alison Kesby, *The Right to Have Rights: Citizenship, Humanity, and International Law* (OUP 2012), 43–6.

[113] *Nottebohm Case, ibid.*, 21, see also Krähenmann, *supra* note 28, at 249.

[114] Art. 15 Universal Declaration of Human Rights. See also International Convention on the Elimination of All Forms of Racial Discrimination Art. 5 (d) (iii); European Convention on Nationality, Art. 4 (a): American Convention on Human Rights, Art. 20.

[115] Although children receive particular protection as they may find themselves without nationality due to the interplay between different municipal law rules regulating the acquisition of nationality, see Art. 24 (3) International Covenant on Civil and Political Rights, Art. 7 Convention on the Rights of the Child; Art. 29 International Convention on the Protection of the Rights of All Migrant Workers and Members of Their Families; Art. 18 Convention on the Rights of Persons with Disabilities. See also UNHRC 'Impact of Arbitrary Deprivation of Nationality on the Enjoyment of the Rights of Children Concerned, and Existing Law and Practices on Accessibility for Children to Acquire Nationality, inter alia, of the Country in which They Are Born, if They Otherwise Would be Stateless. Report of the Secretary-General' (16 December 2015) UN Doc A/HRC/31/29; CRC, 'Concluding Observations on the Combined Third and Fourth Periodic Report of Canada, Adopted by the Committee at its Sixty-First Session (17 September–5 October 2012)' (6 December 2012), UN Doc CRC/C/CAN/CO73-4, paras 40 and 41; IACtHR *Expelled Dominicans and Haitians v Dominican Republic* (28 August 2014) Series C No. 282, paras 258–261. In this context, it deserves to be underlined that the Australian Allegiance to Australia Act 2015 provides for loss of citizenship for persons aged fourteen or older.

[116] *Karassev and Family v Finland* App No 31414/96 (ECtHR, Admissibility Decision, 12 January 1999). *Petropavlovskis v Latvia* App No 44230/06 (ECtHR, 13 January 2015) paras 73 and 83.

[117] UNHRC 'Human Rights and Arbitrary Deprivation of Nationality. Report of the Secretary-General' (19 December 2013) UN Doc A/HRC/25/28, para. 4; UNHCR 'Human Rights and Arbitrary Deprivation of Nationality. Report of the Secretary-General' (14 December 2009) UN Doc A/HRC/13/34, para. 21. For an overview of how this is interpreted, see Krähenmann, *supra* note 28 and Laura van Waas, 'Foreign Fighters and the Deprivation of Nationality: National Practices and International Law Implications', in de Guttry et al., *supra* note 12, 476–80.

[118] Krähenmann, *supra* note 36, 55ff; van Waas, *supra* note 117, 476ff.

[119] van Waas, *ibid.*, 475.

permitting their deportation.[120] Deprivation of citizenship as a counterterrorism measure has been widely criticized as ineffective and counterproductive[121] as well as inconsistent with the obligations enshrined in resolution 2178 (2014) because it amounts to exporting the risk posed by individuals suspected of involvement in terrorist activities to other countries rather than investigating and prosecuting them.[122] Recently, the European Court had the opportunity to address deprivation of citizenship of a suspected British-Sudanese 'foreign fighter' in the case of *K2 v the United Kingdom*.[123] The Court rejected the application as manifestly ill-founded, amongst others because deprivation of citizenship did not have a 'significant adverse impact' on the applicant's right to family and private life as he had left the country voluntarily and his wife and children appeared no longer to be living there.[124] Moreover, due to a failure to exhaust local remedies, the Court did not need to address the fundamental question whether limitation of citizenship deprivation powers in such circumstances to dual citizens was discriminatory.[125] The Court recognized that deprivation of citizenship 'might lead to a similar—if not greater—interference'[126] with the right to respect for family and private life as arbitrary denial of citizenship, but did not seem to consider whether such 'greater' interference required a higher level of scrutiny than denial of citizenship. In particular, loss of legal status as a citizen under national law amounts to revocation of a series of acquired rights and entitlements tied to citizenship under national law, most notably, but not exclusively,[127] the full exercise of political rights, the right to return,[128] and protection against expulsion. More generally, deprivation

[120] According to the International Law Commission, revocation of citizenship for the 'sole purpose' of expulsion is arbitrary, see UNGA 'Report of the International Law Commission' (66th session, 5 May–6 June and 7 July–8 August 2014) UN Doc A/69/10 32.

[121] Anderson, *supra* note 104, para. 3.6. See also the various contributions in Audrey Macklin and Rainer Bauböck (eds), *The Return of Banishment: Do the New Denationalisation Policies Weaken Citizenship?* EUI Working Paper 2015/14.

[122] Rainer Bauböck and Vesco Paskalev 'Citizenship Deprivation. A Normative Analysis' *CEPS Paper in Liberty and Security in Europe* 2015 2.

[123] *K2 v United Kingdom* App No 42387/13 (ECtHR, Admissibility Decision, 7 January 2017). The applicant may be described as a 'foreign fighter' because he was a dual citizen and had been permanently residing in the United Kingdom before he allegedly travelled to Somalia and became involved with al-Shabaab; see para. 5.

[124] *Ibid.*, para. 62.

[125] *Ibid.*, para. 69. See also Shaheed Fatima QC 'Keeping K2 (European Human Rights Court Decision on Citizenship-Stripping) in Perspective' (*Just Security*, 10 March 2017) <https://www.justsecurity.org/38647/keeping-k2-european-human-rights-court-decision-citizenship-stripping-perspective/> accessed 28 April 2019. Similarly, the distinction between naturalized and non-naturalized citizens for the purposes of citizenship stripping power is problematic under the equality before the law principle, see van Waas, *supra* note 118, 482–4; see also Mantu, *supra* note 29, at 348.

[126] *K2 v United Kingdom, supra* note 123, para. 49.

[127] A 2011 Report by the UN Secretary General addresses exclusively how deprivation of citizenship affects a range of human rights, including in more indirect ways; see UNHRC 'Human Rights and Arbitrary Deprivation of Nationality. Report of the Secretary-General' (19 December 2011) UN Doc A/HRC/19/43. See also Kesby, *supra* note 112, 50ff, who argues that in practice many rights are still linked to citizenship.

[128] However, according to the practice of the UN Human Rights Committee, the right to enter one's own country in Art. 12 ICCPR covers not only nationals but also long-term residents and 'at the very

of citizenship places the now foreign individual in a significantly more vulnerable position than before.[129] Without entering into a detailed discussion of various conceptions of citizenship and the implications entailed for powers of deprivation,[130] the resurgence of powers of deprivation of citizenship against individuals suspected of involvement in terrorist activities during recent years, including so-called foreign fighters, illustrates a renewed focus on citizenship conceptualized 'as a privilege, not a right.'[131] A pledge of allegiance or loyalty[132] not only plays a role in the decision to grant citizenship,[133] but, even once citizenship is acquired, it continues to be dependent on loyalty and allegiance to the state and its people.[134] Conduct that is incompatible with national values, such as purported involvement in terrorist activities, breaches this bond of allegiance[135] and allows for revocation of citizenship.[136]

least, an individual who, because of his or her special ties to or claims in relation to a given country, cannot be considered to be a mere alien. This would be the case, e.g., of nationals of a country who have been stripped of their nationality in violation of international law.' See HRC 'CCPR General Comment No. 27: Art. 27 (Freedom of Movement)' 2 November 1999, UN Doc CCPR/C/21Rev.1/Add.9, para. 20.

[129] UNHRC 'Human Rights and Arbitrary Deprivation of Nationality. Report of the Secretary-General', *supra* note 127.

[130] For such a discussion, see, e.g., Kesby, *supra* note 112, in particular 68ff; Mantu, *supra* note 29, 15ff; Bauböck and Paskalev, *supra* note 122, 8–15.

[131] Press Association, 'Theresa May Strips Citizenship from 20 Britons Fighting in Syria' *The Guardian* (23 December 2013) <http://www.theguardian.com/politics/2013/dec/23/theresa-may-strips-citizenship-britons-syria> accessed 28 April 2019; Sabra Lane, 'Citizenship is a Privilege not a Right Says New Minister Assisting PM on Counter Terrorism' *Australian Broadcasting Corporation* (25 May 2015) <http://www.abc.net.au/7.30/content/2015/s4242230.htm> accessed 28 April 2019.

[132] While nationality is often described as a bond of allegiance, in this sense see the *Nottebohm Case, supra* note 112, at 24. However, as Sandra Mantu argues, 'today these two notions are no longer congruent', see Mantu, *supra* note 29, at 5.

[133] See analysis of a pledge of loyalty for the purposes of acquiring citizenship in *Petropavloskis v Latvia, supra* note 116, para. 80 ff.

[134] Mantu, *supra* note 29, 15ff and 347ff.

[135] For example, the 2015 Australian Citizenship Amendment (Allegiance to Australia) Act provides that the Purpose of the Act is to recognize that 'Australian citizenship is a common bond, involving reciprocal rights and obligations, and that citizens may, through certain conduct incompatible with the shared values of the Australian community, demonstrate that they have severed that bond and repudiated their allegiance to Australia.' Similarly, the British government argued that the distinction between naturalized and non-naturalized mono-nationals for the purposes of deprivation of citizenship for conduct seriously prejudicial to the vital interests of the United Kingdom was not discriminatory because 'there was and is an objective basis for such a restriction in relation to a measure which is intended to protect the vital interests of the UK. Naturalised citizens have chosen British values and have been granted citizenship on the basis of their good character. It is therefore appropriate to restrict a measure with such serious consequences as becoming stateless to naturalized citizens.' See Home Office, 'Immigration Bill. European Convention on Human Rights. Supplementary Memorandum by the Home Office' January 2014 <https://www.gov.uk/government/uploads/system/uploads/attachment_data/file/276660/Deprivation_ECHR_memo.pdf> accessed 28 April 2019, para. 15. See also Mantu, *supra* note 29, at 203.

[136] Patrick Sykes, 'Denaturalisation and Conceptions of Citizenship in the "War on Terror"' (2016) *Citizenship Studies* <http://dx.doi.org/10.1080/13621025.2016.1191433> accessed 28 April 2019. He argues that recasting citizenship as conditioned upon good conduct opens up exceptions within the conceptualization of citizenship as a right.

5 Conclusion

The response to the 'foreign fighter' phenomenon has been quite extraordinary. On the international level, the Security Council adopted resolution 2178, a legislative resolution that imposes sweeping obligations on states, including by creating a new offence of travel for terrorist purposes. Moreover, in resolution 2178, the Security Council endorsed countering violent extremism as a conceptual framework to address the threat of 'foreign fighters' and terrorism more generally. Amongst the measures taken by states to curtail the phenomenon of 'foreign fighters', two kinds of measures stand out, also when compared to the previous wave of counterterrorism measures in the aftermath of 9/11. First, under the guise of countering violent extremism, states curtail freedom of expression, in particular in digital space, by banning, removing, or otherwise rendering inaccessible 'terrorist' content. Second, the use of deprivation of citizenship of suspected 'foreign fighters' and other individuals suspected of involvement with terrorist activities has increased. Both measures illustrate a trend to exclude and delimit the normative space available to individuals to conduct and opinions that are within the norm accepted by the majority. Failure to be a 'good' citizen may lead to exclusion in the form of deprivation of citizenship. Similarly, while digital communication and information technology have been hailed for their potential to empower individuals by enabling them to share and exchange critical views and to find otherwise unattainable information, sweeping measures to counter violent extremism limit this space and can be used to stifle dissent and prevent discussion of important social issues. Moreover, the effectiveness—and hence the necessity—of both measures for counterterrorism purposes is doubtful. Radicalization theories tend to overemphasize the link between extremist ideas, including exposure to such ideas, and resort to violence.[137] Moreover, the limited available data suggest that online radicalization without other external influences, including peer groups, is extremely rare.[138] Similarly, resort to deprivation of citizenship as a counterterrorism tool appears not only ineffective but also incoherent: rather than cooperating to bring to justice those involved in terrorist activities, states are trying to prevent the return of those individuals.[139] Finally, such measures may

[137] UNHRC 'Report of the Special Rapporteur on the Promotion and Protection of Human Rights and Fundamental Freedoms While Countering Terrorism', *supra* note 14, para. 40. Most studies on 'terrorist' use of the internet focus on the 'supply' side, i.e., the availability of terrorist and extremist material, but not how individuals consume and interact with such material and the role it plays in individual paths of radicalization. See C. Edwards and L. Gribbon, 'Pathways to Violent Extremism in the Digital Era' (2013) 158(5) *The RUSI Journal* 41.

[138] Reynolds and Hafez, *supra* note 91, at 20.

[139] See references in notes 121 and 122 *supra*.

also further foster feelings of exclusion and marginalization, which is consistently identified as a condition conducive to violent extremism.[140]

Postscript: in December 2017, the Security Council adopted Resolution 2396 (2017) which focuses on a series of measures to address returning 'foreign terrorist fighters' and their accompanying family members, including their rehabilitation and reintegration.

[140] UNGA 'Plan of Action to Prevent Violent Extremism', *supra* note 17, paras 27–28.

Multiple Actors in Framing EU External Policy

The Case of the EU Global Security Strategy

Ilze Ruse

1 Introduction

In recent years the EU has been exposed to various external and internal challenges. Overcoming crises has become a routine modus operandi of the EU and its Member States. The question of the capability of the EU to respond to crisis situations in a rapid and coherent manner has thus become increasingly important.

The foreign policy of the European Union has been a reactive rather than a proactive policy area of the EU because of the Member States' reluctance to give up national competence over this policy area, which stands at the heart of high politics.[1] The early days of European foreign policy cooperation, starting with the missed opportunity of the European Defence Community in 1952, political cooperation in 1970, and the gradual establishment of the Common Foreign and Security Policy (CFSP) with the Maastricht Treaty, were marked by slow but deliberate steps.

The CFSP is neither an exclusive nor a shared competence under the Treaty on the Functioning of the European Union (TFEU), which explains that legally competence is divided between the Member States and EU institutions in a *sui generis* manner. Article 2(4) TFEU confers on the Union competence, in accordance with the provisions of the TEU, to define and implement a common foreign and security policy, including the progressive framing of a defence policy.[2] The nature of that competence is not clarified. Article 24(1) TFEU provides that Union competence covers all areas of foreign policy and all questions relating to the Union's security. Further, Article 24(3) TEU instructs the Member States to support the policy actively and unreservedly in a spirit of loyalty, and to comply with Union action in this area. Decisions on operational action commit the Member States to the positions they adopt and in the conduct of their activity (Article 28(2) TEU). Member States must also ensure that their national policies conform to the Union's

[1] Charlotte Bretherton and John Volger, *The European Union as a Global Actor* (Routledge 2006) 1–12.
[2] Art. 2(4) TFEU.

Ilze Ruse, *Multiple Actors in Framing EU External Policy: The Case of the EU Global Security Strategy* In: *How International Law Works in Times of Crisis*. Edited by: George Ulrich and Ineta Ziemele, Oxford University Press (2019).
DOI: 10.1093/oso/9780198849667.003.0005

positions (Article 29 TEU). They are required to consult one another within the European Council, and the Council of the European Union on any matter of foreign and security policy of general interest in order to determine a common approach (Article 32 TEU). It can be stated that the European Council and the Council of the European Union are the most important institutions for the conduct of the CFSP.

This explains why the Member States play such a substantial role among multiple actors in determining EU decisions in the field of external action, along with the External Action Service (EEAS) that has been given a prominent role under the Lisbon Treaty.

This chapter argues that the institutional set-up and interaction between the Member States and the EEAS matters for policy output in the field of CFSP and influences the effectiveness of the EU to decide and take action in responding to external challenges. In spite of the EEAS leadership in framing action in foreign policy, the Member States retain their role and closely monitor the mandate that has been granted to the EEAS through delegation of policy-framing functions.

As a *sui generis* bureaucratic body, the EEAS has gained significant attention after its establishment under the Lisbon Treaty from academics and practitioners alike, with a frequent focus on assessing its potential in delivering the intended optimization, efficiency, and coherence of EU foreign policy.[3] Consisting of civil servants from two EU institutions and Member State diplomatic services, the EEAS has become a laboratory for solving the EU's 'capacity expectations gap'[4] and fascinates or frightens supporters and opponents, respectively, as a new type of 'foreign ministry'.[5]

According to the Council Decision establishing the service in 2010, the EEAS 'shall support'[6] the High Representative and Vice President of the European Commission (HR/VP) in ensuring coherency and consistency in the EU's external action and implementing the CFSP, as well as supporting her under her mandate as the HR/VP.[7] After fierce inter-institutional negotiations over form and content, it was decided in 2010 that the EEAS would stand outside the Commission or Council bodies, and consist of civil servants from the European

[3] Bart Van Vooren, 'A Legal-Institutional Perspective on the European External Action Service' (2011) 48 *Common Market Law Review* 475–502, at 478; Poul Jonas , 'EU Foreign Policy After Lisbon: Will the New High Representative and the External Action Service Make a Difference?' (2008) 2 *CAP Policy Analysis* 32.

[4] Christopher Hill, 'The Capability–Expectations Gap or Conceptualising Europe's International Role' (1993) 31(3) *Journal of Common Market Studies* 305–28.

[5] Federica Bindi, 'One Year On: Assessing the European Foreign Policy and the European External Action Service' (2011) 17(2) *Brown Journal of World Affairs* 129.

[6] Council of the European Union, 'Council Decision of 26 July 2010 establishing the organisation and functioning of the European External Action Service', 2010/427/EU, Brussels, 26 July 2010.

[7] Van Vooren, *supra* note 3; Simon Duke, 'The European External Action Service: Antidote against Incoherence?' (2012) 17(1) *European Foreign Affairs Review* 45.

Commission, the diplomatic services of the Member States, and the Council Secretariat. By depriving the Commission of DG Relex and the Union's delegations, the EEAS stripped the Commission both in terms of competence and staff. Significant institutional changes were undertaken in the name of less duplication and enhanced efficiency and coherence in the EU's external representation.[8]

Although the Member States were able to ensure their place in the new institutional arrangements, it is far from clear who dominates the interaction. Some studies consider that at the EEAS dominance is weakened because of conflicting working cultures between the Commission staff and Member State diplomatic servants inside the EEAS.[9] Others argue that in the long run, there is a possibility of the service wandering off on its own orbit. From the legal perspective, the definition of the EEAS in the Lisbon Treaty is very short and general: it 'shall support' the HR/VP in fulfilling the mandate.[10] There is no clear list of EEAS internal rules of procedure. This arms the service with a margin of manoeuvre that it can potentially use for pursuing its own intentions and shaping its own identity in the long run.[11]

This chapter aims to investigate—with the help of political science tools—the extent to which the Member States are willing and able to keep control over the EEAS. Using the political science approach to explain the institutional structure of the CFSP actors contributes to the interdisciplinary approach to studying the EU's responsiveness towards external challenges.

Foreign policy is often explained through the lens of rational choice theories, as states are seen as self-interested agents that in the international system aim to achieve their preferred policy outcomes. Member States have their own policy preferences that they are willing to attain through the CFSP. Accordingly, there exists a 'delegation pattern' in trying to influence the EEAS to frame the policy output for it to align as closely as possible with Member States' expectations. In this regard, political science theory of the Principal–Agent (P-A) relationship in the institutional system fits the purpose of explaining the delegation pattern to the EEAS on the one hand, and control mechanisms by Member States on the other. According to the theory, the Member States are seen as *principals* and the EEAS as an *agent*.

[8] Van Vooren, *supra* note 3, at 478; Zuzana Murdoch, 'Negotiating the European External Action Service (EEEAS): Analysing the External Effects of Internal (Dis) Agreement' (2012) 50(6) *Journal of Common Market Studies* 1011.

[9] Bindi, *supra* note 5, at 129.

[10] Treaty on the Functioning of the European Union.

[11] David Spence, 'The Early Days of the European External Action Service: A Practitioner's View' (2012) 7 *The Hague Journal of Diplomacy* 116.

2 Principal–Agent Theory and its Application to Assessing the EEAS

Principal–Agent theory is a newcomer to EU studies in political science, originating in the United States in the 1980s in the form of economic governance literature.[12] It is based on the act of delegation, which is defined as 'a conditional grant of authority from a principal to an agent in which the latter is empowered to act on behalf of the former'.[13] Although it traditionally stood under the rubric of comparative politics, recent application of the theory to explaining delegation from EU Member States to its institutions, such as the European Commission,[14] the European Court of Justice, or the European Central Bank[15] has been remarkably fruitful. Applying principal–agent theory to the study of the EU has become popular in the last decade. Previous literature has focused on delegation to the European Commission, mostly in terms of internal policy areas.[16] With the entry into force of the Lisbon Treaty, an additional bureaucratic actor entered the already complex web of delegation. As a new agent in the foreign policy arena with a loosely defined mandate, the EEAS has recently thrilled advocates of principal–agent theory with its potential for strengthening or upgrading theoretical premises with new empirical evidence. The following section will outline our interpretation of the ways in which the EEAS can be mapped into principal–agent theory, and what potential insight or explanatory capacity the theory carries for the service and its engagement in drafting the European Global Strategy, the case study for this chapter.

Principal–Agent theory shares its ontological features with rational choice theory. The three key presumptions are: first, that actors—both principals and agents—are self-interested and seek to maximize their utility.[17] Second, the theory stipulates that a conflict of interest tends to occur between the principal and the agent. The third feature is an asymmetry of information between the principal and the agent, which is in favour of the latter by virtue of its specialization in the given policy domain.[18]

Principal–Agent theory suggests that the act of delegation to a third party is not random; there are strong reasons for such a cost-bearing act. Majone proposes 'two

[12] Robert Elgie, 'The Politics of the European Central Bank: Principal–Agent Theory and the Democratic Deficit' (2002) 9(2) *Journal of European Public Policy* 186–200.

[13] Darren G. Hawkins et al., 'Delegation under Anarchy: States, International Organisations, and Principal–Agent Theory' in Darren G. Hawkins et al. (eds), *Delegation and Agency in International Organizations* (CUP 2006) 3.

[14] Fabio Franchino, 'Efficiency or Credibility? Testing the Two Logics of Delegation to the European Commission' (2002) 9(5) *Journal of European Public Policy* 677–84.

[15] Elgie, *supra* note 12.

[16] Franchino, *supra* note 14.

[17] Fabrizio Gilardi, 'Principal–Agent Models Go to Europe: Independent Regulatory Agencies as Ultimate Step of Delegation' *ECPR General Conference Paper* 6–8 September 2001, at 5.

[18] *Ibid.*

logics of delegation', from which the first rationale is for the principal to gain credibility in policy commitments that is only attainable by delegating the task to the agent.[19] The second 'logic' for delegation is to delegate for the purpose of gaining policy-relevant expertise, as the agent is in a position to specialize in a subject area. In other words, the relationship between principal and agent is marked by an asymmetry of information.[20] The author suggests that delegation for credibility reasons means that the agent is granted more autonomy than when delegation takes place for reasons of policy-relevant expertise. Nevertheless, separating the two forms of delegation based on varied autonomy has been criticized by Pollack,[21] Franchino,[22] and Grant and Keohane.[23] In other words, some—but never unlimited—in-built autonomy is present *in every* form of delegation.[24] Furthermore, when principals sign a 'contract' of delegation, they often leave parts of the mandate on purpose to be completed by the agent. This is referred to as 'discretion'.[25] Hawkins and colleagues suggest that discretion is particularly employed where uncertainty exists over future developments in a constantly changing policy area, when a degree of specialization is needed that only the agent can provide, or in the scenario in which there are multiple principals with heterogonous preferences.[26]

This in-built autonomy, deliberate or not, forms the so called Principal–Agent problem.[27] Because agents are utility-maximizing actors with arguably diverging preferences from their principals, they seek to follow their own intentions where possible, and to expand their autonomy even further. The agent's abuse of its empowered position is referred to as 'slippage'.[28] As already established, agents will always have some degree of autonomy, and 'too much control … undermines the purpose of the delegation'.[29] After having made a cost–benefit analysis, principals will select a type of control mechanism that will ensure that the agent does not diverge from the principal's initial preferences too radically. This chapter will apply the list of control mechanisms from work by Gilardi,[30] who identifies several types of control:

1. Oversight: the constant monitoring of the agent's behaviour;
2. Administrative procedures: determining the agent's role in decision-making;

[19] Giandomenico Majone, 'Two Logics of Delegation: Agency and Fiduciary Relations in EU Governance' (2001) 2(1) *European Union Politics* 103–21.
[20] *Ibid.*
[21] Mark A. Pollack, 'Delegation, Agency, and Agenda-setting in the European Community' (1997) 51(1) *International Organization* 99–134 at 10.
[22] Franchino, *supra* note 14.
[23] Ruth W. Grant and Robert O. Keohane, 'Accountability and Abuses of Power in World Politics' (2005) 99(1) *American Political Science Review* 29–43.
[24] Hawkins et al., *supra* note 13, at 4.
[25] Grant and Keohane, *supra* note 23, at 31.
[26] Hawkins, *supra* note 13, at 29.
[27] *Ibid.*
[28] Pollack, *supra* note 21.
[29] Hawkins et al., *supra* note 13, at 33.
[30] Gilardi, *supra* note 17.

3. Appointments: a like-minded agent is granted power over appointees of head positions;
4. Legislation: the threat to change laws and procedures; and
5. Institutional checks by creating multiple agents that would compete and mutually control each other.

3 Who is Taking the Lead in the EU's External Action?

Over recent years the global security situation has posed numerous challenges for the EU. Europe's security environment has changed with a more militarily assertive Russia, instability in the Middle East, increased terrorist activity with the rise of the so-called Islamic State, as well as migration flows to Europe from regions of instability. The EU needs rapid and decisive action to respond to these developments. In spite of numerous crises internally and externally during the past decade, the EU has for a long time now not been able to agree on an updated strategy for its external action. Therefore, adoption of the EU Global Security strategy by the European Council on 28 June 2016 marked a significant step in regard to the EU desire to adopt a role as an external actor. But in reality, who is taking the lead in framing the action? P–A theory can assist us in providing an explanation.

With the entry into force of the Lisbon Treaty, the Member States paved the way for the creation of a new foreign policy agent in the EU architecture. In particular, Articles 18 and 27 of the Treaty of the European Union (TEU) outline the creation and mandate of the High Representative/Vice President of the European Commission, supported by the EEAS.

Because the EEAS and its head are legally and structurally linked, they can be placed within principal–agent theory as a single agent. This section will highlight the aspects of the EEAS that are most relevant to questions of delegation.

As outlined in the previous section, the reasons for delegation can be various; for example, for the purpose of enhancing credibility, and gaining policy-relevant expertise.[31] These two logics of delegation can both be applied to the EEAS. The Council Decision of 2010 establishing the organization and functioning of the EEAS explains that the formal objective for its creation was to enhance the consistency and coordination of the various external action policy areas.[32] The introduction of a single position of High Representative/Vice President of the Commission (HR/VP) was meant to allow for more coherence and dialogue between the EU institutions and the Member States.

[31] Majone, *supra* note 19.

[32] Council of the European Union, Council Decision of 26 July 2010 establishing the organization and functioning of the European External Action Service, 2010/427/EU, Brussels, para. 2.

Second, the policy delegations to the EEAS also contribute to building policy-relevant expertise by virtue of the EEAS now holding EU delegations in third countries, which are important sources of information on the ground. Furthermore, the EEAS has to stand between the EU institutions in a brokering role,[33] a position that allows the EEAS to obtain more information. Overall, an initial assessment of the creation of the EEAS supports both logics of delegation with an emphasis on credibility logic.

According to P–A theory it can be expected that principal(s) (here the Member States) will try to strike a balance between pre-emptive control and a healthy degree of discretion by the agent (here the EEAS). This largely depends on the intentions of the principal(s). Greater discretion can be desirable for an agent such as the EEAS because it consists of multiple and heterogeneous actors and also because the policy area in which delegation takes place requires flexibility that accommodates unanticipated changes of events at a global scale. In the case of leaving greater discretion to the agent (EEAS), more oversight and corrective control will be needed in the future by the principals, the Member States. So, the institutional challenge arises here. In spite of the fact that the EEAS is mandated to take action and define policy, the Member States will keep close control of the EEAS and not allow the EEAS to 'glide away' from the policy preferences of the Member States. This argument is further tested on the basis of a case study on framing the EU Global Strategy. The research question addressed is: To what extent have the Member States exerted their control over EEAS in deliberations on European Global Strategy?

4 The Case of the EU Global Strategy

The case study draws on the Principal–Agent relationship between the Member States (principals) and the EEAS (agent) in deliberating the European Global Strategy and argues that Member States have applied several types of control mechanisms as provided in Gillardi's model.[34]

Its full name, Global Strategy for the European Union' s Foreign and Security Policy (EUGS), indicates that the strategy addresses the EU's role as a global actor. The strategy deals with both internal and external threats. Compared to the European Security Strategy (ESS) of 2003, the EUGS offers 'a new overall approach to foreign and security policy'.[35] Instead of only listing the threats, as the ESS did, the new strategy for the first time outlines the interests of the EU's externally focused activity. This is done against the backdrop of current global challenges and

[33] Richard G. Whitman, 'The Rise of the European External Action Service: Putting the Strategy into EU Diplomacy?' *12th Biennial Conference of the European Union Studies Association* (EUSA), 2011.

[34] Gilardi, *supra* note 17, at 5.

[35] Sven Biscop, 'The EU Global Strategy: Realpolitik with European Characteristics', *Working paper*, Egmont Institute, June, 2016.

thus frames long-term guidelines for foreign policy and external action. The five main objectives of the EUGS are: (i) the internal security of the EU; (ii) security beyond the borders—neighbourhood; (iii) measures in times of crisis; (iv) regional stability; and (v) effective global governance.[36]

The aim of this chapter is to focus on the process of deliberations on the EUGS rather than scrutinizing its contents. At the same time, it has to be noted that in the context of its overarching nature, the EUGS frames a foreign policy strategy that merges European interests with the national interests of Member States as well as citizens. Accordingly, throughout the deliberation process we can trace the interaction between the EEAS and the Member States in integrating a set of various interests in the final document.

Work on the EUGS started with a mandate given to the High Representative by the June European Council in 2015 during the Latvian Presidency of the Council of the EU. The Council Conclusions tasked the High Representative to 'continue the process of strategic reflections with a view to preparing an EU global strategy on foreign and security policy in close cooperation with Member States, to be submitted to the European Council by June 2016'.[37] With respect to the Principal–Agent theoretical framework, this quotation bears a significant empirical value as it reveals the relationship between the actors involved in framing the new policy document. The European Council, here the principal, tasks the High Representative, the agent, to draft a strategic document for EU external action to be submitted to the European Council, the principal. Delegation logic here corresponds to the rationale for gaining policy-relevant expertise through giving the task to the EEAS. Delegation can also be justified for the purpose of enhanced credibility on policy commitments as the EUGS was supposed to become a tool for the EU's role in global foreign affairs.

In the light of the legal basis for the CFSP, adoption of a new 'foreign policy strategy' for the EU's global activity would have taken place with strong engagement by the Member States and the Council. In reality, the whole process was largely owned by the High Representative and the EEAS.

The mandate from the European Council was implemented by the High Representative through organizing the preparatory work under the EEAS institutional framework. The main body—'a task force' for collecting input from the Member States and stakeholders—was established under close supervision of the High Representative herself. In 2015, a Special Advisor to the High Representative was nominated, Dr Nathalie Tocci, the former advisor on international strategies to Federica Mogherini during her time as the Italian Foreign Minister. The special task force on drafting the EUGS included twenty-eight focal points from the Member States, which were supposed to give an input with respect to the various

[36] EU Global Strategy <https://europa.eu/globalstrategy/en> accessed 28 April 2019.
[37] European Council Conclusions, 25–26 June, 2015.

national interests of each of the Member States. This period between September 2015 and May 2016 was, by and large, the only direct involvement in the drafting of the strategy by the Member States. The Council as an EU institution was not involved in deliberations. Instead, the High Representative actively engaged various stakeholders in the consultation process. The EUGS was discussed at numerous seminars with think-tanks in the EU capitals and beyond EU borders. According to external relations law, the High Representative has competence to make proposals (Arts 18(2), 22(2), 27(1), and 43(3) of the TFEU).[38] Apart from initiating policies, the High Representative has a role in implementing and supervising the CFSP (Arts 24, 27(1), and 26(3) of the TFEU). Finally, there is an obligation to ensure consistency in the EU's external action by enhancing coordination between the Council, the EEAS, and the Commission (Arts 18(4) and 21(3) of the TFEU). The post of High Representative aims to ensure coherence and efficiency. Some scholars argue that the complexity of the relationship between the actors can sometimes lead to 'institutional schizophrenia'.[39]

Application of principal–agent theory helps to explain the relationship between the High Representative and the Council in adoption of the EUGS. The Member States have already been urging adoption of a new strategy for the EU as a global actor for some time. The previous security strategy of 2003 has become largely outdated due to changes in the international security environment, the 2004 enlargement, as well as the treaty change in 2009. The Member States have been genuinely interested in securing their preferences in the EUGS draft. However, throughout the drafting process the Member States as principals had a limited influence in delegating the policy mandate to the agent (here the EEAS) due to the fact that the Council was not engaged in that process.

The theoretical framework of this chapter hypothesizes that principals will select a type of control mechanism to ensure that the agent does not diverge from the principal's initial preferences. Indeed, this could be observed throughout the deliberation process. The Member States used the whole set of control mechanisms, as suggested in the theory—oversight, administrative procedures, appointments, legislation, and institutional checks. First, the mandate from the European Council ensured the legal basis of the Principal–Agent delegation. The final document of the EUGS was supposed to be adopted by the European Council a year later, to ensure feedback. With respect to appointments, each country nominated a responsible focal point who would interact with the EEAS taskforce. The network of focal points worked closely together to avoid asymmetries in information distribution between principal and agent. With the whole process concentrated in the EEAS, the risk was that the agent could 'glide away' and form preferences of its own. Oversight was ensured through submitting non-papers to the EEAS with

[38] Treaty on the Functioning of the European Union.

[39] Paul Craig, *The Lisbon Treaty. Law Politics and Treaty Reform* (OUP 2010) at 111.

the clearly defined interests of the governments or like-minded groups of Member States. These Member State inputs contained clear guidelines for the contents that the principal was willing to see in the final document drafted by the agent. Finally, there were additional institutional checks by the Member State governments through multiple agents. The deliberation process involved deep engagement of civil society and think-tanks in the Member States. These formats were used by respective foreign ministers to signal the preferences of their countries. For instance, the Estonian Foreign Minister called for more intensive cooperation in the field of cyber security during a conference in Tallinn,[40] the Portuguese Minister of Defence gave a special address on defence issues while speaking in Lisbon,[41] while the Latvian Foreign Minister stressed the role of Central Asia in the regional context during a discussion in Riga,[42] and so on. This ministerial input balanced the absence of the Council as an institution in drafting the strategy. The consultation process concluded with an exchange of views on the EUGS in an informal Council of foreign ministers (*Gimnich*) during the Dutch Presidency to ensure that the multiple interests involved were properly integrated in the EUGS.

4 Legal Explanations on the Limits of 'Slippage' by the EEAS

Application of principal–agent theory places the discussion in the political science domain. The aim of this section is to involve legal analysis in addressing the limits of discretion by the EEAS. The Member States, as principals, may find themselves concerned with 'slippage' by the EEAS, their agent. Thus, by virtue of the principle of conferral, any action by the Union is constrained by the limits imposed on it by the Member States.[43] This implies that in theory, as a matter of EU law, the EEAS cannot gain such behavioural autonomy that its actions fall beyond what the Member States have conferred in the Treaties. Yet this tells just half the story, given the 'uneasy relationship'[44] between the CFSP and other areas of EU law. Having developed as a separate pillar in EU law, the CFSP retained its *sui generis* nature in the Lisbon Treaty. One of the most striking features of the CFSP can be found in the last paragraph of Article 24(1) TEU, coupled with Article 275 TFEU, which takes

[40] <https://europa.eu/globalstrategy/en/estonian-fm-kaljurand-calls-more-inclusivity-international-cyber-cooperation-cyber-security> accessed 28 April 2019.

[41] <https://europa.eu/globalstrategy/en/portuguese-minister-defence-stresses-importance-european-project-defence-lisbon-conference> accessed 28 April 2019.

[42] <https://europa.eu/globalstrategy/en/latvian-fm-rinkevics-and-kazakh-deputy-fm-vassilenko-address-eu-central-asian-relations-eu-global> accessed 28 April 2019.

[43] Art. 5(1) TFEU stipulates that 'the Union shall act only within the limits of the competences conferred upon it by the Member States in the Treaties to attain the objectives set out therein'.

[44] Damian Chalmers, Gareth Davies, and Giorgio Monti, *European Union Law, 2nd edn* (OUP 2010) at 660.

the CFSP outside the jurisdiction of the Court of Justice of the European Union (CJEU). However, while the CJEU may be deprived of jurisdiction on matters of substance in CFSP actions, the aforementioned provisions make clear that the Court will have jurisdiction to 'monitor compliance with Article 40 [TEU]'. In accordance with Article 40 TEU, the CFSP must be implemented in light of the principle of conferral, the CJEU maintaining jurisdiction to assure that action is taken within the correct legal basis.[45] In other words, from the perspective of attribution of conduct, the Treaties ensure that the Agent does not glide away from the mandate given by the Principal. Applying Gillard's model, the legal basis serves here as an additional control mechanism to avoid slippage by the Agent.

This principle of responsibility was made clear by the Court in the *ECOWAS* case,[46] which concerned the Cotonou Agreement concluded by the EU with a number of African, Pacific, and Caribbean states. Drawing reference to a UN-backed prohibition, certain actions under the Agreement were taken under the auspices of the CFSP, rather than under the corresponding legal basis empowering the EU institutions. Given the *sui generis* nature of the CFSP, the Court held that any measure which can be adopted under either the Community or CFSP pillar must be adopted under the Community pillar.[47] This is potentially a remarkable limitation on the action of the EEAS, which finds itself at the crossroads of competences in the Treaties.[48] This means that unless a measure finds itself fully under the CFSP, it must be taken under its corresponding *Union* legal basis and is reviewable by the CJEU, a rule that has recently been extended to include review of actions by the Head of an EU Mission formed under the CFSP.[49] Such legal constraints could be seen as having the dual consequence of ensuring that the EEAS does not 'slip' too far away from the preferences of the Member States, at the same time placing a limit on the scope of the CFSP and, consequently, the ability of the EU to act in global foreign affairs.

5 Conclusions

This chapter aimed to analyse policy delegation in the complex relationship between the European External Action Service and the Member States in carrying out external relations policy. Interaction between the EEAS and the Member States is crucial in terms of effectively responding to various external challenges that the

[45] *Ibid.*

[46] Case C-91/05 *Commission v Council* ECLI:EU:C:2008:288.

[47] *Ibid.*, para. 77.

[48] Geert De Baere and Ramses Wassel, 'EU Law and the EEAS: Of Complex Competences and Constitutional Consequences', paper presented at the conference *The EU's Diplomatic System: Post-Westphalia and the European External Action Service*, London, 19 November 2013, at 7.

[49] Case C-455/14 P *H v Council and Commission* (2016), not yet reported.

EU is facing. Any kind of 'slippage' from the mandate can create an internal contest and distrust between the principal (the Member States) and the agent (the EEAS) and drive policy output to the level of lowest common denominator.

Adoption of the European Global Security Strategy offers great potential in testing the effect of the institutional structure of the CFSP on policy output, in particular when there is a demand for action by the EU in responding to an external crisis. Through the lens of principal–agent theory, the chapter assessed the control mechanisms through which the Member States (principals) have reacted to performance by the EEAS (agent) in deliberating the new comprehensive strategy for the future of the EU as a global actor. The study hypothesized that the principals would use different control mechanisms to avoid 'slippage' by the agent. Too much discretion by the EEAS would leave the Member States with less influence in drafting a new security vision for the EU.

Empirical findings demonstrate that in spite of the fact that the EEAS appeared to demonstrate a high level of leadership throughout the drafting process, the Member States managed to integrate their preferences in the document successfully through appointing their focal points, sharing input-papers, and actively engaging foreign ministers throughout the multiple agent network during the consultation process. Accordingly, through various control mechanisms the Member States ensured that their preferences were taken into account by making the strategy more concrete and operational. The chapter notes the legal limits to the CFSP under EU law, which simultaneously operates as a legal safeguard against agent 'slippage'.

In conclusion, the EUGS is one of the most significant policy documents in recent years in the field of EU external relations. The process of deliberations between 2015 and 2016 showed impressive work by the EEAS under the direct leadership of the High Representative. Yet, the final result has to be viewed as collaboration between various stakeholders. The Member States actively communicated their preferences through multiple channels, to ensure that the new EUGS document accommodates the preferences of all actors. The chapter reveals a significant aspect with regard to the institutional architecture within the CFSP, in that the Lisbon Treaty granted the High Representative/Deputy Commission President significant power in framing EU foreign policy, although the Member States are reluctant to acknowledge this fully and view foreign policy as their own exclusive realm of action. This poses a challenge to the EU's influence as an external actor in global affairs, in particular in times of crisis. There is only one way forward: the complex institutional set-up of multiple actors in the field of EU external relations requires a high level of coordination and complementarity among all relevant actors.

Activating the Mutual Assistance Clause of the Treaty on the European Union and the Right of Self-defence

*Carlos Espaliú Berdud**

1 Introduction

As a result of the train attacks in Spain in 2004, the European Union (EU) inserted mutual defence measures into the Lisbon Treaty. Thus, Article 42(7) of the Treaty on European Union (TEU) stipulates that 'if a Member State is the victim of armed aggression on its territory, the other Member States shall have towards it an obligation of aid and assistance by all the means in their power, in accordance with Article 51 of the United Nations Charter'. After the terrorist attacks in Paris on 13 November 2015, French President François Hollande invoked Article 42(7) TEU, requesting bilateral aid and assistance from other EU Member States. During meeting 3426 of the Foreign Affairs Council of the EU on 17 November 2015, defence ministers expressed their unanimous and full support for France and their readiness to provide all necessary aid and assistance to that country.[1] This was the first time in EU history that the defence ministers unanimously decided to activate Article 42 (7) TEU, also called the 'mutual assistance clause'.

In the current crisis in the aftermath of the 2015 Paris attacks, not dissimilar to the terrorist acts of 11 September 2001, one of the most discussed issues is whether the Paris incidents constitute an 'armed attack' requisite to trigger the right to self-defence in the light of the wording of Article 51 of the United Nations Charter of 1945 (hereinafter UN Charter).

The question arises due to the absence in the UN Charter of any definition of the expression 'armed attack', and in particular to Article 51's silence on the personality of those committing such an attack, or the authority on behalf of whom such an

* The author gratefully acknowledges Dr Edward Cavanagh, Fellow of Downing College, University of Cambridge, for his commentaries on this work.

[1] Council of the European Union, Meeting No. 3426, Brussels, 16 November 2015, available at: <http://www.consilium.europa.eu/en/meetings/fac/2015/11/16-17/> accessed 28 April 2019.

Carlos Espaliú Berdud, *Activating the Mutual Assistance Clause of the Treaty on the European Union and the Right of Self-defence* In: *How International Law Works in Times of Crisis.* Edited by: George Ulrich and Ineta Ziemele, Oxford University Press (2019).
DOI: 10.1093/oso/9780198849667.003.0006

attack was committed, that might justify self-defence. Traditionally, it was understood that armed attacks had to emanate from a state, but some have seen UN Security Council Resolutions 1368 (2001) and 1373 (2001), which recognized—in the context of the 2001 terrorist attacks upon New York, Washington, DC, and Pennsylvania—'the inherent right of individual or collective self-defence in accordance with the Charter',[2] a first step in the direction to claim the right of self-defence in response to terrorist attacks.

Should the responses of the EU Member States to the Paris attacks, activating the mutual assistance clause, be seen as a move towards the formation of a new customary rule reshaping the content of the right of individual or collective self-defence in accordance with Article 51 of the UN Charter and customary law? Or rather, should that invocation of Article 42 (7) TEU be considered a violation of the UN Charter as to the law of self-defence? On these questions, it should be noted from the outset that the right of self-defence is not rooted solely within conventional international law through Article 51 of the UN Charter. Of course, the right of self-defence was a regular feature in discussions about war and peace, within natural law and *ius gentium* traditions, even before the 'state' had become the normative authority in international affairs.[3] More recently though, it is significant that the 1986 decision of the International Court of Justice (ICJ) in *Nicaragua v USA* appears to confirm that the right of self-defence also exists within customary international law. The Court sustained that opinion on the basis that the UN Charter itself employs the term 'inherent right' in Article 51,[4] and on the consensus shown by adoption of the Declaration on the Principles of International Law concerning Friendly Relations and Cooperation among States in accordance with the Charter of the United Nations (UN General Assembly Resolution 2625 (XXV) of 24 October 1970). For the Court, that resolution 'demonstrates that the States represented in the General Assembly regard the exception to the prohibition of force constituted by the right of individual or collective self-defence as already a matter of customary international law'.[5]

In order to clarify these matters, this chapter will address, first, the scope of '*ratione personae*' under Article 51 of the UN Charter. Second, we will review the practice of states before the 2001 terrorist attacks in the context of the activity of the UN Security Council, for its great responsibilities regarding security issues and in particular with regard to Article 51 of the UN Charter. Third, we are going

[2] UNSC Res 1368 (12 September 2001). For its part, Resolution 1373 (2001) reaffirmed 'the inherent right of individual or collective self-defence as recognized by the Charter of the United Nations as reiterated in resolution 1368 (2001)'; see: UNSC Res 1373 (28 September 2001).

[3] Stephen C. Neff, *War and the Law of Nations: A General History* (CUP 2008) 7–158.

[4] *Military and Paramilitary Activities in and against Nicaragua (Nicaragua v United States of America)* (Merits) [1986] ICJ Rep 102, para. 193.

[5] *Ibid.*, 103, para. 193.

to weigh the practice of states with respect to the right of self-defence, mainly in the framework of UN Security Council activity after the Twin Towers attacks of 2001. Fourth, we will see new developments regarding the definition of aggression and new collective self-defence pacts. Fifth, we are going to examine the question of the right of terrorist groups to self-defence in cases *before* the ICJ after the Twin Towers attacks of 2001. Finally, we will try to come up with some conclusions regarding the controversial issue of the emergence of a new norm of customary law allowing states to exercise the right to self-defence against terrorist attacks in international law.

2 Scope of '*Ratione Personae*' of the Right of Self-defence under Article 51 of the UN Charter

From the point of view of methodology, in order to ascertain whether the interpretation of the expression 'armed attack' embodied in Article 51 of the UN Charter can trigger the right of self-defence in the context of terrorism, we should develop an interpretation of this expression in relation to the rules set out in Articles 31 and 32 of the Vienna Convention on the Law of Treaties. For the sake of clarity, in this section we will deal only with the interpretation of the expression 'armed attack' following most of the elements foreseen in Articles 31 and 32 of the Vienna Convention on the Law of Treaties and we shall leave examination of state practice for the following sections.

Nevertheless, before focusing on the discussion about the '*ratione personae*' scope of the expression 'armed attack', it will be necessary to explore the '*ratione materiae*' of that expression, at least to come to grips with its basic content.

Analysis of the text of Article 51 of the UN Charter appears to encourage an interpretation that the expression 'armed attack' should be interchangeable with the word 'aggression' (noting that the French wording used in Article 51 is 'aggression armée', even if their meanings are not exactly the same). In fact, due to the absence of any relevant treaty law definition of the former, extensive use has been made of the Definition of Aggression annexed to Resolution 3314 of the UN General Assembly of 14 December 1974 in the context of self-defence.[6] The ICJ itself, in the *Nicaragua Case*, noted that '[t]here appears now to be general agreement on the nature of the acts which can be treated as constituting armed attacks'[7], and advanced—with the aim of illustrating that agreement—the description contained in Article 3 para. (g) of the Definition of Aggression[8] annexed to UN General

6 It has also been the case in connection with the definition of the crime of aggression in the context of criminal international law. In this regard, see *infra* the section on new developments in defining aggression and adoption of new obligations of mutual assistance.

7 *Nicaragua v United States of America*, *supra* note 4, para. 195.

8 *Ibid.*, 103–4.

Assembly Resolution 3314. Thus, it is clear that the Court uses the criterion of the gravity, 'scale and effects', of use of force to legitimize recourse to self-defence.[9]

Turning now to the scope '*ratione personae*' of the expression 'armed attack' included in Article 51 of the UN Charter and the possibility to cover acts by terrorist groups, it seems clear that, in view of the precedent elements, mainly Article 3 (g) of the Definition of Aggression annexed to Resolution 3314 (XXIX), terrorist acts can absolutely be considered as armed attacks if they present sufficient gravity, as long as they can be attributed to a state.[10]

This interpretation is consistent with ICJ jurisprudence, which has always refused to extend the right to self-defence against non-state actors. Only when acts by non-state entities amount to aggression and engage the responsibility of a state can the victim state have recourse to self-defence. Indeed, in the *Nicaragua* case, the Court saw self-defence as a relation between states exclusively, but in its advisory opinion for the case concerning the *Legality of the Threat or Use of Nuclear Weapons* the Court took into consideration only the possibility of states possessing nuclear weapons to use them in self-defence.[11] For instance, in the *Nicaragua* case, the Court pointed out that it saw no reason to deny that:

> in customary law, the prohibition of armed attacks may apply to the sending by a State of armed bands to the territory of another State, if such an operation, because of its scale and effects, would have been classified as an armed attack rather than as a mere frontier incident had it been carried out by regular armed forces. [12]

Here the Court places the problem of classifying armed attacks in the context of the criteria for attributing responsibility to a state for acts by a person or a group of persons. The Court itself has contributed to delimiting those criteria that were finally embodied in Article 8 of the International Law Commission's Draft Articles on Responsibility of States for Internationally Wrongful Acts[13] putting emphasis upon 'effective control'.[14] According to that provision: 'The conduct of a person or group of persons shall be considered an act of a State under international law if the person or group of persons is in fact acting on the instructions of, or under the direction or control of, that State in carrying out the conduct.'

[9] *Ibid.*, 103, para. 195 and also 127, para. 247.

[10] In that sense see, e.g.: Vianney Silvy, *Le recours à la légitime défense contre le terrorisme international* (Connaissances et Savoirs 2013) 93.

[11] For the Court, 'In order to lessen or eliminate the risk of unlawful attack, States sometimes signal that they possess certain weapons to use in self-defence against any State violating their territorial integrity or political independence' (see *Legality of the Threat or Use of Nuclear Weapons* (Advisory Opinion) [1996] ICJ Rep 226, at 246, para. 47).

[12] See *Nicaragua v United States of America, supra* note 4, para. 195.

[13] See *Yearbook of the International Law Commission, 2001*, Vol. II (Part Two).

[14] See *Nicaragua v United States of America, supra* note 4, para. 115.

In regard to the context of Article 51, it has to be stressed that this provides little help in concluding once and for all whether there is room for the right of self-defence in the face of armed attacks committed by terrorist groups. In general lines, the context of the Charter speaks against any expansion of the right to use force in international law and in favour of placing the management of a security crisis in the hands of the Security Council. That interpretation coincides with the object and purpose of the Charter. It is well known that the principal aim of the Charter is to create an organization and a correlative system in order to avoid war and maintain international security as much as possible, as is stated mainly in paragraph 1 of Article 1 of the Charter (purposes of the UN). Nevertheless, at the same time, Article 51 of the Charter considers temporary self-defence as a use of force not inconsistent with the purposes of the UN, in the words of Article 2 (4). This argument is reinforced by the fact that the Charter itself qualifies the right of self-defence as 'inherent', which implies something that existed before the Charter and is independent of it. Moreover, by using the expression 'armed attack' in the text of Article 51 and forgetting to signal who has to be the author of it, it is clear that the Charter is stressing the factor of the gravity of the use of force suffered and placing in second or third place the question of the '*ratione personae*' scope of the right of self-defence.

In view of this, it is useful to have recourse to the preparatory works of the UN Charter and the circumstances in which it was drafted. These seem to support the interpretation of Article 51 according to which armed attacks can only be directed by states, due to the common perception of international peace and security at the time in relation to the conduct of two World Wars waged by state combatants. The origin of this provision lies in the context of the intent to harmonize the operation of regional arrangements and agencies with the general provisions of the future Charter, in particular with those relating to the use of force. More precisely, the goal was to discover the best means of incorporating the prevailing Inter-American system within the new UN model, with special reference to the solidarity obligations that had been assumed under the Act of Chapultepec of 6 March 1945.[15] According to the third point of that declaration:

> every *attack of a State* against the integrity or the inviolability of the territory, or against the sovereignty or political independence of an American State, shall, conformably to Part III hereof, be considered as an act of aggression against the other States which sign this Act. In any case invasion by armed forces of one *State*

[15] In this regard, see Leland M. Goodrich and Edvard Hambro, *Charter of the United Nations. Commentary and Documents* (World Peace Foundation 1946) 175.

into the territory of another trespassing boundaries established by treaty and demarcated in accordance therewith shall constitute an act of aggression.[16]

From the wording of this text it seems clear that only actions and reactions by states were taken into consideration at the time.[17] Therefore, during the drafting of the Charter at the San Francisco Conference, the possibility to foresee extending the right of self-defence to cases of armed attacks committed by non-state actors was inconceivable.

3 Practice of States in the Context of the Activity of the UN Security Council before 2001

During the decades that followed adoption of the UN Charter, the practice of states regarding Article 51 took place mainly in the context of decolonization.

In the 1950s and 1960s, states invoked the right of self-defence in response to attacks by armed bands that were considered to be acting as instruments of other states. This was the case, for example, with regard to the Israeli occupation of the whole Sinaï Peninsula on the grounds that armed units were carrying out recurring raids into its territory from Egyptian *fedayeen* bases.[18] In that case there was no official position on the part of the Security Council because a draft resolution by the United States[19] noting that the forces of Israel had penetrated deeply into Egyptian territory in violation of the armistice agreement between Egypt and Israel was vetoed by France and the United Kingdom.[20] It should not be forgotten, moreover, that this period also witnessed the United States justifying its intervention in Vietnam as an exercise of collective self-defence, for the reason that South Vietnam had been subjected to armed attacks that were both indirect and direct.[21]

From this point onwards, during the global period of decolonization, states newly justified cross-border interventions in respect of their right of self-defence against attacks by national liberation movements from abroad. In that sense,

[16] Inter-American Reciprocal Assistance and Solidarity (Act of Chapultepec), 6 March 1945, Resolution approved by the Inter-American Conference on Problems of War and Peace at Mexico, 6 March 1945. Emphasis added.

[17] In this sense, see also *Foreign Relations of the United States: Diplomatic Papers, 1945, General: The United Nations, Vol. I* (United States Government Printing Office 1967) 665–6.

[18] UN Doc S/PV.749, 30 October 1956, § 33 (Israel).

[19] Letter dated 29 October 1956 from the representative of the United States of America to the President of the Security Council concerning 'The Palestine question: steps for the immediate cessation of the military action of Israel in Egypt' (S/3710).

[20] See UN Doc S/PV.749. The result of the vote was seven in favour, two against, with two abstentions.

[21] On this matter, see 'The legality of United States participation in the defense of Viet-Nam', Department of State bulletin (Vol. v. 54, Jan–Mar 1966) 82, <http://chssp.ucdavis.edu/programs/teaching-democracy/programs/teaching-democracy/copy_of_teaching-democracy/td-042512-1966-legality-of-u.s.-participation> accessed 28 April 2019.

we can mention interventions by Portugal, Israel, South Africa, and Southern Rhodesia in different countries.[22] In most of these cases, the Security Council denounced the interventions but based its responses on grounds other than the right of self-defence.[23] Only in very few cases did the Security Council refer to the right of self-defence. In Resolution 546 (1984) of 6 January 1984, the Security Council manifested its concern about 'the renewed escalation of unprovoked bombing and persistent acts of aggression, including the continued military occupation, committed by the racist regime of South Africa in violation of the sovereignty, airspace and territorial integrity of Angola', and reaffirmed 'the right of Angola, in accordance with the relevant provisions of the Charter of the United Nations and, in particular, Article 51, to take all the measures necessary to defend and safeguard its sovereignty, territorial integrity and independence'.[24] In its Resolution 574 (1985) of 7 October 1985, the Security Council reaffirmed the right of Angola to take all the measures necessary to defend itself in accordance with Article 51 of UN Charter.[25]

Geopolitical conditions unique to the 1970s and early 1980s provided states with greater confidence to invoke explicitly the right of self-defence in the context of 'terrorism', which represented a shift in global conflict. That was the case, for instance, for Israel, which commenced justifying its right of self-defence based on

[22] See: (1) Portugal: Complaint by Senegal concerning Portugal: (1963) UNYB 24-26; Communications concerning Portuguese Guinea (1964) UNYB 120–1; Complaints by Senegal and Portugal (1965) UNYB 134–6; Relations between other African States and Portugal (1966) UNYB 121–2; Relations between Portugal and Guinea, Portugal and Senegal, Portugal and Zambia (1967) UNYB 131–2; Relations between African States and Portugal (1968) UNYB 159–60; Relations between African States and Portugal (1969) UNYB 135–45; (2) Israel: The situation in the Middle East (1968) UNYB 191–232; The situation in the Middle East (1970) UNYB 223–40; The situation in the Middle East (1971) UNYB 177–8; The situation in the Middle East (1972) UNYB 157–71; The situation in the Middle East (1973) UNYB 178–82; Questions related to the Middle East (1978) UNYB 295 ff.; Questions related to the Middle East (1979) UNYB 325 ff.; Questions related to the Middle East (1980) UNYB 347 ff.; Middle East (1982) UNYB 428 ff.; Middle East (1985) UNYB 285–93; Middle East (1988) UNYB 217-220; (3) South Africa and Southern Rhodesia: Matters relating to Africa (1976) UNYB 163–71; Matters relating to Africa (1977) UNYB 206-221; Matters relating to Africa (1979) UNYB at 218 ff.; (1980) UNYB 252-266; Africa (1981) UNYB 214–22; Africa (1982) UNYB 310–18; Africa (1983) UNYB 169–80; Africa (1984) UNYB 177–84; Africa (1985) UNYB 178–96; Africa (1986) UNYB 155–68; Africa (1987) UNYB 163–76; Africa (1988) UNYB 158–61.

[23] (1) Portuguese interventions: UNSC Res 178 (24 April 1963); UNSC Res 204 (19 May 1965); UNSC Res 268 (28 July 1969); UNSC Res 273 (9 December 1969); UNSC Res 275 (22 December 1969); (2) Israeli interventions: UNSC Res 248 (24 March 1968); UNSC Res 256 (16 August 1968); UNSC Res 262 (31 December 1968); UNSC Res 280 (19 May 1970); UNSC Res 316 (26 June 1972); UNSC Res 332 (21 April 1973);UNSC Res 450 (14 June 1979); UNSC Res 467 (24 April 1980); UNSC Res 573 (4 October 1985); (3) South African or Southern Rhodesian interventions: UNSC Res 393 (30 July 1976); UNSC Res 403 (14 January 1977); UNSC Res 455 (23 November 1979); UNSC Res 447 (28 March 1979); UNSC Res 454 (2 November 1979); UNSC Res 475 (27 June 1980); UNSC Res 466 (11 April 1980); UNSC Res 527 (15 December 1982); UNSC Res 545 (20 December 1983); UNSC Res 546 (6 January 1984); UNSC Res 567 (20 June 1985); UNSC Res 571 (20 September); UNSC Res. 574 (7 October 1985); UNSC Res 568 (21 June 1985); UNSC Res 577 (6 December 1985); UNSC Res 580 (30 December 1985); UNSC Res 581 (13 February 1986); UNSC Res 602 (25 November 1987); UNSC Res 606 (23 December 1987).

[24] UNSC Res 546 (6 January 1984).

[25] UNSC Res 574 (7 October 1985).

the recurrent terrorist attacks that it was suffering from Lebanese territory and on the admitted helplessness of the Lebanese authorities to control their own territory.[26] Nevertheless, the Security Council did not accept Israeli arguments and by Resolution 313 (1972), 'demanded that Israel immediately desist and refrain from any ground and air military action against Lebanon and forthwith withdraw all its military forces from Lebanese territory'.[27] This was also the case for the United States, which justified some interventions in the Middle East as self-defence as well, for example the seizure of its embassy in Teheran on 4 November 1979.[28] The United States also coined the so-called Shultz doctrine, according to which those states which did not want to prevent terrorist attacks from their territories would be liable to a forcible response in the exercise of the right of self-defence. The Security Council, in the case of the American hostages in Teheran, did not elaborate upon the principles of self-defence but rather developed its interpretation in relation to the violation of international obligations arising from diplomatic and consular conventions, calling upon 'the Government of Iran to release immediately the personnel of the Embassy of the United States of America being held at Teheran, to provide them with protection and to allow them to leave the country'.[29]

Another important case of alleged self-defence was the repeated incursions by Turkey, and to a lesser extent by Iran, against Kurdish fighters operating from Iraqi soil after the 1990–1991 Gulf War. Following the presentation of some claims before the Security Council by Iraq, Turkey argued that its incursions in the territory of Iraq were due to the incapacity of that country to prevent the use of its territory for staging terrorist acts against Turkey.[30] By contrast, Iraq condemned those actions and categorically rejected the justifications advanced by Turkey for its open aggression, namely, its right to protect its national security by moving against terrorist elements, specifically the Kurdish Workers' Party, even going so far as to push them into Iraqi territory, where they were to face extirpation.[31] In response to these developments, the Security Council did not seize the opportunity to make any reference to the right of self-defence in connection to terrorist attacks, abstaining from doing so perhaps sensibly, however, amid the complicated political upheavals that followed the Second Gulf War.

Finally, in the framework of the events in the African Great Lakes and the conflict in the Democratic Republic of the Congo (DRC) between its government, supported by Angola, Namibia, and Zimbabwe, and various rebel groups, loosely allied with the neighbouring countries of Burundi, Rwanda, and Uganda in the

[26] (1972) UNYB 239.

[27] UNSC Res 313 (28 February 1972).

[28] On this matter see: Relations between Iran and the United States (1979) UNYB 307–12.

[29] UNSC Res 457 (4 December 1979).

[30] *Letter dated 24 July 1995 from the Charge d'Affaires a.i. of the permanent mission of Turkey to the United Nations addressed to the President of the Security Council*, UN Doc S1995/605, 24 July 1995.

[31] (1996) UNYB 237.

early 2000s,[32] both the DRC and Rwanda claimed to be acting in accordance with Article 51 of the UN Charter. Rwanda stated before the Security Council that the Government of the DRC had 'allied itself with the planners and perpetrators of the Rwandan genocide'. Therefore, Rwanda asked the Security Council to re-examine the circumstances which had led Rwanda 'to intervene militarily in the [DRC], in exercise of the inherent right of self-defence, pursuant to Article 51 of the Charter of the United Nations'.[33] By contrast, the DRC reaffirmed that it was within its legitimate rights to take all necessary measures to respond to the Rwandese armed aggression in accordance with Article 51 of the Charter, which included soliciting assistance from the Member States of the Southern Africa Development Community by invoking a natural right to collective and individual self-defence.[34] In the end, the Security Council, by Resolution 1304 (2000), affirmed that Rwanda had violated the sovereignty and territorial integrity of the DRC, and demanded that Rwanda withdraw all its forces from the territory of the DRC without further delay, again without elaborating upon the right of self-defence.[35]

Therefore, it appears difficult to identify within these cases—which concern armed attacks carried out by groups considered to be 'terrorists'—any customary rule recognizing the right of self-defence. While some states would continue to justify repelling terrorist activity through unilateral agreements and recourse to a customary right, they did so without the agreement of the majority of states or the Security Council's acceptance.[36]

4 Practice of States as to the Right of Self-defence, Mainly in the Framework of UN Security Council Activity after the Twin Towers Attacks of 2001

The international trend of responding to terrorist attacks in relation to self-defence carried into the new Millennium, largely due to the catastrophe of the 2001 attacks. As is well known, on 11 September 2001 (9/11), four civilian airplanes were hijacked by terrorists in the United States and deliberately crashed in New York, Washington, DC, and Pennsylvania, resulting in the loss of thousands of innocent lives.[37] Almost immediately, the UN Security Council condemned the terrorist attacks by Resolution 1368 (2001) of 12 September 2001, adopted unanimously. It also expressed its readiness to take all necessary steps to respond

[32] (2000) UNYB 114.
[33] Repertoire of the practice of the Security Council 2000–2003, 1007.
[34] *Ibid.*
[35] UNSC Res 1304 (16 June 2000).
[36] According to Vianney Silvy, state terrorism, the employment of terrorism by the state, can be equated to aggression, while purely private terrorism was traditionally considered as a simple crime to be prosecuted and punished through international cooperation, see: Silvy, *supra* note 10, at 139.
[37] (2001) UNYB 60.

to the 9/11 terrorist attacks and to combat all forms of terrorism, in accordance with its responsibilities under the UN Charter. The Council also recognized 'the inherent right of individual or collective self-defence in accordance with the Charter'.[38] A couple of weeks later, by Resolution 1373 (2001) of 28 September 2001 (also adopted unanimously), the Security Council asserted that terrorist acts constituted a threat to international peace and security and expressed its deep concern about the increase in acts of terrorism in various regions of the world. Moreover, it decided that all states were to prevent and suppress the financing of terrorist acts and called on states to work together urgently to achieve these goals. In that respect, the Security Council reaffirmed 'the inherent right of individual or collective self-defence as recognized by the Charter of the United Nations as reiterated in resolution 1368 (2001)'.[39] However, it must be highlighted that the Security Council seems to have taken those decisions under the conviction that the 9/11 attacks implied the responsibility of a state for its involvement in terrorist attacks. It has to be recalled that the Security Council had already on different occasions called upon the Taliban regime to refrain from harbouring and training terrorists and their organizations.[40] That is probably why the Security Council, in Resolution 1372 (2001), reaffirmed the principle established by the General Assembly in its declaration of October 1970 (resolution 2625 (XXV))[41] according to which 'every State has the duty to refrain from organizing, instigating, assisting or participating in terrorist acts in another State or acquiescing in organized activities within its territory directed towards the commission of such acts'.[42]

Some weeks afterwards, on 7 October 2001, the United States and the United Kingdom commenced a military operation called 'Enduring Freedom' against the Taliban in Afghanistan. By letter dated the same day, the United States announced to the President of the Security Council that, together with other states, it had already initiated actions in the exercise of its inherent right of individual and collective self-defence following the armed attacks that were carried out against the United States on 9/11 by Al-Qaeda with the support of the Taliban regime in Afghanistan.[43] It is also worth mentioning that a group of other states—the United Kingdom, Canada, France, Australia, Germany, the Netherlands, New Zealand, and Poland—were prepared to inform the Security Council in this period that they, too, had participated in military action led by the United States against Al-Qaeda

[38] UNSC Res 1368 (12 September 2001).

[39] UNSC Res 1373 (28 September 2001).

[40] See, e.g., UNSC Res 1193 (28 August 1998); UNSC Res 1214 (8 December 1998); UNSC Res 1267 (15 October 1999); UNSC Res 1333 (19 December 2000).

[41] Before 2001, the Security Council had already reiterated that principle in its resolution 1189 (1998) of 13 August 1998.

[42] UNSC Res 1373 (28 September 2001).

[43] UN Doc S/2001/946.

and the Taliban regime in Afghanistan, allegedly in accordance with the inherent right of individual or collective self-defence.[44]

In regard to the North Atlantic Treaty Organization (NATO), it has to be noted that its North Atlantic Council met on the same day of the terrorist attacks in the United States. On the following day, the Council agreed that if it was determined that the attacks were directed from abroad against the United States, they should be regarded as an action covered by Article 5 of the Washington Treaty which declares, we recall, that an armed attack against one or more of the Allies in Europe or North America shall be considered an attack against them all.[45] In that sense, on 2 October 2001, the United States informed the North Atlantic Council that an investigation had clearly determined that the individuals who carried out the attacks belonged to the worldwide terrorist network of Al-Qaeda, headed by Osama bin Laden and protected by the Taliban regime in Afghanistan.[46] Therefore, on 4 October, the North Atlantic Council decided—at the request of the United States—to take eight measures, individually and collectively, to fight against terrorism, operationalizing Article 5 of the Washington Treaty for the first time in the history of the organization.[47] On 8 October 2001, the North Atlantic Council met to review the situation and stated that even if operation 'Enduring Freedom' was not a military operation by the organization itself but a military operation led by the United States and the United Kingdom with military support from other NATO Allies, the Alliance itself would continue to provide military and other support, taking whatever defensive measures were considered by them to be necessary.[48] The invocation of Article 5 of the Washington Treaty and the measures undertaken by the organization constituted an event of tremendous relevance because these measures suppose materialization of the right of collective self-defence in the face of an attack of considerable proportions committed by a terrorist organization.

Additional support came from the EU which, through two letters addressed by the representative of Belgium to the UN Secretary-General dated 8 and 17 October 2001, conveyed its profound sympathy to the United States. For the EU, the 9/11 terrorist attacks represented an assault upon the open, democratic, tolerant, and multicultural institutions of its Member States. In this frame the EU declared its full solidarity with the United States and offered its wholehearted support for the action taken in self-defence, in conformity with the UN Charter and Security Council resolution 1368 (2001).[49]

[44] Repertoire of the practice of the Security Council 2000–2003, 1005–6.

[45] Statement by the North Atlantic Council, Press Release (2001)124, 12 September 2001.

[46] Statement by NATO Secretary General, Lord Robertson, 2 October 2001.

[47] Statement to the Press by NATO Secretary General, Lord Robertson, on the North Atlantic Council Decision on Implementation of Art. 5 of the Washington Treaty following the 11 September Attacks against the United States.

[48] Statement by NATO Secretary General, Lord Robertson, Press Release (2001) 138, 8 October 2001.

[49] Annex to the letter dated 8 October 2001 from the Permanent Representative of Belgium to the United Nations addressed to the Secretary-General, UN Doc S/2001/967. In addition, by a letter dated 20 November 2001 addressed to the UN Secretary-General, the representative of Belgium presented

For its part, the Organization of American States also supported the military operation in Afghanistan by a resolution of the ministers of foreign affairs of Member States acting as an organ of consultation in application of the Inter-American Treaty of Reciprocal Assistance (Rio Treaty). That declaration stated that the 9/11 attacks were in fact attacks against all American states and that in accordance with all the relevant provisions of the Rio Treaty and the principle of continental solidarity, all states parties to the Rio Treaty should provide effective reciprocal assistance to address such attacks. At the same time, that resolution recalled the inherent right of states to act in the exercise of the right of individual and collective self-defence in accordance with the UN Charter and with the Rio Treaty.[50]

This interpretation could also be seen to prevail in parts of Europe and Africa at this time. At its 4414th meeting on 13 November 2001, the UN Security Council held an open debate on the situation in Afghanistan in which the representatives of Norway and Egypt, for example, were at pains to stress that military operations were being pursued in Afghanistan in connection with individual and/or collective self-defence.[51]

Therefore, the popular support shown for military operations against Al-Qaeda in Afghanistan among the community of national states, and the heightened inclination to consider these actions in the framework of self-defence, appeared to create the conditions for development of a customary rule in relation to self-defence in response to terrorist attacks—attacks of a similar nature, it was increasingly accepted, to 'armed attacks' set out in Article 51 of the UN Charter. The extent to which this interpretation was confirmed through subsequent state practice remains now to be seen.

For instance, as conflict began to engulf Lebanon and northern Israel in July 2006, following the crisis of the Hezbollah attack across the Blue Line (the border demarcation set up after Israel withdrew from Lebanon in 2000), Israel became prepared to claim before the UN Security Council that it should act to uphold its 'right to act in accordance with Article 51 of the Charter of the United Nations and exercise its right of self-defence' when attacked.[52] During subsequent debates held at the Security Council regarding the reactions by Israel and the situation in Lebanon, several states representatives recognized Israel's right to act in self-defence, but cautioned at the same time that Israel should ensure that its actions were proportionate and measured, in accordance with international law.[53] Lebanon

the conclusions of the General Affairs Council of the European Union on Afghanistan, highlighting its unreserved support for coalition action undertaken in self-defence and in conformity with Security Council resolution 1368 (2001) of 12 September 2001, (see Repertoire of the practice of the Security Council 2000–2003, 1006).

[50] Twenty-Fourth Meeting of Consultation of Ministers of Foreign, Doc EA/Ser.F/II.24 RC.24/RES.1/01, 21 September 2001.

[51] Repertoire of the practice of the Security Council 2000–2003, 1005–6.

[52] Repertoire of the Practice of the Security Council 2004–2007, 1024.

[53] *Ibid.*

qualified the Israeli action/reaction as 'disproportionate aggression'.[54] At a meeting held on 20 July 2006, the Council heard a briefing by the Secretary-General in relation to the crisis in Lebanon in which the Secretary-General, while reiterating his condemnation of Hezbollah's attacks on Israel and acknowledging Israel's right to self-defence under Article 51 of the UN Charter, warned about the excessive use of force.[55] At a subsequent meeting, several state representatives recognized Israel's right to self-defence against terrorism but at the same time required from Israel a commitment to caution and restraint in the exercise of this right.[56] It is also worth mentioning that the Middle East situation was raised during the G8 2006 summit in Saint Petersburg. In that respect, the G8 leaders, while recognizing the responsibility of Hamas and Hezbollah at the origin of the upheaval, called upon Israel to exercise its right to self-defence with utmost restraint,[57] being mindful of the strategic and humanitarian consequences of its actions.[58]

Similarly, amid the crisis that befell Mali in 2012, the right of self-defence was also invoked in the face of attacks committed by terrorist groups. In January 2012, a Tuareg movement known as the 'Mouvement national pour la libération de l'Azawad', along with Islamic armed groups including Ansar Dine, Al-Qaeda in the Islamic Maghreb, and the 'Mouvement pour l'unicité et le jihad en Afrique de l'Ouest', in addition to deserters from the Malian armed forces, initiated a series of attacks against government forces in the north of the country.[59] In March 2012, a mutiny led by disaffected soldiers formerly defeated by armed groups in the north resulted in a military *coup d'état*. Once this military 'junta' took power, it suspended the constitution and dissolved the government institutions. Only through the mediation of the Economic Community of West African States (ECOWAS), in August 2012 was a Government of National Unity formed.[60] The precarious situation in Mali faced compromise when in January 2013 several terrorist elements took control of a series of towns. The deterioration in the political situation in Mali led the transitional authorities to request the assistance of France to defend state sovereignty and to restore its territorial integrity.[61] In response, on 11 January 2013, a French-led military operation called 'Operation Serval' was launched against terrorist and associated elements, which turned out to be instrumental for improving

[54] *Ibid.*

[55] UN Doc S/PV. 5492, 20 July 2006.

[56] UN Doc S/PV.5493, 19 (Slovakia); UN Doc S/PV.5493 (Resumption 1), 4 (Peru); 7 (Denmark); 12 (France); 19 (Brazil); 27 (Australia); 39 (Canada); and 41 (Guatemala).

[57] G8 2006 Summit, Middle East, St Petersburg, 16 July 2006.

[58] For Tatiana Waisberg, 'The overwhelming international community support of Israel's claim of self-defense against Lebanese territory confirms the dramatic shift promoted by reactions to the September 11, 2001, terrorist attacks.' (see: Tatiana Waisberg, *War on Terror and the New International Order: Shaping International Law Use of Force Discourse at the 21st Century* (CreateSpace 2012) 187–8.

[59] MINUSMA, United Nations Stabilization Mission in Mali, Background, available at: <https://peacekeeping.un.org/en/mission/minusma>.

[60] *Ibid.*

[61] *Ibid.*

the security of the country.[62] When this new situation in Mali, and moreover the French intervention in relation to it, was later discussed in the Security Council on 22 January 2013, the representative of Niger maintained that the intervention by France in Mali was legitimate and legal by virtue of the specific request made by the authorities of Mali under the relevant provisions of the UN Charter, mainly Article 51, 'which enshrines the principle of individual and collective self-defence'.[63] For its part, in letters to the President of the Security Council, France made no explicit reference to Article 51 of the UN Charter but offered the assurance that its actions were offered in response to a request for assistance from the Interim President of the Republic of Mali.[64] More precisely, France informed the Security Council that its armed forces supported Malian units in destroying terrorist elements from the north perceived to be threatening the very existence of Mali and the lives of its population.[65]

Finally, in the face of recurrent terrorist attacks by Islamic State (also known as Da'esh) in Iraq and the Levant, the Security Council affirmed in Resolution 2249 (2015), adopted on 20 November 2015, a week after the Paris attacks and the invocation by France of the mutual assistance clause embodied in Article 42 (7) of the TEU, that Da'esh 'constitutes a global and unprecedented threat to international peace and security'.[66] However, after condemning the long series of horrifying terrorist attacks perpetrated by Da'esh in the strongest terms,[67] the Security Council went little further than to reaffirm 'that those responsible for committing or otherwise responsible for terrorist acts, violations of international humanitarian law or violations or abuses of human rights must be held accountable'.[68] Still, the Security Council was prepared to call upon UN Member States to take all necessary measures, in compliance with international law (and in particular the UN Charter) as well as international human rights, refugee, and humanitarian law, on the territory under the control of Da'esh in Syria and Iraq, to redouble and coordinate their efforts to prevent and suppress terrorist acts and to destroy the safe havens they had established over significant parts of Iraq and Syria.[69] This resolution refrained from any invocation or recognition of the right to self-defence, as indeed it had in its resolutions of 2001 after the terrorist attacks by Al-Qaeda in the United States.[70]

[62] *Ibid.*

[63] UN Doc S/PV. 6905, 22 January 2013, 14.

[64] Repertoire of the Practice of the Security Council 2012–2013, 91.

[65] *Ibid.*, 92.

[66] UNSC Res 2249 (20 November 2015).

[67] *Ibid.*, para. 1.

[68] *Ibid.*, para. 4

[69] *Ibid.*, para. 5.

[70] A commentary on the Security Council resolution can be found in: Marc Weller, 'Permanent Imminence of Armed Attacks: Resolution 2249 (2015) and the Right to Self Defence Against Designated Terrorist Groups', (2015) November, *European Journal of International Law Analysis*, available at: <http://www.ejiltalk.org/permanent-imminence-of-armed-attacks-resolution-2249-2015-and-the-right-to-self-defence-against-designated-terrorist-groups/?> accessed 28 April 2019.

Nevertheless, in that context, some states—such as France[71] and Germany[72]—had already declared that they can resort to the use of force based on the right of self-defence.

Even if this account of state practice is not exhaustive, it shows increasing support for extending the right to self-defence in the face of attacks by terrorist groups, which probably represents another manifestation of the growing relevance of non-state actors in the international society of our time.

5 Practice of States: New Developments in Defining Aggression and New Collective Self-defence Pacts

After the 2001 terrorist attacks, some substantial developments have occurred in the African continent in regard to the definition of aggression in international law and adoption of new pacts including mutual assistance obligations.

On the one hand, on 31 January 2005, the Assembly of the African Union adopted the African Union Non-Aggression and Common Defence Pact, which contains a definition of aggression in which armed attacks committed by non-state actors are taken into account. Indeed, in its Article 1 the following definition figures:

> 'Aggression' means the use, intentionally and knowingly, of armed force or any other hostile act by a State, a group of States, an organization of States or *non-State actor(s)* or by any foreign or external entity, against the sovereignty, political independence, territorial integrity and human security of the population of a State Party to this Pact, which are incompatible with the Charter of the United Nations or the Constitutive Act of the African Union. The following shall constitute acts of aggression, regardless of a declaration of war by a State, group of States, organization of States, or *non-State actor(s)* or by any foreign entity: […] xi. the encouragement, support, harbouring or provision of any assistance for the commission of *terrorist acts* and other violent trans-national organized crimes against a Member State.[73]

[71] *Identical letters dated 8 September 2015 from the Permanent Representative of France to the United Nations addressed to the Secretary-General and the President of the Security Council*, UN Doc S/2015/745, 9 September 2015.

[72] On this point see: Anne Peters, 'German Parliament Decides to Send Troops to Combat ISIS—Based on Collective Self-Defense "in conjunction with" SC Res. 2249', (2015) December, *European Journal of International Law Analysis*, available at: <http://www.ejiltalk.org/german-parlament-decides-to-send-troops-to-combat-isis-%E2%88%92-based-on-collective-self-defense-in-conjunction-with-sc-res-2249/> accessed 28 April 2019.

[73] Emphasis added.

On top of the definition, Article 4 of the Pact states that: 'a) State Parties undertake to provide mutual assistance towards their common defence and security vis-à-vis any aggression or threats of aggression'. This declaration seems quite similar to the mutual assistance clause embodied in Article 42 (7) of the TEU and is very rich in significance in the context of this research. Theoretically at least, a state party to this pact that is the object of a terrorist attack will be entitled to have recourse to the right of self-defence and to call upon the assistance of the other states parties.

On the other hand, but along the same lines, some months later some African states adopted the Protocol on Non-Aggression and Mutual Defence in the Great Lakes Region.[74] This text contains another definition of aggression that takes into consideration acts by non-state actors.[75] Moreover, in Article 8 (10), the signatory states affirmed that: 'Nothing in the provisions of this Article shall affect the right of individual or collective self-defence in the event of an armed attack, or the failure, after notification or request, to intercept and disarm members of an armed group pursued by the defence and security forces of a Member State.'[76]

The above-mentioned instruments possess great relevance both in conventional law and in customary law as long as they show the *opinio juris* of African states which did not take part in the alliance against Al-Qaeda and Afghanistan in 2001 but clearly consider that the right of self-defence can be used in the face of attacks committed by non-state actors in general and by terrorist groups in particular.

In the universal sphere, the definition of the crime of aggression adopted by amending the Rome Statute of the International Criminal Court (ICC) at the first Review Conference of the Statute in Kampala, Uganda, in 2010 also sheds some light over the status of *opinio iuris* regarding possible extension of the right of self-defence to attacks committed by non-state actors.

It was originally foreseen that the ICC would have jurisdiction from the beginning over the crime of aggression. However, due to the circumstances of adoption of the Statute during the Rome Conference, in particular discussion of the issue of the relationship between the Security Council and the ICC, that outcome was postponed.[77] Thus, Article 5 (1)(d) of the Rome Statute determined that the ICC would have jurisdiction over the crime of aggression, while Article 5 (2) set out that this

[74] Second Summit of the International Conference on the Great Lakes Region, Protocol on Non-Aggression and Mutual Defence in the Great Lakes Region.

[75] 'Aggression: the use, intentionally and knowingly, of armed force or any hostile act, as referred to in Article 1(3)(g to k), perpetrated by a State, a group of States, an organization of States or an armed group or by any foreign or external entity, against the sovereignty, political independence, territorial integrity and human security of the population of a Member State, contrary to the Constitutive Act of the African Union, the African Union Non-Aggression and Common Defence Pact or the Charter of the United Nations.'

[76] Second Summit of the International Conference on the Great Lakes Region, Protocol on Non-Aggression and Mutual Defence in the Great Lakes Region.

[77] See Draft Statute for the International Criminal Court, United Nations Diplomatic Conference of Plenipotentiaries on the Establishment of an International Criminal Court, Rome, Italy, 15 June–17 July 1998, A/CONF.183/2/Add.1, 14 April 1998.

jurisdiction was to be exercised only once a provision had been adopted defining the crime and setting out the conditions under which such jurisdiction should be exercised.[78] According to Article 123, seven years after the entry into force of the Statute, a Review Conference was to be convened by the UN Secretary-General to consider amendments to the Statute, including the list of crimes contained in Article 5. The conference was held in Kampala, Uganda, 31 May–11 June 2010, and adopted a definition of the crime of aggression.[79] Therefore, under the new Article 8 bis (1) of the Rome Statue the crime of aggression consists of 'the planning, preparation, initiation or execution by a person in a position effectively to exercise control over or to direct the political or military action of a state, of an act of an aggression which, by its character, gravity and scale, constitutes a manifest violation of the Charter of the United Nations'. Moreover, Article 8 bis (2) also considers an act of aggression 'the use of armed force by a state against the sovereignty, territorial integrity or political independence of another state, or in any manner inconsistent with the Charter of the United Nations'. The Article then lists the same acts as the UN General Assembly's resolution 3314 (XXIX) qualifying as acts of aggression.

Importantly, then, for those states which have adopted this definition of aggression, this reflects a crime committed by a political or military leader of a state. According to that definition the crime of aggression cannot be committed by non-governmental actors such as organized armed groups or terrorist groups. It may therefore be implied that, according to a strict reading of the Statute, terrorist groups cannot commit acts of aggression and therefore it follows that their actions cannot provide the necessary condition for exercise of the right of self-defence in response on the part of states.

6 The Question of the Right to Self-defence in Cases before the ICJ after the Twin Towers Attacks of 2001

After the Twin Towers attacks and UN Security Council resolutions 1368 (2001) and 1373 (2001), the ICJ continues to defend its previous position according to which self-defence is only a right of states.

In the *Wall* case, Israel raised the question of the exercise of self-defence against 'private' terrorist attacks coming from Palestinian territory, as Palestine remains

[78] The actual exercise of jurisdiction is subject to a decision to be taken after 1 January 2017 by the same majority of States parties to the Rome Statute as is required for the adoption of an amendment to the Statute, and one year after the ratification or acceptance of the amendments by thirty States parties, whichever is later (see Review conference of the Rome Statute of the International Criminal Court, Kampala, 31 May–11 June 2010, Official Records, at 6).

[79] Review conference of the Rome Statute of the International Criminal Court, Kampala, 31 May–11 June 2010, Official Records, Resolution RC/Res.6 of 11 June 2010, Annex I, Amendments to the Rome Statute of the International Criminal Court on the Crime of Aggression.

to be considered a state in international law. Indeed, for Israel, the construction of a fence in order to halt terrorist attacks was a measure wholly consistent with the right of states to self-defence enshrined in Article 51 of the UN Charter and Security Council resolutions 1368 (2001) and 1373 (2001).[80] In its advisory opinion of 9 July 2004, the Court refused to take Article 51 of the UN Charter into consideration in the case, above all because Israel did not claim that the attacks against it were imputable to a foreign state, and affirmed explicitly that 'Article 51 of the Charter […] recognizes the existence of an inherent right of self-defence *in the case of armed attack by one State against another State*'.[81] Furthermore, regarding UN Security Council resolutions 1368 (2001) and 1373 (2001), the Court noted that Israel exercises control in the Occupied Palestinian Territory and, as Israel itself stated, the threat which it regarded as justifying construction of the wall originated within, and not outside, that territory. This situation differed from those hypothesized by the Security Council resolutions, leaving Israel incapable of invoking those resolutions in support of its claim to be exercising the right of self-defence.[82]

Upon concluding that Article 51 of the Charter had no relevance in the *Wall* case, the Court moved on to consider whether Israel could rely on a state of necessity, which would preclude the wrongfulness of constructing the wall.[83] Beginning with the acknowledgement that Israel had to face numerous indiscriminate and deadly acts of violence against its civilian population, the Court noted that Israel had the right, and indeed the duty, to respond in order to protect the life of its citizens, but the measures that it should take were bound nonetheless to remain in conformity with applicable international law.[84] To sum up, the Court found that Israel could not rely on the right of self-defence or on a state of necessity in order to preclude the wrongfulness of constructing the wall, and its associated 'regime'.[85]

The Court's findings in this case may allow us to refine the present status of the right to self-defence and those circumstances in which that right can be exercised. To the Court, it seems that states have an inherent right, even a duty, to defend themselves from attack. Under certain circumstances, if an attack amounts to aggression and if, therefore, in line with the Charter, that aggression emanates directly or indirectly from another state, the defensive reaction by the victim state can be considered a legitimate exercise of self-defence. In other circumstances, the

[80] *Legal Consequences of the Construction of a Wall in the Occupied Palestinian Territory* (Advisory Opinion) (2004) ICJ Rep 194, para. 138.

[81] *Ibid.*, para. 139. Emphasis added.

[82] *Ibid.*

[83] *Ibid.*, 194, para. 140.

[84] *Ibid.*, 195, para. 141.

[85] *Ibid.*, para. 142. These measures were previously declared by the Court to be contrary to international law, as they were seen to severely impede the progress of the Palestinian people towards self-determination; moreover they constituted breaches of several of Israel's obligations under international humanitarian law and human rights instruments applicable to it, see *ibid.*, 184, para. 122, and *ibid.*, 193–4, para. 137.

defensive reaction by the victim state could be legitimate in international law but would not be considered as exercise of the right of self-defence.

Some judges, in their separate opinions and declarations appended to the advisory opinion, were quite critical of the Court's advisory opinion in light of the Court's interpretation of Article 51 of the UN Charter according to which states can have recourse to self-defence only in cases of armed attacks committed by states. For Judge Kooijmans, it was true that it had been the generally accepted interpretation for more than fifty years that 'armed attacks' should be committed by states in order to legitimize recourse to self-defence.[86] However, resolutions 1368 (2001) and 1373 (2001) have introduced a new element regarding 'acts of international terrorism' that should be taken into consideration. For their part, judges Buergenthal and Higgins underlined that nothing in Article 51 of the UN Charter should be read as reserving the right to self-defence for cases or armed attacks by states.[87] Finally, Judge Buergenthal stressed that resolutions 1368 (2001) and 1373 (2001) supported a more flexible construction of Article 51 than the formalistic one that the Court followed in its advisory opinion.[88]

In *Armed Activities on the Territory of the Congo (Democratic Republic of the Congo v Uganda)*, the DRC argued that Uganda had violated the principle of both conventional and customary law of non-use of force in international relations, including the prohibition of aggression. For the Congolese, Uganda had perpetrated that violation by engaging in military and paramilitary activities against the DRC by occupying its territory and by actively extending military, logistic, economic, and financial support to irregular forces having operated there.[89] By contrast, according to the Court, while Uganda claimed to have acted in self-defence, it did not ever claim that it had been subjected to an armed attack by the armed forces of the DRC.[90] To the Court, there was no satisfactory proof of involvement in the alleged attacks, direct or indirect, by the government of the DRC. The attacks did not emanate from armed bands or irregulars sent by the DRC or on behalf of that state, within the sense of Article 3 *(g)* of General Assembly resolution 3314 (XXIX) on the definition of aggression, adopted on 14 December 1974.[91] Judge Kooijmans was critical of this opinion: 'If armed attacks are carried out by irregular bands from such territory against a neighbouring State, they are still armed attacks even if they cannot be attributed to the territorial State.'[92]

[86] *Legal Consequences of the Construction of a Wall in the Occupied Palestinian Territory* (Advisory Opinion) [2004] ICJ Rep, Separate opinion of Judge Kooijmans, 230, para. 35.

[87] *Ibid.*, Declaration of Judge Buergenthal, 242, para. 6; and *ibid.*, separate opinion of Judge Higgins, 215, para. 33.

[88] *Ibid.*, Declaration of Judge Buergenthal, § 6.

[89] *Armed Activities on the Territory of the Congo* (*Democratic Republic of the Congo v Uganda*) (2005) ICJ Rep 187, para. 25.

[90] *Ibid.*, at 222, para. 146.

[91] *Ibid.*, at 223, para. 146.

[92] *Democratic Republic of the Congo v Uganda*, *supra* note 89, Separate opinion of Judge Kooijmans, 314, para. 30.

For all those reasons, the Court found that the legal and factual circumstances for exercise of the right of self-defence by Uganda against the DRC were not present. Having replied that the circumstances of the case did not allow for any recourse to the right of self-defence, the Court avoided responding to the contentions of the parties as to whether and under what conditions contemporary international law provides for a right of self-defence against large-scale attacks by irregular forces.[93]

7 Conclusions

To appreciate the novelty of the EU Member States' response to the Paris terrorist attacks, activating the mutual assistance clause embodied in Article 42 (7) TEU and thereby moving closer towards forming a new customary rule as to individual and collective rights of self-defence in accordance with Article 51 of the UN Charter and customary law, it is necessary to develop familiarity with the textual and contextual elements of that provision, and the practice of states since then, mainly in the context of the activity of the UN Security Council. The text of the UN Charter requires, as a necessary condition for exercising the right to self-defence, exclusively to be the presence of an 'armed attack', which is the use of force of considerable dimensions. By contrast, the drafters of the Charter did not take into consideration any '*ratione personae*' requirements for the exercise of that right, which is the reason for continuing discussion regarding the international subjectivity of the authors of acts allowing self-defence by the victim state. On that basis, recourse was needed to examine the circumstances of and the preparatory works for Article 51. At the time of drafting, only states could be the authors of armed attacks, and therefore only their acts could trigger the exercise of any right to self-defence. Composed in 1945, Article 51 was designed to harmonize the operation of regional arrangements and agencies with other general provisions within the UN Charter, in particular with regard to the use of force. More precisely, the drafters of Article 51 had in mind the solidarity obligations assumed under the Act of Chapultepec of 6 March 1945 in the Inter-American system, which expressly mentioned that acts of aggression should be committed by states.

There exists, then, a need to become more conscious of the idiosyncratic practice of states in the context of twenty-first century conflicts. Before the 2001 terrorist attacks in the United States, it cannot be argued that any customary rule recognized the right of self-defence in cases of armed attacks carried out by terrorist groups. Nor was it possible to understand that the subsequent practice of the parties to the UN Charter allowed such an interpretation of Article 51. That possibility

[93] *Democratic Republic of the Congo v Uganda, supra* note 89, para. 147.

had been increasingly claimed unilaterally by some states from the last decades of the past century, once the decolonization wave ended, but without agreement by the majority of states or acceptance by the Security Council.

The overwhelming support for the United States and United Kingdom intervention in Afghanistan after the 9/11 terrorist attacks on US soil, coming from many states as well as from some international organizations, provides evidence of increasing support for extending the right of self-defence to serious terrorist attacks. Great weight should be given to the fact that, on 4 October, the North Atlantic Council decided—at the request of the United States—to take eight measures, individually and collectively, to combat terrorism, operationalizing Article 5 of the Washington Treaty for the first time in the history of the organization. It must also be highlighted that the UN Security Council itself recognized in that context 'the inherent right of individual or collective self-defence in accordance with the Charter' in resolutions 1368 (2001) and 1373 (2001). In my view, the fact that there was a connection between the terrorist group Al-Qaeda and the Taliban regime in Afghanistan, and that Afghanistan could share some responsibility for those terrorist attacks accordingly, dispossess this event of part of its relevance as a precedent for forming a new customary rule, but not completely.

The definition of the crime of aggression adopted by amending the Rome Statute of the ICC at the first Review Conference of the Statute in Kampala, Uganda, in 2010, appears to suggest that those states which have adopted the definition of the crime of aggression have to acknowledge that these acts are committed by a political or military leader of a state. The crime of aggression cannot, therefore, be committed by non-governmental actors such as organized armed groups or terrorist groups. It follows, then, that the justification of retaliation by victim states as 'self-defence' is not possible in the strictest sense, even if this reading flies in the face of what appears to be the development of customary rules to provide for self-defence in response to terrorist attacks. By contrast, for the African states that in 2005 adopted the African Union Non-Aggression and Common Defence Pact, and in 2006 the Protocol on Non-Aggression and Mutual Defence in the Great Lakes Region, acts by non-state actors can be considered as aggression and accordingly entail the right of self-defence. Moreover, in the case of the 2005 African Union Pact, the states parties are obliged to come to the aid of the state attacked, much in the line of the obligation assumed in European Law with Article 42 (7) TEU.

Another central element in this analysis is the jurisprudence of the ICJ. In this regard, it should be noted that after the Twin Towers attacks and UN Security Council resolutions 1368 (2001) and 1373 (2001), the ICJ continues to defend its previous position according to which self-defence is only a right of states. Indeed, neither in the *Wall* case of 2004 nor in the 2005 case concerning the *Democratic Republic of the Congo v Uganda* did the Court recognize the possibility of extending that right to non-state actors. Dissenting judges have begun to point out in their declarations or separate opinions their feeling that this is an outdated argument, proposing an updated interpretation of the Charter in the current context of terrorism.

Even if it can be said that, for the time being, the existing rule in international law both in conventional law (Article 51 of the UN Charter) and customary law allowing states to have recourse to the use of force in self-defence can only be legally exercised in the presence of an armed attack committed by a state, it can also be argued that the current practice of states appears to be heading in another direction. It has to be recalled that for the drafters of Article 51 of the UN Charter the right of self-defence was already 'inherent'. If they had been in the current situation, perhaps they would have extended this right to cases of terrorist attacks of considerable dimensions.

In that light, invoking Article 42 (7) TEU in response to a serious terrorist attack, like those which unfortunately occurred in Paris in November 2015, cannot be considered a violation of Article 51 of the UN Charter. The unanimous support of the EU Member States is telling, with many of them seemingly prepared to entertain a new interpretation of that provision, at least the part about the scope of '*ratione personae*'.[94]

[94] It has to be noted that the European Parliament had already expressed its conviction that the mutual assistance clause embodied in Art. 42 (7) of the UN Charter should have a broad scope. Indeed, for the Parliament: 'even non-armed attacks, e.g., cyberattacks against critical infrastructure, that are launched with the aim of causing severe damage and disruption to a Member State and are identified as coming from an external entity could qualify for being covered by the clause, if the Member State's security is significantly threatened by its consequences, while fully respecting the principle of proportionality'. (European Parliament resolution of 22 November 2012 on the EU's mutual defence and solidarity clauses: political and operational dimensions, para. 13).

The Policy Effects of the Decisions of European Courts on Targeted Sanctions

Whither Human Rights?

*Kushtrim Istrefi**

> Judges, too, must display that doubt, caution, and prudence, that not being 'too sure' of oneself.
>
> Justice Breyer

1 Introduction

Decades ago, Sir Hersch Lauterpacht argued that 'international courts not only give a decision in a particular dispute, but that they are also are fundamental to making international law a more complete and effective law'.[1] Philippe Sands maintains that international courts should also contribute to raising public consciousness and contribute to offering working, effective solutions backed up by the special authority of the law.[2]

This role of international courts also applies, at times, in the context of national and regional courts. This can be said of cases where courts respond to issues of international community interest,[3] or where they examine, even if indirectly, laws

* Assistant Professor of Public International Law and Human Rights at Utrecht University. Parts of this contribution will appear in his forthcoming book, *European Judicial Responses to Security Council Resolutions: A Consequentialist Assessment* (Brill | Nijhoff 2019).

[1] Hersch Lauterpacht, *The Function of International Law in the International Community* (Clarendon Press 1933) 423–5.

[2] Philippe Sands, 'Climate Change & Rule of Law' (lecture held at the UK Supreme Court, 17 September 2015) <https://www.supremecourt.uk/news/climate-change-and-the-rule-of-law.html> accessed 28 April 2019.

[3] C/09/295241/HA ZA 07-2973 (The Hague District Court 2014) <http://uitspraken.rechtspraak.nl/inziendocument?id=ECLI:NL:RBDHA:2014:8748> accessed 28 April 2019; C/09/456689/HA ZA 13-1396 (The Hague District Court 2015) <http://uitspraken.rechtspraak.nl/inziendocument?id=ECLI:NL:RBDHA:2015:7196&keyword=urgenda> accessed 28 April 2019.

Kushtrim Istrefi, *The Policy Effects of the Decisions of European Courts on Targeted Sanctions: Whither Human Rights?* In: *How International Law Works in Times of Crisis*. Edited by: George Ulrich and Ineta Ziemele, Oxford University Press (2019).
DOI: 10.1093/oso/9780198849667.003.0007

or policies affecting other legal regimes.[4] Such judicial responses may have a twofold purpose. According to Dworkin, by applying arguments of principle, courts aim to establish an individual right and, by applying arguments of policy, they aim to establish a collective goal.[5] While arguments of principle may be relevant to the individual concerned and the domestic legal order, arguments of policy may aim to reach other legal regimes or the international community as a whole.

Such legal and policy significance can be seen in the European jurisprudence of Security Council targeted sanctions, as the measures triggering the respective proceedings were rooted in another legal order, namely, that of the United Nations. Through their findings in such cases, the European courts have conveyed certain messages to the UN and other legal regimes. They have also contributed to the debate on the value-based system of international law, given that the proceedings concerned international security and human rights.[6] They have raised global awareness about human rights, particularly in the context of counterterrorism. As 'megaphones of the truth',[7] they have courageously pointed to the flaws of Security Council sanctions decision-making, even when unable to uphold human rights in the normative realm.[8] As Eyal Benvenisti observed:

> the ways in which [...] courts have reacted to their executive's security-related claims since 11 September 2001, . . . speak of a new phase in the way democracies are addressing the threat of terrorism: executive unilateralism is being challenged by [...] courts in what could perhaps be a globally coordinated move.[9]

At the same time, 'all litigation runs the risk of unintended consequences and this is true too in respect of restrictive measures'.[10] Such consequences have largely been discussed through the notions of hierarchy of norms, constitutional pluralism, and the autonomy of legal regimes.[11] However, this contribution does not add to those

[4] *Al-Jedda v The United Kingdom* App No 27021/08 (ECHR, 7 July 2011); *Nada v Switzerland* App No 10593/08 (ECtHR, 12 September 2012); Joined Cases C-402/05 P and C-415/05 P *Kadi and Al Barakaat International Foundation v Council and Commission* ECLI:EU:C:2008:461.

[5] Ronald Dworkin, 'Hard Cases' (1975) 88(6) *Harvard Law Review* 1067.

[6] See Erika de Wet, 'The Emergence of International and Regional Value Systems as a Manifestation of the Emerging International Constitutional Order' (2006) 19 *Leiden Journal of International Law* 611–32.

[7] Philip Allott, 'The Idealist's Dilemma: Re-Imagining International Society' (*EJIL Talk!*, 9 June 2014) <http://www.ejiltalk.org/the-idealists-dilemma-re-imagining-international-society/#more-11047> accessed 28 April 2019.

[8] See, e.g., *Kadi and Al Barakaat International Foundation v Council and Commission* ECLI:EU:C:2008:461, *supra* note 4; *Al-Jedda v The United Kingdom, supra* note 4; *Youssef Nada v State Secretariat for Economic Affairs and Federal Department of Economic Affairs* [2007] BGE 133 II 450, 1A 45/2007, para. 8.

[9] Eyal Benvenisti, 'United We Stand: National Courts Reviewing Counterterrorism Measures' in Andrea Bianchi and Alexis Keller (eds), *Counterterrorism: Democracy's Challenge* (Hart Publishing 2008) 254.

[10] Cian C. Murphy, 'Counter-terrorism Law and Judicial Review: The CJEU' in Fergal Davis and Fiona de Londras (eds), *Critical Debates on Counter-Terrorism Judicial Review* (CUP 2014) 301.

[11] See, e.g., Andre Nollkaemper, 'Rethinking the Supremacy of International Law' (2010) 65 *Zeitschrift für ausländisches öffentliches Recht und Völkerrecht* 65–85; Erika de Wet and Jure Vidmar

discussions. Instead, it aims to examine the policy effects of the European courts on Security Council due process reform and genuine realization of human rights, the two concerns which triggered their judicial responses. To determine these policy effects, the assessment is consequentialist[12] in nature as it aims to (i) identify the ultimate value and (ii) encourage actions that maximize the value in question.[13] With respect to the former, the present chapter considers that genuine protection of human rights is the ultimate value. Following this, it considers actions which advance Security Council due process reform to be those which maximize that value. The review mechanism within the Security Council remains, in the author's view, an essential avenue capable of maximizing the value of genuine human rights protection.[14]

European judicial responses to Security Council measures are scrutinized in the context of targeted sanctions, in particular those regarding counterterrorism, which, at the time of writing, seem to have no endpoint. In order to justify harsh measures affecting individual rights, executive and legislative bodies have referred to terrorism, whether real or perceived, as a crisis and emergency.[15] Against this background, discussion of the policy effects of decisions by European courts regarding due process reveals the broader role of courts and human rights in times of crisis.

The chapter commences by examining the question whether Security Council due process reform has been stimulated by a more courageous response by the CJEU in *Kadi II* or the cautious response of the ECtHR in *Al-Dulimi*. Then, in the light of the latter judgment, the chapter looks at the role

(eds), *Hierarchy in International Law: The Place of Human Rights* (OUP 2012); Antonios Tzanakopoulos, *Disobeying the Security Council Countermeasures against Wrongful Sanctions* (OUP 2013); Ramses A. Wessel and Steven Blockmans, *Between Autonomy and Dependence: The EU Legal Order Under the Influence of International Organizations* (T.M.C. Asser Press 2013); Matej Avbelj, Filippo Fontanelli, and Giuseppe Martinico (eds), *Kadi on Trial: A Multifaceted Analysis of the Kadi Trial* (Routledge 2014); Inge Govaere, 'The Importance of International Developments in the Case-law of the European Court of Justice: Kadi and the Autonomy of the EC Legal Order' (2009) *Research Papers in Law of the College of Europe No. 1/2009*; Gráinne de Búrca, 'The European Court of Justice and the International Legal Order After *Kadi*' (2010) 51 *Harvard International Law Journal* 1–49.

---

[12] For the purpose of this contribution, consequentialism is not employed to adhere to or engage with a strict theory of moral philosophy. It is applied, as Paul Hurley writes, 'beyond philosophy consequentialism' in the area of contemporary jurisprudence to assess, *inter alia*, the right strategy taken to maximize the overall benefit. As Justice Breyer argues, the focus on consequences 'allows us to gauge whether and to what extent we have succeeded in facilitating workable outcomes'. See Paul Hurley, *Beyond Consequentialism* (OUP 2009) 2; Stephen Breyer, *Active Liberty: Interpreting Our Democratic Constitution* (Alfred A. Knopf 2005) 115.

[13] Paul Hurley, 'Consequentializing and Deontologizing: Clogging the Consequentialist Vacuum' in Mark Timmons (ed.), *Oxford Studies in Normative Ethics: Vol. III* (OUP 2013) 127.

[14] The assessment of policy effects of European jurisprudence on targeted sanctions through the notion of consequentialism is not applied to deny the existence of other ultimate values, or actions that could maximize them. Furthermore, the author rejects a radical reading of consequentialism by which any action or policy that achieves the desired aim could be justified.

[15] Oren Gross and Fionnuala Ní Aoláin, *Law in Times of Crisis* (CUP 2006) 4; Mary Dudziak, *War Time* (OUP 2013) 4.

of courts in pressing national authorities to further such due process reform and to ensure the practical realization of human rights. Finally, the concluding remarks highlight the correlation between judicial activism and the desired policy impact by European courts on due process reform and genuine realization of human rights.

2 EU Courts—The Rise and Fall of Their Impact on Due Process Reform

2.1 A Brief Overview of *Kadi II*

Before the CJEU rendered its judgment in *Kadi II*, Mr Kadi had been delisted from the UN sanctions list upon the recommendation of the Office of the Ombudsperson. In that light, Advocate General Bot invited the CJEU to take into account, *inter alia*, procedural improvements within the Office of the Ombudsperson.[16] Bot proposed that the CJEU should perform a lower intensity and not full judicial review of Security Council measures.[17]

The CJEU in *Kadi II* disregarded the calls of Advocate General Bot and decided to reinforce its earlier position on two issues.[18] First, it reiterated that Security Council measures when implemented at the European level were subject to the primacy of EU constitutional guarantees, and, second, that it would continue to perform a full judicial review of such measures for at least as long as Security Council sanction mechanisms lacked effective judicial protection.[19] On the latter issue, the Court made it clear that Security Council due process reform was incomplete and without effect as long a court was lacking. The CJEU held:

> [t]he essence of effective judicial protection must be that it should enable the person concerned to obtain declaration from a court, by means of a judgment ordering annulment whereby the contested measure is retroactively erased from the legal order and is deemed never to have existed, that the listing of his name, or the continued listing of his name, on the list concerned was vitiated by illegality, the recognition of which may re-establish the reputation of that person or constitute for him a form of reparation for the non-material harm he has suffered.[20]

[16] Joined Cases C-584/10 P, C-593/10 P, and C-595/10 P *European Commission and Others v Yassin Abdullah Kadi (No. 2)* ECLI:EU:C:2013:176. Opinion of AG Bot, paras 5, 61, 67, 76, 80, 81.

[17] *Ibid.*, paras 10, 68, 69, 71, 81.

[18] Joined Cases C-584/10 P, C-593/10 P, C-595/10 P. Appeals brought on 10 December 2010.

[19] Joined Cases C-584/10 P, C-593/10 P, and C-595/10 P *European Commission and Others v Yassin Abdullah Kadi (No. 2)* ECLI:EU:C:2013:518, paras 22 and 119.

[20] *Ibid.*, para. 134 (emphasis added).

It has been argued that the CJEU in *Kadi II* transformed the 'act of rebellion by the ECJ in *Kadi* [*I*] into an enduring normative approach'.[21] In maintaining this approach, the CJEU did not accept context-based procedures that could be suitable for other organizations, including the United Nations.

2.2 Policy Effects

A challenge is inherent in identifying individuals supporting terrorism due to the secret nature of their operation. By targeting 'unknowns', the Security Council inevitably runs the risk of erroneous designations. As Lord Rodger observed in *Ahmed*, 'sooner or later, someone will be designated who has not actually been committing or facilitating terrorist acts'.[22] These concerns have been realized, and the Security Council Al-Qaeda sanctions regime has recognized that erroneous or toxic designations have occurred.[23] In addition, the Council has also blamed the wrong organization for terrorist attacks.[24]

In response to these challenges, there is a growing consensus in the Security Council that the individuals and entities concerned should have access to a review mechanism that is independent and impartial.[25] The earlier jurisprudence of the EU courts has contributed to the formation of this consensus and to the initiative on establishing the Office of the Ombudsperson.[26] However, since the establishment of the Office of the Ombudsperson, the impact of decisions by the EU courts appears to have diminished. This is in part due to the position of the EU courts differing from not only that of the Security Council but also from some of the UN actors working on due process reform, including the Special Rapporteur on counterterrorism and human rights, the Group of Like-Minded States, and the Office of the Ombudsperson.[27]

[21] Devika Hovell, 'Kadi: King-Slayer or King-Maker? The Shifting Allocation of Decision-Making Power between the UN Security Council and Courts' [2016] *Modern Law Review* 160.

[22] *Her Majesty's Treasury (Respondent) v Mohammed Jabar Ahmed and others (FC) (Appellants); Her Majesty's Treasury (Respondent) v Mohammed al-Ghabra (FC) (Appellant); R (on the application of Hani El Sayed Sabaei Youssef) (Respondent) v Her Majesty's Treasury (Appellant)* [2010] UKSC 5 (hereinafter *Ahmed*), para. 174.

[23] See SC Res. 1822 (2008) paras 15, 25, 26 regarding the review of 'toxic designations'. In its two-year work of reviewing so-called toxic designations, the Security Council 1267 Sanctions Committee identified forty-five names of individuals and entities listed erroneously.

[24] The Security Council in its Resolution 1530 (2004) mistakenly identified the Basque group ETA as responsible for the 2004 Madrid bombings. See also Therese O'Donnell, 'Naming and Shaming: The Sorry Tale of Security Council Resolution 1530 (2004)' (2007) 17 *European Journal of International Law*.

[25] See SC Res. 1989 (2011) para. 21; SC Res. 2083 (2012), para. 19.

[26] Kimberly Prost, Ombudsperson of the Security Council Al-Qaida Sanctions Committee, Remarks to the 49th meeting of the Committee of Legal Advisors on Public International Law (CAHDI) of the Council of Europe (Strasbourg, 20 March 2015) <https://www.un.org/securitycouncil/sites/www.un.org.securitycouncil/files/cahdi.pdf>.

[27] *Ibid.* See also 'Report of the Special Rapporteur on the promotion and protection of human rights and fundamental freedoms while countering terrorism: Report to the General Assembly' (26 September 2012) UN Doc A/67/396; 'Report of the United Nations High Commissioner for Human Rights on

According to the EU courts, the Security Council should establish nothing short of a full-blown court.[28] It is, however, clear that for Security Council and UN actors working on human rights, the due process reform may only go as far as modifying and enhancing the mandate of the Office of the Ombudsperson.[29] It has been noted that 'full judicial review is not always within reach'.[30] The entrenchment of these positions has resulted in a debate which 'increasingly resembles a conversation of the deaf'.[31]

Devika Hovell has recently suggested that the EU courts should overcome the fixation on a court-based adjudicatory model of due process for Security Council sanctions. Since due process is not a 'one-size-fits-all' principle, the Security Council may legitimately require 'different procedural standards and operate according to different principles and values'.[32] Hovell rightly argues that a 'formalist legal approach has failed to persuade the Security Council, a body that operates in a setting in which the relationship between law and politics is notoriously complex'.[33]

The fixation of the EU courts on the notion of a court has been viewed as counterproductive to due process reform. In her speech delivered in March 2015 in Strasbourg, the then UN Ombudsperson, Kimberly Prost, explained that one of the key reasons for setbacks of her institution at the time emanated from the EU courts. She stated that the absence of recognition by the CJEU in *Kadi II* of the Office of the Ombudsperson '[had] had a damaging effect in terms of the motivation at the political level to maintain and to expand the Ombudsperson position'.[34] The Ombudsperson found it regrettable that 'the [CJEU] [would] independently decide on what [was] necessary in terms of fair process according to its analysis and law'.[35] The position of the CJEU, according to Prost, could only

the protection of human rights and fundamental freedoms while countering terrorism' (15 December 2010) UN Doc A/HRC/16/50; Letter dated 17 April 2014 from the Permanent Representatives of Austria, Belgium, Costa Rica, Denmark, Finland, Germany, Liechtenstein, the Netherlands, Norway, Sweden, and Switzerland to the United Nations addressed to the President of the Security Council, S/2014/286 <https://digitallibrary.un.org/record/769545>.

[28] T-85/09 *Kadi v Commission* ECLI:EU:T:2010:418; Joined Cases C-584/10 P, C-593/10 P, and C-595/10 P *European Commission and Others v Yassin Abdullah Kadi* [2013] ECR 00000 (hereinafter *Kadi II*), 13.

[29] Report of the Special Rapporteur, *supra* note 27; UN General Assembly Res 60/1 'World Summit Outcome' of 24 October 2005; Non-paper of the Secretary General referred to in the debate on 'Strengthening international law: rule of law and maintenance of peace and security' (22 June 2006) UN Doc S/PV.5474. The International Commission of Jurists has also advocated the establishment of an 'independent or quasi-judicial complain mechanism' into Security Council targeted sanctions. See International Commission of Jurists, *Assessing Damage, Urging Action: Report of the Eminent Jurists Panel on Terrorism, Counter-Terrorism and Human Rights* (2009).

[30] Katja Creutz, 'Balancing Targeted Sanctions: Effectiveness Through a Climate of Legality' (2015) *FIIA Briefing Paper* 169, 8.

[31] Devika Hovell, *The Power of Process* (OUP 2016) 1–2.

[32] *Ibid.*

[33] *Ibid.*, 3.

[34] Ombudsperson Prost, *supra* note 26, 4.

[35] *Ibid.*

encourage the Security Council to consider its reform independently from the EU courts.[36]

These remarks reveal a concern about the future impact of EU jurisprudence on Security Council due process reform. While the initial rebellion of the EU courts might have had a positive impact by raising awareness at the UN of the need to have an adequate review mechanism, the courts entrenchment now runs the risk of losing that impact. As Antonios Tzanakopoulos argued, 'after procuring some progress, … [the EU courts are] now sending the [Security Council] into regression and may end up being counterproductive'.[37] Thus, by taking a consequentialist assessment, the ability of the Herculean approach to maximize due process reform and human rights protection appears to be limited.

3 Strasbourg Court—Revitalizing UN Due Process Reform through National Authorities

3.1 Al-Dulimi Test on Arbitrariness of UN Listings: Regime Compatibility under Limited Judicial Supervision

On 21 June 2016, the Grand Chamber of the Strasbourg Court confirmed the Chamber judgment that Switzerland had violated Article 6 of the ECHR.[38] However, the legal reasoning of the individual judges differed substantially. Unlike the Chamber, it found 'the question [of] whether the equivalent protection test should be applied' to be nugatory,[39] given that the case did not concern a conflict of obligations under the UN Charter and the Convention system. The Grand Chamber maintained its *Al-Jedda* presumption 'that the Security Council does not intend to impose any obligation on Member States to breach fundamental principles of human rights'.[40] Despite this presumption, it noted that 'sanctions imposed by the Security Council entails practical interferences that may be extremely serious for the Convention rights'[41] and, for that reason, courts must perform adequate judicial review to ensure that sanctions are applied in close harmony with the Convention. In particular:

[36] *Ibid.* Prost argued that the purpose of her Office and Security Council due process reform is not 'to satisfy any individual Court or body … [but] to ensure that the use of the Security Council powers is in conformity with Article 1 of the Charter, which includes respecting international law and human rights principles'.

[37] Antonios Tzanakopoulos: 'The Solange argument as a justification for disobeying the Security Council in the *Kadi* judgments' in Avbelj et al., *supra* note 11, at 134.

[38] *Al-Dulimi and Montana Management Inc. v Switzerland* App No 5809/08 (ECtHR 21 June 2016).

[39] *Ibid.*, para. 149.

[40] *Ibid.*, para. 140.

[41] *Ibid.*, para. 145.

> in view of the seriousness of the consequences for the Convention rights of those persons, where a resolution such as that in the present case, namely Resolution 1483, [did] not contain any clear or explicit wording excluding the possibility of judicial supervision of the measures taken for its implementation, it must always be understood as authorising the courts of the respondent State to exercise sufficient scrutiny so that any arbitrariness can be avoided. By limiting that scrutiny to arbitrariness, the Court takes account of the nature and purpose of the measures provided for by the Resolution in question, in order to strike a fair balance between the necessity of ensuring respect for human rights and the imperatives of the protection of international peace and security.[42]

As regards application of the new arbitrariness test, the Grand Chamber indicated that the national authorities:

> had a duty to ensure that the listing was not arbitrary ... The applicants should ... have been afforded at least a genuine opportunity to submit appropriate evidence to a court, for examination on the merits, to seek to show that their inclusion on the impugned lists had been arbitrary.[43]

Overall, the Grand Chamber left unanswered the normative concern regarding the place in the Convention system of Article 103 of the UN Charter. However, the judgment deserves a closer assessment for its policy objectives. As Anne Peters observes, '[t]he functions of the domestic courts as stop-gaps for securing the legitimacy of Security Council action will be crucially strengthened by *Al-Dulimi*'.[44]

3.2 Implementation of the Al-Dulimi Judgment by Switzerland

In November 2016, the Swiss Government submitted an action report to the Committee of Ministers of the Council of Europe outlining the measures they had undertaken with a view to executing the *Al-Dulimi* judgment.[45] The measures included submission of the *Al-Dulimi* judgment to the relevant national authorities, including the Federal Tribunal before which three sets of proceedings were

[42] *Ibid.*, para. 146.

[43] *Ibid.*, paras 150–151.

[44] Anne Peters, 'The New Arbitrariness and Competing Constitutionalisms: Remarks on ECtHR Grand Cahmber Al-Dulimi' *EJIL Talk!* 30 June 2016 <http://www.ejiltalk.org/the-new-arbitrariness-and-competing-constitutionalisms-remarks-on-ecthr-grand-chamber-al-dulimi/#comments> accessed 28 April 2019.

[45] Communication de la Suisse concernant l'affaire Al-Dulimi et Montana Management Inc. contre Suisse (Requête n° 5809/08), Bilan d'action 22 November 2016, para. 3 <https://search.coe.int/cm/Pages/result_details.aspx?ObjectId=09000016806d4af7> accessed 28 April 2019.

pending at the time with regard to implementation of the *Al-Dulimi* judgment. The action report indicated that the domestic authorities and tribunals would give full effect to the *Al-Dulimi* judgment, and, therefore, no additional measures appeared necessary.[46] At the same time, the Swiss Government referred to some further measures aimed at improving due process guarantees in the context of Security Council targeted sanctions, in particular:

> le Conseil fédéral a chargé, en mars 2016, l'administration fédérale d'entamer des réflexions portant sur l'amélioration des garanties procédurales dans le cadre de la mise en œuvre des sanctions adoptées par le Conseil de sécurité de l'ONU, les conclusions devant lui être soumises dans un délai échéant douze mois après l'arrêt de la Grande Chambre dans la présente affaire.[47]

While these further measures have not yet concluded, two early observations can be drawn from the action report on the execution of the *Al-Dulimi* judgment. First, the Government did not consider that application of the arbitrariness test by national courts would be at odds with the state's commitment to implement Security Council measures. The Government sent a clear signal to the national institutions, including the courts, to give full effect, *comme d'habitude*, to the judgment.[48] Second, the Swiss Government saw the *Al-Dulimi* principles as a call for proactive engagement in improving procedural guarantees in the context of targeted sanctions.

3.3 Policy Effects

Unlike the CJEU, the Strasbourg Court has been more cautious about the wider implications of its judgments. In the *Al-Dulimi* judgment, the Grand Chamber omitted a firm position on whether a court in the UN was necessary in order to ensure due process guarantees with regard to targeted sanctions.[49] The Strasbourg Court appears to have left that issue to the UN itself, as it avoided the notion of a court. It also made no reference to full or intensive judicial review as a precondition for due process in the context of targeted sanctions.[50] This approach, however, does not mean that the ECtHR would rubber stamp decisions on sanctions or leave

[46] *Ibid.*, para. 3.3.

[47] *Ibid.* EN: 'In March 2016, the Federal Council commissioned the federal government to initiate reflections on improving procedural safeguards in the framework of the implementation of the sanctions adopted by the UN Security Council, the conclusions to be submitted within a period of 12 months after the judgment of the Grand Chamber in this case.'

[48] *Ibid.*

[49] *Al-Dulimi and Montana Management Inc.*, *supra* note 38.

[50] *Ibid.*, para. 153. The deficiencies of the current delisting procedure in the UN are looked at through the reports of the UN Special Rapporteurs as well as other actors.

the matter of procedural guarantees unaddressed. The Strasbourg Court has reiterated 'very serious . . . and consistent criticisms' about the current review mechanism and has sent a clear message that adequate procedural guarantees should be put in place.[51] Judge Pinto de Albuquerque, joined by three other judges, noted 'if the legal reasoning [in *Al-Dulimi*] is fragile, the message is not: the Court is determined not to accept UN sanctions without adequate procedural guarantees'.[52]

The strength of *Al-Dulimi* lies in the arbitrariness test established by the ECtHR therein, for the policy developments it prompts. According to this test, national courts should perform a limited review of whether individuals were given 'at least a genuine opportunity to submit appropriate evidence to a court, for examination on the merits, to seek to show that their inclusion on the lists had been arbitrary'.[53] This, in turn, urges not only the national courts but also executives and legislatures, as appropriate, to request and provide evidence for listings. In addition to this action, national executives may apply political pressure on a designating state and legislatures may adopt laws that limit the effects of certain Security Council measures at the domestic level. It is through these actions that the desired policy consequences of judicial action—that is, due process reform and human rights protection—may be realized.

With regard to the approach adopted by the Strasbourg Court in *Al-Dulimi*, it is relevant to note that a similar type of pressure by national authorities has, in some cases, proved to be effective. In the cases concerning Mr Sayadi, Ms Vinck, and Mr Nada, examined later in this chapter, the national courts prompted the national executives and legislatures to condition—by reference to procedural guarantees—their cooperation with the Security Council in the area of targeted sanctions.

3.3.1 The role of national authorities in the delisting of Mr Sayadi and Ms Vinck

Mr Sayadi and Ms Vinck, a couple of Belgian nationality, were placed on Security Council targeted sanctions in January 2003.[54] At the European level, the Security Council measures against Mr Sayadi and Ms Vinck were implemented through an EU regulation[55] and a Belgian ministerial order.[56] Mr Sayadi and Ms Vinck challenged their listing before the UN Human Rights Committee[57] and the Belgian

[51] *Ibid.*

[52] *Ibid.* Concurring opinion of Judge Pinto de Albuquerque, joined by Judges Hajiyev, Pejchal, and Dedov, para. 58.

[53] *Al-Dulimi and Montana Management Inc., supra* note 38, para. 151.

[54] Concerning the facts of the case see Communication No. 1472/2006 [2008], UN Doc CCPR/C/94/D/1472/2006, para. 2.

[55] Commission Regulation (EC) No. 145/2003 of 27 January 2003 amending Regulation (EC) No. 881/2002.

[56] Belgian Ministerial Order of 31 January 2003 amending the ministerial order of 15 June 2000 implementing the Royal Decree of 17 February 2000 concerning the restrictive measures directed against the Taliban in Afghanistan.

[57] The UN Human Rights Committee found violations of Arts 12 and 17 ICCPR in Communication No. 1472/2006 [2008], *supra* note 54, para. 11.

courts. In 2005, the Belgian courts ordered the Government to 'urgently initiate a de-listing procedure with the United Nations Sanctions Committee'.[58]

Following this judicial decision, the Belgian Government requested the Security Council Sanctions Committee to delist their two nationals.[59] After the Sanctions Committee rejected that request, the Belgian Ambassador to the UN met a few times with diplomats of the designating state, namely the United States, to discuss the delisting of Mr Sayadi and Ms Vinck. The confidential communication between the two diplomats, subsequently disclosed by *Wikileaks*, showed the significance of political factors which eventually led to the delisting of Mr Sayadi and Ms Vinck.[60]

In 2008, the Belgian Ambassador, who at the time was Chairman of the 1267 Sanctions Committee, noted to a US diplomat that a negative response could have certain consequences for the efficacy of targeted sanctions. In particular, he:

> underscored that representatives of many UN [M]ember [S]tates have told him that they are reluctant to submit names to the Committee for sanctions because they perceive the Committee takes little action to remove parties from the list, even when warranted, and that there is little likelihood of reversing sanctions once a party had been listed.[61]

The Belgian Ambassador signalled that cases such as that of Mr Sayadi and Ms Vinck may prompt a wave of political distrust in the area of targeted sanctions which could result in unwillingness on the part of states to submit new names to the Sanctions Committee.

In view of these remarks, the US diplomat recommended:

> [the Belgian Ambassador's] … point that [S]tates are increasingly unwilling to submit new listings to the Committee because 1267 sanctions are viewed as a life-sentence is worth consideration. The 1267 Monitoring Team has found in consecutive reports that the list is becoming increasingly outdated as the threat of [A]l-Qaeda and the Taliban evolves. Without new listings, the 1267 regime will become increasingly irrelevant to global counter-terrorism actions. Appropriate delistings could serve as an important incentive to keep [S]tates engaged in improving the 1267 list.[62]

[58] *Sayadi & Vick v l'Etat Belge* [2005] Decision of the Tribunal de Première Instance de Bruxelles.

[59] Communication No. 1472/2006, *supra* note 54, para. 2.5.

[60] 'Belgium reluctant to take CTC or 1267 Chairs', Canonical ID: 06USUNNEWYORK2182_a (*Wikileaks*, 22 November 2006) <https://www.wikileaks.org/plusd/cables/06USUNNEWYORK2182_a.html> accessed 28 April 2019; 'UN/1267 Sanctions: Belgians request U.S. reconsider case to delist Sayadi and Vinck', Canonical ID: 08USUNNEWYORK209_a (*Wikileaks*, 6 March 2008) <https://www.wikileaks.org/plusd/cables/08USUNNEWYORK209_a.html> accessed 28 April 2019.

[61] *Ibid. Wikileaks* 'UN/1267 Sanctions: Belgians request U.S. reconsider case to delist Sayadi and Vinck'.

[62] *Ibid.*

A few months later the Security Council delisted Mr Sayadi and Ms Vinck and established the Office of the Ombudsperson.[63] Given the lack of clear reasons by the Security Council Sanctions Committee for the delisting of the Belgian couple, it is hard to identify whether it was the national courts, public opinion, diplomacy, or other factors that had a decisive impact. However, the aforementioned diplomatic documents show that the Belgian executive, pressurized also by the national courts and the public, triggered the delisting of Mr Sayadi and Ms Vinck. They also reveal that the US diplomat may have been receptive to the idea of delisting after having realized that active participation by states in the sanctions regime is dependent on the existence of due process guarantees. In light of these consequences, the *Sayadi and Vinck* case reveals the role that national authorities may have in advancing sanctions decision-making reform.

3.3.2 The role of national authorities in delisting Mr Nada

The influence of national authorities on the processes of the Security Council Sanctions Committee can also be revealed through the case of Mr Nada.

Mr Nada was listed by the Security Council Sanctions Committee two months after 9/11.[64] He brought a case before the Swiss courts in 2007 in relation to this listing. Although the Swiss courts gave effect to Article 103 of the UN Charter, they noted that sanctions decision-making lacked sufficient procedural guarantees.[65] The Swiss and Italian authorities requested the Sanctions Committee to delist Mr Nada, without success.

Unexpectedly, in 2009 the Sanctions Committee decided to delist him. It is interesting to observe that it was precisely during that time that there was an important legislative initiative within the Swiss Parliament. On 12 June 2009, the Swiss Council of States—the upper house of the Federal Parliament—adopted a motion urging the state to refrain from implementing Security Council sanctions in certain cases:[66]

> to cease implementing sanctions against individuals included on the 1267 Consolidated List in cases where the individual: (1) has been on the list for more than 3 years and not been brought before the court, (2) has not had the possibility to resort to an independent institution for a remedy, (3) has had no indictment

[63] See Decision of the Security Council Al-Qaida and Taliban Sanctions Committee SC/9711 of 21 July 2009 <http://www.un.org/press/en/2009/sc9711.doc.htm> accessed 28 April 2019.

[64] For more details regarding the arrest and transfer, travel ban and asset freeze of Mr Nada and his company see *Nada v Switzerland, supra* note 4, paras 21–25.

[65] *Youssef Nada v State Secretariat, supra* note 8, para. 8.

[66] Motion 09.3719 Submitted to the Swiss Council of States by Dick Marty (12 June 2009) passed in the upper house on 8 September 2009. The motion was adopted by the lower chamber on 1 March 2010. See also *Nada v Switzerland, supra* note 4, paras 54 and 56.

issued, and (4) has not had new incriminating evidence brought forward since listing.[67]

The Swiss Council of States referred to the case of Mr Nada to justify non-implementation of Security Council targeted sanctions.[68] It is significant that, three months after the motion, the Sanctions Committee delisted Mr Nada. These events are a further demonstration of the power that national authorities may have with regard to the work of the Sanctions Committee.

3.3.3 The inherent limitations of national courts

Yuval Shany observed that 'the more the executive is likely to adopt counterterrorism policies which are under-protective of the rights and interests of terror suspects, the more it is likely to try to render courts and other oversight bodies incapable of serving as effective corrective mechanisms'.[69] Such an observation is poignant in the present context.

Given the aforementioned relationship between national executives and judiciary, and the subordinate position of courts, the latter may have unavoidable limitations in achieving the desired results. By way of example, the UK Supreme Court faced such limitations in cases concerning the freezing of Mr Ahmed's assets and the revocation of Al-Jedda's citizenship.[70] In the case of *Ahmed*, on 27 January 2010, the UK Supreme Court decided that Government measures were *ultra vires*. The decision clarified that the measures including an asset freeze on, *inter alia*, Mr Ahmed had been imposed without authority and were of no effect in law. In practice, this meant that Mr Ahmed could access his funds held in UK banks. A week later, the UK Government applied for suspension of the quashing of the asset-freezing legislation until Parliament introduced new primary legislation.[71]

[67] Cited in Thomas Biersteker and Sue Eckert, 'Addressing Challenges to Targeted Sanctions', An Update of the Watson Report, October 2009, 9. It is interesting to note that in July 2009, the Dutch Parliament received proposals for amendment of the Constitution, in particular on the place of the international legal order in the Dutch Constitution. The proposal explicitly referred to the 1267 regime as an example of international rules that were drafted outside a proper rule of law context. See *Staatscourant* 10354, 9 July 2009.

[68] *Nada v Switzerland, supra* note 4, para. 63.

[69] Yuval Shany, 'Guarding the Guards in the War on Terrorism' in Christopher A. Ford and Amichai Cohen (eds), *Rethinking the Law of Armed Conflict in an Age of Terrorism* (Lexington Books 2012) 118.

[70] Then UK Home Secretary Theresa May 'told the House of Commons that she had decided the laws needed to change after losing a long-running court case to strip the Iraqi-born Hilal al Jedda of his British citizenship'. She further stated 'since we saw the result of the al Jedda case ... I specifically asked officials whether there was anything that we could do to ensure that we would be able to take action against people whose activities, particularly those related to terrorism, were seriously prejudicial to the [S]tate. See Alice Ross and Olivia Rudgard, 'How one man was stripped of his UK citizenship—twice', (*openDemocracy*, 11 July 2014) <https://www.opendemocracy.net/opensecurity/alice-ross-olivia-rudgard/how-one-man-was-stripped-of-his-uk-citizenship%E2%80%94twice> accessed 28 April 2019.

[71] *Her Majesty's Treasury (Respondent) v Mohammed Jabar Ahmed and others (FC) (Appellants); Her Majesty's Treasury (Respondent) v Mohammed al-Ghabra (FC) (Appellant); R (on the application of Hani*

The Government submitted to the UK Supreme Court that 'refusing a suspension would give rise to the risk of those assets being disbursed and used for the purposes of terrorism, with the attendant risk of causing serious and irreparable harm to the national interest of the United Kingdom'. [72]

The UK Supreme Court did not suspend operation of the orders and considered that granting the Government's request would 'obfuscate the effect of its judgment'.[73] While the UK Supreme Court made efforts to preserve the effects of its judgment, it subsequently became apparent that the UK Government had utilized EU legislation to limit its effects. In that regard, in the *Youssef* judgment Lord Carnwath, with whom Lord Neuberger, Lord Mance, Lord Wilson, and Lord Sumption agreed, noted:

> [f]rom the victim's point of view it may seem strange that a process which, as applied under domestic legislation, was found to involve an unacceptable interference with his property rights, should be capable of automatic and immediate reinstatement by the indirect route of a European regulation. Indeed, it is unclear from the substantive judgments in *Ahmed* to what extent the court was made aware of the limited practical effects of its decision.[74]

The *Ahmed* case demonstrates the limitations inherent in the role of courts in upholding human rights in cases of targeted sanctions. Despite the possibilities of restrained judicial activism prompting due process reform, when national executives turn out to be uncooperative such activism falls on deaf ears and reform is prevented.

4 Conclusions

The jurisprudence of the European courts reveals their mixed blessing effect on Security Council due process reform and genuine realization of human rights. When examining the effects of *Kadi II* it appears that bold and formalistic legal assessments may not always lead to the desired effects of the court decision,[75] and in the long run may weaken the EU courts' authority[76] and effectiveness.[77]

El Sayed Sabaei Youssef) (Respondent) v Her Majesty's Treasury (Appellant) [2010] UKSC 2 of 27 January 2010 (hereinafter *Ahmed II*).

[72] Press Summary of *Ahmed II*, available at <https://www.supremecourt.uk/cases/docs/uksc-2009-0015-press-summary.pdf> accessed 28 April 2019.

[73] *Ahmed II, supra* note 71, *Lord Philips, with whom Lord Rodger, Lord Walker, Lady Hale, Lord Brown and Lord Mance agree,* para. 8.

[74] *Youssef v Secretary of State for Foreign and Commonwealth Affairs* [2016] UKSC 3, para. 48.

[75] Ombudsperson Prost, *supra* note 26.

[76] Karen J. Alter, Laurence R. Helfer, and Mikael Rask Madsen, How Context Shapes the Authority of International Courts (2016) 79 *Law and Contemporary Problems* 1–36, 7.

[77] Report of the Special Rapporteur, *supra* note 27, para. 22.

With regard to the authority of the courts, Alter, Helfer, and Madsen have argued that de facto authority can be measured by 'two key components—(1) recognising an obligation to comply with court rulings, and (2) engaging in meaningful action pushing toward giving full effect to those rulings'. Application of these criteria to the context of European courts illustrates the limited effect of the approach by the EU court. The latter component, engagement in giving effect to the rules, which according to the authors is particularly essential, can hardly be seen in the actions of EU Member States taken with regard to *Kadi II*.[78] Despite initial success, continued Herculean judicial activism muted the response and engagement of the Security Council.

In addition, the *Kadi* approach also has consequences for the Courts' effectiveness. Ben Emmerson has rightly observed that national or regional courts are unable to carry out an effective judicial review of measures emanating from the Security Council as long as the designating state does not reveal information concerning the listing.[79] In the *Kadi* case the CJEU's lack of access to the evidence for the listing of Mr Kadi represents such an undermining of effectiveness.

The result of these challenges to the EU courts' authority and effectiveness may be that affected persons are discouraged from bringing claims before the Court. The absence of litigation following from such discouragement may bring an end to judicial dialogue in the field of targeted sanctions. Such a cessation of judicial dialogue highlights the possibility of counterproductivity of the approach.

The limited effects of *Kadi II* raise the question whether, in the long run, a form of judicial restraint could prove to be more successful. Such an approach, according to Justice Breyer, 'will take account of the constitutional role of other institutions, including their responsibilities, their disabilities and the ways in which they function'.[80] This would allow the courts to consider the various actors which have a role within the sanctions regime and seek ways to impact the due process reform through such actors in so far as possible.

Such a cautious approach, as seen in the ECtHR *Al-Dulimi* judgment, preserves the authority and effectiveness which hinders the courageous approach. Switzerland has acknowledged the binding effect of the *Al-Dulimi* judgment. It has also committed to undertake further measures to improve procedural guarantees concerning implementation of Security Council targeted sanctions. These may be seen as engagement in meaningful actions pushing towards giving full effect to the judgment, attesting to the continued authority of the court.

[78] *Ibid.*, they argue that '[a] simple public statement that a judgment is legally binding is, without more, inadequate'.

[79] The Special Rapporteur Ben Emmerson considers that 'even if [domestic judicial review is considered … an adequate substitute for due process at the United Nations level] … it may not have the designating State's consent to reveal the information. This can obstruct the ability of national or regional courts to carry out an effective judicial review.' See Report of the Special Rapporteur, *supra* note 27, para. 22.

[80] Stephen Breyer, *America's Supreme Court* (OUP 2010) 216.

In so far as the effectiveness of the ECtHR's judicial review is concerned, there are still limitations to the approach. The arbitrariness test introduced in *Al-Dulimi* may prove to be ineffective if a designating state chooses not to provide evidence for listing. Despite this possible limitation of effectiveness, *Al-Dulimi* seeks to overcome obstacles to judicial review by calling on states to secure the evidence for listing. Furthermore, its observations with regard to the sanctions regime encourage states to work on improving procedural guarantees. Thus, through greater restraint, the approach of the ECtHR may ultimately preserve the effectiveness of its judicial review.

While the Security Council is the ultimate authority to decide on due process reform, continual judicial activism revitalizes the concerns of the legitimacy and legality deficit within the Security Council. A setback to such due process reform may discourage states from submitting new listings and lead to resistance on the part of national authorities to give effect to certain Security Council measures. As the analysis in this chapter has shown, a Herculean judicial approach may ultimately result in such a setback. In contrast, a more cautious approach may be preferable, as it preserves the authority and effectiveness necessary to achieving a productive dialogue which actuates the desired Security Council due process reform and genuine realization of human rights.

The Crisis of Privacy and Sacrifice of Personal Data in the Name of National Security

CJEU Rulings Strengthening EU Data Protection Standards

Irena Nesterova

1 Introduction

Edward Snowden's surveillance revelations in 2013 thrust the issue of privacy and security into the public spotlight. These revelations underlined the need for a strong data protection framework. At the same time, the pressing demand to address security concerns and the threat of terrorist attacks weaken privacy and data protection standards.

The Court of Justice of the European Union (CJEU) has made significant steps in promoting the right to privacy in the context of mass digital surveillance for the purpose of national security. The CJEU has adopted a number of landmark judgments evaluating whether the processing and collection of personal data is consistent with the right to privacy and data protection enshrined in Articles 7 and 8 of the Charter of Fundamental Rights of the European Union (the Charter). In the *Digital Rights Ireland* judgment[1] of April 2014, the CJEU annulled the Data Retention Directive,[2] finding that interference with fundamental rights went beyond what is strictly necessary for the protection of national security and thus did not comply with the principle of proportionality enshrined in Article 52 (1) of the Charter. In the *Schrems* judgment[3] of October 2015, the CJEU invalidated the

[1] Joined cases C-293/12 and C-594/12, *Digital Rights Ireland and Seitlinger and Others* ECLI:EU:C:2014:238.
[2] Directive 2006/24/EC of the European Parliament and of the Council of 15 March 2006 on the retention of data generated or processed in connection with the provision of publicly available electronic communications services or of public communications networks and amending Directive 2002/58/EC (2006) OJ L 105.
[3] Case C-362/14, *Maximillian Schrems v Data Protection Commissioner* ECLI:EU:C:2015:650.

Irena Nesterova, *The Crisis of Privacy and Sacrifice of Personal Data in the Name of National Security: CJEU Rulings Strengthening EU Data Protection Standards* In: *How International Law Works in Times of Crisis.* Edited by: George Ulrich and Ineta Ziemele, Oxford University Press (2019).
DOI: 10.1093/oso/9780198849667.003.0008

European Commission's Safe Harbour Decision[4] which allowed transfers of personal data from the European Union (EU) to the United States. It concluded that the Decision did not comply with the requirement of adequate levels of protection because the data transferred under the Safe Harbour Decision could be accessed and further processed by the US authorities beyond what is strictly necessary and proportionate to the protection of national security.

Through the lens of the CJEU, this chapter seeks to reveal the essential issues and challenges related to privacy and national security that need to be addressed in developing data protection laws both at national and EU level. The analysis begins by briefly outlining how the necessity to fight against terrorism, in particular after the 9/11 attacks, has led to the introduction of mass surveillance practices both in the EU and the United States. It reveals how EU data protection rules have become not only an important economic development tool but also an enabler of national security objectives in serious tension with the right to privacy. Further, the chapter analyses the CJEU landmark cases. It summarizes the main findings of the *Digital Rights Ireland* and the *Schrems* judgments and then proceeds to examine the CJEU position on justifying interference with the fundamental rights to privacy and data protection in the interests of national security. Finally, the chapter discusses the implications of the CJEU judgments for EU Member States' data protection regimes, as well for EU data protection law and policy, including regulation of international data transfers. The chapter reveals the key challenges that data protection law and policy face at national and EU level and that have to be overcome in response to mass digital surveillance in order to maintain a proper balance between privacy and national security.

2 Security as an Objective of the EU Data Protection Rules

The rapid development of the information and communication technologies (ICT) sector has brought emerging opportunities but also new challenges. The ability to access information with no borders has become crucial for social and economic interactions and technological advancement. However, the growing economic importance of data processing has raised concerns over effective protection of fundamental rights in the information society.

The final adoption of the new EU data protection rules has made a significant step in strengthening EU citizens' fundamental rights in the digital age. The data

[4] European Commission Decision 2000/520 of 26 July 2000 pursuant to Directive 95/46 of the European Parliament and of the Council on the adequacy of the protection provided by the Safe Harbour privacy principles and related frequently asked questions issued by the US Department of Commerce, (2000) OJ L 215/7.

protection package includes the General Data Protection Regulation (the GDPR),[5] which entered into force on 24 May 2016, and applies from 25 May 2018. It also includes the Data Protection Directive for Police and Criminal Justice Authorities,[6] which entered into force on 5 May 2016 and which EU Member States were due to transpose into national law by 6 May 2018. The last aims to ensure a high level of data protection while improving cooperation in the fight against terrorism and other serious crime across Europe. Thus, the new EU rules for personal data protection are key enablers of the Digital Single Market Strategy[7] as well the EU Agenda on Security.[8]

Likewise, the necessity to combat terrorism had previously led to the introduction of data retention regimes permitting state surveillance of communications for security purposes. The Data Retention Directive was introduced as an urgent counterterrorism measure responding to the terrorist attacks in Madrid (2004) and London (2005). Despite concerns about compliance with fundamental rights, the Directive was rapidly adopted under huge political pressure and entered into force in 2006.[9] The Data Retention Directive required Member States to oblige telecommunications and internet service providers to retain traffic and location data regarding fixed and mobile telephony, internet access, and email communications for a period of at least six months and no more than two years, and to make it available on request to law enforcement authorities for the purpose of investigation, detection, and prosecution of serious crime and terrorism. However, in the *Digital Rights Ireland* case, the CJEU declared the Data Retention Directive invalid on the basis that it entails unjustified interference with fundamental rights.

Retention of communication data as a means of fighting terrorism has been widely applied across the Atlantic. Following the 9/11 terrorist attacks, the United States unilaterally began to use its economic power to 'exploit the vulnerability of digital communication technologies to electronic surveillance and interception of communication both in the US and in countries across the globe'.[10] The disclosures in 2013 by former US National Security Agency (NSA) contractor Edward

[5] Regulation (EU) 2016/679 of the European Parliament and of the Council of 27 April 2016 on the protection of natural persons with regard to the processing of personal data and on the free movement of such data, and repealing Directive 95/46/EC (General Data Protection Regulation) (2016) OJ L 119.

[6] Directive (EU) 2016/680 of the European Parliament and of the Council of 27 April 2016 on the protection of natural persons with regard to the processing of personal data by competent authorities for the purposes of the prevention, investigation, detection, or prosecution of criminal offences or the execution of criminal penalties, and on the free movement of such data, and repealing Council Framework Decision 2008/977/JHA (2016) OJ L 119.

[7] Commission, 'A Digital Single Market Strategy for Europe' (Communication) COM/2015/0192 final.

[8] Commission, 'The European Agenda on Security' (Communication) COM(2015) 185 final.

[9] See Niklas Vainio and Samuli Miettinen, 'Telecommunications Data Retention after *Digital Rights Ireland*: Legislative and Judicial Reactions in the Member States' (2015) 23 *International Journal of Law and Information Technology* 291–2.

[10] UN General Assembly, 'The Right to Privacy in the Digital Age', Resolution 68/167. UN Doc A/RES/68/167, 18 December 2013.

Snowden revealed mass surveillance of global telecommunication and data flows of both US citizens and other (foreign) individuals on a previously unimaginable scale.[11] It was revealed that the NSA tapped directly into the servers of internet companies, including Facebook, Google, Microsoft, and Yahoo, to track online communication in a surveillance programme known as PRISM.[12] Moreover, they revealed widespread data sharing among the so-called Five Eyes intelligence-sharing network comprising the United Kingdom, the United States, Australia, Canada, and New Zealand, dominated by the NSA, as well as extensive collaboration between different EU member states' intelligence authorities—in particular the United Kingdom and Germany—and the United States.[13]

These revelations sparked global concern about the negative impact of surveillance practices on human rights.[14] The international community—in particular, UN bodies—have addressed serious concerns about the negative impact that surveillance and interception of communications as well as the collection of personal data, in particular when carried out on a mass scale, may have on the exercise and enjoyment of human rights.[15] The UN emphasizes that unlawful or arbitrary surveillance and interception of communications, as well as unlawful or arbitrary collection of personal data, as highly intrusive acts, violate the rights to privacy and to freedom of expression and may contradict the tenets of a democratic society and called upon all Member States to respect and protect the right to privacy in digital communication.

Furthermore, surveillance and interception of digital communication technologies undermine trust, which is a particularly important tool for reducing uncertainty and enabling reliance on others in the global online environment. The risks of unlawful or arbitrary surveillance and interception of digital communication technologies can discourage innovation and undermine the opportunities presented by the digital economy, as the protection of privacy is seen as critical for trust.[16]

[11] See Glenn Greenwald and Ewen MacAskill, 'NSA Prism program taps in to user data of Apple, Google and others', (*The Guardian*, 7 June 2013) <http://www.theguardian.com/world/2013/jun/06/us-tech-giants-nsa-data> accessed 28 April 2019; Spencer Ackerman and Dominic Rushe, 'The Microsoft, Facebook, Google and Yahoo release US surveillance requests' (*The Guardian*, 3 February 2014) <http://www.theguardian.com/world/2014/feb/03/microsoft-facebook-google-yahoo-fisa-surveillance-requests> accessed 28 April 2019.

[12] See, e.g., Greenwald and MacAskill, *supra* note 11; Ackerman and Rushe, *supra* note 11.

[13] See Council of Europe, Committee on Legal Affairs and Human Rights, Rapporteur Mr Pieter Omtzigt, Netherlands, EPP/CD (2015), Report Doc13734, Mass surveillance, 18 March 2015.

[14] After 2013 revelations over one thousand academics signed against mass surveillance. See Academics Against Mass Surveillance, 2014 <https://pure.uva.nl/ws/files/2333271/161678_Academics_Against_Mass_Surveillance.pdf>.

[15] UN General Assembly, *supra* note 10; Report of the Office of the United Nations High Commissioner for Human Rights 'The right to privacy in the digital age', UN Doc A/HRC/27/37, 30 June 2014.

[16] OECD Digital Economy Outlook 2015, 30, 209.

The revelations about extraterritorial digital mass surveillance have also influenced the transatlantic relationship and raised questions about the lawfulness of long-term agreements on data transfer between the United States and the EU. The main rules on transfers of personal data to third countries are contained in Chapter 5 of the GDPR setting up the general principle according to which the transfer of personal data may take place only if the third country ensures an adequate level of protection. This was at the heart of the *Schrems* case, in that the basic question in that case was whether the United States ensures an adequate level of data protection in order to prevent the abuse of personal data of EU citizens as the Safe Harbour rules could be overridden by national security requirements.

As shown earlier, the CJEU has been largely involved in the heated debate about the impact of security measures and surveillance practices on privacy.

3 CJEU Judgments Striking a Balance between the Right to Privacy and National Security

The following analysis aims to summarize the main findings of the *Digital Rights Ireland* and *Schrems* judgments and then examines the CJEU position on the justification of interference with the fundamental rights to privacy and protection of personal data in the interests of national security.

3.1 The *Digital Rights Ireland* Judgment

The High Court of Ireland and the Constitutional Court of Austria (*Verfassungsgerichtshof*) submitted references for a preliminary ruling to the CJEU for determination of the validity of the Data Retention Directive. Both courts had to resolve disputes regarding the legality of national measures concerning retention of data relating to electronic communications.

The CJEU declared the Data Retention Directive invalid on the ground that it does not comply with the principle of proportionality in the light of Articles 7, 8, and 52 (1) of the Charter (paragraph 69).

The CJEU, first of all, observed that, by imposing obligations on providers to retain traffic and location data and by allowing the competent national authorities to access them, the Data Retention Directive constituted a wide-ranging and particularly serious interference with respect to private life and the protection of personal data (paragraph 37).

The CJEU then examined whether such an interference with the fundamental rights at issue is justified. The CJEU found that the retention of data required by the Data Retention Directive is not such as to affect the essence of the right to private life adversely as it does not permit the acquisition of knowledge of the content of electronic communications as such (paragraph 39). Nor is that retention of data such as to affect the essence of the right to the protection of personal data adversely, as it provides certain principles of data protection and data security that must be respected by providers, which require Member States to adopt appropriate technical and organizational measures against accidental or unlawful destruction, accidental loss, or alteration of data (paragraph 40).

The CJEU further stated that the interference satisfies an objective of general interest, namely the fight against serious crime and thus, ultimately, public security (paragraphs 41–44). The CJEU emphasized that EU legislation must lay down clear and precise rules governing the extent of interference with fundamental rights and impose minimal safeguards to guarantee effective protection of retained data (paragraph 54). However, it found that the interference with fundamental rights goes beyond what is strictly necessary. In support of that finding, the CJEU pointed to the five following shortcomings of the Data Retention Directive.

First, the Data Retention Directive covers, in a generalized manner, all persons and all means of electronic communication as well as traffic data without any differentiation, limitation or exception being made in the light of the objective of combating serious crime (paragraph 57). Second, it does not lay down any objective criteria by which to determine the limits on the possibility of national authorities accessing data retained by private companies, and it failed to specify conditions that justify the use of these data for law enforcement purposes (paragraphs 60 and 61). Third, the Data Retention Directive does not set a sufficiently restrictive time frame for retention of data. It imposes a period of at least six months, without making any distinction between categories of data on the basis of the persons concerned or the possible usefulness of the data in relation to the objective pursued (paragraph 63). Fourth, the Data Retention Directive does not provide sufficient safeguards relating to the security and protection of data retained by private providers of electronic communications (paragraph 66). Finally, it does not require data to be retained within the EU, thus it does not fully ensure control of compliance with the requirements of protection and security by an independent authority (paragraph 68).

The CJEU largely relied on the *Digital Rights Ireland* judgment to support its reasoning in the Schrems judgment.

3.2 The *Schrems* Judgment

Maximillian Schrems, an Austrian Facebook user, brought a complaint before the Irish Data Protection Commissioner, taking the view that in the light of Edward Snowden's revelations the Irish supervisory authority should order Facebook to cease transferring his personal data to servers in the United States. The supervisor rejected the complaint. Mr Schrems challenged the authority's decision before the High Court, which decided to request a preliminary ruling on the question whether national supervisory authorities are absolutely bound by the Safe Harbour Decision.

The CJEU, first, considered the powers of the national supervisory authorities. It held that in accordance with Article 8(3) of the Charter each of them has the power to check, with complete independence, whether a transfer of data from its own Member State to a third country complies with the requirements laid down by the Data Protection Directive (paragraphs 45–47). The Safe Harbour Decision cannot prevent persons whose personal data has been or could be transferred to a third country from lodging a claim with the national supervisory authorities in order to protect their fundamental rights (paragraph 53).

The CJEU then examined the validity of the Safe Harbour Decision and noted that solely self-certified US organizations receiving personal data from the EU, but not the US public authorities, are bound by the safe harbour principles (paragraph 82). Moreover, national security, public interest, or law enforcement requirements have primacy over the safe harbour principles pursuant to which self-certified US organizations receiving personal data from the EU are bound to disregard those principles without limitation where they conflict with those requirements (paragraph 86). The Safe Harbour Decision does not refer either to the existence, in the United States, of rules intended to limit interference by US public authorities with the fundamental rights of persons or to the existence of effective legal protection against such interference (paragraphs 88–89).

The CJEU found that under EU law, legislation is not limited to what is strictly necessary where, on a generalized basis, it authorizes storage of all the personal data of all the persons whose data is transferred from the EU to the United States without any differentiation, limitation, or exception being made in the light of the objective pursued and without an objective criterion being laid down for determining the limits of access by the public authorities to the data and of its subsequent use (paragraph 93). In particular, legislation permitting the public authorities to have access on a generalized basis to the content of electronic communications must be regarded as compromising the essence of the fundamental right to respect for private life (paragraph 94). Likewise, legislation not providing any possibility for an individual to pursue legal remedies in order to have access to personal data relating to them, or to obtain rectification or erasure of such data, compromises the essence of the fundamental right to effective judicial protection, the existence of such a possibility being inherent in the existence of the rule of law (paragraph 95).

The CJEU further noted that the Commission did not find in the Safe Harbour Decision that the United States in fact ensures an adequate level of protection by reason of its domestic law or its international commitments; that is, a level of protection of fundamental rights and freedoms that is essentially equivalent, but not identical, to that guaranteed within the EU (paragraphs 73 and 96). Therefore, without there being any need to examine the content of the safe harbour principles, the Safe Harbour Decision was declared invalid (paragraph 96).

3.3 Justification of Interference with the Right to Privacy and Data Protection in the Interests of National Security

The CJEU in both cases admitted that interference with the right to privacy and data protection requires a strict necessity and proportionality test under Article 52 (1) of the Charter. According to this Article, limitations may be imposed on the exercise of fundamental rights and freedoms such as those set forth in Articles 7 and 8 of the Charter, as long as those limitations are provided for by law, respect the essence of those rights and freedoms, and, subject to the principle of proportionality, are necessary and genuinely meet objectives of general interest recognized by the EU or the need to protect the rights and freedoms of others.

The CJEU has not taken a clear stand regarding the requirement to respect the essence of fundamental rights enshrined in Articles 7 and 8 of the Charter. In the *Digital Rights Ireland* case, the CJEU found that mass metadata surveillance, unlike the content of communication, does not affect the essence of the right to privacy enshrined in Article 7.[17] The CJEU also separately found that the Data Retention Directive does not affect the essence of the right to data protection under Article 8 of the Charter, referring to the principles of data protection and data security,[18] thus emphasizing the differences between the concepts of privacy and data protection in line with the theory that the right to privacy is 'an optical tool' that prohibits intrusion in the private sphere, while the right to data protection is a 'transparency tool' that relates to the management of personal information and empowers the individual with a certain level of control over his or her data and the ways it is used.[19] The CJEU subsequently referred to this finding in the *Schrems* case, stating that as regards US legislation, access on a generalized basis to the content of communications data by the public authorities compromises the essence of the right to privacy.[20]

Such a differentiation nowadays no longer seems to be justified given the rapid changes in how society communicates; that is, increasingly preferring use of portable devices (smartphones and tablets) that cover all of our communications (calls, emails, web searches).[21] These changes have made metadata surveillance a unique and valuable tool for both law enforcement and commercial purposes, as it may

[17] *Digital Rights Ireland, supra* note 1, para. 39.

[18] *Ibid.*, para. 40.

[19] Paul de Hertz and Serge Gutwirth 'Privacy, Data Protection and Law Enforcement. Opacity of the Individual and Transparency of Power' in E.E. Claes, A. Duff, and S. Gutwirth (eds), *Privacy and the Criminal Law* (Intersentia 2006) 61–104.

[20] Schrems, *supra* note 3, para. 95.

[21] See Nora Ni Loideain, 'EU Law and Mass Internet Metadata Surveillance in the Post-Snowden Era' (2015) 3(2) *Media and Communication* 54; Frederik J. Zuiderveen Borgesius and Axel Arnbak, 'New

provide very precise information on every communication and movement of individuals, as has also been recognized by the CJEU.[22]

At the same time, the CJEU in both cases pointed to the necessity to include 'differentiation, limitation or exception' in legislation as regards persons, means of electronic communication, and traffic data covered by it,[23] as well to lay down 'objective criteria by which to determine the limits of the access of the competent national authorities to the data'.[24] The CJEU reaffirmed that general and indiscriminate retention of traffic and location data is illegal in its judgment adopted on 21 December 2016 in joined cases C-203/15 and C-698/15 *Tele2 Sverige* and *Davis and Others*[25] related to Swedish and UK data retention laws.

The CJEU in the *Digital Rights Ireland* judgment made references to the case law of the European Court of Human Rights (the ECtHR) concerning interpretation of Article 8 of the European Convention on Human Rights (the ECHR) in the context of data retention measures.[26] Article 8 of the ECHR provides the right to respect for private life. The right to protection of personal data, although not explicitly mentioned, also forms part of the rights protected under Article 8 of the ECHR.[27] Conditions for lawful processing in Article 52 (1) of the Charter are in tune with Article 8 (2) of the ECHR which includes a limitation clause to the right to respect for private life set out in the first part, Article 8 (1). According to Article 52 (3) of the Charter, in so far as the Charter contains rights which correspond to rights guaranteed by the ECHR, the meaning and scope of those rights shall be the same as those laid down by the latter; however, this provision shall not prevent EU law providing more extensive protection. Thus, the conditions for justified interference according to Article 8 (2) of the ECHR are the minimum requirements for lawful limitations of the right to privacy enshrined in the Charter.

The ECtHR has constantly extended a margin of appreciation to the Member States when privacy rights have clashed with national security concerns by recognizing that they have 'a fairly wide margin of appreciation in choosing the means for achieving the legitimate aim of protecting national security'[28] when assessing the necessity of a measure. Moreover, the ECtHR has also recognized that intelligence gathering can be a legitimate aim in processing personal data including the

Data Security Requirements and the Proceduralization of Mass Surveillance Law after the European Data Retention Case' Amsterdam Law School Legal Studies Research Paper No. 2015-41, 35.

---

[22] *Digital Rights Ireland, supra* note 1, paras 26–27.

[23] *Ibid.*, para. 57.

[24] *Digital Rights Ireland, supra* note 1, paras 57, 60; Schrems, *supra* note 3, para. 93.

[25] Joined Cases C-203/15 and C-698/15 *Tele2 Sverige AB and Secretary of State for the Home Department v Post-och telestyrelsen and Others* ECLI:EU:C:2016:970, para. 112.

[26] *Digital Rights Ireland, supra* note 1, paras 35, 47, 54–5.

[27] European Union Agency for Fundamental Rights, Council of Europe, 'Handbook on European Data Protection Law', June 2014, 15 <http://fra.europa.eu/sites/default/files/fra-2014-handbook-data-protection-law-2nd-ed_en.pdf> accessed 28 April 2019.

[28] *Weber and Saravia v Germany*, ECtHR, App No 54934/00, 29 June 2006 [106].

use of secret surveillance measures, as long as adequate and effective guarantees against abuse are in place preventing surveillance from 'undermine[ing] or even destroy[ing] democracy under the cloak of defending it'.[29] Likewise, the CJEU has emphasized the necessity to provide sufficient guarantees to protect personal data effectively against the risk of abuse and against any unlawful access and use of that data.[30] EU law, in particular through the judgments of the CJEU, has significantly enhanced the right to privacy.[31]

The case law of the CJEU as well of the ECtHR has to be regarded as a valuable tool for developing data protection policies both nationally and within the EU. The judgments of the CJEU irreversibly link the two legal orders more closely and open the possibility to interpret Article 8 ECHR and Articles 7 and 8 of the Charter in a parallel way.[32] Moreover, it should be recognized that both the *Digital Rights Ireland* judgment and the *Schrems* judgment will influence not only the European human rights system but also the global international human rights systems,[33] taking into account the serious efforts taken by the international community after the Snowden revelations, in particular UN bodies, in addressing the issue of data privacy and extraterritorial surveillance interception of communications, as well as collection of personal data on a mass scale.[34]

The Article 29 Working Party—a European advisory body on data protection that was replaced by the European Data Protection Board on 25 May 2018—has prepared a survey which analyses the jurisprudence of the CJEU and the ECtHR in order to provide guidance when assessing whether interference with fundamental rights can be justified in the case of a data processing operation. It concludes that there are four European Essential Guarantees:

1. Processing should be based on clear, precise, and accessible rules.
2. Necessity and proportionality need to be demonstrated with regard to legitimate objectives pursued.
3. An independent oversight mechanism should exist.
4. Effective remedies need to be available to the individual.[35]

[29] *Szábo and Vissy v Hungary*, ECtHR, App No 37138/14, 12 January 2016 [57].

[30] *Digital Rights Ireland, supra* note 1, para. 54 and the case law cited.

[31] Federico Fabbrini 'Human Rights in the Digital Age: The European Court of Justice Ruling in the Data Retention Case and Its Lessons for Privacy and Surveillance in the United States' (2015) 28 *Harvard Human Rights Journal* 67–8.

[32] Franziska Boehm and Mark D. Cole, 'Data Retention after the Judgement of the Court of Justice of the European Union' (Münster/Luxembourg, 30 June 2014), 7 <http://www.zar.kit.edu/DATA/veroeffentlichungen/237_237_Boehm_Cole-Data_Retention_Study-June_2014_1a1c2f6_9906a8c.pdf>.

[33] See Monika Zalnieriute, 'An international constitutional moment for data privacy in the times of mass-surveillance' (2015) 23 (2) *International Journal of Law and Information Technology* 99.

[34] Report of the Office of the United Nations High Commissioner for Human Rights 'The right to privacy in the digital age', A/HRC/27/37, 30 June 2014.

[35] Article 29 Working Party, Working Document 01/2016 on the justification of interferences with the fundamental rights to privacy and data protection through surveillance measures when transferring

However, despite these guarantees, mass surveillance still remains an unresolved problem. Even with procedural guarantees, massive and indiscriminate surveillance of individuals for the purpose of national security cannot be considered justified.[36] The UN Special Rapporteur has concluded that 'it is incompatible with existing concepts of privacy for states to collect all communications or metadata all the time indiscriminately. The very essence of the right to the privacy of communication is that infringements must be exceptional and justified on a case-by-case basis.'[37]

4 Implications of the Judgments

Further analysis of the implications of the *Digital Rights Ireland* and *Schrems* judgments aims to identify the key challenges that data protection law and policy face both at Member State and EU level that have to be overcome in order to maintain a proper balance between privacy and national security.

4.1 Implications for Data Protection in the Member States

The CJEU judgments will have a significant and long-standing influence on national data retention laws as well as on data transfer practices in the Member States.

The *Digital Rights Ireland* judgment has induced different judicial and legislative responses among the Member States with regard to national data retention laws. As such, national transposition measures based on the invalidated Data Retention Directive are not directly affected by the judgment.[38] Thus, each Member State will need to review the compatibility of existing national measures with the standards set by the CJEU.

Initiation of legal proceedings in national courts has proved to be the most effective way to have national data retention laws reviewed in the light of fundamental

personal data (European Essential Guarantees); Article 29 Working Party, Adequacy Referential (updated), 28 November 2017.

[36] See Zuiderveen Borgesius and Arnbak, *supra* note 19, 34–6; Article 29 Working Party, Opinion 01/2016 on the EU–US Privacy Shield draft adequacy decision, 13 April 2016.

[37] UN Special Rapporteur on the promotion and protection of human rights and fundamental freedoms while countering terrorism, 'Report of the Special Rapporteur on the promotion and protection of human rights and fundamental freedoms while countering terrorism' UN Doc A/69/397, 23 September 2014.

[38] Art. 15 (1) of Directive 2002/58/EC still provides a possibility to adopt data retention obligations 'when such restriction constitutes a necessary, appropriate and proportionate measure within a democratic society to safeguard national security.' Directive 2002/58/EC of the European Parliament and of the Council of 12 July 2002 concerning the processing of personal data and the protection of privacy in the electronic communications sector (Directive on privacy and electronic communications) (2002) OJ L 201.

rights set out in Articles 7 and 8 of the Charter, Article 8 of the ECHR, and the respective provisions of national constitutions. Even before review by the CJEU, national provisions implementing the Data Retention Directive were successfully challenged before the highest administrative and constitutional courts in Bulgaria, Romania, Germany, Cyprus, and the Czech Republic.[39] Just after the *Digital Rights Ireland* judgment, national implementation laws were quickly annulled by constitutional courts in Austria, Slovenia, Romania, and Bulgaria.[40] In Belgium and the Netherlands, national data retention laws were also invalidated after complaints by public interest groups.[41] Thus, national courts have represented themselves as strict protectors of fundamental rights.[42]

There have also been different legislative responses among the Member States, but most have been slow to uphold the human rights standards set by the judgment without waiting for the urging of national courts. A number of Member States immediately initiated the review process and have changed or plan to change their data retention regimes, mostly by introducing additional safeguards. However, many states have not yet reacted to the CJEU judgment.[43] Some governments or parliaments—for example, in Sweden, Finland, and the United Kingdom—have expressed the view that the CJEU judgment does not prohibit implementation of mass surveillance nationally if proper safeguards are in place.[44]

These different responses indicate the need to maintain a common position among the Member States in respect of the scope of state surveillance in the name of national security.[45] Although national security remains in the sole responsibility of each Member State,[46] governments need to implement and review surveillance measures in the context of protection of private data from a human rights perspective.

[39] Bulgarian Supreme Administrative Court, No. 13627, 11 December 2008; Romanian Constitutional Court, No. 1258, 8 October 2009; German Constitutional Court, 1 BvR 256/08, 1 BvR 263/08, 1 BvR 586/08, 2 March 2010; Czech Constitutional Court, Pl. ÚS 24/10, 22 March 2011; Cypriot Supreme Court, 65/2009, 78/2009, 82/2009, 15/2010-22/2010, 1 February 2011; for further analysis, see Niklas and Miettinen, *supra* note 9, 293–5.

[40] Austrian Constitutional Court, No. G 47/2012, 27 June 2014; Constitutional Court of the Republic of Slovenia, No. U-I-65/13-19, 3 July 2014; Romanian Constitutional Court, No. 440, 8 July 2014; Constitutional Court of the Republic of Bulgaria, No. 8/2014, 12 March 2015.

[41] Belgian Constitutional Court, No. 84/2015, 11 June 2015; District Court of The Hague, ECLI:NL:RBDHA:2015:2498.

[42] For detailed analysis on national courts decisions see European Union Agency for Fundamental Rights, Fundamental rights: Annual activity report 2015, June 2016, 124–5 <http://fra.europa.eu/sites/default/files/fra_uploads/fra-2016-annual-activity-report-2015_en.pdf> accessed 28 April 2019.

[43] For detailed analysis on the impact of the *Digital Rights Ireland* judgment on national data retention legislation and policy, see *ibid.* 125–6.

[44] Niklas and Miettinen, *supra* note 9, at 303.

[45] For analysis of the legal frameworks on surveillance in EU Member States, see European Union Agency for Fundamental Rights, Surveillance by intelligence services: fundamental rights safeguards and remedies in the European Union—Mapping Member States' legal frameworks, November 2015, <http://fra.europa.eu/en/publication/2015/surveillance-intelligence-services> accessed 28 April 2019.

[46] Treaty of Lisbon Amending the Treaty on European Union and the Treaty Establishing the European Community, (2007) OJC 306 1, Art. 4 (2).

The *Schrems* judgment also calls for the necessity to reach a political agreement between Member States on state surveillance issues. The CJEU has substantially strengthened the role of data protection authorities by empowering them to examine the level of data protection in third countries in order to deal with individual claims alleging infringement of fundamental rights. Authorities may restrict data transfers in cases where they find a violation of fundamental rights. However, concerns have been expressed about the capability of the data protection authorities to fulfil such a complicated task due to the lack of available resources as well as about the possibility of different views among them on the level of protection in third countries. The judgment could thus lead to legal uncertainty as different standards of protection of personal data could be applied throughout the EU.[47]

As shown earlier, the CJEU judgments call for a political agreement between EU Member States on state surveillance issues in the light of the legal standards for data protection in order to express a common position on national data retention measures, as well as on EU measures concerning mass surveillance.[48]

4.2 Implications for Data Protection in the EU

The principles outlined in the CJEU judgments have to be taken into consideration with regard to data retention schemes. These schemes relying on exchange of intelligence-led information, mass data collection, and creation of large-scale databases within the EU form a crucial part of EU counterterrorism policy.[49]

Existing and planned EU measures such as the EU PNR (Passenger Name Record) system and the Entry/Exit System (EES) proposal[50] need to be tested for compliance with the requirements set out in the CJEU judgments. Namely, an assessment is needed as to whether access and use by the competent national authorities of data originally collected for another purpose is limited to what is strictly necessary in terms of categories of data and persons concerned and subject to procedural safeguards, such as an independent oversight mechanism and control of access to data.

[47] Christopher Kuner, 'Reality and Illusion in EU Data Transfer Regulation Post *Schrems*' (2016) University of Cambridge Faculty of Law Research Paper No. 14/2016, 12.

[48] See Marina Škrinjar Vidović, 'Schrems v Data Protection Commissioner (Case C-362/14): Empowering National Data Protection Authorities', (2015) 11(11) *Croatian Yearbook of European Law and Policy* 275.

[49] See Didier Bigo et al., 'The EU Counter-Terrorism Policy Responses to the Attacks in Paris: Towards an EU Security and Liberty Agenda', (2015) 81 CEPS Paper in Liberty and Security in Europe <https://www.ceps.eu/system/files/LSE81Counterterrorism.pdf> accessed 28 April 2019.

[50] Proposal for a Regulation of the European Parliament and of the Council establishing an Entry/Exit System (EES) to register entry and exit data and refusal of entry data of third country nationals crossing the external borders of the Member States of the European Union and determining the conditions for access to the EES for law enforcement purposes and amending Regulation (EC) No. 767/2008 and Regulation (EU) No. 1077/2011, COM(2016) 194 final.

The highly controversial EU policy response to the tragic terrorist attacks around the world and in Europe, notably in Paris and Brussels, is the EU PNR system, which was repeatedly proposed in 2015. On 21 April 2016 the Council of the EU adopted the PNR Directive,[51] which entered into force on 24 May 2016 and was to be transposed into national legislation by 25 May 2018. The Directive obliges airlines to transfer their passenger data to EU Member States in order to help the authorities fight terrorism and serious crime. The scope of data retention has been reduced in comparison with the previous proposal of the PNR Directive, which was rejected by the European Parliament in 2013. However, the necessity and proportionality of indiscriminate bulk data collection in PNR systems in the light of the *Digital Rights Ireland* judgment still remains in question. The CJEU requires a link between the data retained and a threat to public security that cannot be established if the data of unsuspicious persons is retained in bulk.[52]

The CJEU judgments also have a strong influence on agreements with third countries allowing for transfer of personal data. Examples include PNR agreements with the United States,[53] Canada,[54] and Australia,[55] and the EU–US Terrorist Finance Tracking Programme Agreement.[56] On 26 July 2017, the CJEU issued Opinion A-1/15[57] on the validity of the EU–Canada PNR agreement, largely relying on the previously adopted *Digital rights Ireland* and *Schrems* judgments. The CJEU declared that the EU–Canada PNR agreement has to be revised because several provisions, such as allowing transfer of sensitive data, are incompatible with fundamental rights and listed necessary guarantees that have to be provided by the agreement. At the same time, the CJEU concluded that systematic transfer, retention, and use of all passenger data does not adversely affect the essence of the right to private life and data protection enshrined in Articles 7 and 8 of the Charter. Opinion A-1/15 will have a major impact on other agreements as well as on the new PNR Directive. Human rights experts have expressed deep concerns about

[51] Directive (EU) 2016/681 of the European Parliament and of the Council of 27 April 2016 on the use of passenger name record (PNR) data for the prevention, detection, investigation, and prosecution of terrorist offences and serious crime (2016) OJ L 119.

[52] See EDRi, Annual Report 2015, <https://edri.org/files/Annual_Report_2015_Final.pdf> accessed 28 April 2019; European Union Agency for Fundamental Rights, Embedding fundamental rights in the security agenda, February 2015, <http://fra.europa.eu/en/publication/2015/embedding-fundamental-rights-security-agenda> accessed 28 April 2019; Boehm, Cole, *supra* note 33, at 8, 65–72.

[53] Agreement between the European Community and the United States of America on the processing and transfer of PNR data by air carriers to the United States Department of Homeland Security, Bureau of Customs and Border Protection, (2012) OJ L 215/5.

[54] Agreement between the European Community and the Government of Canada on the processing of Advance Passenger Information and Passenger Name Record data, (2006) OJ L 82.

[55] Agreement between the European Union and Australia on the processing and transfer of Passenger Name Record (PNR) data by air carriers to the Australian Customs and Border Protection Service (2012), OJ L 186.

[56] Agreement between the European Union and the United States of America on the processing and transfer of Financial Messaging Data from the European Union to the United States for the purposes of the Terrorist Finance Tracking Program (2010), OJ L 8.

[57] Case A-1/15, Opinion of the Court ECLI:EU:C:2016:656.

these measures arguing, in particular, that undifferentiated bulk data collection and transfer of flight passenger and bank data have considerable shortcomings in relation to compliance with the fundamental rights standards set by the CJEU.[58]

Moreover, counterterrorism policy applied unilaterally in other parts of the world, namely by the United States, can lead to mass surveillance of EU citizens through international data transfers made purely for commercial purposes. The *Schrems* judgment significantly speeded up negotiations on the new data protection regime for transatlantic exchanges of personal data. On 12 July 2016, the European Commission adopted the EU–US Privacy Shield,[59] which replaced the previous Safe Harbour Decision invalidated by the CJEU. Its validity is already being challenged before the CJEU in the *Digital Rights Ireland v Commission* case T-670/16. However, the CJEU on 22 November 2017 ruled the EU–US Privacy Shield invalidation action inadmissible.[60] Alternative data transfer mechanisms, such as standard contractual clauses and binding corporate rules, are also being challenged.[61]

According to the opinion of the Article 29 Working Party, the new Privacy Shield offers major improvements compared to the invalidated Safe Harbour Decision. However, a number of shortcomings need to be addressed to ensure that the level of protection of fundamental rights offered by the Privacy Shield is indeed essentially equivalent to that of the EU.[62] In particular, the Working Party doubts whether the role of the new Ombudsperson mechanism would be truly independent in order to offer an effective remedy to non-compliant data processing. It also expresses concerns that the adequacy decision does not set an obligation for organizations to delete data if they are no longer necessary. However, one of the greatest concerns is that the US administration does not fully exclude continued collection of massive and indiscriminate data, which is an unjustified interference with the fundamental rights of individuals.

The new Privacy Shield has also been criticized by academic experts. Professor Christopher Kuner has noted that it includes 'verbose documentation and procedural mechanisms that are lengthy, untransparent, formalistic and unintelligible to the average individual', and has been negotiated in a secret and hurried procedure without proper debate.[63] He also finds that it is an illusion that the EU

[58] Boehm, Cole, *supra* note 33, at 8.

[59] Commission Implementing Decision (EU) 2016/1250 of 12 July 2016 pursuant to Directive 95/46/EC of the European Parliament and of the Council on the adequacy of the protection provided by the EU–US Privacy Shield, (2016) OJ L 207.

[60] Case T-670/16, *Digital Rights Ireland v Commission* ECLI:EU:T:2017:838.

[61] Article 29 Working Party, Statement on the implementation of the judgment of the Court of Justice of the European Union of 6 October 2015 in the *Maximilian Schrems v Data Protection Commissioner* case (C-362-14), 16 October 2015; See M. Carolan, 'High Court sets out 11 questions for ECJ on EU–US data transfers (*Irish Times*, 12 April 2018) <https://www.irishtimes.com/business/technology/high-court-sets-out-11-questions-for-ecj-on-eu-us-data-transfers-1.3459549> accessed 28 April 2019.

[62] Article 29 Working Party (*supra* note 39); Article 29 Working Party, EU–US Privacy Shield—First Annual Joint Review, 28 November 2017.

[63] See Kuner, *supra* n 48, at 4, 37.

data protection law by itself can provide effective protection of EU personal data transferred around the world, as evidenced by reactions to the *Schrems* judgment. Procedural mechanisms cannot provide effective protection against surveillance for national security, and there is a need for further reform regarding intelligence-gathering practice.[64] As pointed out by human rights expert Anthony Dworkin: 'A transatlantic dialogue is needed not only on guiding principles for intelligence collaboration, but more generally on the appropriate limits of surveillance in the age of big data.'[65]

The above-mentioned challenges that the EU faces have to be viewed in the current international context, where the emergence of 'big data' and growing security needs call for new solutions. Global initiatives for development of new international norms regarding surveillance and international privacy standards[66] could have the benefit of establishing a commonly agreed balance between national security and privacy.

5 Conclusions

EU data protection rules have become not only an important economic development tool but also an enabler of national security. Growing security threats have led to domestic and extraterritorial mass digital surveillance over EU citizens' personal data, raising serious concerns about effective protection of fundamental rights. These concerns have reached the CJEU. The landmark judgments on mass surveillance in the name of national security—the *Digital Rights Ireland* judgment and the *Schrems* judgment—are of great significance for strengthening the rights to privacy and data protection enshrined in Articles 7 and 8 of the Charter.

The CJEU in both cases requires a strict necessity and proportionality test when assessing interference with these fundamental rights in the interests of national security, and encourages application of strong procedural safeguards, such as independent oversight mechanisms and effective remedies in the case of mass collection and exchange of personal data. However, despite these guarantees, massive and indiscriminate surveillance of individuals for the purposes of national security cannot be considered justified.

[64] *Ibid.*

[65] Anthony Dworkin, 'Surveillance, Privacy, and Security: Europe's Confused Response to Snowden' (European Council on Foreign Relations, 20 January 2015) <http://www.ecfr.eu/publications/summary/mass_surveillance_privacy_and_security_europes_confused_response329> accessed 28 April 2019.

[66] The first UN Special Rapporteur on the right to privacy, Juseph Cannataci, has indicated that defining the notion of privacy and developing universal surveillance law are among the main areas requiring particular attention. See 'Digital surveillance "worse than Orwell", says new UN privacy chief' (*The Guardian*, 24 August 2015) <https://www.theguardian.com/world/2015/aug/24/we-need-geneva-convention-for-the-internet-says-new-un-privacy-chief> accessed 28 April 2019.

Besides, the CJEU's position on differentiation between the content of communications data and mass metadata surveillance is nowadays no longer justified. The way society communicates has rapidly changed, increasingly preferring use of portable devices that cover all of our communications. These changes have made metadata surveillance a unique and valuable tool both for law enforcement and commercial purposes, as it may provide very precise information on every communication and movement of individuals.

The CJEU judgments call for a political agreement between EU Member States on mass surveillance issues. The *Digital Rights Ireland* judgment has caused different judicial and legislative responses in EU Member States. However, they have been slow to review national data retention laws in the light of the set fundamental rights standards. Similarly, the *Schrems* judgment, by empowering national data protection authorities to examine the level of data protection in third countries in the case of data transfers, could lead to application of different personal data protection standards. These implications indicate the need to maintain a common position in respect of the scope of state surveillance in the name of national security among the Member States and encourage governments to implement and review surveillance measures in the context of protection of private data from a human rights perspective without waiting for court decisions.

The CJEU judgments have to be taken into consideration with regard to any existing or planned EU legislation involving large-scale collection and processing of personal data. It remains to be seen whether data retention mechanisms within the EU—in particular the EU PNR Directive, as well as PNR agreements with third countries—comply with the requirements set out in the CJEU judgment, in particular taking into account CJEU Opinion A-1/15 declaring the draft EU–Canada PNR agreement incompatible with the fundamental rights of the EU. Considering the impact the CJEU judgments will have on the transatlantic data transfer framework, the EU–US Privacy Shield, although introducing new procedural safeguards, will not be able to provide effective protection against surveillance for national security purposes. Procedural mechanisms cannot provide effective protection against surveillance for national security without further reform regarding intelligence-gathering practice and agreement on guiding principles for intelligence collaboration. These challenges require new approaches both within the EU and beyond to set appropriate limits to mass digital surveillance and to find a commonly agreed balance between national security and privacy.

PART II
IMMUNITIES THEMES

Recent Opposing Trends in the Conceptualization of the Law of Immunities

Some Reflections

*Stefano Dominelli**

1 Scope of the Investigation

As recalled by Professor van Aaken during the opening ceremony of the 12th Annual Conference of the European Society of International Law, 'crisis' is commonly defined by dictionaries as a period of insecurity where a decision—for better or worse—is urgently needed. The question 'is international law in a state of crisis?' is different in meaning from the question 'how does international law work in times of crisis?' Neither of these two questions could easily be answered briefly since the scope of investigations has vast—possibly unlimited—boundaries.

The present chapter will start from some generally accepted conclusions related to the first question ('Is international law in crisis?') to address this issue under a very specific lens related to the second question ('How does international law work in times of crisis?').

In this sense, recent developments before the Italian courts in the field of state immunity from civil jurisdiction will be reconstructed and analysed so as to detect a new conceptualization of sovereignty at the domestic level and under a domestic law point of view. This emerging trend will be juxtaposed with others, followed by international and regional courts, namely the International Court of Justice and the European Court of Human Rights, which—as emblems of the Westphalian order—still favour immunity in the context of *jus cogens* violations, even though this might lead to impunity.

This comparison will raise the question whether or not the international law of immunities is in a state of crisis. Nonetheless, as will be argued, whilst there is little doubt that rules on immunity are fragmented and in a higher state of flux

* An early version of the present work was presented at the 12th Annual Conference of the European Society of International Law in Riga. The Author wishes to thank the participants at the conference, the reviewers, and editors for their useful comments.

Stefano Dominelli, *Recent Opposing Trends in the Conceptualization of the Law of Immunities: Some Reflections* In: *How International Law Works in Times of Crisis*. Edited by: George Ulrich and Ineta Ziemele, Oxford University Press (2019).
DOI: 10.1093/oso/9780198849667.003.0009

than usual, it does not seem they have yet reached a state that can unanimously be accepted by all as a 'crisis'. Hence, the intent is to reflect on what will remain of the traditional principles of immunity of international actors depending on the degree of acceptance of what will here be described as the 'Italian trend'. This trend is to be added to the existing rules, which, drawing their reasoning on different conceptualizations, could in the long run deconstruct the customary principle of immunity itself.

2 Immunities and the 'Italian Trend'

Absolute immunity was the expression of the state paradigm that followed the Westphalian construction,[1] which is 'predicated on the co-equal sovereignty of States'.[2] This conceptualization of the rules on state immunity has lost consensus within the international community,[3] and today most states adhere to the so-called restrictive theory.[4] As argued by Italian and Belgian courts,[5] 'States acting as a private individual were regarded as having submitted themselves to all the civil consequences of the contract, including its judicial enforcement'.[6]

[1] Noting that 'internal exclusive competence coupled with external equality with and independence from other States were the hallmarks of the Westphalian State', Hazel Fox and Philippa Webb, *The Law of State Immunity, 3rd edn* (OUP 2015) 26.

[2] Cherif Bassiouni, 'The Discipline of International Criminal Law' in Cherif Bassiouni (ed.), *International Criminal Law, Vol. I Sources, Subjects, and Contents, 3rd edn* (Brill 2008) 1, at 51. See also Antonio Cassese, *International Law, 2nd edn* (OUP 2005) 28.

[3] See European Court of Human Rights, ECtHR *Oleynikov v Russia*, App No 36703/04, 14 March 2013, and Hong Kong Court of Final Appeal, 8 September 2011, *Democratic Republic of the Congo and others v FG Hemisphere Associates LLC*, in 150 ILR 684.

[4] Corte di Cassazione, Sezioni Unite, 27 May 2005, No. 11225, *Borri v Repubblica Argentina*, in (2005) *Rivista di diritto internazionale* 856. A partial English translation of the decision is available at: <http://www.geneva-academy.ch/RULAC/pdf_State/Borri-v-Argentina.pdf> accessed 28 April 2019. See also LG Frankfurt/Main, 14 March 2003—2-21 O 294/02, in [2003] *Zeitschrift für Wirtschafts- und Bankrecht* 783; OLG Frankfurt, 13 June 2006—8 U 107/03, in (2007) *Zeitschrift für Wirtschafts- und Bankrecht* 929, and Bundesgerichtshof, 08 March 2016—VI ZR 516/14, in (2016) *Zeitschrift für Wirtschaftsrecht* 789.

[5] Corte d'Appello Lucca, 1887, *Hamspohn v Bey di Tunisi*, [1887] *Foro it.* I, 474; Tribunal civil of Brussels, *Société pour la fabrication de cartouches v Colonel Mutkuroff, Ministre de la guerre de la principaute de Bulgarie* (1888), in [1889] *Pandectes periodiques* 350; Tribunale Firenze, 8 June 1906, in [1907] *Rivista di diritto internazionale* 379; Corte di Cassazione, 13 March 1926, in [1926] *Rivista di diritto internazionale* 250; Corte d'Appello di Napoli, 16 July 1926, in [1927] *Rivista di diritto internazionale* 104; Corte d'Appello di Milano, 23 January 1932, in [1932] *Rivista di diritto internazionale* 549; Corte di Cassazione, 18 January 1933, in [1933] *Rivista di diritto internazionale* 241; Court of Cassation, 11 June 1903, in [1904] *Journal de Droit International Privé* 136; Court of Appeal of Brussels, 24 June 1920, in [1922] *Pasicrisie Belge* II, 122, and Court of Appeal of Brussels, 24 May 1933, in [1933] *Journal de Droit International* 1034.

[6] Ilaria Queirolo, 'Immunity', in Jurgen Basedow, Franco Ferrari, Pedro de Miguel Asensio, and Gisela Rühl (eds), *Encyclopedia of Private International Law* (Edward Elgar Publishing 2017), 896, at 897.

This (r)evolution is already consistent with what today appears to be a decline of the 'state paradigm':[7] the international community is moving towards a system that also recognizes other actors. It is against this background that some current decisions in the field of state immunity must be analysed. Featuring amongst these is the series of decisions that have been issued in the context of the controversy between Germany and Italy, ultimately leading to a judgment by the Italian Constitutional Court that expresses a 'new trend' in the conceptualization of immunities and sovereignty.

The controversy between Germany and Italy that led to the 2012 judgment of the International Court of Justice (ICJ) is known, and can be recalled here *quatenus opus est*, as well as the judgment itself. Starting with the *Ferrini* case of the Italian Supreme Court,[8] Italian courts have denied immunity to Germany in the actions of individuals (or their heirs) who suffered damage caused by the Third Reich in the Second World War. *Ferrini* came as a *revirement* of Italian domestic case law that, prior to that day, always recognized state immunity for Germany.[9] In *Ferrini*, the *Corte di Cassazione* rationalized the principles and rules of public international law related to international criminal law, humanitarian law, and human rights laws so as to support its view that the law of state immunity witnessed a further evolution

[7] Angela Del Vecchio, *Giurisdizione internazionale e globalizzazione: i tribunali internazionali tra globalizzazione e frammentazione* (Giuffrè 2003); Luigi Ferrajoli, *Principia iuris. Teoria del diritto e della democrazia, Vol. 2, Teoria della democrazia* (Laterza 2007) 490 ff; Giuseppe Palmisano, 'Dal diritto internazionale al diritto cosmopolitico? Riflessioni a margine de La democrazia nell'età della globalizzazione', in (2010) *Jura Gentium* 114 ff, and Ziccardi Capaldo, *Diritto globale. Il nuovo diritto internazionale* (Giuffrè 2010).

[8] Cass. Civ. Sezioni unite, 11 March 2004, No. 5044, *Luigi Ferrini v Rep fed di Germania*, in (2004) *Rivista di diritto internazionale* 540, on which see *ex multis*, Giuseppe Serranò, 'Immunità degli Stati stranieri e crimini internazionali nella recente giurisprudenza della Corte di Cassazione' (2009) *Rivista di diritto internazionale privato e processuale* 605; Francesca De Vittor, 'Immunità degli Stati dalla giurisdizione e risarcimento del danno per violazione dei diritti fondamentali: il caso Mantelli' (2008) *Diritti umani e diritto internazionale* 632; Carlo Focarelli, 'Diniego dell'immunità giurisdizionale degli Stati stranieri per crimini, jus cogens e dinamica del diritto internazionale' (2008) *Rivista di diritto internazionale* 738; Claudio Consolo, 'La Cassazione "vertice imminente", non "ambiguo". Fra jus cogens prevalente sulla immunità giurisdizionale degli Stati (caso greco-tedesco risalente all'eccidio di Distomo e altri crimini bellici) e libertà di vivere con dignità fino all'ultimo (caso Engl)' (2008) *Il Corriere giuridico* 1041; Marina Castellaneta, 'Impossibile un'azione di risarcimento se l'atto deriva dal potere sovrano dello Stato' (2007) 2 *Guida al diritto - Diritto comunitario e internazionale* 45; Pasquale De Sena, Francesca De Vittor, 'Immunità degli Stati dalla giurisdizione e violazioni di diritti dell'uomo: la sentenza della Cassazione italiana nel caso Ferrini' (2005) *Giurisprudenza italiana* 255; Pasquale De Sena and Francesca De Vittor, 'State Immunity and Human Rights: The Italian Supreme Court Decision on the Ferrini Case' (2005) 16 *European Journal of International Law* 89; Alessandra Gianelli, 'Crimini internazionali ed immunità degli Stati della giurisdizione nella sentenza Ferrini' (2004) *Rivista di diritto internazionale* 643; Andrea Atteritano, 'Immunity of States and their Organs: the Contribution of Italian Jurisprudence over the Past Ten Years' (2010) 19 *Italian Yearbook of International Law* 33; Riccardo Pavoni, 'A Decade of Italian Case Law on the Immunity of Foreign States: Lights And Shadows' *ibid.*, at 73; Paolo Palchetti, 'Some Remarks on the Scope of Immunity of Foreign State Officials in the Light of Recent Judgments of Italian Courts' *ibid.*, at 83; Micaela Frulli, 'Some Reflections on the Functional Immunity of State Officials' *ibid.*, at 91.

[9] Prior to *Ferrini*, see Massimo Iovane, 'The Ferrini Judgment of the Italian Supreme Court: Opening Up Domestic Courts to Claims of Reparation for Victims of Serious Violations of Fundamental Human Rights' (2005) *Italian Yearbook of International Law* 165.

in respect to the *Bey of Tunisi* jurisprudence. As is known, this reconstruction of public international law was rejected in 2012 by the ICJ.[10]

According to the ICJ: (i) immunity must be granted (this being the international wrongdoing on which the Court was called to rule[11]) for *acta iure imperii*;[12] (ii) serious violations of international law are no ground to overcome state immunity (it being impossible to detect a contrast between a mere procedural rule and a substantive rule); and (iii) immunity is also granted where there is no other reasonable alternative judicial protection.[13]

The decision of the ICJ has been subject to a number of critiques not only by courts but also by scholars. Amongst the different critiques, some have pointed out that the court has not dwelled on the legitimacy of the substantive conduct to be adjudicated by Italian courts (war crimes).[14] In his dissenting opinion, Judge

[10] ICJ, Jurisdictional Immunities of the State (*Germany v Italy: Greece intervening*), Judgment, ICJ Reports 2012, at 99, para. 54. On the decision see *ex multis* Benedetto Conforti, 'The Judgment of the International Court of Justice on the Immunity of Foreign States: A Missed Opportunity' (2011) 21 *Italian Yearbook of International Law* 135; Riccardo Pavoni, 'An American Anomaly? On the ICJ's Selective Reading of United States Practice in Jurisdictional Immunities of the State' *ibid.*, at 143; Carlos Espósito, 'Jus Cogens and Jurisdictional Immunities of States at the International Court of Justice: "A Conflict Does Exist"' *ibidem* 161; Mirko Sossai, 'Are Italian Courts Directly Bound to Give Effect to the Jurisdictional Immunities Judgment?' *ibid.*, at 175; Lee Walker, 'Case Note: Jurisdictional Immunities of the State (*Germany v Italy—Greece Intervening*) (Judgment) (International Court of Justice, General List No 143, 3 February 2012)' (2012) 19 *Australian International Law Journal* 251; Stefania Negri, 'Sovereign Immunity v. Redress for War Crimes: The Judgment of the International Court of Justice in the Case Concerning Jurisdictional Immunities of the State (Germany v. Italy)' (2014) 16 *International Community Law Review* 123; Paul C. Bornkamm, 'State Immunity against Claims Arising from War Crimes: The Judgment of the International Court of Justice in Jurisdictional Immunities of the State Developments' (2012) 13 *German Law Journal* 773; J. Craig Barker, 'International Court of Justice: Jurisdictional Immunities of the State (Germany V Italy) Judgment of 3 February 2012' (2013) 62 *International and Comparative Law Quarterly* 741; Blanke Hermann-Josef and Lara Falkenberg, 'Is There State Immunity in Cases of War Crimes Committed in the Forum State: On the Decision of the International Court of Justice (ICJ) of 3 February 2012 in Jurisdictional Immunities of the State (Germany v. Italy: Greece Intervening) Developments' (2013) 14 *German Law Journal* 1817; Harvey Jarrad, '(R)evolution of State Immunity following Jurisdictional Immunities of the State (Germany v Italy)—Winds of Change or Hot Air' (2013) 32 *University of Tasmania Law Review* 208; Rosanne van Alebeek, 'Jurisdictional Immunities for the State (Germany v. Italy): On Right Outcomes and Wrong Terms' (2015) 55 *German Yearbook of International Law* 281; Lorna McGregor, 'State Immunity and Human Rights Is There a Future after Germany v. Italy?' (2012) *Journal of International Criminal Justice* 1; Giuseppe Nesi, 'The Quest for a 'Full' Execution of the ICJ Judgment in Germany v. Italy' (2013) 11 *Journal of International Criminal Justice* 185; Stefan Talmon, 'Jus Cogens after Germany v. Italy: Substantive and Procedural Rules Distinguished' (2012) 25 *Leiden Journal of International Law* 979; Alexander Orakhelashvili, 'Jurisdictional Immunities of the State (Germany v. Italy; Greece Intervening)' (2012) 106 *The American Journal of International Law* 609; Sangeeta Shah, 'Jurisdictional Immunities of the State: Germany v Italy' (2012) 12 *Human Rights Law Review* 555, and Markus Krajewski and Christopher Singer, 'Should Judges be Front-Runners? The ICJ, State Immunity and the Protection of Fundamental Human Rights' (2012) 16 *Max Planck Yearbook of United Nations Law* 1.

[11] ICJ, Jurisdictional Immunities of the State (*Germany v Italy: Greece intervening*), Judgment, *supra* note 10, para. 44.

[12] ICJ, Jurisdictional Immunities of the State, *supra* note 10, paras 65 and 77; cf. Fox and Webb, *supra* note 1, at 478.

[13] ICJ, Jurisdictional Immunities of the State (*Germany v. Italy: Greece intervening*), Judgment, *supra* note 10, para. 104.

[14] Krajewski and Singer, *supra* note 10, at 18.

Cançado Trindade suggests the 'absence or inadmissibility of state immunity in the face of *delicta imperii*, of international crimes in breach of *jus cogens*'. The ICJ appears to adhere strictly to the Westphalian understanding of the international community and its founding principles, making its decisions rather 'conservative'[15] in nature.[16] By not using at least a language giving credit to a state of flux in the topic,[17] the ICJ seems to have taken advantage of current international law to avoid any departure from traditional theories and concepts.

In particular, the ICJ could have taken a less rigid approach.[18] Even if it is true that immunities are a preliminary matter, the ICJ could have argued that where the gravity of the conduct is not contested, evaluation of that conduct for the purposes of excluding immunity would not violate the legal or logical reasoning that courts must follow in applying the principles related to immunities.

To comply with the decision of the ICJ, the Italian lawmaker enacted law No. 5 of 14 January 2013,[19] Law for the ratification of the 2004 UN Convention on Immunity, whose Article 3 placed upon courts an obligation to declare by their own motion a lack of jurisdiction in all those cases in which the ICJ determines a state's lack of civil jurisdiction. At the same time, the provision introduced a legal ground to revoke judicial decisions, even *res judicata*, in the same circumstances.

The Italian Constitutional Court was then called to rule on the constitutional validity of such provisions. The Court, by recalling the necessity to ensure effective judicial protection,[20] concluded that a customary norm, as ascertained by the ICJ,

[15] Cf. Winston P. Nagan and Joshua L. Root, 'The Emerging Restrictions on Sovereign Immunity: Peremptory Norms of International Law, the UN Charter, and the Application of Modern Communications Theory' (2013) 38 *North Carolina Journal of International Law and Commercial Regulation* 377, 453.

[16] Jurisdictional Immunities of the State (*Ger. v It., Greece Intervening*), the Separate opinion of Judge Bennouna, para. 18. Cf. also Christian Tomuschat, 'The Case of Germany v. Italy before the ICJ', in Anne Peters, Evelyne Lagrange, Stefan Oeter, and Christian Tomuschat (eds), *Immunities in the Age of Global Constitutionalism* (Brill 2015) 87 ff, summarizing general critiques.

[17] Krajewski and Singer, *supra* note 10, at 31, and Anne Peters, 'Immune Against Constitutionalisation?', in Peters et al., *supra* (note 16) at 1, 9.

[18] Cf. Michael Bothe, 'Remedies of Victims of War Crimes and Crimes against Humanity: Some Critical Remarks on the ICJ's Judgment on the Jurisdictional Immunity of States', in Peters et al., *supra* note 16, at 99, 108.

[19] GU No. 24 del 29 gennaio 2013. On which cf. Chantal Meloni, 'Jurisdictional Immunity of States: The Italian Constitutional Court v. the International Court of Justice? Brief notes on the Judgment no. 238 of 22 October 2014 of the Italian Constitutional Court' (2015) *Zeitschrift für Internationale Strafrechtsdogmatik* 348, at 349 ff.

[20] Judgment 238/2014: 'With an eye to the effectiveness of judicial protection of fundamental rights, this Court also noted that "the recognition of rights goes hand in hand with the recognition of the power to invoke them before a judge in judicial proceedings." Therefore, "the recourse to a legal remedy in defense of one's right is a right in itself, protected by Arts 24 and 113 of the Constitution. [This right is] inviolable in character and distinctive of a democratic State based on the rule of law." (Judgment No. 26/1999, as well as No. 120/2014, No. 386/2004, No. 29/2003). Further, there is little doubt that the right to a judge and to an effective judicial protection of inviolable rights is one of the greatest principles of legal culture in democratic systems of our times.'

cannot enter[21] the Italian legal order because compression of the right to defence exceeds the acceptability that is usually admitted in the field of state immunity, leading in the case at hand to impunity. Additionally, the Court argued that:

> [t]he immunity […] protects the [sovereign] function [of the state]. It does not protect behaviours that do not represent the typical exercise of governmental powers, but are explicitly considered and qualified as unlawful, since they are in breach of inviolable rights, as was recognized, in the present case, by the ICJ itself, and—before that Court—by the [Federal Republic of Germany].

The Constitutional Court clearly stated that its own 2014 decision is inconsistent with international law, but this follows the necessity to protect non-renounceable constitutional principles.[22] This position is one of the purest expressions of the Westphalian construction: the dualism between international and national law was employed by the Court to ensure an overruling nature in relation to domestic rules. On the other side, however, it seems that such a national conceptualization of sovereignty has also been developed to challenge traditional theories of international law through domestic practice. The decision does not 'aim' to convince lower courts of the reconstruction of international principles but rather opposes—from a domestic law perspective—the current state of the art, it being the first possible element of a Pandora's box[23] where principles to overcome traditional rules can be found and referenced by other courts.[24]

Nonetheless, the decision's ability to influence the development of international law in the conceptualization of sovereignty should be excluded. The relevance of domestic decisions for the reconstruction of international customary law must be analysed in light of whether they express a clear internal practice shared by other states.[25]

[21] On the matter, see Lorenzo Gradoni, 'Corte costituzionale italiana e Corte internazionale di giustizia in rotta di collisione sull'immunità dello Stato straniero dalla giurisdizione civile' (2014) *SIDI Blog* 183, 188.

[22] Gradoni, *supra* note 21, at 192. It should also be noted that the general theory of counter-limits in Italy has been developed by the Constitutional Court with regard to the domestic-EU law relationship (Italian Constitutional court, Judgment 183/173). Nontheless, the first time the theory has been applied has been the field of domestic–international law relationships in the matter at hand. More recently, in the 'Taricco Saga' (Judgment of the Court (Grand Chamber) of 5 December 2017, *Criminal proceedings against M.A.S. and M.B.*, Case C-42/17, in *Electronic Reports*), the counter-limits theory was invoked by some, but due to the cooperation of the Italian Constitutional Court and the Court of Justice of the European Union, such application has not been deemed necessary.

[23] Also of this view, Jerzy Kranz, L'affaire *Allemagne contre Italie* ou les dilemmes du droit et de la justice, in Peters et al., *supra* note 16, at 116, 125.

[24] In general, on the role of domestic courts in the evolution see Peters, *supra* note 16, at 6 (also noting at 7 that references to foreign decisions by domestic courts in immunity matters are a persistent feature), and Editorial, 'Jurisdiction of Municipal Courts over Foreign States in Actions Arising out of Their Commercial Activities' (1931) *The Yale Law Journal* 786.

[25] Editorial, *supra* note 24, at 788.

With regard to the 'internal' effects of the ruling, Italian practice might not be particularly clear. Whereas courts are implementing the ruling in similar cases involving claims against Germany,[26] or have apparently extended the Constitutional Court's golden rule[27] in a criminal and civil action[28] against Serbian military forces for the wrecking of an EC helicopter in Podrute (here the *Corte di Cassazione*, dealing with civil claims against Serbia as the successor state, argued that in no way did the Italian Constitutional Court require a complete lack of alternative means of protection to deny the applicability of the rules on state immunity[29]), the political consequences of this case law should be borne in mind.

Immediately after the ruling by the Constitutional Court, the Italian Parliament passed a law[30] recognizing immunity from execution of diplomatic bank accounts that are declared by a foreign state (not by the Italian courts) as used for foreign public functions (a declaration that was solicited by the Italian Government right after the entry into force of the law[31]). Additionally,[32] Italian internal judicial practice might not be upheld by the Italian Government should Italy be sued before the courts of other states. In circumstances where the immunity of the Italian state might become relevant[33]—should private parties to proceedings invoke the Italian Constitutional Court's doctrine against Italy itself before a court of a foreign state—in order to preserve its prerogatives, the Italian Government might still

[26] See Cass. Civ. Sezioni Unite, 29 July 2016, No. 15812, in *Dejure*, also raising an international diplomatic law point, as it excludes notes from the German embassy sent directly to the court and not via the lawyer granted power of attorney.

[27] On the 'spill-over' effect of the decision, see Enzo Cannizzaro, 'Jurisdictional Immunities and Judicial Protection: the Decision of the Italian Constitutional Court No. 238 of 2014' (2015) *Rivista di diritto internazionale* 126, at 132 ff.

[28] Cassazione, Prima sezione penale, 14 September 2015, No. 43696, in [2016] *Rivista di diritto internazionale* 629 ff, on which see for a first reading, Matteo Sarzo, 'La Cassazione penale e il crimine di guerra di Podrute: un divorzio dal diritto internazionale?' *ibid.*, at 523 ff. The case concerned a criminal action for the unlawful killing of some members of the European monitoring mission in Yugoslavia, when members of the Yugoslavian army fired at a helicopter in Podrute in 1991. By addressing criminal aspects, the Italian court allowed a civil action by the parents of the victims seeking compensation against the successor state. Such actions against the successor state of Serbia have been admitted after rejecting the applicability of rules on state immunity for *acta iure imperii*.

[29] Cassazione, Prima sezione penale, 43696/2015, *supra* note 28, at 651ff.

[30] Art. 19-bis, l. 10 novembre 2014 No. 16, on which see Benedetto Conforti, 'Il legislatore torna indietro di circa novant'anni: la nuova norma sull'esecuzione sui conti correnti di Stati stranieri' (2015) *Rivista di diritto internazionale* 558.

[31] Conforti, *supra* note 30, at 560.

[32] I would like to thank the reviewers for stimulating further reasoning on this point.

[33] Other than cases connected to the Second World War where Italy might be sued, one could perhaps also think of more current scenarios where Italian military forces are involved in the use of force, such as the fight against piracy. Should the Italian navy catch pirates, and commit gross human rights violations on board, and afterwards transfer the pirates to a third processing state, the courts of that state, if seised, might need to address the issue of state immunity and the possible effectiveness of a right to access an Italian court whilst incarcerated abroad. In general, on issues of piracy, human rights violations, third country processing states, and immunity, see Anna Petrig, 'Arrest, Detention and Transfer of Piracy Suspects: A Critical Appraisal of the German Courier Case Decision' in Gemma Andreone, Giorgia Bevilacqua, Giuseppe Cataldi, and Claudia Cinelli (eds), *Insecurity at Sea: Piracy and other Risks to Navigation* (Giannini Editore 2013) 153, 169.

invoke immunity, possibly arguing that the doctrine involved is based on internal laws rather than on international principles. Should this happen, the practice of Italy as a state would become too inconsistent to argue that it could concur in the possible formation of a new customary rule.

With regard to the 'external' value of the Italian ruling, it has to be recalled that domestic decisions contribute to the creation of international customs inasmuch as they 'start a process in which other nations intervene by either following suit, by rejecting the proposed innovation, or by reserving their response until consequential implications become clearer'.[34] In light of this consideration, the relevant state practice is still uncertain, even though diplomatic responses from Germany lean towards refusal of the principle created by the Italian Constitutional Court: the German Government has declared that, even though cooperation continues to take place between the two states,[35] Italy is still bound by the ruling of the ICJ,[36] and no compensation will be paid to individuals by the German Government.[37]

In light of this, it seems premature to argue that other courts or other legal systems have accepted a solution that differs from the one proposed by the ICJ, Germany *in primis*.

However, it appears that inconsistencies at the domestic level seem destined to become more important in time: as noted in the legal literature, the law of immunities is driven by courts, not by governments,[38] and the 'attribution of one uniform legal "opinion" to the state is a fiction. This fiction is becoming increasingly problematic in a global order that promotes the rule of law at the national and international level.'[39]

In this sense, it seems that for the time being the 'Italian Trend' will clash with the judgment of the ICJ, one of the latest iconic bastions of the vestiges of state sovereignty.

3 Immunities and Human Rights

Admitting that *jus cogens* rules are a peculiar feature in the ICJ's eyes, it remains to be determined how the 'fundamental human rights factor' has been taken into consideration by human rights courts.

[34] Tomuschat, *supra* note 16, at 88.

[35] Deutscher Bundestag Drucksache 18/3492, 18. Wahlperiode 09 December 2014, Antwort der Bundesregierung auf die Kleine Anfrage der Abgeordneten Ulla Jelpke, Jan Korte, Sevim Dağdelen, weiterer Abgeordneter und der Fraktion DIE LINKE—Drucksache 18/3333—Entschädigung für NS-Opfer in Italien, question 8.

[36] *Ibid.*, question 10.

[37] *Ibid.*, question 4.

[38] Peters, *supra* note 17, at 6.

[39] *Ibid.*, 8.

The European Court of Human Rights (ECtHR) has ruled on a number of occasions on the compatibility of immunities with the right to access justice. However, most of these decisions relate to human rights violations, not to *jus cogens* violations.

In general terms, the court stated that:

> [i]t would not be consistent with the rule of law in a democratic society or with the basic principle underlying Article 6 § 1—namely that civil claims must be capable of being submitted to a judge for adjudication—if a state could, without restraint or control by the Convention enforcement bodies, remove from the jurisdiction of the courts a whole range of civil claims or confer immunities from civil liability on categories of persons.[40]

Following this idea, in the context of labour cases[41] the Court has always admitted a compression of the right to seise a court of law, subject to the condition that the core right is not prejudiced, and the limitation pursues a legitimate state interest.

Such an approach has strongly influenced the case law[42] of the state parties to the ECHR up to the point that a number of domestic courts have granted immunity to

[40] ECtHR, 11 June 2013, *Stichting Mothers of Srebrenica and Others v the Netherlands*, App No 65542/12, para. 139, on which see Beatrice I Bonafè, 'L'esistenza di rimedi alternativi ai fini del riconoscimento dell'immunità delle organizzazioni internazionali: la sentenza della Corte suprema olandese nel caso delle Madri di Srebrenica' (2012) *Rivista di diritto internazionale* 826; Maria I. Papa, 'Immunità delle Nazioni Unite dalla giurisdizione e rapporti tra CEDU e diritto delle Nazioni Unite: la decisione della Corte europea dei diritti umani nel caso dell' "Associazione Madri di Srebrenica" ' (2014) Diritti umani e diritto internazionale 27; Valentina Spiga, 'Effective Limitations and Illusory Rights: A Comment on the Mothers of Srebrenica Decision of the European Court of Human Rights' (2014) 23 *The Italian Yearbook of International Law* 269; Otto Spijkers, 'Responsibility of the Netherlands for the Genocide in Srebrenica. The Nuhanović and Mothers of Srebrenica Cases Compared' (2014) 18 *Journal of International Peacekeeping* 281; Nico Schrijver, 'Beyond Srebrenica and Haiti: Exploring Alternative Remedies against the United Nations' in Niels Blokker and Nico Schrijver (eds), *Immunity of International Organizations* (Brill 2015) 329, and Kirsten Schmalenbach, 'Preserving the Gordian Knot: UN Legal Accountability in the Aftermath of Srebrenica' (2015) 62 *Netherlands International Law Review* 313.

[41] As noted in legal scholarship, case law that has been delivered in cases of acts that cannot be considered *acta iure imperii* is also likely to have relevance on the case law where acts of a foreign state or of an international organization can be qualified as such: Raffaella Nigro, 'Immunità degli Stati esteri e diritto di accesso al giudici: un nuovo approccio nel diritto internazionale?' (2013) *Rivista di diritto internazionale* 812, 843. In general, on the relationship between immunity of international organizations and the right to access a court of law, or forms of compensation, see Marcello Di Filippo, 'Immunità dalla giurisdizione versus diritto di accesso alla giustizia: il caso delle organizzazioni internazionali (Giappichelli 2012); Bonafè, *supra* note 40; August Reinisch, 'The Immunity of International Organizations and the Jurisdiction of their Administrative Tribunals' (2008) 7 *Chinese Journal of International Law* 285 suggesting, following a human rights-based approach, that immunity from jurisdiction of international organizations might be conditional upon the respect of allowing a form of redress. With specific regard to UN peacekeeping operations, see Rosa Freedman, 'UN Immunity or Impunity? A Human Rights Based Challenge' (2014) 25 *European Journal of International Law* 239, arguing that in the cholera outbreak in Haiti, the UN's approach—which invokes immunity—'to disputes arising from peacekeeping operations can and does lead to violations of individuals' rights to access a court and to a remedy', 254.

[42] Bearing in mind that 'Very few supreme courts in the world have tackled the question of immunity of international organizations, and even fewer have addressed the tension between the immunity of the

international organizations only after[43] a check of the adequacy of the international organization's system of protection of rights[44] (since some states such as Italy are more cautious when it comes to denying immunity to foreign states:[45] the Italian *Corte di Cassazione* has indeed noted that foreign states must respect the core right to defence by instituting an impartial judicial system, it being unnecessary for the seised court to verify on a case-by-case basis that the right to defence as enshrined in the Italian Constitution and in Italian procedural safeguards has identical protection in the foreign state).[46]

However, the ECtHR has also dealt with *jus cogens* violations. Contrary to what one could expect from a human rights court, the ECtHR followed the line of argument of the ICJ, rather than that of the Italian Constitutional Court, which gave significant value to the right to access (any form of) justice. According to the ECtHR, states, if they wish, are free to uphold the immunity[47] of both states[48] and state officials[49] in civil cases[50] for reparation of damages suffered from the occasion

organization and the individual's right of access to a court' (Jan Wouters, Cedric Ryngaert, and Pierre Schmitt, 'Western European Union v. Siedler; General Secretariat of the ACP Group v. Lutchmaya; General Secretariat of the ACP Group v. B.D.: Belgian Supreme Court Decisions on the Immunities of International Institutions in Labor and Employment Matters' (2011) 105 *American Journal of International Law* 560, 562).

[43] On which see August Reinisch and Ulf A. Weber, 'The Jurisdictional Immunity of International Organizations, The Individual's Right of Access to the Courts and Administrative Tribunals as Alternative Means of Dispute Settlement' (2004) *International Organizations Law Review* 59, 68.

[44] August Reinisch, 'Transnational Judicial Conversations on the Personality, Privileges, and Immunities of International Organizations—An Introduction' in August Reinisch (ed.), *The Privileges and Immunities of International Organizations in Domestic Courts* (OUP 2013) 1, 11.

[45] Riccardo Pavoni, 'L'immunità degli Stati nelle controversie di lavoro', in Natalino Ronzitti and Gabriella Venturini (eds), *Le immunità giurisdizionali degli Stati e degli altri enti internazionali* (Cedam 2008) 29, 43. This does not, however, mean that no hesitation has followed in applying the principle stated by the ECtHR. For a comparative study on such hesitations, see Fox and Webb, *supra* note 1, 461 ff.

[46] Corte Cost., 2 February 1982, No. 18, Di Filippo e altro c. Gospodinoff e altro, in [1982] *Rivista di diritto internazionale* 667; Corte Cost., 27 December 1965, No. 98, Società Acciaierie San Michele c. Comunità europea del carbone e dell'acciaio, in *consultaonline*; Cass. Civ. Sezioni unite, 8 June 1994, No. 5565, Nacci c. Istituto di Bari del Centre International De Hautes Agronomiques Mediterraeennes, in [1995] *Rivista di diritto internazionale privato e processuale* 402. Recently, in the scholarship, see Beatrice I Bonafè, 'Italian Courts and the Immunity of International Organizations' in Niels Blokker and Nico Schrijver (eds), *Immunity of International Organizations* (Brill 2015) 246.

[47] Cedric Ryngaert, 'Jones v United Kingdom: The European Court of Human Rights Restricts Individual Accountability for Torture' (2014) 30 *Utrecht Journal of International and European Law* 47, at 49, noting that the Court does not impose recognition of state immunity. Additionally, in other cases concerning civil actions for torture, the court has admitted that State Parties are not obliged under international law to recognize universal civil jurisdiction (ECtHR, 21 June 2016, *Naït-Liman v Switzerland*, App No 51357/07, now under appeal before the Great Chamber).

[48] Cf. ECtHR, 21 November 2001, *Al-Adsani v the United Kingdom*, App No 35763/97.

[49] Cfr. ECtHR, 14 January 2014, *Jones et al v United Kingdom*, App Nos 4356/06 and 40528/06.

[50] Whilst some argue that in criminal cases, with specific reference to the crime of torture, the 1984 Convention against Torture and Other Cruel, Inhuman or Degrading Treatment or Punishment, 1465 UNTS, 85, overrules functional immunity by providing that 'Each State Party shall ensure in its legal system that the victim of an act of torture obtains redress and has an enforceable right to fair and adequate compensation, including the means for as full rehabilitation as possible. In the event of the death

of international crimes, such as torture. A decision that finds comfort in the ICJ immunity case since immunity knows no exception even for breaches of imperative international norms,[51] but that, by realigning state immunity and immunity of state agents departs from said ruling which is 'confined […] to the state "leaving the law on the immunity of State officials in respect of the commission of the same acts to develop independently" '.[52]

The same conclusions have been reached in connection to actions for damages following peacekeeping operations. In general, immunity for international organizations is seen as a corollary to the establishment of an alternative system of protection.[53] With specific reference to the UN, the creation of such a system has been seen as a necessary condition for ensuring consistency of the organization with its goals.[54] Nonetheless, international practice has shown that a system for the internal management of claims has not in all cases been created by the UN. In dealing with the question whether the Netherlands violated the ECHR by recognizing the immunity of the UN for the events in Srebrenica, the ECtHR addressed for the first time (in its case law) the issue of individual actions against the UN. Here the Court noted that since

> operations established by United Nations Security Council resolutions […] are fundamental to the mission of the United Nations to secure international peace and security, the Convention cannot be interpreted in a manner which would subject the acts and omissions of the Security Council to domestic jurisdiction without the accord of the United Nations.[55]

With the consequence that it does not necessarily follow that the 'absence of an alternative remedy the recognition of immunity is *ipso facto* constitutive of a violation of the right of access to a court',[56] in particular if the action of ensuring

of the victim as a result of an act of torture, his dependents shall be entitled to compensation' (Art. 14), (cf. *ex multis* Enzo Cannizzaro, *Corso di diritto internazionale* (Giuffré 2011) 338).

[51] Dapo Akande, 'European Court of Human Rights Upholds State Immunity in Case Involving Allegations of Torture—Jones v United Kingdom', in *EJIL:Talk!*, 14 January 2014, and ECtHR, 14 January 2014, *Jones et al v United Kingdom, supra* note 49, para. 198.

[52] Philippa Webb, 'Jones v UK: The re-integration of State and official immunity?', in *EJIL:Talk!*, 14 January 2014.

[53] Cf. Fourth report on relations between States and international organizations (second part of the topic), by Mr Leonardo Díaz-González, Special Rapporteur on Status, privileges and immunities of international organizations, their officials, experts, para. 58 ff.

[54] ICJ Effect of awards of compensation made by the UN Administrative Tribunal, Advisory Opinion of 13 July 1954, in ICJ Rep 1954, 47.

[55] ECtHR, 11 June 2013, *Stichting Mothers of Srebrenica and Others v the Netherlands, supra* note 40, para. 154.

[56] ECtHR, 11 June 2013, *Stichting Mothers of Srebrenica and Others v the Netherlands, supra* note 40, para. 164.

international peace and security is at stake.[57] In fact, as noted by some scholars, 'allowing suits against an international organization in relation to wrongful acts committed in the context of peace operations may weaken the willingness of its Member States to contribute troops to peace operations, and ultimately weaken the world's peace and security structures'.[58]

This decision, which expresses a trend of protecting the UN and which seems to present some common lines with the case law developed as regards immunity of states for violation of *jus cogens*, surely serves a legitimate interest, and—even though it prejudices the core of the human right at stake[59]—it could be argued that this is justifiable in light of the principle of proportionality: individual interests to access a court of law must be balanced with collective and public interests in international peace and security.[60] In this sense, the decision of the ECtHR seems in line with the decision of the ICJ:[61] immunity cannot be prevailed over by the gravity of the conduct to adjudicate[62] (alleged omission to prevent genocide[63]), and alternative means of protection are not seen as strictly necessary to apply the rules on immunity.[64]

The ECtHR decision finds comfort in international practice as well. The US District Court, Southern District of New York clearly wrote that 'nothing in the text of the [Convention on the Privileges and Immunities of the United Nations] suggests that the absolute immunity of section 2 is conditioned on the UN's providing the alternative modes of settlement contemplated by section 29'.[65] This decision

[57] Recently, on the immunity of the UN, see Kristen E. Boon, 'The United Nations as Good Samaritan: Immunity and Responsibility' (2016) 16 *Chicago Journal of International Law* 341 ff, also arguing, at 377, that immunity should be recognized only in so far as immunity involves a core mission or a 'constitutional question'.

[58] Cedric Ryngaert, 'The Immunity of International Organizations before Domestic Courts: Recent Trends' (2009) 7 *International Organizations Law Review* 121, 147.

[59] Whose respect is necessary in commercial disputes involving a foreign state or an international organization, cf. *ex multis*, *Waite and Kennedy v Federal Republic of Germany* App No 26083/94 (ECtHR, 18 February 1999), [2000] *Rivista di diritto internazionale* 168, para. 59 ff.

[60] I would like to thank the reviewers for stimulating further reasoning on this point.

[61] Jacob Katz Cogan, 'Stichting Mothers of Srebrenica v. Netherlands' (2013) 107 *American Journal of International* 884, 887.

[62] ECtHR, 11 June 2013, *Stichting Mothers of Srebrenica and Others v the Netherlands*, *supra* note 40, para. 158.

[63] On the difference between commission and prevention of genocide, and *jus cogens*, see ICJ Application of the Convention on the Prevention and Punishment of the Crime of Genocide (*Bosnia and Herzegovina v Serbia and Montenegro*), Judgment, in ICJ Rep 2007, 43.

[64] Fox and Webb, *supra* note 1, at 583, fn. 38. Wondering on whether the combined case law of the two courts might in the future lead domestic courts to take a more cautious approach, August Reinisch, 'To What Extent Can and Should National Courts' Fill the Accountability Gap'?', in Niels Blokker and Nico Schrijver (eds), *Immunity of International Organizations* (Brill 2015) 313, 317.

[65] US District Court, Southern District of New York, *Delama Georges, et al., v United Nations*, et al., 13-CV-7146 (JPO), 9 January 2015. For a preliminary reading on the material facts of the case, see prior to the decision, Freedman, *supra* note 41, and Schrijver, *supra* note 40; Stephan Hollenberg, 'Immunity of the UN in the Case of Haitian Cholera Victims' (2015) 19 *Journal of International Peacekeeping* 118; Thomas G. Bode, 'Cholera in Haiti: United Nations Immunity and Accountability' (2016) 47 *Georgetown Journal Of International Law* 759, and Kristen E. Boon, 'The United Nations as Good Samaritan: Immunity and Responsibility', *supra* note 57.

has been confirmed by the court of appeals[66] even though the UN seems to be currently admitting the necessity for some restoration in connection to the cholera epidemic in Haiti (and other conduct committed by peacekeeping forces).[67]

In general, international practice seems consistent in recognizing an absolute 'blanket of immunity'[68] for the UN even when it comes to alleged serious human rights violations or alleged *jus cogens* violations.

In this sense, it appears quite clear that the UN (to the extent it acts to maintain international peace and security) does enjoy a status that might be inconsistent with the new 'Italian Trend', that could induce states in 'shifting the attribution of the alleged wrongful acts from themselves to the (immune) organization' and, at the same time, might have the effect that '[v]ictims who seek to assign blame directly to international organizations will need to lobby for the establishment of non-judicial panels (such as commissions of inquiry) to investigate and issue findings concerning their alleged wrongful acts'.[69]

4 The Coexistence of Opposing Trends: Some Reflections

As mentioned earlier, the aim of this chapter is to reflect on the effects on the principle of immunity of different trends in the conceptualization of sovereignty. From this, it is clear that the case law of the Italian Constitutional Court stands alone (as Greek decisions in the Distomo case are prior to the ICJ's ruling). Even though the decision is based upon strict considerations of domestic law, the general idea that

[66] United States Court of Appeals for the Second Circuit, *Delama Georges, et al., v United Nations, et al.*, Case 15-455, Decided 18 August 2016, on which see Riccardo Pavoni, 'Immunità e responsabilità dell'ONU per l'introduzione del colera ad Haiti: la sentenza d'appello nel caso "Georges", il "rapporto Alston" e le "scuse" del Segretario generale' (2017) *Rivista di diritto internazionale* 133 ff.

[67] As reported by the *New York Times,* '[t]he deputy spokesman for the secretary general, Farhan Haq, said in an email this week that "over the past year, the UN has become convinced that it needs to do much more regarding its own involvement in the initial outbreak and the suffering of those affected by cholera." He added that a "new response will be presented publicly within the next two months, once it has been fully elaborated, agreed with the Haitian authorities and discussed with member States"' (Jonathan M. Katz, 'U.N. Admits Role in Cholera Epidemic in Haiti', 17 August 2016, available at: <http://www.nytimes.com/2016/08/18/world/americas/united-nations-haiti-cholera.html?_r=1>; accessed 28 April 2019). On the latest position of the UN in respect to the Haiti epidemic, see Kristen E. Boon, 'Haiti Cholera Update', in *Opinio Juris* (20 September 2016). More recently, the UN Secretary General apologised for the UN role in the outbreak of Cholera in Haiti (see Kristen E. Boon, 'UN Apologizes for Role in Cholera Outbreak', in *Opinio Juris* (7 December 2016)) and has proposed a 'New Approach to Cholera in Haiti' (Deputy Secretary-General's remarks to the General Assembly on Haiti, 14 June 2017, available at: <https://www.un.org/sg/en/content/dsg/statement/2017-06-14/deputy-secretary-generals-remarks-general-assembly-haiti-prepared>, accessed 28 April 2019).

[68] Kimberly Faith, 'Stichting Mothers of Srebrenica v. Netherlands: Does U.N. Immunity Trump the Right of Access to a Court?' (2014) 22 *Tulane Journal of International and Comparative Law* 359, at 372. Cf. also Freedman, *supra* note 41, at 243, also noting that, even where some courts have followed a different approach, a certain distinguishing in favour of the UN has most often been made.

[69] Cogan, *supra* note 61, at 889.

immunity 'does not protect behaviours that do not represent the typical exercise of governmental powers' is still not followed, at least where alleged *jus cogens* violations are involved. As far as *jus congens* is concerned, immunity is on the contrary held admissible by both the ICJ and the ECtHR, even if there are no alternative means of protection. The idea that under the ECHR immunity is only admissible as long as alternatives for protection are guaranteed has not been transposed in the context of alleged *jus cogens* violations.

Additionally, the Italian domestic case law has stressed the importance of the autonomy between immunity from jurisdiction and immunity from execution. With a recent decision (Judgment No. 14885/2018, 8 June 2018), the Italian *Corte di Cassazione* rejected the enforceability of a foreign (Greek) judgment against Germany—for events that occurred during the Second World War—against German immovable property in Italy if this is used for public functions (even where the foreign state does not directly manage or use the building).

In general terms, it does not seem surprising that the voices calling for an (explicit or implicit) re-evaluation of the Westphalian vestiges of the international community are coming from domestic courts, which are called on to apply domestic law, rather than from international courts or states themselves, given that these might be—on a number of occasions—less willing to abandon traditional legal conceptualizations of international law, at least where these are too interconnected with sovereignty.

The question thus is what consequences the 'Italian Trend' might have in the future.

It seems unlikely, but it cannot be excluded, that domestic courts of other states could still follow the Italian example and thus contribute to changing customary international law over time, even though, as we have seen, it does not seem that this decision alone has been able to change current principles so far. In this possible process of evolution, the 2004 UN Convention could play a significant role in the understanding of the relationship between immunity and the right to access a court (at least in non-military operations). It must also be pointed out that human rights are gradually acquiring significant importance, as testified by the *Kadi* case law of the CJEU that—as is known—has also been recognized for adopting an (unusual for the Court) dualist approach.[70] However, up until that (indefinite)[71] point

[70] Case C-402/05 P and C-415/05, *P. Kadi and Al Barakaat International Foundation v Council and Commission* [2008] ECR I-6351, on which see *ex multis* Juliane Kokott and Christoph Sobotta, 'The Kadi Case—Constitutional Core Values and International Law—Finding the Balance?' (2012) 23 *European Journal of International Law* 1015. Also, for a comparison between the Italian decision and the Kadi judgment of the CJEU, see Chimène I. Keitner, 'Authority and Dialogue: State and Official Immunity in Domestic and International Courts', in Chiara Giorgetti and Guglielmo Verdirame (eds), *Concepts of International Law in Europe and the United States* (CUP forthcoming), and *ibid.*, 'Constitutional Courts and International Law: Revisiting The Transatlantic Divide' (2016) 129 *Harvard Law Review* 1362. But cf. Martin Scheinin, 'The Italian Constitutional Court's Judgment 238 of 2014 Is Not Another Kadi Case' (2016) 14 *Journal of International Criminal Justice* 615.

[71] Should this take place, it will probably be a long path: domestic courts might exercise self-restraint in this respect. However, this long path is now open. Domestic courts willing to change their case law

in time where a sufficient number of domestic courts oppose international law and thus shape customary international law in general, the Westphalian construction will hold.

Yet, the coexistence of different trends seems to raise concerns on the very foundations of immunity. Should *jus cogens not* become a widely accepted limit to immunity, but nonetheless find at least *some consensus* amongst other states, what will be left of state immunity? Can the growth of different rules applied within domestic systems deconstruct the customary principle itself? As of today there are a number of different conceptualizations: those who grant absolute immunity; those who grant restricted immunity, without exceptions to *acta iure imperii*; those who grant limited immunity, but for cases of states sponsoring terrorism;[72] and those who grant restricted immunity, unless the foreign conduct to adjudicate is in breach of fundamental values of domestic systems and expresses non-legitimate governmental functions.[73]

In such a scenario, could it still be possible to speak of an international custom or could this fragmentation—if aggravated—be the very negation of the principle of state immunity so to argue that this derives its legitimacy from a rule that is not state sovereignty, but rather from a more general obligation of states not to interfere in foreign domestic affairs without due reason?[74]

On the contrary, should *jus cogens* become a widely accepted limit to immunity,[75] what will remain of state sovereignty itself if each state unilaterally

now have a model decision to which they could make reference, and contextualize in a broader legal framework of international fundamental human rights protection and constitutional provisions. (The specification seems important: having adopted a rigid dualist approach, the decision alone—whose aim is not to provide a new rationalization of the rules of international law, as it was in previous cases—could not be a sufficiently convincing element for foreign courts, since the focus of the Constitutional Court is domestic law alone, and how rules of international law are admitted within the Italian system. Also critical regarding the possibility for the Constitutional Court to promote a shift in international law after having changed its scope of investigation, Cannizzaro, *supra* note 45, at 128).

---

72 See Iranian application before the ICJ, Certain Iranian Assets (*Islamic Republic of Iran v United States of America*) with regard to a dispute concerning alleged violations of the 1955 Treaty of Amity. Other than the well-known examples of the United States of America (Justice Against Sponsors of Terrorism Act (JASTA), entered into force on 28 September 2016), and of Canada, Italian courts have also recently affirmed that states supporting terrorism act in violation of international law and actions for damages following violations of fundamental human rights do not enjoy immunity (Cass. Civ., 28 October 2015, No. 21964, in [2016] *Rivista di diritto internazionale* 292 ff).

73 For a recent study on the comparative perspective of cases where domestic constitutional provisions have been invoked in general to avoid domestic implementation of international law, and thus that pose the domestic constitution as a limit to international law, see Keitner, *supra* note 70.

74 Riccardo Luzzatto, 'La giurisdizione sugli Stati stranieri tra Convenzione di New York, norme internazionali, generali e diritto interno' (2007) XXIII *Comunicazioni e studi* 7ff. Still taking into consideration—for a different purpose—the mentioned fragmentation, so to argue that immunity no longer expresses a 'rule' of public international law, but rather a 'principle', see Jasper Finke, 'Sovereign Immunity: Rule, Comity or Something Else?' (2011) 21 *European Journal of International Law* 853.

75 In general on human rights as a possible exception to immunity, see Andrea Bianchi, 'Denying State Immunity to Violators of Human Rights' (1994) 46 *Austrian Journal of Public and International Law* 195.

determines preconditions for foreign states to enjoy immunity, or will there be a centralized organ to determine uniformly when a state act is in compliance with international law (thus entitled to immunity)?

In the long run, it appears that this question will press for answers, and domestic courts eventually ruling following the indications of the Italian Constitutional Court should not be blind to the issue of sovereignty[76] and to what the international community will look like[77] if states are no longer sovereign, especially if the deconstruction of the Westphalian model follows a case-by-case approach[78] adopted by domestic courts under the lens of domestic constitutional provisions.

In this last sense, whilst the ideological outcome of the Italian Constitutional Court's ruling can be praised in some respects, this *modus operandi* that seeks to promote new international law concepts under a domestic perspective might lead to excessive fragmentation of law, which would suggest a more systemic and systematic assessment of all issues related to immunity.

5 Conclusions

To conclude, in light of all this, it does not seem that today, it is possible to speak undisputedly of a clear and definite crisis in international law on state immunity.

There are indeed different conceptualizations, a number of rules that coexist but that do not yet lead to a significant fragmentation of rules capable of denying the very existence of the principle underlying immunity itself. In this sense, the opposing trends in the law of immunities do not seem to have reached the state of 'crisis' intended as a 'time of great disagreement, confusion, or suffering' as defined by the *Oxford Dictionary of English*.

Today, there is little doubt that customary law is crystallized in the ICJ decision, and that Italy is in violation of international law. Of course, this might change

[76] Also suggesting caution in the elaboration of extraordinary measures of reparation for cases of grave breaches of international law, Tomuschat, *supra* note 16, at 91 ff, additionally noting '[s]hould every state be entitled to pursue its own sanctioning strategy or is some kind of international coordination necessary?'

[77] It is indeed acknowledged that state immunity 'provides a valuable case study of the present nature of the international community and in particular the interaction of international law and national law, and on the formation of customary international law from national sources. Ultimately the extent to which international law requires, and national legislations and courts afford, immunity to a foreign state as a defendant before another State's courts depends on the underlying structure of the international community and the degree to which one state may adjudicate the disputes of another state. In order to understand the structure of international law, theory must be tested against reality, and the significance of trends and patterns must be discerned. A study of state immunity directs attention to the central issues of the international legal system' (Fox and Webb, *The Law of State Immunity*, *supra* note 1, at 7). Cf. also in the same terms, Peters, *supra* note 17, at 2, and Stefan Oeter, 'The Law of Immunities as a Focal Point of the Evolution of International Law', in Peters et al., *supra* note 23, at 355, 358.

[78] Arguing that 'due regard to the requirements of international cooperation within a world without central authority', Robert Uerpmann-Wittzack, 'Serious Human Rights Violations as Potential Exceptions to Immunity: Conceptual Challenges', in Peters et al., *supra* note 23, 236, 243.

if further domestic courts determine that it is becoming necessary to challenge and oppose international law as it stands, up until that point in time where international law actually evolves.

Nonetheless, current tensions, whilst not expressing a crisis in their own specific field, could play an additional role in the ongoing assessment of a possible crisis in the Westphalian model, which still predicates the privilege of states not to be judged by others, at least when they exercise sovereign acts, and that still sees in states—rather than in others—the most important and preponderant international actors. This is a static vision that every day seems less able to adapt to a changing world where individuals seem to move to the centre stage[79] of international law.

[79] Jurisdictional Immunities of the State (*Germany v Italy, Greece Intervening*), separate opinion of Judge Bennouna, *supra* note 16, para. 18.

How to Limit Immunity of State Officials from Foreign Criminal Jurisdiction

Pavel Šturma

This chapter aims to shed more light on the question whether international law on immunities is in crisis and, if so, how to overcome the crisis. It will not deal with all kinds of immunities under international law but will focus only on immunity of state officials.

Immunity of state officials from foreign criminal jurisdiction is governed by customary international law, whose exact scope is often debatable both in theory and practice, particularly in connection with the reinvigorated international effort to end impunity for the most serious crimes under international law, such as genocide, war crimes, crimes against humanity, including torture, abduction, and enforced disappearances.

The development of international criminal law and justice, from the International Military Tribunal at Nürnberg[1] to the permanent International Criminal Court, indicates exceptions; that is, excluding the official status of perpetrators of crimes under international law as the reason for their immunity from the jurisdiction of these international courts.[2] The argument that immunities do not apply to the perpetrators of crimes under international law, preventing them from sheltering behind their official position, was unequivocally expressed in the judgment of the Nürnberg Tribunal.[3]

[1] See Art. 7, Charter of the International Military Tribunal annexed to Agreement for the Prosecution and Punishment of the Major War Criminals of the European Axis (signed 8 August 1945, entered into force 8 August 1945) 82 UNTS 279: 'The official position of defendants, whether as Heads of State or responsible officials in Government Departments, shall not be considered as freeing them from responsibility or mitigating punishment.' See also A.-M., La Rosa, *Dictionnaire de droit international pénal* (PUF 1998) 91.

[2] See, e.g., Art. 27 of the Rome Statute of the International Criminal Court (adopted 17 July 1998, entered into force 1 July 2002) 2187 UNTS 90: '1. This Statute shall apply equally to all persons without any distinction based on official capacity. In particular, official capacity as a Head of State or Government, a member of a Government or parliament, an elected representative or a government official shall in no case exempt a person from criminal responsibility under this Statute, nor shall it, in and of itself, constitute a ground for reduction of sentence. 2. Immunities or special procedural rules which may attach to the official capacity of a person, whether under national or international law, shall not bar the Court from exercising its jurisdiction over such a person.'

[3] See Judgment of the Nuremberg International Military Tribunal 1946 (1947) 41 AJIL 172, 221: 'The principle of international law, which under certain circumstances protects the representative of a state,

Pavel Šturma, *How to Limit Immunity of State Officials from Foreign Criminal Jurisdiction* In: *How International Law Works in Times of Crisis*. Edited by: George Ulrich and Ineta Ziemele, Oxford University Press (2019).
DOI: 10.1093/oso/9780198849667.003.0010

In the following years this idea was confirmed both in the work of the International Law Commission (ILC), and in the statutes of ad hoc international criminal tribunals. The ILC addressed this issue in 1950 when it drafted the Principles of International Law recognized in the Charter of the Nürnberg Tribunal and in the Judgment of the Tribunal,[4] specifically in Principle III: 'The fact that a person who committed an act which constitutes a crime under international law acted as Head of State or responsible Government official does not relieve him from responsibility under international law.'[5]

Shortly afterwards, the ILC started working on the draft Code of Crimes against the Peace and Security of Mankind, whose first version was submitted to the UN General Assembly in 1954.[6] After reinvigorating the work on this topic in 1981, the ILC adopted the final draft of the Code in 1996.[7] Both versions ensure that the official position of a perpetrator does not free the perpetrator (even if acting as the head of state or government) from criminal responsibility.[8]

As regards further development of international criminal law after the Second World War, a similar rule was incorporated in the statutes of a number of tribunals, including Law No. 10 of the Allied Control Council on Punishment of Persons Guilty of War Crimes, Crimes against Peace and against Humanity (of 20 December 1945),[9] the statutes of the International Criminal Tribunal for the former Yugoslavia (ICTY, 1993),[10] the International Criminal Tribunal for

cannot be applied to acts which are condemned as criminal by international law. The authors of these acts cannot shelter themselves behind their official position in order to be freed from punishment in appropriate proceedings.'

[4] See International Law Commission, *Yearbook of the International Law Commission* (1950) Vol. II, 374 ff.

[5] See also J. Mrázek, *K boji s mezinárodní zločinností z hlediska mezinárodního práva* [*On the Fight against International Crime from the Perspective of International Law*] (Academia 1979) 90–2; P. Šturma, *Mezinárodní trestní soud a stíhání zločinů podle mezinárodního práva* [*The International Criminal Court and Suppression of Crimes under International Law*] (Karolinum 2002) 46–8.

[6] See ILC, Report of the International Law Commission covering the work of its sixth session (3 June–28 July 1954) UN Doc A/2693, 149.

[7] Draft Code of Crimes against the Peace and Security of Mankind in *Yearbook of the International Law Commission* (1996) Vol. II (Part Two), 15 ff.

[8] See Art. 3 of the Draft Code of Offences against the Peace and Security of Mankind in *Yearbook of the International Law Commission* (1954) Vol II., 149 ff or Art. 7 of the Draft Code of Crimes against the Peace and Security of Mankind (1996). See also P. Šturma, *supra* note 5, at 58.

[9] See Art. 4 of Law No. 10 of the Allied Control Council on Punishment of Persons Guilty of War Crimes, Crimes against Peace and against Humanity (20 December 1945) 3 Official Gazette Control Council for Germany (31 January 1946), 50–5.

[10] See Art. 7(2) of the Statute of the International Tribunal for the Prosecution of Persons Responsible for Serious Violations of international humanitarian law Committed in the Territory of the former Yugoslavia since 1991 annexed to Report of the Secretary-General pursuant to paragraph 2 of Security Council Resolution 808 (1993), UN Doc S/25704 (3 May 1993) adopted by UNSC Res (25 May 1993) UN Doc S/Res./827.

Rwanda (ICTR, 1994),[11] and the Statute of the Special Court for Sierra Leone (SCSL, 2000).[12]

The main question is whether the exclusion of immunity for prosecution of crimes under international law also applies in proceedings before the national courts of another state. To what extent have the concept of individual criminal responsibility and the development of international criminal law impacted on the immunity of foreign state officials? This issue has been addressed in several cases before national and international courts, with different results and different reasoning, which further divided the approach to immunity of state officials in respect of the criminal jurisdiction of another state.[13] These cases include the well-known case of *Pinochet*, decided by the House of Lords (1999), the ICJ judgment in the *Arrest Warrant Case* (2002), and the SCSL judgment in *Taylor* (2004).

Before embarking on a brief analysis of these cases it should be pointed out that this issue has been considered at various levels of courts: national courts, the ICJ as the main UN court, and a special international (hybrid) criminal court (SCSL). Moreover, various types of immunity have been discussed.

International law and its theory distinguish functional immunity (immunity *ratione materiae*) and personal immunity (immunity *ratione personae*). The former is based on the principle that a state may not exercise its jurisdiction over the officials or civil servants of another state where the officials/civil servants acted in their official capacity. Such acts are considered as acts by the state itself.

By contrast, immunities *ratione personae* embody the principle that a certain group of state officials and civil servants (notably heads of state, heads of government, ministers of foreign affairs, members of special missions, and diplomats) who represent a state externally enjoy immunity from the jurisdiction of other states while in office, in respect of their official and private acts, in order to preclude any interference in the affairs of the state which they represent.[14]

Customary law-based immunities of other officials are still unclear, giving rise to uncertainties which could be resolved by future codification. After a brief analysis of the three cases mentioned earlier, we will explore the current work on this topic undertaken by the ILC.

[11] See Art. 6(2) of International Criminal Tribunal for Rwanda annexed to UNSC Res 955 (8 November 1994) UN Doc S/Res./955.

[12] See Art. 6(2) of Statute of the Special Court for Sierra Leone annexed to the Agreement between the United Nations and the Government of Sierra Leone on the Establishment of a Special Court for Sierra Leone (signed 16 January 2002, entered into force 12 April 2002) 2178 UNTS 138.

[13] See R. van Alebeek, *The Immunity of States and Their Officials in International Criminal Law and International Human Rights Law* (OUP 2008) 218.

[14] See P. Caban, *Jurisdikční imunity státu [Jurisdictional Immunities of States]* (Praha 2007) 102–3, and the cited literature.

1 The Arrest Warrant Case (*Yerodia*)

After having considered an individual application, a Belgian judge issued an international arrest warrant on 11 April 2000 in absentia against the former minister of foreign affairs of the Democratic Republic of Congo (DRC), Mr Abdualaye Yerodia Ndombasi, containing charges of committing or complicity in crimes giving rise to grave breaches of the Geneva Conventions (1949) and Additional Protocols (1977) and crimes against humanity. On 17 October 2000 the DRC initiated proceedings against Belgium before the ICJ, asking the court to order that Belgium annul the international arrest warrant. The Congolese government argued that the international arrest warrant was, *inter alia*, in breach of the principle that states may not exercise their jurisdiction in the territory of another state, the principle of sovereign equality between UN member states, and the diplomatic immunity of the minister of foreign affairs of a sovereign state.

The ICJ issued its judgment in February 2002.[15] The DRC insisted that an incumbent minister of foreign affairs of a sovereign state had an absolute right to inviolability and immunity from criminal proceedings.[16] Belgium argued that while an incumbent minister of foreign affairs generally enjoyed immunity from the jurisdiction of another state´s court, that immunity could only be applied in respect of acts performed in an official capacity, but not in a private capacity or otherwise than in an official capacity.[17]

In its conclusions the Court pointed out that 'in international law it is firmly established that, as also diplomatic and consular agents, certain holders of high-ranking office in a State, such as the Head of State, Head of Government and Minister for Foreign Affairs, enjoy immunities from jurisdiction in other States, both civil and criminal'.[18]

Because conventional instruments, such as the Vienna Convention on Diplomatic Relations (1961) or the Convention on Special Missions (1969), do not specifically define the immunities enjoyed by a minister of foreign affairs, the Court had to decide on the basis of customary international law.[19]

According to the judgment,

> in customary international law, the immunities accorded to Ministers for Foreign Affairs are not granted for their personal benefit, but to ensure the effective performance of their functions on behalf of their respective States... He or she is

[15] *Arrest Warrant of 11 April 2000 (Democratic Republic of Congo v Belgium)* [2002] ICJ Rep 3. See also S. Wirth, 'Immunity for Core Crimes? The ICJ's Judgment in the Congo v. Belgium Case' (2002) 13 *European Journal of International Law* 877.

[16] *Ibid.*, para. 11.

[17] *Ibid.*, para. 22.

[18] *Ibid.*, para. 51.

[19] *Ibid.*, para. 52.

> in charge of his or her Government's diplomatic activities and generally acts as its representative in international negotiations and intergovernmental meetings... His or her acts may bind the State represented... In the performance of these functions, he or she is frequently required to travel internationally, and thus must be in a position freely to do so whenever the need should arise.[20]

Therefore, the Court concluded that for the performance of their responsibilities, a minister of foreign affairs 'when abroad enjoys full immunity from criminal jurisdiction and inviolability. That immunity and that inviolability protect the individual concerned against any act of authority of another State which would hinder him or her in the performance of his or her duties.'[21] In this respect, no distinction could be drawn between acts performed by a minister of foreign affairs in an 'official capacity', and those claimed to have been performed in a 'private capacity', or, for that matter, between acts performed before the person concerned assumed office as minister of foreign affairs and acts committed during the period of office.[22]

The ICJ decided that the arrest warrant had been issued in violation of customary international law, which grants absolute inviolability and immunity from criminal proceedings to an incumbent minister of foreign affairs, and in this way the arrest warrant had been inconsistent with the principle of sovereign equality of states.[23]

At the same time, the Court concluded *obiter dictum* that immunity did not mean impunity but a procedural restriction precluding prosecution before another state's courts. However, immunity does not preclude prosecution before the courts of the domestic state or before international criminal courts or tribunals. Moreover, immunity *ratione personae*, which is at stake here, does not protect state officials (a minister of foreign affairs) when they are no longer in office.

2 The *Pinochet* Case

A slightly different type of immunity was considered by the English courts in the well-known case concerning an arrest warrant and a Spanish request to extradite the former Chilean president, General Augusto Pinochet Ugarte, in 1998/99. The issue was whether the crimes he was accused of were covered by functional immunity (*ratione materiae*).[24]

[20] *Ibid.*, para. 53.
[21] *Ibid.*, para. 54.
[22] *Ibid.*, para. 55.
[23] *Ibid.*, para. 76.
[24] See A. Bianchi, 'Immunity versus Human Rights: The Pinochet Case' (1999) 10 *European Journal of International Law* 237. Cf. also Ch. Dominicé, 'Quelques observations sur l'immunité de juridiction pénale de l'ancien Chef d'État' (1999) 2 *Revue générale de droit international public*, No. 2, 297; M. Cosnard, 'Quelques observations sur les décisions de la Chambre des Lords du 25 novembre 1998 et du 24 mars 1999 dans l'affaire Pinochet' (1999) 2 *Revue générale de droit international public* 309.

Pinochet led the *coup d'état* that overthrew the Chilean Government in 1973. He subsequently led the military junta, from 1973 until 1981 held the office of president, responsible for systematic violations of human rights in Chile. In autumn 1998, when no longer in office (merely a senator for life), he stayed in London as a private individual, for the purposes of medical treatment. On 16 October 1998, Spanish Judge Garzón, on the application of several injured persons, issued an international arrest warrant for Pinochet, who was arrested on the following day. On the basis of the Spanish application, British judges issued two provisional arrest warrants, one based on murder charges for Spanish citizens murdered in Chile, the second containing charges of torture, hostage-taking, and murder.

After the Divisional Court quashed both arrest warrants,[25] an appeal was lodged with the House of Lords (the predecessor of the Supreme Court of the United Kingdom). The Law Lords considered the case on two occasions, for the first decision of 25 November 1998[26] was set aside on 17 December 1998 because the Appellate Committee was improperly constituted (exclusion of Lord Hoffmann).[27] The final judgment (*Pinochet No. 3*) was issued on 24 March 1999.[28]

The majority of the Law Lords (six to one) decided that a former head of state could have no functional immunity for crimes of torture (Lord Goff dissenting). However, the reasoning of individual judges differed. Only three justices unequivocally agreed that there was no immunity for crimes under international law. Two of them, Lord Hope and Lord Philips, relied on the Convention against Torture (1984) which established universal jurisdiction in respect of that crime. Only Lord Hutton argued that there was no functional immunity from the jurisdiction of national courts with respect to all crimes under international law. Lord Saville of Newdigate and Lord Browne-Wilkinson justified their rejection of immunity by specific conditions of the Torture Convention.

It is noteworthy that only Lord Browne-Wilkinson and Lord Hutton argued that torture could not represent a 'public function' or 'government function'. In their opinion such acts were of a private character. By contrast, other justices believed that although torture could be of an official character, it was still a crime. Only Lord Goff (dissenting) considered it to be a decisive factor for functional immunity whether the relevant acts were performed while exercising public powers. The definition of torture in Article 1(1) implies that the torture must be committed by a public official or another person acting in an official capacity. Lord Goff then inferred that immunity could not be excluded on the basis of the Torture

[25] *R v Bow Street Metropolitan Stipendiary Magistrate and others*, ex parte Pinochet Ugarte [1998] All ER (D) 509 (UK, The Divisional Court of the Queen's Bench Division, 1998).

[26] *R v Bow Street Metropolitan Stipendiary Magistrate and others*, ex parte Pinochet Ugarte (Amnesty International and others intervening) [1998] 4 All ER 897 (UK, HL, 1998).

[27] *R v Bow Street Metropolitan Stipendiary Magistrate and others*, ex parte Pinochet Ugarte [1999] 1 All ER 577 (UK, HL, 1999), (Pinochet No. 2).

[28] *R v Bow Street Metropolitan Stipendiary Magistrate and others*, ex parte Pinochet Ugarte (No. 3), [2000] 1 AC 147 (UK, HL, 1999).

Convention because such an exception would have to be expressly provided in the Convention.[29]

Despite a certain disunity and slightly inconsistent opinions among the justices (unlike the clear position in *Pinochet No. 1*), the judgment of the House of Lords in *Pinochet No. 3* is one of the most important decisions in respect of immunities *ratione materiae*. Although its scope was limited to torture, the judgment showed that state officials enjoy no functional immunities from the criminal jurisdiction of another state if they face charges for crimes under international law.

3 The *Taylor* Case

The third well-known case addressing immunities from criminal jurisdiction (and the exemptions from prosecution of crimes under international law) concerned the prosecution of Charles Taylor, the former president of Liberia, before the Special Court for Sierra Leone (SCSL).

Charles Ghankay Taylor was the president of the Republic of Liberia from 1997 until August 2003. On 3 March 2003, during his term of office, the SCSL brought charges against him for committing crimes against humanity and grave breaches of the Geneva Conventions to obtain access to the mineral wealth of Sierra Leone, in particular its diamonds, and to destabilize the country.[30] Taylor was accused of providing financial support, military training, personnel, arms, and other support to rebel factions during the Sierra Leone armed conflict.

The defendant filed a complaint against the indictment and the arrest warrant (when Taylor was visiting Ghana), arguing absolute immunity from criminal prosecution which he enjoyed as a head of state at the time of the indictment. This preliminary motion was determined by the Appeals Chamber of the SCSL. In its decision on immunity from jurisdiction of 31 May 2004, the chamber addressed all the objections of the defence. The chamber also took into account the expert submissions of *amici curiae* (Professor Ph. Sands, Professor D. Orentlicher, and the African Bar Association).

The Appeals Chamber first considered the legal basis and the status of the SCSL. It noted that the establishment of the court was extensively addressed in its previous decisions, in particular the Constitutionality Decision[31] and the Lomé Amnesty Decision.[32] The chamber further stated that the SCSL was set up by the

[29] *Ibid.*, 122–3.

[30] *Prosecutor v Charles Ghankay Taylor*, Case No. SCSL-2003-01, Indictment (3 March 2003).

[31] *Prosecutor v Norman, Kallon and Kamara*, Case Nos SCSL-2004-14-AR72(E), SCSL-2004-15-AR72(E), SCSL-2004-16-AR72(E), Decision on Constitutionality and Lack of Jurisdiction (13 March 2004) (*Constitutionality Decision*).

[32] *Prosecutor v Kallon and Kamara*, Case Nos SCSL-2004-15-AR72(E), SCSL-2004-16-AR72(E), Decision on Challenge to Jurisdiction: Lomé Accord Amnesty (13 March 2004) (*Lomé Amnesty Decision*).

Agreement between the United Nations and Sierra Leone which was entered into pursuant to Resolution 1315(2000) of the Security Council for the purpose of prosecuting persons who bear the greatest responsibility for serious violations of international humanitarian law and Sierra Leonean law committed in the territory of Sierra Leone.[33] Commencement of the operations of the SCSL was authorized by the UN Secretary-General, who notified his intention to do so to the President of the Security Council in a letter dated 2 March 2002.[34]

Although the SCSL was established by treaty (unlike the ICTY and the ICTR which were each established by a resolution of the Security Council in its exercise of powers by virtue of Chapter VII of the UN Charter), it was clear that the Security Council's power to conclude an agreement for the establishment of the court was derived from the Charter, both in regard to the general purposes of the UN under Article 1 and the specific powers of the Security Council under Articles 39 and 41. These powers are wide enough to empower the Security Council to initiate the establishment of the SCSL by Agreement with Sierra Leone.[35] In carrying out its duties for the maintenance of international peace and security, the Security Council acts on behalf of the members of the United Nations. The agreement between the UN and Sierra Leone is thus an agreement between all UN members and Sierra Leone. Consequently, the SCSL established in such circumstances is truly international.[36] The Appeals Chamber found sufficient arguments in the constitutive instruments of the court and Professor Sands' report to conclude that it was an international criminal court.[37]

As regards the issue of jurisdictional immunity, the chamber made a comparison between Article 6(2) of the Statute of the SCSL which provides that '[t]he official position of any accused persons, whether as Head of State or Government or as a responsible government official, shall not relieve such person of criminal responsibility nor mitigate punishment', and similar provisions from the Statutes of the ICTY, ICTR, and ICC.[38] Then the court compared the relevant provision with older documents, such as Article 7 of the Charter of the International Military Tribunal and Principle III of the Principles of International Law recognized in the Charter of the Nürnberg Tribunal and in the Judgment of the Tribunal. The court noted that as early as in 1950, when the General Assembly adopted the wording proposed by the ILC, this principle became firmly established.[39]

The SCSL's decision further stated that the nature of the tribunals had always been a relevant consideration in the question whether there was an exception to

[33] *Prosecutor v Charles Ghankay Taylor, supra* note 30, para. 35.
[34] *Ibid.*, para. 36.
[35] *Ibid.*, para. 37.
[36] *Ibid.*, para. 38.
[37] *Ibid.*, paras 40–42.
[38] *Ibid.*, paras 44–45.
[39] *Ibid.*, para. 47.

the principle of immunity. It highlighted the ICJ decision in the *Yerodia* case (arrest warrant) which upheld immunities *ratione personae* before national courts even in respect of war crimes and crimes against humanity.[40] However, in that judgment the ICJ also confirmed that 'an incumbent or former Minister for Foreign Affairs may be subject to criminal proceedings before certain international criminal courts, where they have jurisdiction'.[41] The ICJ provided the examples of the ICTY, the ICTR, and the ICC.

The Appeals Chamber of the SCSL concluded that Article 6(2) of the Statute was not in conflict with any peremptory norm of general international law and its provisions had to be given effect by the court. Although the applicant was an incumbent head of state at the time when the criminal proceedings were initiated, he could be tried before the SCSL. As the SCSL is not a national court, the Chamber did not consider it necessary to discuss the cases in which immunity was claimed before national courts.[42]

This SCSL decision is consistent with the ICJ's decision on the arrest warrant (2002), expressly confirming that immunities *ratione personae* cannot be successfully raised where a person has been charged with crimes under international law before a relevant international court or tribunal. It can be inferred *a fortiori* that no functional immunities of a former head of state or other officials can be applied before such tribunals. Yet, the decision does not deal with exceptions to functional immunities (*ratione materiae*) of state officials before national courts of other states.

4 Current Work of the ILC

This analysis clearly shows that the ILC deals with highly complex issues under the topic 'immunity of state officials from foreign criminal jurisdiction', which has been on its programme since 2007 when Roman Kolodkin was appointed Special Rapporteur. The Special Rapporteur submitted three reports which were considered by the ILC in 2008 and 2011. The ILC could not deal with this issue at its sessions of 2009 and 2010. At its meeting in 2012 the ILC appointed Concepción Escobar Hernández as its Special Rapporteur, because Roman Kolodkin was no longer a member of the ILC.[43] She submitted a preliminary report[44] and four reports between 2012 and 2016.[45]

[40] *Ibid.*, paras 49–50.

[41] Arrest Warrant case, *supra* note 15, para. 61.

[42] *Prosecutor v Charles Ghankay Taylor*, *supra* note 30, paras 53–54.

[43] See ILC, Report of the International Law Commission on the work of its sixty-sixth session (2014) UN Doc A/69/10, 229 (*ILC 2014 Report*).

[44] C. Escobar-Hernández, Preliminary report on the immunity of State officials from foreign criminal jurisdiction, (2012) UN Doc A/CN.4/654.

[45] C. Escobar-Hernández, Second report on the immunity of State officials from foreign criminal jurisdiction (2013) UN Doc A/CN.4/661; C. Escobar-Hernández, Third report on the immunity of

4.1 General Issues and Personal Immunities of State Officials

In 2013, on the basis of the second report, the concepts of jurisdiction and immunity were discussed, as well as a distinction between immunity *ratione personae* and *ratione materiae*, and the normative elements of personal immunity. The third report presented an analysis of the normative elements of immunity *ratione materiae* and, notably, the definition of persons who could enjoy that immunity. In 2015 the fourth report was discussed, dealing with the material and temporal scope of immunity *ratione materiae*, particularly the definition of an 'official act'.

Until 2014, the ILC provisionally adopted five draft articles, and other provisions were discussed at its session in 2015, both in plenary and in the Drafting Committee, pending their formal adoption at the following session (2016). Under Article 1(1) the present draft articles 'apply to the immunity of State officials from the criminal jurisdiction of another State'. Paragraph 2 specifies that these draft articles do not affect the immunity from criminal jurisdiction enjoyed under special rules of international law, in particular 'by persons connected with diplomatic missions, consular posts, special missions, international organizations and military forces of a State'.[46]

A challenging task (more linguistic than substantive) was to define a 'State official' in Article 2(e) of the draft, because that expression has a different scope of meaning in different languages. Other languages use *représentant de l'État* (French), *funcionario del Estado* (Spanish), or *dolžostnoje lico gosudarstva* (Russian). Despite the various expressions used, those words are presumed to have the same meaning for the purposes of these draft articles.[47] The definition of a state official is 'any individual who represents the State or who exercises State functions'.[48] This is because immunities apply to a wide range of persons, from the monarch in a constitutional monarchy who represents the state although he or she does not rule, to civil servants at various levels who carry out various types of government or state functions.

A key element of the draft articles is the distinction between personal and functional immunities. A relatively easier task was to define immunity *ratione personae*, although the range of persons covered by such immunity was also subject to much discussion. Finally, the majority of the members agreed that immunity applies to three senior state officials who—consistently with the ICJ judgment in

State officials from foreign criminal jurisdiction (2014) UN Doc A/CN.4/673; C. Escobar-Hernández, Fourth report on the immunity of State officials from foreign criminal jurisdiction (2015) UN Doc A/CN.4/686; Fifth report on the immunity of State officials from foreign criminal jurisdiction (2016) UN Doc A/CN.4/701.

[46] ILC 2014 Report, *supra* note 43, at 230.
[47] *Ibid.*, 236.
[48] *Ibid.*, 231.

Yerodia—represent the state in international relations. Thus, under draft Article 3 'Heads of State, Heads of Government and Ministers for Foreign Affairs enjoy immunity *ratione personae* from the exercise of foreign criminal jurisdiction'.[49]

Under draft Article 4(1) these persons enjoy immunity *ratione personae* only during their term of office. Immunity covers all acts performed, whether in a private or official capacity, by heads of state, heads of government, and ministers of foreign affairs during or prior to their term of office (paragraph 2). Under paragraph 3, the cessation of immunity *ratione personae* is without prejudice to application of the rules of international law concerning immunity *ratione materiae*.[50]

This provision characterizes personal immunities which protect a limited group of senior state officials only during their term of office.[51] The last paragraph notes that once their term of office is over, the officials still enjoy residual immunity which is, however, of a functional character; that is, covering their official acts only.

It is beyond doubt that personal immunity applies to heads of state under customary international law.[52] This does not mean, however, that the personal scope of immunity *ratione personae* (the so-called troika) has always been accepted, including in the debates of the ILC. On the one hand, there are views that immunity *ratione personae* should be limited to the head of state and head of government, where removing immunity goes to the root of the principle of equality of states, and should not be applied to ministers for foreign affairs or even to other ministers.[53]

On the other hand, there is also a tendency in practice in a sense to expand the categories of high-ranking officials benefiting from immunity *ratione personae*. This may go beyond the traditional three representatives of states to include other ministers. As stated by the ICJ in *Congo v Rwanda*:

> with increasing frequency in modern times other persons representing a State in specific fields may be authorized by that State to bind it by their statements in respect of matters falling within their purview. This may be true, for example, of holders of technical ministerial portfolios exercising powers in their field of competence in the area of foreign relations, and even of certain officials.[54]

[49] *Ibid.*

[50] *Ibid.*

[51] This is consistent with the case law and the prevailing doctrinal approach; see, e.g., D. Akande and S. Shah, 'Immunities of State Officials, International Crimes, and Foreign Domestic Courts' (2010) 21 *European Journal of International Law* 815, 851.

[52] See H. Fox and Ph. Webb, *The Law of State Immunity, 3rd edn* (Oxford 2015) 564.

[53] See D. Akande and S. Shah, *supra* note 51, at 825.

[54] *Armed Activities on the Territory of the Congo (Democratic Republic of Congo v Rwanda)*, ICJ Jurisdiction and Admissibility of the Claim, [2006] ICJ Rep 6, para. 47.

However, in another case the ICJ agreed with France, which rejected Djibouti's contention that the Prosecutor (*Procureur de la République*) and head of national security of Djibouti enjoyed immunity *ratione personae*.[55]

The current practices of states, case law, and prevailing doctrinal approaches suggest that a limited group of senior state officials are, during their term of office, protected by immunity *ratione personae*, which is of an absolute character. This means that, within its scope, that immunity protects those persons against prosecution by the bodies of other states, even if those persons are suspected of having committed crimes under international law. No exceptions were found in customary or conventional international law for the exercise of jurisdiction by other states. However, that does not preclude the exercise of criminal jurisdiction by the suspect´s own state or by a competent international criminal court or tribunal. Moreover, such immunity does not protect former heads of state and other senior state officials after their term of office is over.

4.2 Functional Immunities and Exceptions to Functional Immunities

Clearly the most complex immunities are immunities *ratione materiae*, which apply to a wide range of persons or official acts. The ILC must deal with this issue appropriately. The definition of persons enjoying such immunity in draft Article 5 is relatively brief and simple: 'State officials acting as such enjoy immunity *ratione materiae* from the exercise of foreign criminal jurisdiction'.[56]

The expression 'acting as such' suggests a functional character of immunity *ratione materiae* which applies only to acts in their official capacity, not their private acts. Clearly, it is crucial for functional immunities to define an 'act performed in an official capacity', which was the focus of the fourth report.[57]

A long discussion at the ILC meeting led to the formulation of two new provisions: the definition of an 'act performed in an official capacity' and draft Article 6 concerned with the scope of immunity *ratione materiae*. The text prepared by the Drafting Committee defines an 'act performed in an official capacity' as any act performed by a state official in the exercise of state authority.

Of particular importance will be the adoption of draft Article 6(1), which confirms that state officials enjoy immunity *ratione materiae* only with respect to acts performed in an official capacity. In this respect it should be remembered that for the distinction between official and private acts in the context of criminal

[55] *Certain Questions of Mutual Assistance in Criminal Matters (Djibouti v France)*, [2008] ICJ Rep 177, paras 185–196, 194.

[56] ILC 2014 Report, *supra* note 43, 236.

[57] See Escobar-Hernández, *supra* note 45.

immunity, it is not possible to mechanically apply by analogy the distinction between the exercise of public authority (*acta jure imperii*) and commercial acts (*acta jure gestionis*) for the purposes of jurisdictional immunity of states, even if the acts of officials are attributed to states. The point is that certain commercial acts may be performed in an official capacity by state officials, and thus be protected by immunity from the exercise of foreign criminal jurisdiction. Of course, functional immunity does not cover acts, including crimes, which are of a private character because such acts are not related to official functions. They include, for example, personal enrichment, corruption, drug trafficking, and crimes of passion.

A more complicated issue arises in *ultra vires* cases; that is, where a civil servant oversteps their authority or acts inconsistently with their service directions. Although *ultra vires* acts are attributed to the state for the purposes of its international responsibility,[58] in the case of immunity *ratione materiae* it will probably be necessary to determine whether the person concerned acted for their own benefit.[59] This suggests that certain *ultra vires* acts, which are wrongful, may be so closely linked to the exercise of the function (rather than private motivation) that they will remain official acts which could be theoretically covered by immunity *ratione materiae*.

This is linked to the problem, already discussed in *Pinochet*, that certain crimes, typically torture, may or even must (in accordance with the treaty definition) be committed by a public official.[60] In other words, if the commission of a crime by a public official is an element of the crime, that act cannot be classified as private. Other definitions of crimes do not specifically require official status of the perpetrator, although such crimes are often committed by public officials. Clearly, this does not imply that commission of crimes belongs to the tasks of such officials. Usually, such acts are performed *ultra vires*. However, in certain cases such acts may have been ordered by the government or a superior. In neither case is there any exclusion of individual criminal responsibility for crimes under international law.

Substantive law regulates individual criminal responsibility, and neither a superior's nor the government's order can be raised as a defence. However, the prosecution of perpetrators could be frustrated by the procedural doctrine of immunities *ratione materiae* of state officials. In such a case there is growing importance of exceptions to functional immunity which could cover at least crimes under international law. This task was addressed by the ILC in 2016. Exceptions to functional immunity are supported by the Resolution of the Institute of International

[58] See Art. 7 of Articles on Responsibility of States for Internationally Wrongful Acts, annexed to UNGA Res 56/83 (28 January 2002) UN Doc A/RES/56/83 as corrected by UN Doc A/56/49(Vol. I)/Corr.4.

[59] See Escobar-Hernández, *supra* note 45, at 113.

[60] See, e.g., Art. 2 of the Convention against Torture and Other Cruel, Inhuman or Degrading Treatment or Punishment (adopted 10 December 1984, entered into force 26 June 1987) 1465 UNTS 85.

Law (Naples, 2009)[61] and many international law academics, although individual authors hold different views as to why immunities do not cover crimes under international law.[62]

In 2016, the Special Rapporteur proposed and the ILC started to discuss draft Article 7 (Crimes in respect of which immunity does not apply). According to paragraph 1, immunity will not apply in relation to the following crimes:

> (a) Genocide, crimes against humanity, war crimes, torture and enforced disappearances; (b) Crimes of corruption; (c) Crimes that cause harm to persons, including death and serious injury, or to property, when such crimes are committed in the territory of the forum State and the State official is present in said territory at the time that such crimes are committed.[63]

While the exception with respect to core crimes under international law seems to follow from this analysis and a number of other cases and state practice, however diverse and heterogeneous, two other proposed exceptions bear on different grounds. It should be noted, however, that those exceptions only affect functional immunities, because paragraph 1 'shall not apply to persons who enjoy immunity *ratione personae* during their term of office'.[64]

The plenary debate of the ILC continued in 2017. In spite of the deep division in the views of members, the Commission sent draft Article 7 to the Drafting Committee. Following in-depth discussion, the revised version of draft Article 7 was adopted. The new paragraph 1 includes an extended list of crimes under international law.[65] On balance, other crimes (corruption and so-called territorial tort) were deleted. In addition, the new paragraph 2 provides that 'the crimes under international law mentioned above are to be understood according to their definition in the treaties enumerated in the annex to the present draft articles'.[66] The redrafted version of draft Article 7 was provisionally adopted by the majority of the ILC. The recorded vote—which is unusual in the work of the Commission—as well

[61] See Institut de Droit International, Resolution on the Immunity from Jurisdiction of the State and of Persons Who Act on Behalf of the State in case of International Crimes (2009) Naples Session.

[62] See D. Akande and S. Shah, *supra* note 51, 815–52; A. Bianchi, *supra* note 24, 237–77; A. Orakhelashvili, 'Immunities of State Officials, International Crimes, and Foreign Domestic Courts: A Reply to Dapo Akande and Sangeeta Shah' (2011) 22 *European Journal of International Law* 849; S Wirth, *supra* note 15, 877–93.

[63] C. Escobar-Hernández, Fifth report on the immunity of State officials from foreign criminal jurisdiction (2016) UN Doc A/CN.4/701, 95.

[64] Draft Art. 7, para. 2; *ibid.*, 99.

[65] Draft Art. 7, para. 1 (UN Doc A/CN.4/L.893 (2017): '1. Immunity *ratione materiae* from the exercise of foreign criminal jurisdiction shall not apply in respect of the following crimes under international law: (a) crime of genocide; (b) crimes against humanity; (c) war crimes; (d) crime of apartheid; (e) torture; (f) enforced disappearance.'

[66] *Ibid.*, 1.

as many statements by individual members, show how difficult discussion on exceptions to immunity was.

4.3 Core International Crimes

The most obvious candidates for exceptions from the immunity of state officials are international crimes.[67] At least three factors support the attempt to single out international crimes in the debate on limitations and exceptions to the immunity of state officials from foreign criminal jurisdiction. First is the connection between international crimes and norms of *jus cogens*. Second, international crimes originate the comparison between immunity and the fight against impunity. Third, the importance of international crimes in the debate on exceptions to immunity is related to the process of institutionalization of international criminal law, as reflected mainly in the establishment of international criminal courts and tribunals.[68]

According to the analysis of the Special Rapporteur (Escobar Hernández), the practice of national courts, although varied, reveals a clear trend towards considering commission of international crimes as a bar to immunity of state officials from foreign criminal jurisdiction. The justification for this trend is twofold: either because such crimes are not considered official acts, or because they are considered an exception to immunity, owing to their gravity or to the fact that they undermine values and principles recognized by the international community as a whole.[69]

On balance, national courts have sometimes recognized immunity from foreign criminal jurisdiction for international crimes, but they have always done so in the context of immunity *ratione personae*. Only in exceptional circumstances have they done so with regard to immunity *ratione materiae*. This fact, in addition to the attitude of international criminal tribunals, led the Special Rapporteur to maintain the distinction of two categories of immunities in general and in particular with respect to possible exceptions from the immunity of state officials.

Therefore the Special Rapporteur and some publicists conclude that contemporary international law recognizes such limitation or exception to the immunity of state officials.[70] On the other hand, some authors take the opposite view.[71]

[67] They are also referred to as 'crimes under international law'. As two other proposed exceptions to immunity (corruption and territorial tort) are different in nature, they will not be addressed in this chapter.

[68] See the Fifth report, *supra* note 63, at 73.

[69] *Ibid.*, 73.

[70] *Ibid.*, 74. Cf. R. Pedretti, *Immunity of Heads of State and State Officials for International Crimes* (Brill 2015) 57–98.

[71] See I. Wuerth, 'Pinochet's Legacy Reassessed' (2012) 106 *American Journal of International Law* 731–68; R. O'Keefe, 'An 'International Crime' Exception to Immunity of State Officials from Foreign Criminal Jurisdiction: Not Currently, Not Likely', in Symposium on the Immunity of State Officials of the American Society of International Law (2015) 109 *American Journal of International Law Unbound*, 167–72.

In short, it seems that the conclusion in the report of the Special Rapporteur on limitation or exception to the immunity of state officials may be based on two sets of arguments: the inductive (ascending) argument and the deductive (descending) argument.[72]

4.3.1 Inductive argument in favour of exception

The first line of argumentation asserts exception based on commission of international crimes as a customary norm of international law. To determine the existence of an international custom, it is necessary to ascertain whether there is a 'general practice that is accepted as law (*opinio juris*)'.[73]

The Special Rapporteur draws conclusions on state practice from analysis of national legislative and judicial practice. In spite of this analysis, there are doubts 'as to whether such practice is sufficiently consistent and uniform to constitute a material element of an international custom'.[74] In the first place, it is important to look at both the position of national courts and recently adopted national laws. However, the position that international crimes constitute a limitation or exception to immunity can also be identified in statements delivered by states and in writings by publicists (doctrine), considered a 'subsidiary means' of identifying custom.

The Special Rapporteur concluded that, despite the diversity of positions taken by national courts, it was possible to identify a trend in favour of the exception to immunity.[75] The analysis reveals certain prevailing trends in case law. First, with regard to decisions on immunity *ratione personae*, almost all national criminal courts held that heads of state (and in some cases other high-ranking officials) enjoy immunity from foreign criminal jurisdiction.[76]

Second, in some cases the courts concluded that immunity *ratione personae* may cease to apply if an international treaty clearly establishes that it has been waived or lifted, or cannot be invoked. This is the case for Article 27 of the Rome Statute of the ICC.[77]

Third, the immunity *ratione materiae* of foreign state officials gave rise to a greater number of judgments that are less uniform. However, in a certain number of cases, domestic courts have been accepting the existence of limitations and exceptions to immunity relating to commission of international crimes.[78]

[72] For this distinction cf. M. Koskenniemi, *From Apology to Utopia: The Structure of International Legal Argument. Reissue with a New Epilogue* (Cambridge 2005), 58–60.

[73] Cf. Art. 38, para. 1b, Statute of the ICJ; and also draft conclusion 2, ILC report on Identification of customary international law, Report of the ILC (2016), 82.

[74] See the Fifth report, *supra* note 63, at 74.

[75] *Ibid.*, 76.

[76] *Ibid.*, 46.

[77] See *Re Sharon and Yaron, HAS v SA (Ariel Sharon) and YA (Amos Yaron)*, Court of Cassation of Belgium, 12 February 2003, 127 ILR, 123–4; *The Hague City Party v Netherlands*, The Hague District Court, judgment of 4 May 2005, LJN AT5152, KG 05/432, para. 3.6.

[78] See, e.g., *R v Bow Street Metropolitan Stipendiary Magistrate ex parte Pinochet Ugarte (No. 3)*, UKHL 17 [2000] 1 AC 147; *Pinochet*, Belgium, Court of First Instance of Brussels, judgment of 6

Finally, national courts have used various arguments to conclude that immunity *ratione materiae* is not applicable, such as the gravity of acts committed by a state official, violation of *jus cogens* norms, or the consideration that the acts in question cannot be regarded as acts performed in an official capacity.[79]

Separate analysis may be needed for decisions by national courts in civil cases. However, similar arguments could be used in these cases by analogy: they concern immunity of the state (but not that of state officials) from foreign civil jurisdiction.

Next, the relevant state practice may be reflected in national legislation. Of course, legislative acts of various states are far from being uniform on the question of immunity of state officials (as well as that of states), but they reflect at least emerging support for certain exceptions from immunity *ratione materiae*. In conformity with the report of the Special Rapporteur, one can distinguish laws expressly governing immunity and laws which, in regulating state jurisdiction in terms of international crimes, also refer to the issue of immunity.[80]

As to the first group, such laws are not frequent and, in addition, most of them refer basically to immunities of states. However, some of them include provisions to be applied to certain state officials, especially heads of state.

In particular, in Spain, the 2015 Organic Act on Privileges and Immunities of Foreign States, International Organizations with Headquarters or Offices in Spain and International Conferences and Meetings held in Spain[81] deals with the immunity of certain officials (head of state, head of government, and minister of foreign affairs). It refers both to immunity *ratione personae* and to immunity *ratione materiae*. For the latter, it introduces an exception based on international crimes. It provides for 'acts performed during a term of office in exercise of official functions … crimes of genocide, forced disappearance, war crimes and crimes against humanity will be excluded from immunity'.[82]

Interesting developments may be traced in special laws in Belgium and the Netherlands, respectively the 1993 Repression of Serious Violations of international humanitarian law Act, as amended in 1999 and 2003, also in response to the Arrest Warrant case (2000),[83] and the 2003 International Crimes Act. Both Article 13 of the Belgian Act and Article 16 of the Dutch Act provide two grounds for the exclusion of criminal jurisdiction (immunity): in relation to foreign heads of state,

November 1998, 119 ILR, 349; *In re Hussein*, Germany, Higher Regional Court of Cologne, judgment of 16 May 2000, 2 Zs 1330/99, para. 11; *Bouterse*, Netherlands, Court of Appeal of Amsterdam, judgment of 20 November 2000; *Fujimori*, Chile, Supreme Court, judge of first instance, judgment of 11 July 2007, Case No. 5646-05, paras 15–17; *FF v. Director of Public Prosecutions (Prince Nasser case)*, High Court of Justice, Queen's Bench Division, Divisional Court, judgment of 7 October 2014 [2014] EWHC 3419 (Admin.).

[79] See the Fifth report, *supra* note 63, at 50.
[80] *Ibid.*, 25.
[81] Organic Act 16/2015, of 27 October, Official Gazette, No. 258.
[82] *Ibid.*, Art. 23, para. 1.
[83] *Arrest Warrant of 11 April 2000 (Democratic Republic of Congo v Belgium)*, *supra* note 15.

heads of government, and ministers for foreign affairs, as long as they are in office, and other persons who have immunity under a treaty binding on the forum state in question. In other words, both acts recognize the absolute immunity *ratione personae*, at least for the 'troika', but do not address immunity *ratione materiae*, which may be interpreted as implicit recognition of applying exceptions to it in connection with crimes against humanity, war crimes, and genocide.[84] Of course, this interpretation is subject to possible immunity under a special treaty.

Next, the issue of immunity has also been addressed in various laws designed to implement in domestic legislation the obligations arising from the Rome Statute of the ICC.[85] The first approach is represented by laws, such as adopted in Burkina Faso, the Comoros, Ireland, Mauritius, and South Africa, recognizing that in general no immunity can be invoked against the exercise of national criminal jurisdiction regarding crimes within the competence of the ICC.[86]

The second approach is reflected in laws adopted in Canada, France, Germany, Kenya, New Zealand, Norway, Switzerland, and Uganda, which do not take into consideration immunity or relevance of official status as grounds for non-compliance with an order to surrender to the ICC.[87]

Next, a sub-category of laws may represent the acts adopted in Iceland, Ireland, Malta, Samoa, and the United Kingdom that deal only with the irrelevance of immunity in relation to nationals of states parties to the Rome Statute and establish a system of consultations with the ICC in case of nationals of the third states.[88]

Finally, some other states (such as Argentina, Australia, Austria, and Liechtenstein) adopted laws that provide not for non-applicability of immunity in all cases but rather for systems of consultation with the Court in order to resolve any dispute on the basis of application of Articles 27 and 98(1) of the Rome Statute.[89]

[84] See 2003 Act amending the Repression of Serious Violations of international humanitarian law Act of 16 June 1993 (Belgium); 2003 International Crimes Act (the Netherlands). Cf. the Fifth report, *supra* note 63, at 29.

[85] Cf. Fifth report, *ibid.*, 24–31.

[86] Burkina Faso: Act No. 52 of 2009 on the determination of competence and procedures for application of the Rome Statute of the ICC by the jurisdictions of Burkina Faso (Arts 7 and 15(1)); Comoros: Act No. 11-022 of 2011 concerning the application of the Rome Statute (Art. 7(2)); Ireland: International Criminal Court Act 2006 (Art. 61(1)); Mauritius: International Criminal Court Act 2001 (Art. 4); South Africa: Act No. 27 of 2002 implementing the Rome Statute of the International Criminal Court, Art. 4(2)(a)(i) and Art. 4(3)(c). E.g., according to the last act, South African courts are competent to prosecute crimes of genocide, crimes against humanity, and war crimes when the presumed perpetrator is in South Africa and any official status claimed by the accused is irrelevant.

[87] E.g. Canada: 1999 Extradition Act (Art. 18); Germany: Courts Constitution Act (Arts 20.1 and 21); Kenya: Act No. 16 of 2008 on International Crimes (Art. 27); New Zealand: International Crimes and International Criminal Court Act 2000 (Art. 31.1).

[88] See, e.g., Iceland: 2003 Act on the International Criminal Court (Art. 20.1); Ireland: International Criminal Court Act No. 30 of 2006 (Art. 6.1).

[89] See, e.g., Argentina: Act No. 26200 implementing the Rome Statute of the International Criminal Court (Arts 40 and 41); Australia: International Criminal Court Act No. 41 of 2002 (Art. 12.4); Austria: Federal Act No. 135 of 2002 on Cooperation with the International Criminal Court and other international tribunals (Arts 9.1 and 9.3).

Last but not least, the positions of states, whether counted as state practice or evidence of *opinio juris*, are also expressed in their statements and comments on the reports of the ILC in the Sixth Committee of the General Assembly. A number of states expressed views in support of certain exceptions to immunity of state officials. Such statements were made, for example, by the Czech Republic.[90] The view that international crimes should be considered *prima facie* as exceptions to immunity was also expressed by the Republic of Korea, Canada, Japan, Norway (on behalf of the Nordic countries), the Netherlands, Poland, and the Republic of the Congo.[91]

At this stage, it is possible to conclude that a large number of states have supported, either in legislative acts or in official statements, the existence of exceptions to immunity *ratione materiae*, mostly those related to international crimes.

4.3.2 Deductive argument in favour of exception

Debates within the ILC and in international legal doctrine at large reveal the fact that limitations and exceptions to immunity of state officials, far from being a purely technical question of stock-taking of treaties and judicial decisions, also involve certain fundamental issues of trends and values reflected in contemporary international law. In addition, in the case of existence of (seemingly) conflicting rules of international law, namely those on jurisdiction and prosecution of international crimes and those on immunity, it is important to adopt an interpretation that leads to the systemic integration of international law as a coherent legal order.[92]

It seems that the following arguments can be advanced in favour of exceptions to immunity *ratione materiae* of state officials: (i) norms *jus cogens* aiming at protection of fundamental values of the international community as a whole; (ii) human rights, access to justice, and the right of victims to reparation; (iii) obligations of individuals resulting from the development of international criminal law; and (4) the obligation of states to establish and exercise jurisdiction over crimes under international law.

[90] See Comments of the Czech Republic, in: <http://legal.un.org/ilc/guide/4_2.shtml#govcoms> accessed 28 April 2019: 'On the other hand, the Czech Republic is aware of the fact that, in the context of criminal jurisdiction, exceptions to the immunity ratione materiae of State officials have been applied or considered, both in the decisions of international and national courts and in the writings of legal scholars: one being a norm of customary international law providing for an exception to immunity ratione materiae in a case where an official has committed a crime under international law (international crime), which is attributed not only to the State but also to the official who performed it; the other being an exception explicitly or implicitly contained in relevant treaties.'

[91] Official Records of the General Assembly, A/C.6/68/SR.18 (Republic of Korea), A/C.6/67/SR.20 (Canada), A/C.6/69/SR.23 (Japan), A/C.6/66/SR.26 (Norway), A/C.6/67/SR.21 (Netherlands), A/C.6/69/SR.23 (Poland), A/C.6/67/SR.21 (Congo).

[92] See the Fifth report, *supra* note 63, 78–88.

4.3.2.1 Norms of jus cogens

This is potentially the most powerful but at the same time the most controversial argument. The starting and non-controversial point is the characterization of (core) international crimes as acts contrary to the fundamental values of the international community. It also constitutes the premise for the fight against impunity as one of the values and objectives of the international community and contemporary international law. This is linked to the assertion that such crimes violate *jus cogens* norms from which no derogation is allowed.[93]

Acceptance of the peremptory nature of underlying norms in the case of international crimes is uncontroversial but not sufficient. What matters, however, is its effect on application of the rules on immunity. The interpretation of *jus cogens* as the basis for limiting or waiving immunity has been accepted by some national courts and many authors.[94] However, it was rejected by the International Court of Justice in the case concerning *Jurisdictional Immunities of the State*.

Although the case concerns state immunity, the Court discussed the argument that certain rules of the law of armed conflict (of which violations constitute war crimes) are rules of *jus cogens*. It concludes that:

> there is no conflict between those rules and the rules on State immunity. The two sets of rules address different matters. The rules of State immunity are procedural in character and are confined to determining whether or not the courts of one State may exercise jurisdiction in respect of another State. They do not bear upon the question whether or not the conduct in respect of which the proceedings are brought was lawful or unlawful.[95]

Nevertheless, this approach by the ICJ, as well as the consequences drawn from it by some commentators, can be criticized. Those who believe in the primacy of *jus cogens* over immunities can easily share the view that '*jus cogens* is about effects and consequences as much as it is about substantive prohibitions'. Well-known examples are the nullity of treaties under Article 53 of the 1969 Vienna Convention or the duty not to recognize situations created through a serious breach of *jus cogens* under the ILC Articles on State responsibility (Articles 40 and 41). Consequently, 'there is no reason why it should be otherwise in relation to jurisdiction and immunities. This outcome becomes even more compelling as *jus cogens* norms relating to international crimes do not just prohibit the relevant conduct but also criminalize it with peremptory effect.'[96]

[93] *Ibid.*, 78.

[94] Cf., e.g., R. Van Alebeek, *supra* note 13, 345–53; A. Bianchi, *supra* note 63; A. Orakhelashvili, 'State Immunity and Hierarchy of Norms: Why the House of Lords Got It Wrong' (2007) 17 *European Journal of International Law* 915; R. Pavoni and S. Beaulac, 'Étude croisée Italie/Canada sur l'immunité des États et le *jus cogens* en droit international'. *EUI Working Papers LAW* 2009/16.

[95] *Jurisdictional Immunities of the State (Germany v Italy)* [2012] ICJ Rep. 38, para. 93.

[96] See A. Orakhelashvili, *supra* note 62, 851–2.

4.3.2.2 *Human rights of victims of crimes*

The second argument is closely related to the *jus cogens* nature of violated rules. Indeed, not all international human rights are protected by *jus cogens*, but most peremptory norms of international law relate to human rights. This seems to be confirmed by the case law of international courts and tribunals.[97] It is particularly relevant for those violations of human rights that amount to international crimes, namely genocide, crimes against humanity, war crimes, torture, and enforced disappearances, listed by the 2016 report as exceptions to the immunity of state officials.

Although protection of human rights—including the right of access to justice and the right of victims to reparation, and the exercise of criminal justice with respect to international crimes—are traditionally considered as two different areas of international law, they pursue similar objectives, in particular in cases of serious and systematic violations of human rights. In such cases, the mere declaration of breach and pecuniary compensation may not represent sufficient legal consequences of wrongful acts. It appears from some decisions of regional courts, especially the Inter-American Court of Human Rights, that in cases of exceptionally serious crimes the state also has the duty to investigate and to punish those responsible for such violations.[98]

Clearly, human rights have to be protected and enforced primarily by courts of the state where violations took place, being usually the state of nationality or residence of victims. Even if invoked in proceedings before the courts of another state, human rights bear mainly on civil jurisdiction and on state immunity, exceptionally on the immunity of foreign officials. However, the immunity of state officials from criminal jurisdiction may also be considered an obstacle to the right of access to justice and the right of victims of international crimes to reparation.[99] Although this is not a necessary conclusion in all cases, it will have this implication only if no other remedy is available.[100]

4.3.2.3 *Obligations of individuals resulting from development of international criminal law*

Next, the emergence of individual criminal responsibility of persons who committed crimes under international law, existing along with the responsibility of

[97] See P. Šturma, 'Human Rights as an Example of Peremptory Norms of General International Law' in P. Šturma and N.L.X. Baez (eds), *International and Internal Mechanisms of Fundamental Rights Effectiveness* (RW&W 2015) 11–21.

[98] See C. Maia, 'Le jus cogens dans la jurisprudence de la Cour interaméricaine des droits de l'homme' in L. Hennebel and H. Tigroudja (eds), *Le particularisme interaméricain des droits de l'homme* (Paris 2009) 278 ff.

[99] According to some views, the right to access to justice is considered as a part of jus cogens. See A.A. Cançado Trindade, *The Access of Individuals to International Justice* (OUP 2011) 197.

[100] See the Fifth report, *supra* note 63, at 84, para. 209.

states, is an important factor affecting the traditional rules on immunity. It was already stated by the Nuremberg Tribunal that:

> the principle of international law which under certain circumstances protects the representatives of a State, cannot be applied to acts which are condemned as criminal by international law. The authors of these acts cannot shelter themselves behind their official position in order to be freed from punishment in appropriate proceedings.[101]

This judgment reflects the principles of individual criminal responsibility and non-relevance of official positions, arising from the Statute of the International Military Tribunal (IMT), and subsequently included in the statutes of all international criminal tribunals. This also explains why Article 27 of the 1998 Rome Statute of the ICC states that official capacity and national and international immunities cannot be invoked before the ICC. This seems hardly compatible with the customary international law of immunity. This is the nature of crimes under international law that prevents state officials from escaping individual criminal responsibility.[102]

On balance, in the *Arrest Warrant Case* the ICJ held that although international conventions 'impose on States obligations of prosecution or extradition, thereby requiring them to extend their criminal jurisdiction, such extension of jurisdiction in no way affects immunities under customary international law, including those of Ministers of Foreign Affairs'.[103] However, the Court referred to the immunity *ratione personae* available to the most senior state officials.

The situation is different with regard to immunity *ratione materiae*, which generally covers any acts of all officials. If not covered by exceptions, immunity of State officials would make the prosecution of most international crimes impossible. This fact has been criticized by some authors from the point of view of modern international law.[104] Indeed, one cannot but agree that 'the very purpose of international criminal law is to attribute responsibility to individuals, including state officials, and to defeat the defence of official capacity or act of state'.[105]

101 *In re Goering and others*, Nuremberg Judgment (International Military Tribunal, 1946) 220–1.

102 See P.-M. Dupuy, 'Crimes et immunité, ou dans quelle mesure la nature des premiers empêche l'exercise des secondes' (1999) 2 *Revue générale de droit international public* 290.

103 *Arrest Warrant case*, *supra* note 15, at para. 59.

104 See, e.g., A. Cassese, 'When May Senior Officials Be Tried for International Crimes? Some Comments on The Congo v. Belgium Case' (2002) 13 *European Journal of International Law* 864–5: 'That such a rule has crystallized in the world community is evidenced by a whole range of elements: not only the provisions of the various treaties or other international instruments on international tribunals, but also international and national case law.'

105 D. Akande and S. Shah, *supra* note 5, at 840.

4.3.2.4 Obligation of states to establish and exercise jurisdiction over international crimes

The final argument seeks to resolve a possible conflict of norms by means of systemic interpretation of international law. This approach has an advantage in comparison with a strict normative hierarchy based on the priority of *jus cogens* norms. The last-mentioned approach works only in the case of direct conflict between two incompatible norms. Such a conflict could be resolved by declaring null and void any norm contrary to the peremptory norms of general international law. This is not, as the ICJ rightly pointed out, the case for rules on immunity that are procedural in nature. It is difficult to see how these rules come into direct conflict with *jus cogens* norms prohibiting acts that constitute crimes under international law.[106]

Even if there is no absolute conflict between two norms as such, there is no doubt that certain consequences of the rules on immunity of state officials may be at odds with the obligation to prosecute international crimes. The dictum of the ICJ that a procedural bar of immunity does not result in impunity is correct only where recourse can be had to a criminal law mechanism other than the courts of the forum state. An alternative mechanism might be the courts of the state of the official or a competent international criminal tribunal.[107]

However, if none of the alternative mechanisms can try perpetrators of international crimes, immunity from foreign criminal jurisdiction loses its exclusively procedural nature. Then the only solution is that, while both rules remain in force, immunity of state officials does not apply, by virtue of exception or waiver, to the prosecution of persons responsible for international crimes. In other words, the general principle of immunity 'does not apply to acts which amount to international crimes, because there is a further, newer, principle that the official position of an individual does not exempt him/her from individual responsibility for international crimes'.[108]

5 Conclusion: Systemic Integration of International Laws

Although state practice, including case law, allows a good number of examples supporting exceptions to the immunity of state officials to be discerned, it is far from being uniform. Therefore, it also provides good arguments to the contrary. This is the reason why the ascending (inductive) arguments have to be completed and balanced by certain descending (deductive) arguments. The latter go clearly to a conclusion in favour of exception.

[106] See the Fifth report, *supra* note 63, at 82.
[107] *Ibid.*, 83.
[108] D. Akande and S. Shah, *supra* note 51, 840.

However, this line of argument may not appear satisfactory for those lawyers (mostly positivists and conservatives) who only rely on ascending arguments, drawing just from state practice which can hardly be uniform in such politically sensitive issues, as immunities undoubtedly are. That is why one additional argument is needed. This is the argument of anti-fragmentation or systemic integration of international law. Put simply, if international law is a legal order (system) and not just bric-à-brac, then it is not acceptable to have two valid rules at the same time, the first requiring states to do something and the other prohibiting them to do so.

However, this would be precisely the result if the interpretation of absolute immunity were admitted. The 1984 Convention against Torture makes acts by a public official part of the definition (elements) of the crime.[109] Similarly, the International Convention for the Protection of All Persons from Enforced Disappearance includes state officials when defining the crime.[110] If states are under obligation, established by the conventions, to criminalize a certain act, to establish their criminal jurisdiction with respect to such crimes and to exercise that jurisdiction (going beyond the principle of territoriality or personality), they cannot at the same time be barred by absolute immunity *ratione materiae*, applied to all official acts of state officials as a matter of customary law. As pointed out by Lord Millet in the *Pinochet* case, 'no rational system of criminal justice can allow an immunity which is coextensive with the offence'.[111]

This argument is supported by the existence of universal jurisdiction (or other form of extra-territorial jurisdiction) and the obligation *aut dedere aut judicare*.[112]

Put differently, although the principle of universal jurisdiction is only permissive under customary international law (but may become mandatory under treaty law), it conflicts with immunity *ratione materiae*.[113] In other words, 'where the application of the prior immunity would deprive the subsequent jurisdictional rule of practically all meaning, then the only logical conclusion must be that the subsequent jurisdictional rule is to be regarded as a removal of the immunity'.[114]

Of course, the fact that international law forms a coherent system should be admitted. Therefore, such conventions can be interpreted at least as *lex specialis* in

[109] Art. 1 of the Convention against Torture and Other Cruel, Inhuman or Degrading Treatment or Punishment (adopted 10 December 1984, entered into force 26 June 1987) 1465 UNTS 85. It defines torture as 'any act by which severe pain or suffering, whether physical or mental, is intentionally inflicted on a person for such purposes as obtaining from him or a third person information or a confession, punishing him for an act he or a third person has committed or is suspect of having committed, or intimidating or coercing him or a third person, or for any reason based on discrimination of any kind, when such pain or suffering is inflicted by or at the instigation of or with the consent or acquiescence of a public official or other person acting in an official capacity'.

[110] Art. 2 of the International Convention for the Protection of All Persons from Enforced Disappearance (New York, 2006, A/RES/61/177).

[111] Cf. also P.-M. Dupuy, Crimes et immunité, *supra* note 102, 292.

[112] Cf. Fox and Webb, *supra* note 52, 43–4.

[113] See P. Caban, Immunity of State Officials from Foreign Criminal Jurisdiction—Exceptions to Immunity ratione materiae, (2016) 7 *Czech Yearbook of Public & Private International Law*, 315–17.

[114] D. Akande and S. Shah, *supra* note 51, at 841.

relation to customary law on immunity and in favour of exceptions to immunity, otherwise the obligations of states under such conventions would be deprived of much of their meaning (*effet utile*). And even more generally, such a trend should be taken into consideration in terms of the progressive development and codification of general international law.

PART III

SUSTAINABLE DEVELOPMENT THEMES

The Future We Want

Sustainable Development as an Inherent Aim of Foreign Investment Protection

*Ilze Dubava**

1 Introduction

In order to achieve the 2030 Agenda for Sustainable Development,[1] one problem that needs to be dealt with is finding a balance between foreign investment protection and the regulatory interests of host states.

At present, the existence of such a balance in the current international investment protection regime is being questioned even by pioneers of that regime such as Germany and France regarding, for instance, Transatlantic Trade and Investment Partnership (TTIP) negotiations. Many states,[1] civil society groups,[2] academics, and investment treaty arbitration practitioners[3] are calling for or proposing reforms to enhance the fairness, legitimacy, and democratic accountability of the regime. Thus, one may say that international investment law is in crisis, implying a reassessment of its postulated aims and values

* The views expressed in this chapter do not represent the official views of the author's current employer.

[1] For instance, Bolivia, Ecuador, and Venezuela are withdrawing from or limiting the jurisdiction of ICSID, see *TDM News*, Issue 1, Week 05, 31 January 2012; available at: <https://www.asil.org/insights/volume/15/issue/22/australian-trade-policy-statement-investor-state-dispute-settlement > accessed 28 April 2019. Australia opposes investor–state dispute settlement in its future IIAs, see J. Kurtz, 'The Australian Trade Policy Statement on Investor–State Dispute Settlement' (2 August 2011) 15(22) *American Society of International Law Insights*; available at.

[2] Regarding TTP, see *220+ Law and Economics Professors Urge Congress to Reject the TPP and Other Prospective Deals that Include Investor–State Dispute Settlement (ISDS)*; available at: <http://www.citizen.org/documents/isds-law-economics-professors-letter-Sept-2016.pdf> accessed 28 April 2019.

[3] J.E. Kalicki and A. Joubin-Bret (eds), *Reshaping the Investor–State Dispute Settlement System: Journeys for the 21st Century* (2015). See also M. Kumm, 'An Empire of Capital? Transatlantic Investment Protection as the Institutionalization of Unjustified Privilege' (25 May 2015) 4(3) *ESIL Reflections* <http://www.esil-sedi.eu/sites/default/files/ESIL%20Reflection%20KUMM%20final_0.pdf> accessed 28 April 2019. For a contrary view: S.W. Schill, 'The Overlooked Role of Arbitration in International Adjudication Theory' (4 May 2015) 4(2) *ESIL Reflections* <http://www.esil-sedi.eu/sites/default/files/Schill%20Reflection%20PDF_0.pdf> accessed 28 April 2019.

Ilze Dubava, *The Future We Want: Sustainable Development as an Inherent Aim of Foreign Investment Protection* In: *How International Law Works in Times of Crisis*. Edited by: George Ulrich and Ineta Ziemele, Oxford University Press (2019).
DOI: 10.1093/oso/9780198849667.003.0011

and the regime's capacity to achieve those aims and further those values in its current form.

The reasons behind this are varied. The structural bias of foreign investment protection law (prescribing rights for foreign investors and duties for host states) and procedural asymmetry of investor–state arbitration (allowing mainly investors to initiate claims in arbitration[4]) has led in some instances to a belief that foreign investment protection is a goal in itself.

The fact that party-appointed investment tribunals have powers to assess the legitimacy of public interest regulations by states, which often involves highly sensitive issues[5] substantially influencing future behaviour by states,[6] has led to questioning the democratic accountability of the regime, particularly when seen in connection with the TTIP and the EU–Canada Comprehensive Economic and Trade Agreement (CETA) negotiations.

Mutually inconsistent, unpredictable awards and varying interpretative practices have led to reservations that international investment law and investment arbitrations may not sufficiently respect the regulatory needs of states, limiting their capacity to address societal interests such as climate change, the environment, and public health. For instance, this perception is

[4] P. Juillard, 'The Law of International Investment. Can the Imbalance Be Redressed?' in K.P. Sauvant (ed.), *Yearbook on International Investment Law & Policy 2008–2009* (OUP 2009) 280.

[5] For example, in the Philip Morris cases against Australia and Uruguay, health protection measures were at issue (in both cases the state prevailed in the arbitration). In *Vattenfall v Germany*, a Swedish nuclear energy company initiated investment proceedings against Germany due to its decision to phase out nuclear power (ICSID, *Vattenfall AB and others v Federal Republic of Germany*, ICSID Case No. ARB/12/12, pending). In *Bilcon Clayton v Canada*, the investor brought Canada to arbitration and won the case after rejection of its quarry terminal project due to the results of the environmental and cultural impact assessment. The majority Tribunal found that the cultural impact assessment was contrary to domestic law and thus violated the legitimate expectations of the investor (NAFTA (UNCITRAL), *William Ralph Clayton, William Richard Clayton, Douglas Clayton, Daniel Clayton and Bilcon of Delaware Inc. v Government of Canada*, PCA Case No. 2009-04, Award on Jurisdiction and Liability, 17 March 2015). In *TransCanada v USA*, Canadian companies went to arbitration in response to the denial of a Presidential Permit for construction of the Keystone XL oil pipeline for environmental and climate change reasons. The claimants insisted their project was rejected because of an arbitrary political calculation, namely because the United States wanted to portray itself as a world leader in combating climate change (NAFTA (ICSID), *TransCanada Corporation & TransCanada PipeLines Limited v USA*, Request for Arbitration, 24 June 2016, ICSID Case No. ARB/16/21, discontinued since president Trump issued a Presidential Permit to construct the pipeline, see L.E. Peterson, 'TransCanada Says It Has Permit for Keystone Pipeline, and ICSID Case is Swiftly Discontinued', *Investment Arbitration Reporter*, 24 March 2017.

[6] NAFTA (UNCITRAL), *Methanex Corporation v United States of America*, Decision on *Amici Curiae*, 15 January 2001, at 9, para. 17; N. Bernasconi-Osterwalder and E. Brown Weiss, 'International Investment Rules and Water: Learning from the NAFTA Experience' in E. Brown Weiss, L. Boisson de Chazournes,, and N. Bernasconi-Osterwalder (eds), *Fresh Water and International Economic Law* (OUP 2005) 263–88; M. Sornarajah, 'Developing Countries in the Investment Treaty System: A Law for Need or a Law for Greed?' in S.W. Schill, C.J. Tams, and R. Hofmann (eds), *International Investment Law and Development. Bridging the Gap* (Edward Elgar Publishing 2015) 48.

recognized in the majority opinion of the *Philip Morris v Uruguay*[7] tribunal, which noted that:

> The principle that the State's reasonable *bona fide* exercise of police powers in such matters as the maintenance of public order, health or morality, excludes compensation even when it causes economic damage to an investor and that the measures taken for that purpose should not be considered as expropriatory did not find immediate recognition in investment treaty decisions.[8]

Thus, to no surprise, states are no longer willing to jump head first into the allegedly unbalanced foreign investment protection system. They are concerned whether their sovereign right to regulate in the public interest will be preserved and, consequently, whether they will be able to achieve their sustainable development goals. Multiple states are withdrawing from the investor–state dispute settlement mechanism (Australia, Ecuador) and from the jurisdiction of the International Centre for Settlement of Investment Disputes (ICSID) system (Bolivia, Venezuela, and Ecuador), while South Africa and several other states have undertaken revision of their foreign investment protection policies.

It is enough to have only a few awards or lines of argumentation that feed the perception that states' regulatory powers are being unduly limited in order to induce their sense of insecurity and distrust of the system as a whole. This distrust is reflected in the reform[9] that the international investment agreement (IIA) regime is currently undergoing, aiming to bring it into line with today's sustainable development imperative[10] and emphasizing the need to preserve states' ability to pursue their public interest objectives while maintaining protection for foreign investors.[11] One may claim that the content of newly drafted IIAs such as the Slovakia–Iran bilateral investment treaty[12] (BIT) has been evolving, partly to improve the loose and unpredictable content of older BITs, and partly in reaction to and criticism of several arbitral awards issued interpreting IIAs concluded in the 1990s which have

[7] ICSID, *Philip Morris Brands SÀRL, Philip Morris Products S.A. and Abal Hermanos S.A. v Oriental Republic of Uruguay*, Award of 8 July 2016, ICSID Case No. ARB/10/7.

[8] *Ibid.*, [295].

[9] E.g., UNCTAD, 'Reform of Investor–State Dispute Settlement: In Search of a Roadmap', *IIA Issues Note*, No. 2, June 2013, 1-4—in addressing 'systemic deficiencies' of investor–state dispute settlement (ISDS) which relate to legitimacy, transparency, consistency, control, independence, and efficiency of ISDS under IIAs. See also recently drafted IIAs such as the Slovakia–Iran BIT, see L.E. Peterson, 'Iran Signs off on a Radical Investment Treaty: Barring Arbitrators from Wearing Two Hats, Narrowing Protections, and Limiting Damages Awards' *Investment Arbitration Reporter*, 27 July 2016.

[10] UNCTAD, *World Investment Report 2016 'Investor Nationality: Policy Challenges'* (2016) 108 (hereinafter WIR 2016).

[11] *Ibid.*, 101.

[12] Peterson, *supra* note 14.

caused a backlash against investment arbitration and against the powers of some arbitrators who have interpreted investment guarantees in the way they have.

In essence, the reform is an attempt to limit the interpretative powers of arbitrators through mechanisms such as more careful elaboration of investment guarantees such as fair and equitable treatment (FET) and indirect expropriation clauses, abolition of others (such as the umbrella clause), or limiting access to investment arbitration. Sustainable development is currently acknowledged as the new paradigm of international investment protection law, and it is to be taken into account in drafting future investment agreements, as proposed by the United Nations Conference on Trade and Development (UNCTAD) Investment Policy Framework for Sustainable Development.[13]

However, there is ambiguity over earlier BITs—most of them drafted in the 1990s—which are rarely redrafted by states but represent the majority of IIAs currently in force[14] ('new generation' IIAs only account for around 8% of all IIAs[15]). Furthermore, even 'new generation' IIAs such as the North American Free Trade Agreement (NAFTA) (1994),[16] which do contain explicit references to sustainable development objectives, are sometimes interpreted as though they were concerned with the investment protection aspect exclusively.[17]

In an effort to resolve some of the ambiguity, this chapter aims to prove that the sustainable development paradigm—and the consequent extension of protected interests in investment law—is already applicable within the existing investment protection regime. In order to accomplish this aim, the chapter allocates enabling objectives to two distinct parts.

First, it asserts that the object and purpose of the investment regime today is sustainable development—being generally understood as pursuing an equitable balance between economic growth, social progress, and environmental protection. A sustainable development paradigm necessitates that the state's regulatory responsibilities are matched by the foreign investor's interests.

[13] UNCTAD, *World Investment Report 2012 'Towards a New Generation of Investment Policies'* (2012).

[14] *Ibid.*, 111.

[15] K. Gordon and J. Pohl, 'Environmental Concerns in International Investment Agreements. A Survey' *OECD Working Papers on International Investment* 2011/01 (2011); available at: https://www.oecd-ilibrary.org/finance-and-investment/environmental-concerns-in-international-investment-agreements_5kg9mq7scrjh-en; UNCTAD, World Investment Report 2012 'Towards a New Generation of Investment Policies' (2012) xxiii.

[16] Where the language of 'old generation' BITs mainly focused on foreign investment facilitation and protection, the wording of 'new generation' IIAs expands to some degree on *prima facie* external issues of investment protection: environmental protection, observance of international labour standards, incorporation of corporate social responsibility guidelines; see K. Vandevelde, 'A Brief History of International Investment Agreements' (2005) 12(157) *University of California Davis Journal of International Law & Policy* 169 ff. See also K. Gordon, 'International Investment Agreements: A Survey of Environmental, Labour and Anti-corruption Issues' in OECD, *International Investment Law: Understanding Concepts and Tracking Innovations* (2008) 135; available at: <http://www.oecd.org/daf/inv/investment-policy/40471550.pdf> accessed 28 April 2019.

[17] E.g., NAFTA (ICSID(AF)), *Metalclad Corporation v the United Mexican States*, ICSID Case No. ARB(AF)/97/1, Award of 30 August 2000, para. 111.

Second, in order to identify where this balance lies, the chapter considers the impact of sustainable development as the object and purpose of investment protection. The author suggests that the sustainable development objective requires a new look at the role that investment arbitrators play. It also alters perceptions of applicable law and guides the contextual and effective interpretations of investment protection standards towards a focus on wider interests than those of foreign investors alone. As a result, the sustainable development paradigm affects the methodologies according to which violations of investment guarantees are established, limiting the discretion and policy choices that adjudicators have while interpreting and filling investment standards with content in specific cases.

2 Sustainable Development as the Object and Purpose of the IIA Network

This chapter argues for a reconceptualization of the current network of IIAs by justifying the evolutionary interpretation of its object and purpose, in particular the term 'economic development'.

2.1 Economic Development as the Principal Objective of Investment Law

The network of 'old-generation' and 'new-generation' IIAs may be treated as a legal regime[18] that also has a common underlying object and purpose. The idea of an inherent object and purpose of the investment regime is expressed in legal doctrine[19] and in the evolving arbitral jurisprudence applying 'old-generation' IIAs that usually remain silent on their objectives.

Arbitral jurisprudence has gradually developed two levels of object and purpose: the 'immediate' and the 'overall'. The 'immediate' object and purpose is explicitly mentioned in a specific IIA, and it predominantly includes foreign investment promotion and protection.[20] The 'overall', or inherent, object and purpose is the promotion of economic development, even if this wider context is not always

[18] J.W. Salacuse, *The Law of Investment Treaties* (OUP 2010) 1–17. See also S.W. Schill, *The Multilateralization of International Investment Law* (CUP 2009) 11–17, 318.

[19] On the theory of the 'innate' purpose of investment protection regime, see T.W. Waelde, 'The Specific Nature of Investment Arbitration' in P. Kahn and T.W. Waelde (eds), *New Aspects of International Investment Law* (Martinus Nijhoff 2007) 109–10; A. van Aaken and T.A. Lehmann, 'Investment and Sustainable Development: Developing a New Conceptual Framework' (2011) *University of St. Gallen Law & Economics Working Paper* No. 2011-10; available at: <http://ssrn.com/abstract=1893692> accessed 28 April 2019, 329: 'the object of the treaty may be investor protection, while the underlying purpose is (sustainable) development'.

[20] Derived from the titles of BITs—treaties between governments concerning the encouragement and reciprocal protection of investment.

explicitly indicated in a given IIA. For instance, the tribunal in *Charles Lemire v Ukraine* interpreted the 'old generation' Ukraine–US BIT (1996) and famously declared: 'The main purpose of the BIT is thus the stimulation of foreign investment and of the accompanying flow of capital... But this main purpose is not sought in abstract; it is inserted in a wider context, the economic development for both signatory countries.'[21]

This focus by the *Lemire* tribunal on the inherent object and purpose (economic development) was logical because promotion and protection of foreign investment is generally associated with economic development-related inputs such as long-term capital inflows to the host state, transfer of technology, access to new markets, and knowledge spillovers.[22] Hence, attracting foreign investment is meant to be one of the principal tools for pursuing economic development in our interconnected world.[23]

As a result, in their awards on 'old-generation' IIAs, some arbitral tribunals have invoked the inherent objective as part of a teleological interpretation of individual IIAs. Concern for the 'overall' object and purpose has made some tribunals shift away from the narrow focus of investment protection as a goal in and of itself,[24] allowing instead an appreciation of investment protection as a tool for the economic development of host states.

In the *Lemire* award, the tribunal not only established that economic development was the overall aim of foreign investment protection, it went so far as to state that '[e]conomic development is an objective which must benefit all, primarily national citizens and national companies, and secondarily foreign investors.'[25]

Hence, the economic development objective allows one to explain why states participate in the network of IIAs that 'might bite'[26] because they impose significant restrictions on a host state's regulatory powers. It also implies that enforcement of international investment protection law goes further than simply protecting foreign investors.

[21] ICSID, *Joseph Charles Lemire v Ukraine*, ICSID Case No. ARB/06/18, Decision on Jurisdiction and Liability of 14 January 2010, paras 272–273. See also UNCITRAL, *Saluka Investments BV v The Czech Republic*, Partial Award of 17 March 2006, paras 298-301. The Tribunal distinguished between an 'immediate' and 'broader' context for interpretation of FET in the Netherlands—Czech/Slovak Federal Republic BIT (1991).

[22] A.T. Guzman, 'Why LDCs Sign Treaties That Hurt Them: Explaining the Popularity of Bilateral Investment Treaties' (1997–1998) *38 Virginia Journal of International Law* 666–86.

[23] UNCTAD, *UNCTAD Report 'Development Implications of International Investment Agreements'* (2007), UNCTAD/WEB/ITE/IIA/2007/2.

[24] As represented in, e.g., ICSID, *Aguas del Tunari S.A. v Republic of Bolivia*, ICSID Case No. ARB/02/3, Decision on Respondent's Objections to Jurisdiction of 21 October 2005, paras 153, 241, 247; ICSID, *Noble Ventures, Inc. v Romania*, ICSID Case No. ARB/01/11, Award of 12 October 2005, para. 52.

[25] *Supra* note 26, para. 273. See also ICSID, *Amco Asia Corporation and others v Republic of Indonesia*, ICSID Case No. ARB/81/1, Decision on Jurisdiction of 25 September 1983, 23 ILM 351 (1984), para. 23: 'To protect investments is to protect the general interest of development and of developing countries.'

[26] Borrowing the phrase from M. Hallward-Driemeier, 'Do Bilateral Investment Treaties Attract FDI? Only a Bit ... and They Could Bite' in (2003) World Bank, *Policy Research Working Papers*, No. WPS 3121; available at: <http://www-wds.worldbank.org> accessed 28 April 2019.

2.2 Economic Development as a Generic Term

Arguably, the notion of economic development fulfils the criteria for being a generic term. Interpretation of a generic term requires it to be adapted to present-day realities at the time of application.

In order to justify an evolutionary interpretation of a treaty, international law requires the fulfilment of certain preconditions: the treaty (of continuing duration) must contain a generic legal term whose meaning over time the treaty parties have intended to change. As a logical consequence, one must identify authoritative statements that incorporate the present-day meaning of the generic term.[27]

First, the presumption regarding the existence of a generic term is strengthened where the treaty is of continuing duration. BITs are in force on average for ten years and their validity is automatically renewed unless one party notifies the other of termination of the treaty. Nonetheless, even in the event of termination, BITs do not cease to apply to established investments for another ten to twenty years, due to so-called sunset clauses. Renegotiations of existing BITs are undertaken hesitantly.[28] When they do occur, BITs are superseded by new BITs or free trade agreements (FTAs) that contain similar investment protection standards with few amendments.[29] Hence, it may be presumed that the network of IIAs functions as a legal regime of continuing duration.

Further, it must be proven that the generic term has content which 'the parties expected would change through time'.[30] The term 'economic development'—like the notions of 'exhaustible natural resources',[31] 'environment',[32] or 'sound recording distribution services'[33]—by its very logic and definition is not a static but a dynamic concept, requiring its interpretation 'in the light of modern day conditions'.[34]

That the meaning of the term 'economic development' was not static but had been evolving in due course of time was first affirmed at the UN Conference on the Human Environment in 1972, where the global community acknowledged economic growth as necessarily being limited by its environmental degradation

[27] R. Gardiner, *Treaty Interpretation, 2nd edn* (OUP 2015) 192–3, 467–78. See also P.-M. Dupuy, 'Evolutionary Interpretation of Treaties: Between Memory and Prophecy' in E. Cannizzaro (ed.) *The Law of Treaties. Beyond the Vienna Convention* (OUP 2011) 123–31.

[28] WIR 2016, 111.

[29] S.W. Schill, *The Multilateralization of International Investment Law* (CUP 2009) 265.

[30] *Case Concerning Kasikili/Sedudu Island (Botswana/Namibia)*, Judgment of 13 December 1999, ICJ Report 1999, 1113, Declaration of Judge Higgins, § 2–3.

[31] WTO, *United States—Import Prohibition of Certain Shrimp and Shrimp Products – Report of the Appellate Body*, WT/DS58/AB/R, 12 October 1998, paras 129–130.

[32] *The Legality of the Threat or Use of Nuclear Weapons*, Advisory Opinion, 6 July 1996, ICJ Reports (1996) 241, § 29.

[33] WTO, *China—Publications and Audiovisual Products—Report of the Appellate Body*, WT/DS363/AB/R, 21 December 2009, para. 398.

[34] R. Gardiner, *Treaty Interpretation* (OUP 2015) 274, using the phrasing in Feldbrugge v Netherlands, ECtHR case no 8/1984/80/127 (Judgment of 23 April 1986), Joint dissenting opinion at paras 23–24.

aspect.[35] This observation was also reflected in the *Gabčikovo-Nagymaros* case, where the International Court of Justice saw a need to reconcile economic development with protection of the environment.[36] Therefore, states participating in the network of IIAs must be presumed to be aware of the inherently generic nature of economic development as a legal term.

Finally, the current meaning of the term stems from the consensus reached at three widely attended UN conferences.[37] Today, the global community is firmly aware that a narrow focus on economic development should give way to a global commitment to promoting sustainable development in an effort to overcome or mitigate the negative externalities that economic development might bring. By way of example, Schreuer, in his commentary on the *Salini* test (which introduced contribution to the host state's economic development as one of the four intrinsic elements making up an investment, although currently the leading opinion treats it merely as a characteristic of investment) writes: 'Any concept of economic development ... should not be restricted to measurable contributions to GDP but should include development of human potential, political and social development and the protection of the local and global environment.'[38]

This contemporary notion of economic development is expressly integrated into the preambles and operative parts of 'new-generation' IIAs. For instance, numerous recent treaties contain 'no lowering of standards' clauses (standards commonly include health, environment, safety, and labour protection) and specific chapters on environmental matters.[39] Several 'new-generation' IIAs actually include explicit preambular references to promotion of sustainable development as being the objective of foreign investment protection: most notably, the Central American Free Trade Agreement (2004), the NAFTA (1994), the COMESA Common Investment Area Agreement (CIAA) 2007, the Slovakia–Iran BIT (2017), and recent Canada and US FTAs such as the Canada–Peru FTA (2009) or the US–Korea FTA (2011). By virtue of Articles 3 and 21 of the Treaty on the Functioning of the European Union, sustainable development is applicable to all internal and external actions

[35] Declaration of the United Nations Conference on the Human Environment, UN Doc A/Conf.48/14/Rev. 1(1973), 11 ILM 1416 (1972), para. 6: 'A point has been reached in history when we must shape our actions throughout the world with a more prudent care for their environmental consequences... To defend and improve the human environment for present and future generations has become an imperative goal for mankind—a goal to be pursued together with, and in harmony with, the established and fundamental goals of peace and of worldwide economic and social development.'

[36] *Gabčíkovo-Nagymaros Project (Hungary/Slovakia)*, Judgment of 25 September 1997, ICJ Reports 1997, 78.

[37] UN Conference on Environment and Development, 'Rio Declaration on Environment and Development', UN Doc A/CONF 151/26/Rev 1 Vol I, 3, 14 June 1992; UN World Summit on Sustainable Development, UN Doc A/AC.257/32, 26 August to 4 September 2002; UN Rio+20 Conference on Sustainable Development, UN Doc A/CONF.216/L.1., 20–22 June 2012.

[38] C.H. Schreuer with L. Malintoppi, A. Reinisch, and A. Sinclair, *The ICSID Convention. A Commentary, 2nd edn* (CUP 2009) 134, para. 174.

[39] S.A. Spears, 'The Quest for Policy Space in a New Generation of International Investment Agreements' (2010) 13 *Journal of International Economic Law* 4, 1037, at 1060–2.

and policies of the EU, including those regarding foreign investment,[40] as reflected in CETA negotiations and its eventual wording.

To conclude, the current sense of the term 'economic development' has evolved with the global community's commitment to harmonising economic development with environmental protection and social development, with evidence for the shift in meaning dating back at least as far as 1972.[41] More than a decade later, this commitment was encapsulated in the now ubiquitous term 'sustainable development'.[42]

This paradigm shift of putting economic development in context with the other pillars of sustainable development is not only reflected in the global commitments expressed by the UN but also mirrored in 'new-generation' IIAs, a number of which shift the focus of investment protection away from economic development in isolation and towards a more comprehensive view of various development factors. Consequently, the object and purpose of IIAs that reflect it narrowly (i.e., purely as economic development) are amenable to evolutionary treaty interpretation. One may claim that this more dynamic interpretation of the economic development purpose of IIAs may affect legal certainty in the eyes of foreign investors. Quite the contrary. It informs the content of their legitimate expectations against a host state.[43] With this in mind, states participating in the network of IIAs and investors enjoying IIA protection should be reasonably presumed to be aware of the inherently generic nature of economic development, which necessitates reasonable adjustments in order to accommodate present-day realities.

2.3 At the Core of Sustainable Development is the Principle of Integration

Identifying the content of sustainable development has turned out to be a complex and highly controversial issue. One way to reveal the term's content is to look at the so-called international law in the field of sustainable development, encompassing *lex lata* and a variety of emergent principles: the duty to cooperate for protection of the environment; the principle of equity and the eradication of poverty; strengthening the rule of law and good governance practices in states; providing

40 Art. 207(1) of the Consolidated version of the Treaty on the Functioning of the European Union, OJ C 326, 26 October 2012, 47–390.

41 *Supra* note 40.

42 The modern term 'sustainable development' was crystallized in the 1987 Report of the World Commission on Environment and Development, see World Commission on Environment and Development, *Our Common Future* (1987).

43 For instance, the *Methanex v US* and *Glamis Gold v US* tribunals rejected investors' expectations of legal stability due to the well-known fact that environmental regulations in California were gradually becoming more stringent, see NAFTA (UNCITRAL), *Methanex v United States of America*, Final Award of 3 August 2005, Part IV—Chapter D—Page 4, paras 7 and 8 and NAFTA (UNCITRAL), *Glamis Gold, Ltd. v The United States of America*, Award of 8 June 2009, para. 800.

civil society with equal access to justice and information; and the duty of states to enforce the sustainable use of natural resources.[44]

Another approach to revealing the content of the term 'sustainable development' involves assessing it as a process rather than a fulfilment of a certain standard of substance.[45] That was the method adopted in this study. One may narrow down the scope of this process to the so-called principle of integration of economic, social, and environmental aspects.[46] For instance, the final document of the Rio+20 Conference, 'The Future We Want',[47] declares in relevant parts: 'We therefore acknowledge the need to further mainstream sustainable development at all levels, integrating economic, social and environmental aspects and recognizing their interlinkages, so as to achieve sustainable development in all its dimensions.'[48]

As a result, one may conclude that the essence of sustainable development is generally agreed to be an equitable balance of economic development, social development, and environmental protection seeking to overcome the negative externalities of sheer economic development. As the inherent object and purpose of the investment protection regime, sustainable development can and should be considered in an effective interpretation of loose investment protection standards and their sub-elements, requiring some revision of the methodologies that arbitral tribunals use to motivate their awards.

3 Influence of the Sustainable Development Objective on Applicable Law and Interpretation of IIAs

This section deals with the role that the sustainable development context should play in applicable law, as well as interpreting (informing the content of) investment protection standards. [49]

[44] International Law Association, 'New Delhi Declaration of Principles of International Law Relating to Sustainable Development' (2002) 49(2) *Netherlands International Law Review* 299; M.-C. Cordonier Segger, 'Sustainable Development in International Law' in H.C. Bugge and C. Voigt (eds), *Sustainable Development in International and National Law* (Europa Law Publishing 2008) 163–76.

[45] A. Boyle and D. Freestone, 'Introduction' in A. Boyle and D. Freestone (eds), *International Law and Sustainable Development. Past Achievements and Future Challenges* (OUP 1999) 17.

[46] See also Principle 7 of the New Delhi Declaration—the principle of integration and interrelationship, in particular in relation to human rights and social, economic and environmental objectives, *supra* note 49: '7.2 All levels of governance—global, regional, national, subnational and local—and all sectors of society should implement the integration principle, which is essential to the achievement of sustainable development.'

[47] United Nations, *Outcome of the Conference 'The Future We Want'*, UN Doc A/CONF.216/L/1/, Rio de Janeiro, Brazil, 20–22 June 2012, para. 3.

[48] *Ibid.*

[49] Pauwelyn indicates the close ties between applicable law and treaty interpretation, which is the reason these elements are often addressed together; see J. Pauwelyn, 'Bridging Fragmentation and Unity: International Law as a Universe of Inter-Connected Islands' (2004) 25 *Michigan Journal of International Law* at 903, 910.

3.1 Applicable Law and Interpretation

Foreign investors have challenged a vast array of general legislative acts and administrative measures of host states that allegedly dealt with protection of non-economic public interests, arguing that they were expropriatory, unreasonable, or discriminatory practices. In response, states often invoke non-investment international law in their defence, whether to justify the rationality of their actions or to excuse alleged IIA violations. For instance, Argentina pointed to a potential conflict between relevant BITs and Argentina's human rights obligations[50] in *Azurix v Argentina*,[51] *Siemens v Argentina*,[52] and *Vivendi v Argentina (Resubmitted)*.[53] The need to safeguard the right to water was invoked by Tanzania and *amici curiae* in *Biwater Gauff v Tanzania*,[54] although the potential conflict of norms argument was entirely skipped by the tribunal. The *Santa Elena v Costa Rica*[55] tribunal ignored Costa Rica's request to take into account the 1972 UNESCO Convention, reliance on which had served as the motivation and justification for expropriating an investor's property.

The possibility that a tribunal might focus exclusively on foreign investment protection, disregarding any other interests involved, has raised concerns about the capacity left for host states to regulate in the public interest.[56]

Current arbitral jurisprudence does not exhibit a clear and predictable attitude vis-à-vis the need to consider and apply non-investment international law.[57] At different times, arbitral tribunals have been 'ignorant' of[58] as well as 'tolerant' towards the invocation of non-investment sources.

There is no longer any doubt that investment protection law is not autonomous from other legal regimes,[59] yet there are 'ignorant' arbitral tribunals that generally fail to recognize a link between external subfields of international law and

[50] These arguments were not addressed by the Tribunals due to alleged insufficient elaboration on the matter by Argentina.

[51] ICSID, *Azurix Corp. v the Argentine Republic*, ICSID Case No. ARB/01/12, Award of 14 July 2006, para. 261.

[52] ICSID, *Siemens A.G. v The Argentine Republic*, ICSID case No. ARB/02/8, Award of 6 February 2007, paras 75, 79, 312, 354.

[53] ICSID, *Compania de Aguas del Aconquija S.A. and Vivendi Universal S.A. v Argentine Republic*, ICSID Case No. ARB/97/3, Award of 20 August 2007, Resubmitted, paras 3.3.3–3.3.5.

[54] ICSID, *Biwater Gauff (Tanzania) Ltd v United Republic of Tanzania*, ICSID Case No. ARB/05/22, Award of 24 July 2008, paras 434, 436, 814.

[55] ICSID, *Compania del Desarrollo de Santa Elena S.A. v Costa Rica*, ICSID Case No. ARB/96/1, Award of 17 February 2000, paras 76 and 77.

[56] F. Francioni, 'Access to Justice, Denial of Justice and International Investment Law' (2009) 20(3) *European Journal of International Law* 729–47, 729.

[57] As also seen in investment cases dealing with intra-EU BITs.

[58] E.g., *Biwater Gauff (Tanzania) Ltd v United Republic of Tanzania, supra* note 59; *Compania de Aguas del Aconquija S.A. and Vivendi Universal S.A. v Argentine Republic, supra* note 58.

[59] Pauwelyn, *supra* note 54 at 903, 904, 915–16; IUSCT, *Amoco International Finance Corp. v Iran*, 15 Iran–USCT Report 189, at 222, para. 112; ICSID, *AAPL v Sri Lanka* (1990) (Award) 4 ICSID Rep 246, para. 21; ICSID, *Phoenix Action, Ltd. v the Czech Republic*, ICSID Case No. ARB/06/5, Award of 15 April 2009, paras 77–78.

specific IIAs.[60] Establishing linkage is not an easy task. It necessarily depends on the boundaries of the dispute involved and on the assertions being expressed by the disputing parties. It is also dependent on the subjective perception of arbitrators as to what scope of international investment protection law would be appropriate. In this respect, the sustainable development context of investment protection law necessarily clarifies what international rules may or may not be relevant for governing the resolution of a case (in other words, which rules would 'lie at the heart of the matter'), since the sustainable development context allows an extension of the applicable law to its three pillars.

3.1.1 'Conflict of norms' in a broad sense

Conflicts of norms can be potential ('in a broad sense') or genuine.[61] A genuine conflict of norms is a situation where the application of one norm excludes the application of another.[62] By contrast, a potential conflict of norms means that the application of a treaty may frustrate the goals of another treaty even though there is no incompatibility between their provisions in a strict sense.[63] The latter sort of conflict can be overcome[64] by the presumption against conflict,[65] or by expressly informing the content of one treaty's norms by reference to the norms of another treaty (interpreting away the conflict through teleological, effective, and evolutionary treaty interpretation),[66] or by applying the systemic integration principle as established by Article 31(3)(c) of the Vienna Convention on the Law of Treaties.[67]

3.1.2 'Informing the content' of investment guarantees by reference to external areas of law

Investment protection guarantees are composed of a variety of sub-elements. For instance, national treatment (NT) and most-favoured nation (MFN) treatment standards require an analysis of the 'in like circumstances' element, whereas FET and indirect expropriation standards contain a 'legitimate investment-backed expectations' element. As the object and purpose of investment law, sustainable development can provide the necessary link between investment law and other, *prima*

[60] J.E. Viñuales, *Foreign Investment and the Environment in International Law* (CUP 2012) 182.

[61] J. Pauwelyn, *Conflict of Norms in Public International Law. How WTO Law Relates to Other Rules of International Law* (CUP 2003) 176–8.

[62] W. Jenks, 'Conflict of Law-Making Treaties' (1953) 30 *British Yearbook of International Law* 401 at 426, 451.

[63] R. Wolfrum and N. Matz, *Conflicts in International Environmental Law* (Springer-Verlag: Berlin 2003) 6–13.

[64] Pauwelyn, *supra* note 66, 165–6.

[65] Pauwelyn, *supra* note 66, 240–4.

[66] *Ibid.*, 244ff

[67] B. Simma and T. Kill, 'Harmonizing Investment Protection and International Human Rights: First Steps Towards a Methodology' in C. Binder, U. Kriebaum, A. Reinisch, and S. Wittich (eds), *International Investment Law for the 21st Century. Essays in Honour of Christoph Schreuer* (OUP 2009) 705.

facie external areas of law to enable reference to these external norms and thereby to inform the content of investment guarantees, in particular their sub-elements.

For example, the *Santa Elena v Costa Rica* tribunal entirely disregarded the possible legal impact of the UNESCO Convention on the content of legitimate expectations that the investor could have regarding the prospective profit of its project.[68] In contrast, in *SPP v Egypt*, the tribunal took into consideration the point in time at which the 1972 UNESCO Convention became effective in Egypt, deciding not to award *lucrum cessans* from the date of inclusion of the project site in the World Heritage List. From that date on, the investment project had effectively been illegal, and the investor was deemed to have lost its legitimate expectations of profit from the intended business activity.[69]

It is therefore evident that investment tribunals may be flexible enough to incorporate arguments from external international law into the process of interpreting investment guarantees. However, this requires a certain mindset from the arbitrators applying investment norms. The sustainable development context arguably calls for them to exercise their inherent powers in a way that references the principle of integration and reveals the pragmatic link between investment protection standards and *prima facie* external norms.

3.2 Influence on the 'Background Theory' of Arbitrators

Koskenniemi explains an adjudicator's 'background theory' as the interaction between the postulated values and goals of the legal system and reflection on them by adjudicators who operate within that legal system.[70] While resolving a legal dispute, adjudicators identify and apply certain principles because their 'background' sets it as their institutional function, part of the expectations set for them.[71]

The context of sustainable development may substantially affect the scope of arbitrators' 'background', driving them to act in a way that applies the purpose and goals of the legal regime, namely the general commitment to promote sustainable development (and its integration principle).

The coexistence of variously 'ignorant' and 'tolerant' approaches towards external areas of law may be explained by the subjective perception that an arbitral tribunal has of its proper role and powers.[72] This diversity in approaching the roles

[68] *Compania del Desarrollo de Santa Elena S.A. v Costa Rica, supra* note 60.

[69] ICSID, *Southern Pacific Properties (SPP) (Middle East) Limited v Arab Republic of Egypt*, ICSID Case No. ARB/84/3, Award of 20 May 1992, paras 190–191.

[70] M. Koskenniemi, 'General Principles: Reflections on Constructivist Thinking in International Law' in M. Koskenniemi (ed.), *Sources of International Law* (2000) 155–6.

[71] *Ibid.*, at 138.

[72] Fauchald distinguishes two extremes—a 'dispute-oriented' tribunal that would focus merely on the relationship between the litigating parties, and a 'legislator-oriented' tribunal, which would also take into account such factors as third party interests, the general functioning of the ICSID system, the potential impact of its reasoning or conclusions for future cases and so on; see O.K. Fauchald,

of investment treaty tribunals also stems from the 'hybrid foundations' of investor–state arbitration, a mixture of public and private international law.[73] Its procedure and enforcement borrows mainly from commercial arbitration, while its content is predominantly governed by public international law,[74] since investor–state arbitration is intended to deal with alleged breaches of a host state's international obligations towards investors.[75]

Some arbitral tribunals have taken the 'service providers' approach similar to that of private commercial arbitration.[76] As a 'service provider', an investment treaty tribunal's engagement is limited to addressing the arguments of the pleading parties without considering the wider context and the consequences of its award.[77]

Conversely, arbitral tribunals that perceive foreign investment protection as 'an emerging system of public law'[78] have instead taken a 'guardians of law' approach recognized in the practice of public law.[79] The public law approach requires them to take into account not only the arguments of pleading parties but also the wider circumstances of a case, such as third party interests, or the effect that the case might have on the legal regime as a whole.[80]

Because the investor–state arbitration mechanism is intended as an effective replacement for national and international courts in adjudicating the legitimacy of national legislative or administrative acts that are challenged by foreign investors, there are grounds for dissatisfaction with the 'service providers' approach.[81] Due to their capacity to review domestic legislative and administrative acts, investor–state arbitrations may, and often do, involve public interests that considerably exceed

'Legal Reasoning of ICSID Tribunals—an Empirical Analysis' *European Journal of International Law* (2008) 2(19) 307.

[73] Z. Douglas, 'The Hybrid Foundations of Investment Treaty Arbitration' *British Yearbook of International Law* 151 (2003 page).

[74] Schreuer et al., *supra* note 43, 560–2, paras 33–36]

[75] ICSID, *Wintershall Aktiengesellschaft v Argentine Republic*, ICSID Case No. ARB/04/14, Award of 8 December 2008, para. 160: 'The ICSID Convention [. . .] combines a public law system of State liability with private arbitration.'

[76] E.g., *Siemens AG v Republic of Argentina, supra* note 57, para. 81.

[77] For favouring the 'service providers' approach, see G. Cordero Moss, 'Tribunal's Powers versus Party Autonomy' in P. Muchlinski, F. Ortino, and C. Schreuer (eds), *The Oxford Handbook of International Investment Law* (OUP 2008); T.W. Waelde, 'Interpreting Investment Treaties: Experiences and Examples, in Investor–state Arbitration' in Binder et al., *supra* note 72.

[78] A. Mills, 'Antinomies of Public and Private at the Foundations of International Investment Law and Arbitration' (2011)14 *Journal of International Economic Law* 2, 469–503, at 500.

[79] *Glamis Gold, Ltd. v The United States of America, supra* note 48, paras 3–9; *Biwater Gauff v Tanzania, supra* note 48; *Methanex v United States, supra* note 11, paras 47, 49.

[80] ICSID, *Saipem S.p.A. v The People's Republic of Bangladesh*, ICSID Case No. ARB/05/07, Decision on Jurisdiction and Recommendation on Provisional Measures of 21 March 2007, para. 67.

[81] For a criticism of the 'service providers' approach, see G. van Harten, *International Treaty Arbitration and Public Law* (xxx 2007) 457; C. Schreuer and U. Kriebaum, 'From Individual to Community Interest in International Investment Law' in U. Fastenrath et al., (eds) *From Bilateralism to Community Interest: Essays in Honour of Bruno Simma* (xxx 2011) 1096.

the interests of the respective pleading parties.[82] Thus, for instance, in *Glamis Gold v United States*, the tribunal noted that 'the decision in this proceeding has been awaited by private and public entities concerned with environmental regulation, the interests of indigenous peoples, and the tension sometimes seen between private rights in property and the need of the State to regulate the use of property'.[83]

Investment litigation may have a significant impact on the future behaviour of host states, their budgets, and the welfare of their citizens.[84] This concern is not addressed if a tribunal reflects on itself as merely a 'service provider' between two litigating parties. Therefore, a group of scholars already insist that the 'service providers' approach is outdated and must be replaced by the 'guardians of law' approach. For instance, Petersmann correlates the need to adopt the 'guardians of law' approach with the customary law duty of adjudicators to decide cases in accordance with the principles of justice.[85] The sustainable development context invites the same conclusion, in addition filling the abstract term 'justice' with specific content requiring rather precise practical implications for the process of interpreting investment guarantees, to balance all three pillars of sustainable development. Consequently, the *Santa Elena v Costa Rica*-like approach to external sources of law would be outdated and no longer in line with the general context of investment protection law.

To conclude, the sustainable development context allows a reassessment of the role of investment treaty tribunals and confers a public law dimension on investment treaty claims. That, in turn, necessitates ensuring that economic interests are not prioritized but balanced and reconciled with competing public interests.

4 Conclusions

International investment law is in a crisis, and essentially there are two options to address it, either by redrafting, terminating IIAs, and radically changing the regime (e.g., withdrawing from investor–state dispute settlement) or, as this study suggests, systemically rethinking the regime from within.

As concerns the latter, foreign investment protection is not a goal unto itself. Rather, it is a tool for achieving a broader aim: economic development in the host country, with its negative social and environmental externalities reined in by accommodating the other two pillars of sustainable development.

[82] H. Mann, *Private Rights, Public Problems: A Guide to NAFTA's Controversial Chapter on Investor Rights* (xxx 2001).

[83] *Glamis Gold, Ltd. v The United States of America*, NAFTA (UNCITRAL), *supra* note 48, para. 8.

[84] *Supra* note 11.

[85] E.-U. Petersmann, 'Multilevel Trade Governance Requires Multilevel Constitutionalism' in C. Joerges and E.U. Petersmann (eds), *Constitutionalism, Multilevel Trade Governance and Social Regulations* (Hart Publishing 2006) 5, 34.

With this reconceptualization in mind, the author has argued that investment law as it stands is capable of achieving the inherent sustainable development objective for the following main reasons. The sustainable development context provides the necessary doctrinal foundation for incorporating *prima facie* non-investment obligations into the investment context. Sustainable development thereby necessitates a 'systemic' thinking of international investment law, implying that investment protection law is not autonomous from other legal regimes, offering a new mechanism of 'defragmentation'. It explicitly requires that competing commercial and public interests are reconciled by choosing appropriate language and argumentation methods, which gives space for weighing conflicting factors such as investment protection and a range of public interests, thereby addressing the structural bias inherent in investment law. Further, arbitral jurisprudence has gradually split investment guarantees into various sub-elements. This facilitates assessment of a compensable political risk, like the legitimate expectations which form part of FET and IE standards. These sub-elements can function as entry points for environmental, human rights, and other kinds of concerns when the content of investment guarantees is informed. If applied in light of the integration principle of sustainable development, they set a higher threshold for gauging the reasonableness of an investor's expectations and provide a broader framework for internalizing the risks of a particular investment activity as non-compensatable commercial risks.

The proposed reconceptualization of the existing network of IIAs would ensure that states retain their policy space, addressing the emergent concerns of the international community from within the current system.

The Paris Agreement and the Future of the Climate Regime

Reflections on an International Law Odyssey

*Annalisa Savaresi**

1 Introduction

Climate change has been described as a risk 'multiplier' exacerbating virtually all crises facing humanity in the twenty-first century,[1] and thus requiring unprecedented levels of international cooperation.[2] International cooperation on climate change has a short but rather eventful history. On other environmental matters, such as protected areas or fresh water, multilateral cooperation is only a relatively recent addition to well-established regulatory and governance[3] arrangements at the national and regional level.[4] Conversely, climate change efforts started at the international level, and only subsequently trickled down to the national and regional level. This peculiarity can be explained by the global nature of climate change and by the relatively recent scientific awareness of the problem. By comparison with other international regimes, therefore, the climate change regime is

* This chapter builds and expands upon the author's previous works, including: Annalisa Savaresi, 'The Paris Agreement: A New Beginning?' (2016) 34 *Journal of Energy & Natural Resources Law* 16; Annalisa Savaresi, 'The Paris Agreement: A Rejoinder' https://www.ejiltalk.org/the-paris-agreement-a-rejoinder/; Annalisa Savaresi, 'A Glimpse into the Future of the Climate Regime: Lessons from the REDD+ Architecture' (2016) 25 *Review of European, Comparative & International Environmental Law* 186.

[1] 'Global Risks 2014' (World Economic Forum), part 1 <http://wef.ch/GJkRdk> accessed 28 April 2019.

[2] David Archer and Stefan Rahmstorf, *The Climate Crisis: An Introductory Guide to Climate Change* (CUP 2009) 230.

[3] Drawing on Laurence E. Lynn Jr, 'The Many Faces of Governance: Adaptation? Transformation? Both? Neither?' in David Levi-Faur (ed.), *The Oxford Handbook of Governance* (OUP 2012), the term governance is used in this chapter to refer to the act of 'directing, guiding, or regulating' state conduct or actions, including through the design of international processes and institutions. *Ibid.*, 49.

[4] In relation to protected areas, see, e.g., Alexander Gillespie, *Protected Areas and International Environmental Law* (Brill 2007) 7–26. In relation to watercourses, see, e.g., Ariel Dinar and others, *Bridges Over Water: Understanding Transboundary Water Conflict, Negotiation and Cooperation* (World Scientific Publishing Company 2013) 58–74.

Annalisa Savaresi, *The Paris Agreement and the Future of the Climate Regime: Reflections on an International Law Odyssey Protection* In: *How International Law Works in Times of Crisis*. Edited by: George Ulrich and Ineta Ziemele, Oxford University Press (2019).
DOI: 10.1093/oso/9780198849667.003.0012

still a relatively new addition to the international law family, and is an especially troubled one. Indeed, the history of international climate change law thus far may be likened to an odyssey.

Since 1992, states have struggled to stabilize greenhouse gas concentrations in the atmosphere 'at a level that would prevent dangerous anthropogenic interference with the climate system'.[5] The treaty laying the foundations of international climate change governance—the 1992 United Nations Framework Convention on Climate Change (UNFCCC)—does not contain much detail on action that parties should undertake to achieve this objective. Instead the UNFCCC rather typically performs a 'constitutional' role,[6] sketching out a series of principles guiding parties' action, and an institutional framework for inter-state cooperation.[7] The main components of this architecture are a set of substantive obligations concerning achievement of the objective of the Convention (i.e., mitigation of climate change and adaptation to the adverse consequences thereof), and procedural obligations to enable the review of implementation of substantive obligations. Furthermore, the UNFCCC sketches a framework to enable international cooperation through provision of finance, capacity building, and exchange of information. The Convention only performs a limited 'regulatory' role,[8] envisioning the progressive development of parties' obligations through the adoption of protocols and the rule-making activities of treaty bodies.[9] This approach is far from unusual, and may rather be regarded as established practice under Multilateral Environmental Agreements (MEAs).[10]

Only one protocol to the Convention has been adopted, namely, the 1997 Kyoto Protocol to the UNFCCC.[11] The protocol was meant to phase out greenhouse gas emissions progressively, pursuant to a 'targets and timetables' approach[12] similar to that embedded in the Montreal Protocol to the 1985 Vienna Convention for the Protection of the Ozone Layer.[13] The Kyoto Protocol, however, has not enjoyed the same success as its model treaty[14] and has largely failed to deliver the hoped-for

[5] United Nations Framework Convention on Climate Change (New York, 9 May 1992; in force 21 March 1994) (*UNFCCC*), Art. 2.

[6] For this use of terminology, see P. Birnie, A. Boyle, and C. Redgwell, *International Law and the Environment, 3rd edn* (OUP 2009) 9.

[7] UNFCCC, Arts 3 and 7–11, respectively.

[8] For this use of terminology, see Birnie, Boyle, and Redgwell, *supra* note 6, at 9.

[9] UNFCCC, Arts 7.1 and 17.

[10] Robin R. Churchill and Geir Ulfstein, 'Autonomous Institutional Arrangements in Multilateral Environmental Agreements: A Little-Noticed Phenomenon in International Law' (2000) 94 *American Journal of International Law* 623.

[11] Kyoto Protocol to the United Nations Framework Convention on Climate Change (Kyoto, 11 December 1997, in force 16 February 2005) ('Kyoto Protocol').

[12] The conceptualization of a targets and timetables, as opposed to a pledge and review, approach to climate governance is operated in the works of Daniel Bodansky, starting with Daniel Bodansky, 'The Emerging Climate Change Regime' (1995) 20 *Annual Review of Energy and the Environment* 425.

[13] Montreal Protocol on Substances that Deplete the Ozone Layer (Montreal, 16 September 1987, in force 1 January 1989).

[14] As noted most famously in Scott Barrett, *Why Cooperate? The Incentive to Supply Global Public Goods, 1st edn* (OUP 2007), at 94–5.

results. Its bifurcated approach to the differentiation between parties' obligations and almost exclusive reliance on developed countries efforts[15] have been superseded by circumstances, most saliently, the dramatic increase of emissions in developing countries.

As parties squabbled over the means to either reform or replace the Kyoto Protocol's architecture, international climate governance has progressively become a highly fragmented affair.[16] This is exemplified by the emergence of a multitude of law-making and governance processes outwith those designed by international climate change treaties.[17] International climate change governance has in this connection been likened to the Cambrian explosion, whereby 'a wide array of diverse institutional forms emerges, and through selection and accident a few are chosen', and where the architecture designed under the UNFCCC and the Kyoto Protocol is 'particularly important' but 'not unrivalled'.[18]

Implementation of climate change treaties has produced important results, when one considers the high level of compliance with parties' reporting obligations, and with the targets embedded in the Kyoto Protocol.[19] Yet the action undertaken to date has undoubtedly been inadequate to tackle climate change, raising concerns about the adequacy of existing governance arrangements.

After much tribulation, and the near collapse of the regime in 2009, the quest for better international cooperation on climate change resulted in the adoption of the 2015 Paris Agreement. Expectations of this new treaty could scarcely be greater: the Paris Agreement is meant to provide a framework to improve international cooperation on climate change, and to keep the world within the global mean temperature-change goal identified by scientists as safe.[20] Yet, whether and how this important objective will be reached largely depends, on the one hand, on the supporting political will and, on the other, on the redesign of the international

[15] Kyoto Protocol, Art. 3 and Annex B.

[16] The literature on this issue is vast. See, e.g.: Oran Young, *The Institutional Dimensions of Environmental Change: Fit, Interplay, and Scale* (MIT Press 2002); Frank Biermann et al., 'The Fragmentation of Global Governance Architectures: A Framework for Analysis' (2009) 9 *Global Environmental Politics* 14; Cinnamon P. Carlarne, 'Good Climate Governance: Only a Fragmented System of International Law Away?' (2008) 30 *Law & Policy* 450; Harro van Asselt, Francesco Sindico, and Michael Mehling, 'Global Climate Change and the Fragmentation of International Law' (2008) 30 *Law & Policy* 423; Harro van Asselt, *The Fragmentation of Global Climate Governance: Consequences and Management of Regime Interactions* (Edward Elgar Publishing 2014).

[17] On the informalization of the climate regime, see Harro van Asselt, Michael Mehling, and Clarisse Siebert, 'The Changing Architecture of International Climate Change Law' in Geert van Calster, Wim Vanderberghe, and Leonie Reins (eds), *Research Handbook on Climate Change Mitigation Law* (Edward Elgar Publishing 2015), at 5; and Duncan French and Lavanya Rajamani, 'Climate Change and International Environmental Law: Musings on a Journey to Somewhere' (2013) 25 *Journal of Environmental Law* 437, at 446.

[18] Robert O. Keohane and David G. Victor, 'The Regime Complex for Climate Change' (2011) 9 *Perspectives on Politics* 7, at 12.

[19] See Michael Grubb, 'Full Legal Compliance with the Kyoto Protocol's First Commitment Period – Some Lessons' (2016) *Climate Policy* 1.

[20] Paris Agreement, Art. 2.1(a).

architecture for climate governance. These rather thorny matters hang in the balance of ongoing negotiations on the so-called rule book of the Paris Agreement, which are meant to conclude by the end of 2018.[21]

This chapter reflects on this ongoing process, in light of the evolution of international climate change law-making and governance to date, focusing on challenges that have faced implementation of existing arrangements, and on the suitability of the Paris Agreement to address these. The chapter follows a two-pronged approach. The first part reflects on international climate change law-making, and on practice since adoption of the Paris Agreement. The second part considers the shift in international climate change governance, from a 'targets and timetables' to a 'pledge and review' approach. Whilst the suitability of the latter approach to deliver the solution to climate change remains to be tested, this chapter looks at the past of the climate regime, to gauge where implementation of the Paris Agreement may lead, as well as to identify potential pitfalls lying ahead.

2 International Climate Law-Making and its Complexities

The Paris Agreement was adopted by consensus at the twenty-first conference of the Parties (COP) to the UNFCCC.[22] The agreement was from the outset meant to be 'a protocol, another legal instrument or an agreed outcome with legal force' under the UNFCCC.[23] The issue of legal form, nevertheless, was an elephant in the room during much of the lengthy negotiation that led to adoption of the new agreement.[24]

At one end of the spectrum, some parties favoured a protocol. This is in keeping with the practice of seeking to perfect and further substantiate parties' obligations under framework conventions, such as the UNFCCC, by adopting ancillary treaties, commonly referred to as protocols.[25] On the other end of the spectrum, other parties were uneasy about the legal form of the Paris Agreement. The United States had domestic political reasons to ask that the agreement's legal form be left undetermined, so as to enable presidential ratification without the approval of the US senate.[26] Other parties too, however, were wary of the legal implications

[21] Decision 1/CMA.1 Matters relating to the implementation of the Paris Agreement, (UN Doc FCCC/PA/CMA/2016/3/Add.1, 31 January 2017), at 5.

[22] Decision 1/CP.21, Adoption of the Paris Agreement, (UN Doc FCCC/CP/2015/10, Add.1, 29 January 2016).

[23] Decision 1/CP.17, Establishment of an Ad Hoc Working Group on the Durban Platform for Enhanced Action (UN Doc FCCC/CP/2011/9/Add, 15 March 2012), at 2.

[24] Annalisa Savaresi, 'UN Climate Change Negotiations: Last Tango in Paris?' <http://www.ejiltalk.org/un-climate-change-negotiations-last-tango-in-paris/> accessed 28 April 2019.

[25] Daniel Bodansky, *The Art and Craft of International Environmental Law* (Harvard University Press 2011), at 151–2.

[26] As noted, e.g., at a hearing before the Environment and Public Works Committee of the United States Senate, Testimony of Julian Ku and Maurice A. Deane 'Examining the International Climate

attached to encapsulating the new architecture enshrined in the Paris Agreement in a treaty.

In spite of some confusion at the time of its adoption,[27] the Paris Agreement is, without doubt, an international treaty. This conclusion is compelled by the fact that the agreement is endowed with typical features of a treaty. For example, the agreement is structured in articles and it includes standard treaty provisions concerning ratification, the depositary, and so on.[28] Most conclusively, the Paris Agreement has been treated as a treaty by its now 174 parties, which brought about its entry in force much earlier than anticipated, following a record-breaking ratification process.[29]

In substance, the Paris Agreement is an ancillary treaty to the UNFCCC, and possibly a protocol in all but name.[30] It hinges on the principles[31] and institutional arrangements established by the Convention,[32] the implementation of which it is mandated to enhance.[33] As such, the agreement is not expected to dismantle the pre-existing international climate change governance architecture but rather to build upon it.[34] While the core ingredients of the regulatory framework have remained the same—that is, substantive obligations concerning mitigation and adaptation, as well as procedural obligations to enable the review of implementation of these—much of the normative content of the Paris Agreement is incompatible with the continued existence of the governance architecture established by the Kyoto Protocol. The agreement is nevertheless silent on the fate of the protocol and of the complex governance arrangements and obligations it established, which therefore hang in the balance.

Another matter that engendered animated debate after adoption of the Paris Agreement is whether or not it is 'legally binding'.[35] Again, there is scarcely any

Negotiations' 18 November 2015; available at: <https://www.epw.senate.gov/public/_cache/files/29525f03-9fc4-4112-9488-701f3dc1e8d1/ku-testimony.pdf> accessed 28 April 2019.

[27] As noted, e.g., in Joust Pauwelyn and Lilliana Andonova, 'A "Legally Binding Treaty" or Not? The Wrong Question for Paris Climate Summit' <https://www.ejiltalk.org/a-legally-binding-treaty-or-not-the-wrong-question-for-paris-climate-summit/> accessed 28 April 2019; and Daniel Bodansky, 'The Legal Character of the Paris Agreement: A Primer' <http://opiniojuris.org/2015/12/02/the-legal-character-of-the-paris-agreement-a-primer/> accessed 28 April 2019.

[28] Paris Agreement, Arts 20 and 27, respectively. See also reflections in Daniel Bodansky, 'The Legal Character of the Paris Agreement' (2016) 25 *Review of European, Comparative & International Environmental Law* 142.

[29] Christina Voigt, 'On the Paris Agreement's Imminent Entry Into Force' <http://www.ejiltalk.org/on-the-paris-agreements-imminent-entry-into-force/> accessed 28 April 2019.

[30] As argued also in Annalisa Savaresi, 'The Paris Agreement: A New Beginning?' (2016) 34 *Journal of Energy & Natural Resources Law* 16, at 20.

[31] Paris Agreement, Preamble and Art. 2.

[32] *Ibid.*, Arts 16–18.

[33] *Ibid.*, Art. 2.1.

[34] See, e.g., Paris Agreement, Art. 13.13 and Decision 1/CP.21, Adoption of the Paris Agreement, UN Doc FCCC/CP/2015/10/Add.1, 29 January 2016, at 98.

[35] As noted, e.g., in Bodansky, *supra* note 28.

doubt that, as any other treaty, the Paris Agreement is formally binding upon its parties. As with any other treaty, however, the scope of parties' obligations clearly depends on the language in each provision. Some provisions establish categorical obligations, such as the obligation to pursue domestic mitigation measures, or to submit 'Nationally Determined Contributions' (NDCs).[36] Others, instead, are expressed in non-categorical terms, like that concerning the move by developing countries towards emission reduction targets.[37] Others again have a merely enabling character, and aim to facilitate internationally coordinated action, rather than prescribe it, such as provisions on the joint implementation of parties' mitigation obligations.[38] In practice, the contours of states' obligations under the Paris Agreement do not depend only on the terms used in each provision. The practice of implementation may turn what sound like hortatory provisions into a sophisticated web of reciprocal state obligations. Conversely, the practice of implementation may turn into a dead letter what were seemingly construed as categorical obligations.

The climate regime provides eloquent examples of both. One example of the first type of practice concerns the body of rules concerning REDD+.[39] These rules have emerged in a tumultuous fashion, from a long string of decisions adopted by the UNFCCC COP,[40] which are *ex se* non-legally binding.[41] These rules nevertheless detail a set of obligations, which are now understood to encumber parties wishing to carry out REDD+ activities.[42]

Conversely, the Kyoto Protocol features several examples of categorically formulated obligations that have progressively descended into irrelevance. The protocol's targets and timelines for the progressive reduction of emissions in developed countries were multilaterally negotiated in a process of political bargaining, which was enshrined in treaty form.[43] But even though the protocol unequivocally requires all developed country parties to adopt successive targets over time,[44] faltering political

[36] Paris Agreement, Art. 4.2.

[37] *Ibid.* Art. 4.4.

[38] *Ibid.*, Art. 6.

[39] The acronym stands for Reducing Emissions from Deforestation and forest Degradation in developing countries, and the scope of activities covered was progressively expanded to cover also the role of conservation, sustainable management of forests, and enhancement of forest carbon stocks in developing countries (hence the '+'). See Decision 1/CP.16, The Cancun Agreements: Outcome of the Work of the Ad Hoc Working Group on Long-term Cooperative Action under the Convention (UN Doc FCCC/CP/2010/7/Add.1, 15 March 2011), at 70.

[40] These decisions are recalled in the Paris Agreement, Art. 5.2.

[41] As noted, e.g., in Jutta Brunnée, 'COPing with Consent: Law-Making Under Multilateral Environmental Agreements' (2002) 15 *Leiden Journal of International Law* 1.

[42] As argued in Christina Voigt and Felipe Ferreira, 'The Warsaw Framework for REDD: Implications for National Implementation and Access to Results-Based Finance' (2015) 9 *Carbon & Climate Law Review* 113; Christina Voigt, 'Introduction: The Kaleidoscopic World of REDD' in Christina Voigt (ed.), *Research Handbook on REDD+ and International Law* (Edward Elgar Publishing 2016); and Annalisa Savaresi, 'The Legal Status and Role of Safeguards' in Christina Voigt (ed.), *Research Handbook on REDD+ and International Law* (Edward Elgar Publishing 2016).

[43] Kyoto Protocol, Art. 3.1 and Annex B.

[44] *Ibid.*, Art. 3.9.

will has made it impossible to continue with this approach. The Doha Amendment to the Kyoto Protocol has never entered into force, which means that the targets enshrined in it are not formally legally binding on parties.[45]

Far from being unique to the climate regime, this fuzziness in sources and in the related normative content is a typical feature of MEAs. So-called autonomous institutional arrangements[46] have rendered MEAs living instruments into which, in Brown Weiss's words, parties 'continuously breathe life and to which they give new directions by acting as informal legislatures'.[47] MEA treaty bodies regularly perform a variety of law-making functions. At times these functions are an emanation of specific delegated rule-making powers.[48] The rationale for entrusting treaty bodies with adopting such rules is to enable the periodical adjustment and review of technical details that would scarcely be suited to be embedded in treaty text.[49] At other times, decisions by treaty bodies may be regarded as authoritative interpretations of the terms of the treaties, and the practice of implementation may render these decisions obligatory.[50] Establishing whether or not the decisions of treaty bodies impose obligations on parties, therefore, requires context-specific assessment.[51]

Even by the standards of MEAs, international climate change law is remarkable for its latitude. The UNFCCC COP, its subsidiary bodies[52] and their homologues under the Kyoto Protocol[53] have been extremely prolific international law-making machines. They have adopted hundreds of decisions and established dozens of institutions, which together constitute one of the largest international environmental bureaucracies in existence. The treaty bodies of the climate regime have thus typically 'amplified' the terms of climate treaties, filling in their 'open-textured'[54] provisions with content. This has been done by adopting both hard rules that parties are expected to uphold,[55] as well as soft guidance. Indeed, the latter may be regarded as 'subsequent practice in the application of the treaty which establishes the agreement of the parties regarding its interpretation,'

[45] Doha Amendment to the Kyoto Protocol, Doha, 8 December 2012, not in force.

[46] See Churchill and Ulfstein, *supra* note 28, at 623.

[47] Edith Brown Weiss, 'The Rise or the Fall of International Law' (2000) 69 *Fordham Law Review* 345, at 352.

[48] See, e.g., Kyoto Protocol, Art. 6.2. Cf. also Churchill and Ulfstein, *supra* note 28, at 639.

[49] As noted in A.E. Boyle and C.M. Chinkin, *The Making of International Law* (OUP 2007) 216; C.C. Shaffer and M.A. Pollack, 'Hard vs. Soft Law: Alternatives, Complements, and Antagonists in International Governance' (2009) 94 *Minnesota Law Review* 706, at 719.

[50] As suggested also in Boyle and Chinkin, *supra* note 49, at 151–2.

[51] As pointed out also in van Asselt, Sindico, and Mehling, *supra* note 16, at 430.

[52] UNFCCC, Art. 7.2(i).

[53] Kyoto Protocol, Art. 13.4.

[54] This use of terminology is borrowed from Alan E. Boyle, 'Some Reflections on the Relationship of Treaties and Soft Law' (1999) 48 *The International and Comparative Law Quarterly* 901.

[55] Building upon specific mandates conferred upon them by the treaties, e.g., Kyoto Protocol, Arts 3.4 and 12.7.

pursuant to Article 31(3)(b) Vienna Convention on the Law of Treaties.[56] The UNFCCC and the Kyoto Protocol are therefore conspicuous examples of living international law instruments, and the negotiated expression of parties' consensus, enshrined in guidance adopted by treaty bodies has become the backbone of the climate regime.[57]

The adoption of the Paris Agreement marked the beginning of a new rule-making process whereby parties are expected to fill with content the open-textured provisions in the treaty, through its so-called rule book, by the end of 2018. The total or partial shelving of the architecture built with the Kyoto Protocol and the building of the institutional and regulatory architecture envisioned in the Paris Agreement requires considerable adjustment in international climate change governance. This gargantuan reform process was always expected to take time and is no mean undertaking for bodies operating on the basis of consensus, in a process with almost 200 parties, where institutional viscosity and 'lowest common denominator outcomes'[58] are the norm.

Prolonged rule-making processes are standard practice after the adoption of constitutional treaties,[59] such as the Paris Agreement. Nevertheless, thus far, the process for making the Paris Agreement's rule book has been marked by much complexity and by a high level of controversy.[60] The remarkable institutional complexity of the climate regime has meant that even the matter of which subsidiary body does what in the drafting of the rule book had to be painstakingly negotiated.[61] The early entry into force of the Paris Agreement complicated matters further, forcing parties to decide which tasks ought to be reserved to the treaty bodies of the agreement, and which could be overseen by UNFCCC treaty bodies.[62] So, even though parties gave themselves until the end of 2018 to agree on the Paris Agreement rule book, delivery of this crucial piece of the climate regime is proving difficult, and time is running short already.

[56] Vienna Convention on the Law of Treaties (Vienna, 23 May 1969, in force 27 January 1980) 115 UNTS 331. On the legal status of treaty bodies decisions, see Boyle, *supra* note 24, at 905 and 903, respectively.

[57] As noted also in Duncan French and Lavanya Rajamani, 'Climate Change and International Environmental Law: Musings on a Journey to Somewhere' (2013) 25 *Journal of Environmental Law* 437, at 445.

[58] As suggested also in Boyle and Chinkin, *supra* note 49, at 159.

[59] On the notion of constitutional treaties, see Birnie et al., *supra* note 6, at 9–10.

[60] As noted also in Jennifer Allan et al., 'Earth Negotiations Bulletin: Summary of the Fiji/Bonn Climate Change Conference' (IISD 2017) <http://enb.iisd.org/vol12/enb12714e.html> accessed 28 April 2019.

[61] Decision 1/CP.21 entrusts some issues to the COP serving as the meeting of the Parties to the Paris Agreement and the UNFCCC subsidiary bodies; others are entrusted to the body charged to prepare for its entry into force, the Ad Hoc Working Group on the Paris Agreement (APA); and others again to the Subsidiary Body for Implementation and the Subsidiary Body for Scientific and Technological Advice.

[62] As reported, e.g., in Anna Schulz et al., 'Summary of the Marrakech Climate Change Conference, 7–18 November 2016, Marrakech, Morocco' 12 *Earth Negotiations Bulletin* 689, 21 November 2016.

2.1 The Role of Non-state Actors

The Paris Agreement has conferred an enhanced role upon non-state actors in international climate governance.[63] As with many other MEAs, non-state actors may attend meetings of the parties, and although they cannot formally participate in international law-making, they may make submissions on matters under consideration by parties.[64] Over the years an increasingly large number of civil society organizations have made ample use of this prerogative.[65]

In the lead-up to adoption of the Paris Agreement, however, much emphasis was placed on voluntary emission reductions by non-state actors, such as companies and subnational governments, as well as on their contribution to provision of climate finance.[66] This is understandable, given the prominent role of corporate actors in engendering the climate problem and in being part of the solution.

Rather belatedly, therefore, the preamble of the Paris Agreement acknowledges for the first time in a climate treaty the importance of engaging 'all levels of government' and 'various actors' in addressing climate change.[67] Furthermore, while the UNFCCC already made generic reference to public participation in addressing climate change and its effects, and developing adequate responses,[68] the Paris Agreement specifically emphasizes the importance of enhanced public and private sector participation in implementing NDCs.[69] These developments largely focus on non-state actors' engagement in making and implementing climate change action at the national, rather than at the international level. Yet, developments at recent party meetings clearly show that momentum is building for finding ways to expand the visibility and active involvement of non-state actors in international climate change governance.[70]

An eloquent sign of this paradigm shift was the establishment of a dedicated platform for local communities and indigenous peoples in 2016.[71] The platform

[63] Paris Agreement, Preamble and Decision 1/CP.21, Adoption of the Paris Agreement, paras 133–135. For an early reflection, see Harro van Asselt, 'The Role of Non-State Actors in Reviewing Ambition, Implementation, and Compliance under the Paris Agreement' (2016) 6 *Climate Law* 91.

[64] UNFCCC, Art. 7.6 and Kyoto Protocol, Art. 13.8.for an early analysis, see B. Arts, *The Political Influence of Global Ngos: Case Studies on the Climate and Biodiversity Conventions* (International Books 1998).

[65] These submissions may be found at: <https://unfccc.int/submissions_and_statements#eq-2> .

[66] See Lima–Paris Action Agenda and the Non-state Actor Zone for Climate Action (NAZCA) platform launched in 2014. For an analysis, see Sander Chan et al., 'Reinvigorating International Climate Policy: A Comprehensive Framework for Effective Non-state Action' (2015) 6(4) *Global Policy* 466; and Sander Chan et al., 'Strengthening Non-state Climate Action: A Progress Assessment of Commitments Launched at the 2014 UN Climate Summit' (London School of Economics, 2015).

[67] Paris Agreement, Preamble.

[68] UNFCCC, Art. 6

[69] Paris Agreement, Art. 6.8.

[70] As noted in Allan et al., *supra* note 60.

[71] Decision 1/CP.21, Adoption of the Paris Agreement, FCCC/CP/2015/10/Add.1 (2015), 135–6; and Report of the Conference of the Parties on its twenty-second session, held in Marrakech from 7–18 November 2016, FCCC/CP/2016/10 (2016), at 163–7.

has been tasked with strengthening the knowledge, technologies, practices, and efforts of local communities and indigenous peoples, facilitating the exchange of experience and the sharing of best practices and lessons learned, and enhancing the engagement of local communities and indigenous peoples in the UNFCCC process.[72] Work towards operationalizing the platform is still ongoing at the time of writing, yet the platform has opened up an unprecedented avenue for the formal involvement of non-state actors in the climate regime, which is reminiscent of similar developments that occurred in the context of the 1992 Convention on Biological Diversity (CBD).[73] The CBD is unique amongst MEAs for having attributed a formal role to indigenous peoples and local communities.[74] While it is too early to tell whether developments in the climate regime will take a turn similar to that observed under the CBD, this is a development which is potentially gravid with momentous consequences for greater involvement of non-state actors in the climate regime.

2.2 Regime Interplay and Institutional Cooperation

Because of the breadth of its subject matter, the climate regime is especially prone to overlap with other international regimes.[75] Parties to the climate regime have nevertheless historically been reluctant to engage in institutional cooperation with other regimes. Even when they have done so—as, for example, in the context of the Joint Liaison Group to enhance coordination between the UNFCCC, the Convention on Biological Diversity, and the UN Convention to Combat Desertification—very limited results have been obtained, based on the argument that the Rio Conventions have a 'distinct legal character, mandate and membership'.[76]

[72] Decision 2/CP.23, Local Communities and Indigenous Peoples Platform, FCCC/CP/2017/11/Add.1 (2018), para. 5.

[73] Convention on Biological Diversity (Rio de Janeiro, 5 June 1992, in force 29 December 1993) 1760 UNTS 79. This argument is reproduced in Annalisa Savaresi, 'Traditional Knowledge and Climate Change: A New Legal Frontier?' (2018) 9 *Journal of Human Rights and the Environment* 32.

[74] Elisa Morgera and Elsa Tsioumani, 'Yesterday, Today, and Tomorrow: Looking Afresh at the Convention on Biological Diversity' (2011) 21 *Yearbook of International Environmental Law* 3.

[75] The literature on this matter is vast. See, e.g., Carlarne, *supra* note 16; Biermann and others, *supra* note 16; Margaret Young, 'Climate Change and Regime Interaction' (2011) 5 *Carbon and Climate Law Review* 147; van Asselt, *supra* note 16.

[76] See, e.g., the position of the United States in 'Views on the Paper on Options for Enhanced Cooperation Among the Three Rio Conventions, Submissions from Parties', (UN Doc FCCC/SBSTA/2006/MISC.4, 23 March 2006), at 16. The same point was made by Australia, *ibid.*, at 5, as observed also in Harro van Asselt, 'Managing the Fragmentation of International Environmental Law: Forests at the Intersection of the Climate and Biodiversity Regimes' (2012) 44 *New York University Journal of International Law and Politics* 1205, at 1266–7.

The Paris Agreement has seemingly opened the way to greater institutional cooperation with other international bodies and processes with a mandate relating to climate change. The COP decision adopting the agreement acknowledges the importance of liaising with international processes that deal with matters such as climate finance[77] and human displacement.[78] Furthermore, the preamble to the Paris Agreement has broken new ground by tracing explicit links between climate change and human rights law. The climate regime has thus become the only body of international environmental law to include a specific reference to parties' existing human rights obligations.[79] While such a reference does not impose new human rights obligations on states, it draws attention to the need to comply with existing ones. Although timid, this reference may have significant implications for the interpretation and further refinement of parties' obligations under the climate regime.[80]

A string of Human Rights Council (HRC) resolutions emphasize the potential for human rights to 'inform and strengthen' climate change law- and policy-making, by 'promoting policy coherence, legitimacy and sustainable outcomes'.[81] Indeed, after having unprecedentedly engaged in the negotiations for the Paris Agreement, human rights bodies have actively sought to influence the making of its rule book[82] with submissions on matters including gender, finance, the sustainable development mechanism, and capacity building.[83] The Office of the High Commissioner on Human Rights has furthermore facilitated a compilation of expert recommendations on climate change and human rights,[84] whereas human rights bodies have started to work as institutionalized pathways to monitor and sanction human rights violations associated with climate change and the implementation of climate change response measures.[85]

[77] Decision 1/CP.21, at 44.

[78] *Ibid.*, at 50.

[79] Paris Agreement, Preamble.

[80] Annalisa Savaresi, 'Climate Change and Human Rights: Fragmentation, Interplay and Institutional Linkages' in Sébastien Duyck, Sébastien Jodoin, and Alyssa Johl (eds), *Routledge Handbook of Human Rights and Climate Governance* (Routledge 2018).

[81] HRC, Human Rights and Climate Change, UN Doc A/HRC/7/78, 29 March 2008; HRC, Human Rights and Climate Change, UN Doc A/HRC/RES/10/4, 25 March 2009, at preamble; HRC, Human Rights and Climate Change, UN Doc A/HRC/RES/18/22, 17 October 2011, at preamble; and HRC, Human Rights and Climate Change, UN Doc A/HRC/RES/26/27, 15 July 2014, at preamble.

[82] As noted also in *ibid.*; Daniel Bodansky, Jutta Brunnée, and Lavanya Rajamani, *International Climate Change Law* (OUP 2017), at 228.

[83] All submissions are available at: <http://www.ohchr.org/EN/Issues/HRAndClimateChange/Pages/UNFCCC.aspx> accessed 28 April 2019.

[84] The OHCHR hosted an expert meeting on climate change and human rights on 6–7 October 2016 in Geneva. The Draft Recommendations elaborated at the meeting are available online at: <http://www.ohchr.org/EN/Issues/HRAndClimateChange/Pages/ClimateChange.aspx> accessed 28 April 2019.

[85] CIEL, 'States' Human Rights Obligations in the Context of Climate Change' (CIEL 2018) <http://www.ciel.org/wp-content/uploads/2018/01/HRTBs-synthesis-report.pdf> accessed 28 April 2019.

3 Turning International Climate Change Governance on its Head

The Paris Agreement enshrines in treaty form the 'bottom up', 'pledge and review' approach to international climate governance which first emerged with the Copenhagen Accord.[86] Ever since the ill-fated 2009 Copenhagen Climate Change Conference, the climate regime has progressively moved away from the 'top down' 'targets and timetable' model embedded in the Kyoto Protocol.[87] The new approach requires that parties unilaterally declare the action they are willing to undertake, with the international climate bureaucracy working as a notary collecting, and eventually enabling, review of parties' pledged action. This 'hybrid' architecture[88] hinges on parties' NDCs, rather than on a set of targets enshrined in a treaty.

The legal character of NDCs was the subject of much speculation during and after the negotiations for the Paris Agreement.[89] Contrary to what some suggested at the time,[90] NDCs can scarcely be regarded as binding unilateral acts, as they miss the 'intention'[91] or 'will to be bound'.[92] Equally, given their unilateral nature, it seems unlikely that NDCs might qualify as subsequent agreements between the parties 'regarding the interpretation of the treaty or the application of its provisions' pursuant to Article 31(3)(a) of the Vienna Convention on the Law of Treaties.[93] Whilst parties' interpretation of the legal character of NDCs will only become clearer with the implementation of the Paris Agreement, the provisions anchoring NDCs in the treaty provide some useful clues in this connection. Article 4.2 of the Paris Agreement says:

Each Party shall prepare, communicate and maintain successive nationally determined contributions that it intends to achieve. Parties shall pursue domestic mitigation measures, with the aim of achieving the objectives of such contributions.

This provision clearly imposes obligations of conduct upon all parties,[94] which are required to submit NDCs detailing action on how they plan to reduce their

[86] Decision 2/CP.15, Copenhagen Accord, UN Doc FCCC/CP/2009/11/Add.1, 30 March 2010. For this use of terminology, see Bodansky, *supra* note 82.

[87] Savaresi, 'The Paris Agreement', *supra* note 30, at 6.

[88] This terminology is used in Bodansky et al., *supra* note 82, at 214.

[89] See, e.g., Daniel Bodansky and Lavanya Rajamani, 'Key Legal Issues in the 2015 Climate Negotiations' (Centre for Climate and Energy Solutions 2015) https://www.ssrn.com/abstract=2652001; Jorge Viñuales, 'The Paris Climate Agreement: An Initial Examination' https://www.ejiltalk.org/the-paris-climate-agreement-an-initial-examination-part-i-of-ii/.

[90] Viñuales, *supra* note 89.

[91] International Court of Justice, *Nuclear Tests Case [Australia v France]* ICJ Reports 1974 253, at 43.

[92] As argued also in Annalisa Savaresi, 'The Paris Agreement: A Rejoinder' <https://www.ejiltalk.org/the-paris-agreement-a-rejoinder/>. For this use of terminology see: International Law Commission, Guiding Principles Applicable to Unilateral Declarations of States Capable of Creating Legal Obligations, 2006, at 1.

[93] Vienna Convention on the Law of Treaties (Vienna, 23 May 1969, in force 27 January 1980) 115 UNTS 331.

[94] For a reflection on the differences between obligations of conduct and obligations of result, see: Rüdiger Wolfrum, 'Obligation of Result Versus Obligation of Conduct: Some Thoughts About the Implementation of International Obligations' in Mahnoush H. Arsanjani and Jacob Cogan (eds),

emissions and by how much.[95] This obligation of conduct[96] is procedural in nature.[97] Whilst no format for (intended) NDCs could be agreed ahead of adoption of the Paris Agreement, the conference of the parties, serving as the meeting of the parties, is expected to adopt specific guidance on this issue.[98]

Quite crucially, therefore, the Paris Agreement does not impose obligations of result, as the Kyoto Protocol did, to achieve specific emission reductions over a certain time frame.[99] Instead, all parties must contribute to achieving the global temperature goal envisioned in the Paris Agreement,[100] and NDCs will be the term of reference to assess their contribution to that goal. The Paris Agreement does not entirely do away with a differentiated approach to parties' obligations but it moves away from the static distinction between developed and developing countries drawn in the UNFCCC, replacing it with a rather more flexible 'self-differentiation' approach.[101]

In many ways, the governance architecture envisioned in the Paris Agreement is very much akin to that embedded in other MEAs, such as the 1992 Convention on Biological Diversity and its so-called Aichi Targets,[102] or indeed in the Sustainable Development Goals.[103] While pursuit of these collective targets/goals is not the subject of enforceable obligations, the expectation is that the process of reporting on progress in achieving these targets/goals will engender a virtuous peer pressure circle, leading parties to deliver the desired outcomes.[104]

Generally, the provision of information is a crucial ingredient of MEAs, both to ensure monitoring of the problems that parties seek to tackle (in the case of the climate regime, emissions of greenhouse gases), as well as to review parties' adherence to the substantive obligations they have undertaken. When compared with other climate treaties, the Paris Agreement attempts to devise a more comprehensive system to review the effectiveness, implementation, and compliance with parties' obligations.[105]

Looking to the Future: Essays on International Law in Honor of W. Michael Reisman (Martinus Nijhoff Publishers 2010); and Pierre-Marie Dupuy, 'Reviewing the Difficulties of Codification: On Ago's Classification of Obligations of Means and Obligations of Result in Relation to State Responsibility' (1999) 10 *European Journal of International Law* 371.

---

95 See e.g. Bodansky, *supra* note 28, at 146; Savaresi, *supra* note 94.
96 Paris Agreement, Art. 4.2.
97 As argued also in Bodansky, *supra* note 28; Savaresi, *supra* note 93.
98 Paris Agreement, Art. 4.13; and Decision 1/CP.21, at 31.
99 Kyoto Protocol, Art. 3.1 and Annex B.
100 Paris Agreement, Art. 2.1(a).
101 For this use of terminology, see Bodansky et al., *supra* note 82, at 223.
102 Decision X/2. Strategic Plan for Biodiversity 2011–2020, UN Doc UNEP/CBD/COP/DEC/X/2, 29 October 2010, Annex.
103 'Transforming Our World: the 2030 Agenda for Sustainable Development', UNGA Res 70/1 (2015).
104 See Norichika Kanie and Frank Biermann (eds), *Governing through Goals—Sustainable Development Goals as Governance Innovation* (MIT Press 2017).
105 This categorization of review processes in borrowed from Bodansky, *supra* note 25, at 242.

Before the adoption of the Paris Agreement, in fact, not only did differentiation in the climate regime apply to parties' substantive obligations concerning emission reductions, but it also affected procedural obligations associated with review of implementation and compliance. Yet the Kyoto Protocol's sophisticated review mechanisms did not encompass a review of the effectiveness of action. This in turn means that the Kyoto Protocol lacked the means to 'ratchet up' ambition over time and align with recommendations received from scientists concerning the pace at which to phase out the emission of greenhouse gases.

Conversely, the UNFCCC only contains skeletal provisions concerning the review of implementation of parties' obligations. Since the Copenhagen debacle, decisions adopted by UNFCCC treaty bodies have increased parties' reporting obligations in frequency and expanded their scope, incorporating new elements, such as information concerning assistance to developing countries.[106] The review of implementation, however, remained differentiated for developed and developing countries.[107] Implementation of these arrangements has evidenced some obvious shortcomings.[108] First, the lack of a standard template to report pledged mitigation action has hindered comparison between parties' efforts.[109] Second, developing countries have struggled to comply with their increased reporting obligations,[110] thus drawing attention to the need for dedicated assistance and capacity building. A review of the effectiveness of action was unsuccessfully attempted with the so-called 2013–15 Review,[111] and did not result in a process to adjust parties' level of ambition.

The Paris Agreement is expected to build and expand on existing review procedures under the UNFCCC,[112] and to address their shortcomings. Its rule book is expected to standardize reporting of information for all parties, largely doing away with the differentiation between developed and developing countries.[113] A Capacity-building Initiative for Transparency is set to support developing country parties in meeting their enhanced reporting obligations.[114] Most crucially, the Paris Agreement has, at least in principle, levelled the process for review of implementation of parties' obligations in relation to mitigation,[115] establishing the

[106] Decision 1/CP.16, at 42.

[107] *Ibid.*, at 44–6 and 63–4.

[108] As noted, e.g., in Jane Ellis and Sarah Moarif, 'Identifying and Addressing Gaps in the UNFCCC Reporting Framework' (OECD 2015) <http://www.oecd.org/environment/cc/Identifying-and-addressing-gaps.pdf> accessed 24 April 2019.

[109] *Ibid.*, at 4.

[110] As of January 2016, only twenty-four developing country Parties had submitted their biennial update reports, whereas all developed country Parties have submitted their biennial reports.

[111] Decision 1/CP.16, at 4 and 138.

[112] Decision 1/CP.21, at 99.

[113] Paris Agreement, Art. 4.13; and *ibid.*, at 31.

[114] Decision 1/CP.21, at 85.

[115] Paris Agreement, Art. 13.

premises for the creation of machinery to periodically scrutinize these at both the individual and the aggregate level.

At the individual level, the review of implementation of the agreement will be coupled with an expert-based, facilitating compliance mechanism.[116] Even though the details of this mechanism remain to be determined, it seems clear that it will follow what has been described as a 'managerial' rather than an 'enforcement' model.[117] Therefore, and in line with arrangements under other MEAs, the Paris Agreement will not so much coerce but rather encourage compliance, enabling parties' consultation, cooperation and peer pressure. It is unlikely that parties will equip this mechanism with the means to attach consequences to instances of non-compliance, as under the Kyoto Protocol. Yet the very existence of a mechanism to consider questions of compliance for all parties, rather than for developed ones only, is a major novelty.

At the aggregate level, alignment with the temperature goal enshrined in the Paris Agreement will be periodically assessed, in the context of a so-called global stocktake exercise.[118] This brand new element in international climate governance aims to review the effectiveness of parties' action and to induce them to adjust their level of ambition over time.[119] The global stocktake is therefore crucial to ensuring that the bottom-up architecture envisioned in the Paris Agreement will deliver the results it was designed to produce. Even though global goals and targets are commonplace in MEAs, effectiveness review procedures to assess parties' alignment with achieving these are not. Therefore, it is currently hard to predict how the global stocktake will work in practice.

Non-state actors can potentially perform an important role in this context, both by contributing to the provision of information as well as by putting pressure upon parties.[120] The Paris Agreement is silent on this matter. However, negotiations on the rule book may open the door to greater involvement by non-state actors, for example by enabling them to partake in the review process, building upon precedents established with other MEAs.[121]

Greater institutional cooperation with other international bodies may also have implications for the review of implementation of parties' obligations under the Paris Agreement. Human rights bodies' emboldened efforts to monitor and sanction human rights violations associated with climate change and the implementation of climate change response measures may already be regarded as a promising development in this connection.

116 *Ibid.*, Art. 15.
117 Bodansky, *supra* note 25, at 242.
118 Paris Agreement, Art. 14.
119 *Ibid.*, Art. 14.3.
120 As suggested in Harro van Asselt, *supra* note 63, at 106.
121 *Ibid.*, at 96.

4 Conclusions

The Paris Agreement laid the foundations for reform of the architecture for international climate change governance. This architecture hinges on a bottom-up, pledge and review approach and, at least in principle, relies on greater non-state actors' involvement and inter-institutional cooperation. Compared with the UNFCCC, the Paris Agreement is a great leveller of parties' obligations, in the sense that now all parties are expected to reduce their emissions, and all are going to be subjected to review of implementation and compliance. Compared with the Kyoto Protocol, less pervasive substantial obligations under the Paris Agreement are compensated for by a universal commitment to emission reductions, as well as by a process for review of the effectiveness of parties' action.

From a law-making perspective, adoption of the Paris Agreement has initiated a new complex rule-making season. This rule-making has engaged parties in a collective exercise to fill in with content the provisions in the treaty concerning crucial elements of the new international climate change governance architecture, such as NDCs, and procedures for reviewing implementation, compliance and effectiveness. The work undertaken thus far has clearly shown how complex this endeavour is. In an ideal world, parties would use this opportunity to simplify the remarkable institutional and regulatory complexity that plagues the climate regime, doing away with rules and institutions which are no longer needed. In reality, thus far, rather than manage this complexity, some parties have used it to throw a spanner in the works for adoption of the Paris Agreement rule book.

From a governance perspective, it is vital that rule-making under the Paris Agreement delivers a robust framework to ensure adequate coordination between parties' actions. As is often the case with international law, the main purpose of the Paris Agreement is to put pressure on parties to adopt measures at the national level suited to tackling a problem. While in and of itself international law cannot deliver a solution to the epochal challenge of climate change, it clearly plays an important part in engendering peer pressure to engage in delivering a solution. Notwithstanding the shift to a bottom-up, pledge and review approach, the job of international rules therefore remains the same: to deliver a robust architecture for review of implementation, compliance and effectiveness, as well as the means to collaborate internationally, through provision of finance, capacity building, and exchange of information.

It would be naïve to expect the Paris Agreement to be a miraculous cure for all the maladies that have affected international cooperation on climate change thus far. Whilst adoption of a new approach to international climate governance was a matter of political necessity, a change in architecture is not in itself a guarantee of success. Indeed, while the rhetorical value of identifying global goals is beyond dispute, their suitability for delivering concrete results is yet to be demonstrated. More generally, the Paris Agreement leaves unsolved a series of unpalatable political questions and complex technical details. The devil clearly is in these details, yet experience accrued with implementation of the UNFCCC and the Kyoto Protocol is a precious term of reference to assist with detecting the pitfalls lying ahead and avoiding repeating the mistakes of the past.

On paper at least, the Paris Agreement has already marked some progress by dismantling the differentiation firewall, replacing it with a more flexible approach, which is cognizant of the need to involve all parties in tackling climate change. It also planted the seeds to establish processes for reviewing implementation, compliance, and effectiveness that involve all parties. The Paris Agreement also seems to have opened up new avenues to involve non-state actors in climate governance and to improve coordination and address synergies between international regimes with mandates that are related to climate change. Indeed, when an issue has overarching implications for a range of different international regimes, it seems wise to emphasize, and vigorously explore, avenues for coordination. All these elements seem to augur well, but only time will tell whether these auspicious signs marked a fresh start for a regime whose journey has thus far been anything but plain sailing.

Investment Law and Renewable Energy

Green Expectations in Grey Times

Fernando Dias Simões

1 A Grey Cloud over Green Investments

Over recent decades, governments all over the world have striven to shift from a model based on fossil fuels to one based on low-carbon sources. The quest for a greener future led to the emergence of an international market for renewable energy technologies and equipment,[1] attracting gigantic flows of capital.[2] Foreign direct investment plays a major role in this endeavour as it provides fresh funds but also induces the transfer of knowledge and technology.[3]

The financial viability of investment in renewable energies is frequently dependent on public support.[4] Many governments designed and implemented renewable energy support mechanisms to encourage private investment, often in the form of subsidies and incentive tariffs.[5] The abundance of economic support mechanisms sparked a boom in investment in the renewable energy sector.[6]

[1] See generally Dirk Assmann, Ulrich Laumanns, and Dieter Uh (eds) *Renewable Energy: A Global Review of Technologies, Policies and Markets* (Earthscan 2006).

[2] See, e.g., Omar Ellabban, Haitham Abu-Rub, and Frede Blaabjerg, 'Renewable Energy Resources: Current Status, Future Prospects and their Enabling Technology' (2014) 39 *Renewable and Sustainable Energy Reviews* 748, 758.

[3] Gaëtan Verhoosel, 'Foreign Direct Investment and Legal Constraints on Domestic Environmental Policies: Striking a Reasonable Balance Between Stability and Change' (1998) 29 *Law and Policy in International Business* 451, 452; Anatole Boute, 'The Potential Contribution of International Investment Protection Law to Combat Climate Change' (2009) 27 *Journal of Energy and Natural Resources Law* 333, 334–5.

[4] World Bank, 'Inclusive Green Growth: The Pathway to Sustainable Development' (2012) 20–2 <http://siteresources.worldbank.org/EXTSDNET/Resources/Inclusive_Green_Growth_May_2012.pdf> accessed 24 April 2019.

[5] See, e.g., Richard Ottinger, Lily Mathews, and Nadia Elizabeth Czachor, 'Renewable Energy in National Legislation: Challenges and Opportunities' in Don Zillman, Catherine Redgwell, Yinka Omorogbe, and Lila Barrera-Hernández (eds) *Beyond the Carbon Economy: Energy Law in Transition* (OUP 2008) 183, 186–206.

[6] See Onno Kuik and Sabine Fuss, 'Renewables in the Energy Market: A Financial-Technological Analysis Considering Risk and Policy Options' in André Dorsman, Wim Westerman, Mehmet Karan, and Özgür Arslan (eds), *Financial Aspects in Energy: a European Perspective* (Springer 2011) 33.

Fernando Dias Simões, *Investment Law and Renewable Energy: Green Expectations in Grey Times* In: *How International Law Works in Times of Crisis*. Edited by: George Ulrich and Ineta Ziemele, Oxford University Press (2019).
DOI: 10.1093/oso/9780198849667.003.0013

By the end of the decade, however, several countries decided to reduce or eliminate those economic support mechanisms.[7] Governments claimed that incentives to renewable energy generation had proven too popular (and therefore, more expensive than anticipated); that they became disproportionate because production costs for the new technology had decreased significantly; or that they simply could not afford them following the 2008 financial crisis.[8]

This wind of change in the renewable energy market unleashed a flurry of investor–state arbitration proceedings. Foreign investors claim that changes to legal frameworks diminished or exhausted the commercial viability of their investments,[9] thus breaching the host states' obligations under international investment agreements, namely the Energy Charter Treaty.[10] International investment law has long attempted to strike a balance between foreign investors' reliance on the regulations that underpin their long-term investments and the host state's right to adapt regulations to new circumstances.[11] Investment protection standards such as the prohibition of expropriation and fair and equitable treatment have, in theory, the potential to shield investors adequately from unexpected changes to legal frameworks. Modification or withdrawal of incentives may frustrate an investor's legitimate expectations to benefit from public support. The crux of the question is whether investors can seek compensation under international investment treaties when governments encourage investments via economic support schemes but decide to reduce or eliminate them after investment costs are already sunk.

The answer to this question is emerging slowly from the decisions of arbitral tribunals. By the end of July 2018, final awards had been rendered in nine cases: *Charanne B.V. and Construction Investments S.A.R.L. v Spain* ('*Charanne v Spain*');[12] *Isolux Infrastructure Netherlands, B.V. v Spain* ('*Isolux v*

[7] See Fernando Dias Simões, 'When Green Incentives Go Pale: Investment Arbitration and Renewable Energy Policymaking' (2017) 45(2) *Denver Journal of International Law and Policy* 251, 258–9.

[8] Nigel Bankes, 'Decarbonising the Economy and International Investment Law' (2012) 30(4) *Journal of Energy and Natural Resources Law* 497, 502; James Prest, 'The Future of Feed-in Tariffs: Capacity Caps, Scheme Closures and Looming Grid Parity' (2012) 2012(1) *Renewable Energy Law and Policy Review* 25, 346; Ioannis Glinavos, 'Solar Eclipse: Investment Treaty Arbitration and Spain's Photovoltaic Troubles' in Constantin Gurdgiev, Liam Leonard, and Maria Alejandra Gonzalez-Perez (eds), *Lessons from the Great Recession: at the Crossroads of Sustainability and Recovery* (Emerald Group Publishing 2016) 251, 254.

[9] Anna De Luca, 'Withdrawing Incentives to Attract FDI: Can Host Countries put the Genie back in the Bottle?' (2014) *Columbia Center on Sustainable International Investment* 2 <http://ccsi.columbia.edu/files/2013/10/No-125-De-Luca-FINAL.pdf> accessed 24 April 2019; Daniel Behn and Ole Fauchald, 'Governments under Cross-fire? Renewable Energy and International Economic Tribunals' (2015) 12(2) *Manchester Journal of International Economic Law* 117, 120.

[10] Energy Charter Treaty <http://www.energycharter.org/fileadmin/DocumentsMedia/Legal/ECTC-en.pdf> accessed 24 April 2019.

[11] See Rudolf Dolzer and Cristoph Schreuer, *Principles of International Investment Law* (OUP 2008) 145–9.

[12] *Charanne B.V. and Construction Investments S.A.R.L. v Spain* (Stockholm Chamber of Commerce, Case No. 62/2012), award of 21 January 2016 (in Spanish) <https://www.italaw.com/sites/default/files/case-documents/italaw7047.pdf> accessed 28 April 2019. An unofficial English translation (by Mena Chambers) can be found at <https://www.italaw.com/sites/default/files/case-documents/italaw7162.pdf> accessed 28 April 2019.

Spain');[13] *Blusun S.A., Jean-Pierre Lecorcier and Michael Stein v Italy* ('*Blusun v Italy*');[14] *Eiser Infrastructure Limited and Energía Solar Luxembourg S.à r.l. v Spain* ('*Eiser v Spain*');[15] Mr Jürgen Wirtgen, Mr Stefan Wirtgen, Mrs Gisela Wirtgen, *JSW Solar (zwei) GmbH & Co. KG v The Czech Republic* ('*JSW Solar v the Czech Republic*');[16] Novenergia II—Energy & Environment (SCA) (*Grand Duchy of Luxembourg*), *SICAR v Spain* ('*Novenergia v Spain*');[17] *Antaris Solar GmbH and Dr Michael Göde v The Czech Republic* ('*Antaris v the Czech Republic*');[18] *Masdar Solar & Wind Cooperatief U.A. v Spain* ('*Masdar v Spain*');[19] and *Antin Infrastructure Services Luxembourg S.à.r.l. and Antin Energia Termosolar B.V. v Spain* ('*Antin v Spain*').[20] At least fifty-three cases are yet to be decided.[21] This number,

[13] *Isolux Infrastructure Netherlands, B.V. v Spain* (Stockholm Chamber of Commerce, Case No. V2013/153), award of 12 July 2016 (in Spanish) <https://www.italaw.com/sites/default/files/case-documents/italaw9219.pdf> accessed 28 April 2019.

[14] *Blusun S.A., Jean-Pierre Lecorcier and Michael Stein v Italy* (ICSID Case No. ARB/14/3), award of 27 December 2016 <https://www.italaw.com/sites/default/files/case-documents/italaw8967.pdf> accessed 28 April 2019.

[15] *Eiser Infrastructure Limited and Energía Solar Luxembourg S.à r.l. v Spain* (ICSID Case No. ARB/13/36), Award of 4 May 2017 <https://energycharter.org/fileadmin/DocumentsMedia/Disputes/ISDSC-043en.pdf> accessed 28 April 2019. The award is also available in Spanish at <https://www.italaw.com/sites/default/files/case-documents/italaw8798_0.pdf> accessed 28 April 2019.

[16] *Mr Jürgen Wirtgen, Mr Stefan Wirtgen, Mrs Gisela Wirtgen, JSW Solar (zwei) GmbH & Co. KG v The Czech Republic* (Permanent Court of Arbitration, Case No. 2014-03), award of 11 October 2017 <https://www.italaw.com/sites/default/files/case-documents/italaw9498.pdf> accessed 28 April 2019.

[17] Novenergia II—Energy & Environment (SCA) (Grand Duchy of Luxembourg), *SICAR v Spain* (Stockholm Chamber of Commerce, Case No. 2015/063), award of 15 February 2018 <https://energycharter.org/fileadmin/DocumentsMedia/Disputes/Final_Award.pdf>, accessed 28 April 2019.

[18] *Antaris Solar GmbH and Dr Michael Göde v The Czech Republic* (Permanent Court of Arbitration, Case No. 2014-01), award of 2 May 2018, <https://www.mfcr.cz/assets/cs/media/Informace-zadost-106_Pr-001_2018-07-03_Info-106-99-MF-12417-2018-10-527-IK.pdf> accessed 28 April 2019.

[19] *Masdar Solar & Wind Cooperatief U.A. v Spain* (ICSID Case No. ARB/14/1), Award of 16 May 2018, <https://energycharter.org/fileadmin/DocumentsMedia/Disputes/Case49-Award.pdf> accessed 28 April 2019.

[20] *Antin Infrastructure Services Luxembourg S.à.r.l. and Antin Energia Termosolar B.V. v Spain* (ICSID Case No. ARB/13/31), award of 15 June 2018, <https://energycharter.org/fileadmin/DocumentsMedia/Disputes/ISDSC-041.pdf> accessed 28 April 2019.

[21] Cases administered by the International Centre for Settlement of Investment Disputes (ICSID): *EVN AG v Bulgaria*, Case No. ARB/13/17; *RREEF Infrastructure (G.P.) Limited & RREEF Pan-European Infrastructure Two Lux S.à.r.l. v Spain*, Case No. ARB/13/30; *NextEra Energy Global Holdings B.V. & NextEra Energy Spain Holdings B.V. v Spain*, Case No. ARB/14/11; *InfraRed Environmental Infrastructure GP Limited & others v Spain*, Case No. ARB/14/12; *RENERGY S.à.r.l. v Spain*, Case No. ARB/14/18; *RWE Innogy GmbH and RWE Innogy Aersa S.A.U. v Spain*, Case No. ARB/14/34; *Stadtwerke München GmbH, RWE Innogy GmbH, & others v Spain*, Case No. ARB/15/1; *STEAG GmbH v Spain*, Case No. ARB/15/4; *9REN Holding S.a.r.l v Spain*, Case No. ARB/15/15; *BayWa r.e. Renewable Energy GmbH & BayWa r.e. Asset Holding GmbH v Spain*, Case No. ARB/15/16; *ENERGO-PRO a.s. v Bulgaria*, Case No. ARB/15/19; *Cube Infrastructure Fund SICAV & others v Spain*, Case No. ARB/15/20; *Matthias Kruck & others v Spain*, Case No. ARB/15/23; *KS Invest GmbH & TLS Invest GmbH v Spain*, Case No. ARB/15/25; *JGC Corporation v Spain*, Case No. ARB/15/27; *Cavalum SGPS, S.A. v Spain*, Case No. ARB/15/34; *E.ON Finanzanlagen GmbH & E.ON Iberia Holding GmbH v Spain*, Case No. ARB/15/35; *OperaFund Eco-Invest SICAV PLC & Schwab Holding AG v Spain*, Case No. ARB/15/36; *Silver Ridge Power BV v Italy*, Case No. ARB/15/37; *SolEs Badajoz GmbH v Spain*, Case No. ARB/15/38; *Belenergia S.A. v Italy*, Case No. ARB/15/40; *Hydro Energy 1 S.à.r.l. & Hydroxana Sweden AB v Spain*, Case No. ARB/15/42; *Watkins Holdings S.à.r.l. & others v Spain*, Case No. ARB/15/44; *Landesbank Baden-Württemberg & others v Spain*, Case No. ARB/15/45; *Eskosol S.p.A. in liquidazione v Italy*, Case No. ARB/15/50; *Eurus Energy Holdings Corporation & Eurus Energy Europe B.V. v Spain*, Case No.

however, may not be totally accurate since arbitral proceedings may be administered by institutions that, differently from the International Centre for Settlement of Investment Disputes (ICSID), do not disclose the initiation of proceedings publicly. Furthermore, they may also be conducted ad hoc, with no supervising institution. Due to this lack of transparency, the exact number of disputes already initiated is unknown and the legal basis on which such claims are made is not totally clear. Still, most of the pending arbitral proceedings seem to arise out of governmental changes in regulatory frameworks for renewable energy.[22] Regardless, it is safe to say that we are witnessing a boom in arbitral proceedings relating to reduction or withdrawal of economic mechanisms in the field of renewable energies.

2 Awards in Favour of Host States

The first award to be rendered in this string of arbitrations was *Charanne v Spain*.[23] The dispute concerned legislative measures introduced by Spain in 2010 scaling

ARB/16/4; *ESPF Beteiligungs GmbH, ESPF Nr. 2 Austria Beteiligungs GmbH, & InfraClass Energie 5 GmbH & Co. KG v Italy*, Case No. ARB/16/5; *Sun-Flower Olmeda GmbH & Co KG and others v Spain*, Case No. ARB/16/17; *Infracapital F1 S.à r.l. and Infracapital Solar B.V. v Spain*, Case No. ARB/16/18; *ČEZ, a.s. v Bulgaria*, Case No. ARB/16/24; *Sevilla Beheer B.V. and others v Spain*, Case No. ARB/16/27; *VC Holding II S.a.r.l. and others v Italy*, Case No. ARB/16/39; *Portigon AG v Spain*, Case No. ARB/17/15; *DCM Energy GmbH & Co. Solar 1 KG and others v Spain*, Case No. ARB/17/41; *ACF Renewable Energy Limited v Bulgaria*, Case No. ARB/18/1; *LSG Building Solutions GmbH and others v Romania*, Case No. ARB/18/19; *Veolia Propreté SAS v Italy*, Case No. ARB/18/20; *Itochu Corporation v Spain*, Case No. ARB/18/25. Cases administered by the Permanent Court of Arbitration: *The PV Investors v Spain*, Case No. 2012–14; *G.I.H.G. Limited, Natland Group Limited, Natland Investment Group NV and Radiance Energy Holding S.A.R.L. v the Czech Republic*, Case No. 2013-35. Cases administered by the Arbitration Institute of the Stockholm Chamber of Commerce (SCC): *CSP Equity Investment Sarl v Spain* (Case No. 094/2013); *Greentech Energy Systems & Novenergia v Italy* (Case No. 095/2015); *Alten Renewable Energy Developments BV v Spain* (registered March 2015); *Greentech Energy System A/S, Foresight Luxembourg Solar 1 S.A.R.L., Foresight Luxembourg Solar 2 S.A.R.L., GWM Renewable Energy I S.P.A, GWM Renewable Energy II S.P.A v Spain* (Case No. 2015/50); *CEF Energia BV vs Italy* (Case No. 158/2015); *Green Power K/S Y Obton A/S v Spain* (Case No. 2016/135); *Sun Reserve Luxco Holdings SRL v Italy* (Case No. 132/2016); *FREIF Eurowind Holdings Ltd v Spain* (Case No. 2017/060). The case of *Solarpark Management GmbH & Co. Atum I KG v Spain* (Case No. V2015/163) was discontinued in 2016. Ad hoc cases: *EDF Energies Nouvelles S.A. v Spain* (UNCITRAL Case No. AA6130); *Voltaic Network GmbH v Czech Republic* (registered 8 May 2013); *ICW Europe Investments Limited v Czech Republic* (registered 8 May 2013); *Photovoltaik Knopf Betriebs-GmbH v Czech Republic* (registered 8 May 2013); *WA Investments-Europa Nova Limited v Czech Republic* (registered 8 May 2013).

[22] The Energy Charter Secretariat defines the subject matter of most of these disputes as 'legal reforms affecting the renewable energy sector'—Energy Charter Secretariat, 'List of all Investment Dispute Settlement Cases' <http://www.energycharter.org/?id=345> accessed 28 April 2019. Two other disputes regarding renewable energy are worth mentioning, even if they do not arise from true 'legal reforms' but rather from some other type of governmental measures: *Mesa Power Group LLC v Canada* (Permanent Court of Arbitration, Case No. 2012-17), award of 24 March 2016 <https://www.italaw.com/sites/default/files/case-documents/italaw7240.pdf> accessed 24 April 2019; and *Tennant Energy, LLC. v Canada* (ad hoc, registered in 2017, pending).

[23] *Charanne v Spain, supra* note 12. See Fernando Dias Simões, 'Charanne and Construction Investments v Spain: Legitimate Expectations and Investments in Renewable Energy' (2017) 26 *Review of European, Comparative and International Environmental Law* 174; Björn Arp, 'Charanne

back the incentives offered to investors in the photovoltaic sector. Investors claimed that, after having attracted their investments through a series of government incentives, Spain changed the regulatory framework, causing such a 'brutal impact' on the economic value of their investments that it amounted to indirect expropriation.[24] The tribunal noted that, despite such measures, the investors continued to be shareholders in the company, which continued to operate and earn revenue;[25] while their profitability had been affected, it was not as serious as to be characterized as expropriation.[26] In addition, the investors submitted that Spain's actions caused them to have legitimate expectations that the regulatory regime would not be modified.[27] The tribunal held that, in the absence of specific commitments, international investment law does not require states to freeze regulatory frameworks. Since Spain had not made any specific commitment with respect to the stability of the incentives regime, the investors could not expect that the regulatory framework would remain unchanged for the lifetime of the photovoltaic plant.[28] The changes introduced by Spain were reasonable, proportional, made in the public interest, and not retroactive.[29]

The *Isolux* case[30] focused on legislative changes introduced by Spain in 2013 and 2014. Investors invoked a breach of fair and equitable treatment and of prohibition of expropriation standards. As regards the first standard, the tribunal held that Spain had not made any specific commitment with respect to the stability of the incentives regime.[31] Furthermore, when investors made their investment, the legal framework had already been modified and several studies were ongoing that made its revision inevitable. Therefore, no reasonable investor could have the expectation that this framework would not be modified in the future and would remain unchanged.[32] The tribunal also held that there was not indirect expropriation because investors continued to be shareholders in the company and the company continued to operate and receive revenue[33] without suffering 'severe' or radical' loss.[34]

B.V. v. Spain', 110(2) *American Journal of International Law* 327 (2016); Iñigo del Guayo, 'Energy Law in Spain' in Martha Roggenkamp, Catherine Redgwell, Anita Ronne, and Inigo del Guayo (eds), *Energy Law in Europe: National, EU and International Regulation, 3rd edn* (OUP 2016) 973.

---

[24] *Charanne v Spain, supra* note 12, paras 280, 283–4.
[25] *Ibid.*, para. 462.
[26] *Charanne v Spain, supra* note 12, para. 465.
[27] *Ibid.*, para. 296. See also paras 297–301.
[28] *Charanne v Spain, supra* note 12, para. 499.
[29] *Ibid.*, para. 539.
[30] *Isolux v Spain, supra* note 13. See Enrique Fernandez Masia, 'Spain before the International Arbitration for the Cut to Renewable Energies: A Representation in Three Acts, for Now' (2017) 9(2) *Cuadernos de Derecho Transnacional* 673–4.
[31] *Isolux v Spain, supra* note 13, paras 769–72, 775.
[32] *Ibid.*, para. 787.
[33] *Isolux v Spain, supra* note 13, para. 840.
[34] *Ibid.*, para. 852.

The *Blusun* case arose because of the so-called *spalmaincentivi* reform implemented by the Italian Government to reduce incentives to producers of renewable energy.[35] The investors claimed that there was a causal link between measures adopted by various public authorities and the project's failure. Because of the legal insecurity created by the Italian state, investors were unable to attract construction project financing.[36] The tribunal quoted the *Charanne* award, highlighting that laws are subject to reasonable change consistently with the fair and equitable treatment standard and that there can be no legitimate expectation to the contrary.[37] The *Blusun* tribunal noted that the fair and equitable treatment standard 'preserves the regulatory authority of the host State to make and change its laws and regulations to adapt to changing needs, including fiscal needs, subject to respect for specific commitments made'.[38] However, if subsidies are lawfully granted and if it becomes necessary to modify them, this should be done in a manner which is not 'disproportionate to the aim of the legislative amendment' and with due regard to the 'reasonable reliance interests of recipients who may have committed substantial resources on the basis of the earlier regime'.[39] The tribunal also found that Italy had significantly changed the applicable legal framework through 'non-discriminatory laws ostensibly passed in the public interest'.[40] The situation was therefore not analogous, still less tantamount, to expropriation.[41] The investors were not subject to expropriation or a similar situation since they never lost title to the land and the premium paid for it was at the investors' risk.[42] The investors applied for annulment of the award.[43]

In an award of 11 October 2017, an arbitral tribunal ruled in favour of the host state in *JSW Solar*.[44] The majority of the tribunal found that the Czech Republic had not provided any specific guarantees to investors and had not 'deliberately attracted' and then harmed solar energy producers.[45] The investors had recognized that, in the absence of a stabilization guarantee, changes to domestic law for a legitimate public purpose are not unlawful. The tribunal held that no such stabilization guarantee existed and that the contested measures were introduced for a legitimate

[35] *Blusun v Italy, supra* note 14. See Fernando Dias Simões, '*Blusun S.A. and others v Italy*: Legal (in)stability and Renewable Energy Investments' (2017) 26(3) *Review of European, Comparative and International Environmental Law* 298; Sondra Faccio, 'The Italian Energy Reform as a Source of International Investment Disputes' (2016) 2 *Rivista di Diritto Internazionale Privato e Processuale* 460, 463–7.

[36] *Blusun v Italy, supra* note 14, para. 310.

[37] *Ibid.*, para. 317.

[38] *Blusun v Italy, supra* note 14, para. 319(4).

[39] *Ibid.*

[40] *Blusun v Italy, supra* note 14, para. 401.

[41] *Ibid.*

[42] *Blusun v Italy, supra* note 14, para. 407.

[43] ICSID, cases Database, <https://icsid.worldbank.org/en/Pages/cases/AdvancedSearch.asp> accessed 24 April 2019.

[44] *JSW Solar v The Czech Republic, supra* note 16.

[45] *Ibid.*, para. 445.

purpose.[46] The Czech Republic had guaranteed that solar photovoltaic plants that met certain requirements could expect a feed-in-tariff set at certain levels and those guarantees were maintained.[47] Finally, the tribunal ruled that the state was not obliged to maintain the tax incentives as they existed at the time of the investment.[48]

The Czech Republic also prevailed in the *Antaris* case.[49] The tribunal agreed with the host state that 'the market which the Claimants were entering was a bubble and that the Czech Government considered that the FiT regime was out of balance and that would have been obvious to anyone who participated in industry discussions, or paid attention to warnings by specialist professionals, or read the local press'.[50] Investors know that regulations may change depending on circumstances and not every modification amounts to a breach of legitimate expectations.[51] The tribunal also rejected the investors' claims of impairment by arbitrary and unreasonable conduct, holding that the Czech Republic 'had the rational objective of reducing excessive profits and sheltering consumers from excessive electricity price rises, and that its actions were not arbitrary or irrational'.[52] The measures adopted by the Czech Government 'dealt with a pressing problem caused by the late entry of many investors ... seeking to take advantage of an incentive regime which was bound to change'.[53]

3 Awards in Favour of Foreign Investors

The award in *Eiser v Spain*[54] was the first to rule in favour of investors. The tribunal found that Spain's 2013 and 2014 legal reforms constituted a breach of the standards of investment protection and deprived the investors of the entire value of their investment. According to the tribunal, while the fair and equitable treatment standard does not give a right to regulatory stability per se,[55] it does 'protect investors from a fundamental change to the regulatory regime in a manner that does not take account of the circumstances of existing investments made in reliance on the prior regime'.[56] Spain had eliminated a favourable regulatory regime, replacing it with an unprecedented and wholly different regulatory approach, based

[46] *JSW Solar v The Czech Republic, supra* note 16, para. 446.
[47] *Ibid.*, para. 451.
[48] *JSW Solar v The Czech Republic, supra* note 16, para. 465.
[49] *Antaris v the Czech Republic, supra* note 18.
[50] *Ibid.*, para. 434.
[51] *Antaris v the Czech Republic, supra* note 18, para 437.
[52] *Ibid.*, para. 444.
[53] *Antaris v the Czech Republic, supra* note 18, para 445.
[54] *Eiser v Spain, supra* note 15. See María José Alonso, 'The Economic Support for Renewable Energies in Spain and the Energy Charter: The Eiser Case Against Spain' (12 June 2017) 69 *Actualidad Jurídica Ambiental* 1; Masia, *supra* note 30, at 675.
[55] *Eiser v Spain, supra* note 15, para. 362.
[56] *Ibid.*, para. 363.

on completely different premises. The tribunal found this new system to be 'profoundly unfair and inequitable ... stripping Claimants of virtually all of the value of their investment'.[57] The tribunal analysed legislative changes introduced between 2013 and 2014, and thus not covered by the *Charanne* award, emphasizing that the 'factual and legal situation' differed 'fundamentally',[58] as the measures challenged by investors 'had far less dramatic effects'[59] in *Charanne*. In *Eiser*, the regulatory changes had a 'devastating' effect on the investments.[60] The tribunal recalled that 'the proportionality requirement is fulfilled inasmuch as the modifications are not random or unnecessary, provided that they do not suddenly and unexpectedly remove the essential features of the regulatory framework in place'.[61] While the tribunal did not question the appropriateness of measures adopted by the Spanish authorities to address its tariff deficit, it noted that Spain had to act in a way that respected its obligation to accord fair and equitable treatment to investors.[62] Spain has applied for annulment of the award.[63]

In February 2018, an arbitral tribunal ruled in favour of investors in *Novenergia v Spain*.[64] The tribunal started by analysing the three previous cases against Spain,[65] claiming to be 'mindful of both similarities and differences'.[66] It recalled that the *Charanne* tribunal only dealt with legislation enacted until 2010, agreeing that those measures did not breach the fair and equitable treatment standard.[67] Furthermore, the tribunal underlined that the *Isolux* case concerned investments made in October of 2012, 'a stage when it must have been clear to the investor that changes were being made to the Special Regime'.[68] The factual and legal context in *Novenergia* was very similar to that of *Eiser*,[69] with an important difference: the 'extent of the harm incurred' by investors in the two cases.[70] The tribunal then moved to analyse legislative measures adopted by Spain in 2013.[71] While the Spanish Government argued that such changes did not have a decisive impact since investors were still able to make a reasonable profit,[72] the tribunal held that the actions of the host state do not have to 'obliterate' the investment entirely to be considered unlawful.[73] The tribunal contended that assessing a breach of the fair and

[57] *Eiser v Spain, supra* note 15, para. 365, footnotes omitted.
[58] *Ibid.*, para. 367.
[59] *Eiser v Spain, supra* note 15, para. 368.
[60] *Ibid.*, para. 409.
[61] *Eiser v Spain, supra* note 15, para. 370, quoting *Charanne v Spain, supra* note 12, para. 517.
[62] *Eiser v Spain, supra* note 15, para. 371.
[63] See ICSID, *supra* note 43.
[64] *Novenergia v Spain, supra* note 17.
[65] *Ibid.*, para. 683.
[66] *Ibid.*, para. 684.
[67] *Ibid.*, paras 685 and 688.
[68] *Ibid.*, para. 686.
[69] *Ibid.*, para. 687.
[70] *Ibid.*, para. 687.
[71] *Ibid.*, para. 691.
[72] *Ibid.*, para. 692.
[73] *Ibid.*, para. 694.

equitable treatment standard is a 'balancing exercise, where the state's regulatory interests are weighed against the investors' legitimate expectations and reliance' and that 'the economic effect on a claimant's investment is an important factor in the balancing exercise'.[74] The tribunal found Spain's legislative measures to be 'radical' and 'unexpected', taking into account its prior statements and assurances. Furthermore, the way they were implemented 'fell 'outside the acceptable range of legislative and regulatory behavior' and 'entirely transform[ed] and alter[ed] the legal and business environment under which the investment was decided and made'.[75] The regulations enacted in 2013 and 2014 have definitely abolished the fixed long-term feed-in-tariff regime in a retroactive manner, thus breaching the fair and equitable treatment standard.[76]

Spain suffered another defeat in the *Masdar* case.[77] The tribunal noted that while host states have the right to amend their legislation,[78] that right is not unrestricted.[79] The panel cited several decisions in support of this position,[80] *inter alia* the *Eiser* award.[81] The essential question was what type of commitments can give rise to legitimate expectations worthy of protection.[82] The tribunal discussed at length two distinct doctrinal and jurisprudential positions: one that considers that commitments can result from general statements in general laws or regulations; and another which argues that commitments need to be specific.[83] The tribunal recalled that the second position, according to which stabilization provisions offered in general legislation or political announcements cannot create legitimate expectations,[84] was espoused by the *Charanne* tribunal.[85] The tribunal moved beyond that discussion, holding that it had to consider not only the totality of the Spanish legislative framework but also the existence of specific commitments.[86] In the end the tribunal concluded that Spain had made specific commitments and therefore investors had legitimate expectations that the benefits afforded by the legal regime would remain unchanged.[87] Modification of that legal framework constituted a breach of the fair and equitable treatment standard.[88]

[74] *Ibid.*, para. 694.
[75] *Ibid.*, para. 695, footnotes omitted.
[76] *Ibid.*, para. 697.
[77] *Masdar v Spain, supra* note 19.
[78] *Ibid.*, para. 485.
[79] *Ibid.*, para 486.
[80] *Ibid.*, para. 487.
[81] *Ibid.*, para 488.
[82] *Ibid.*, para. 489.
[83] *Ibid.*, paras 490–506.
[84] *Ibid.*, para. 507.
[85] *Ibid.*, paras 508–10.
[86] *Ibid.*, para. 511. See also paras 512–20.
[87] *Ibid.*, para 521.
[88] *Ibid.*, para. 522.

Spain was also found to have violated the fair and equitable treatment standard in the *Antin* case.[89] The tribunal started by invoking the *Charanne* and *Eiser* awards to posit that:

> the specific obligation of stability of the conditions for investors ... does not eliminate or strictly limit the regulatory powers of States nor does it prevent [them] from amending existing regulations, provided that the given State does not 'suddenly and unexpectedly eliminate the essential features of the regulatory framework in place'[90]

The tribunal agreed with the *Charanne* tribunal that the requirement of stability does not equate to the immutability of legal frameworks, and that host states are entitled to exercise their sovereign power to amend regulations to respond to changing circumstances in the public interest.[91] However, legislative changes 'must be consistent with the assurances on stability of the regulatory framework' by the State and investment treaties.[92] The tribunal underlined that its position was consistent with the *Charanne* award: investors' legitimate expectations may be frustrated if the host state 'eliminates the essential features of the regulatory framework relied upon by the investor in making a long-term investment'.[93] The tribunal also recalled that while the *Charanne* tribunal only dealt with 2010 regulations, in the *Antin* case the challenged regulations were adopted in 2013 and 2014,[94] concluding that the latter measures 'dismantled all the regime and therefore all the features' of the previous framework,[95] thus breaching the fair and equitable treatment standard.[96]

4 Adjusting Economic Incentives in Times of Crisis: (Preliminary) Lessons

At the time of writing, only nine awards have been rendered out of more than sixty disputes in this rapidly growing sector of investment arbitration jurisprudence. Respondent states prevailed in five disputes (*Charanne v Spain, Isolux v Spain, Blusun v Italy, JSW Solar v the Czech Republic*, and *Antaris v the Czech Republic*) while investors were successful in four cases (*Eiser v Spain, Novenergia v Spain, Masdar v Spain*, and *Antin v Spain*). Drawing any major conclusions would be hasty and ill-advised; attempts at forecasting the outcome of future awards even more so.

[89] *Antin v Spain, supra* note 20.
[90] *Ibid.*, para. 531. Footnotes omitted. See also para. 532.
[91] *Ibid.*, para. 555.
[92] *Ibid.* Footnotes omitted.
[93] *Ibid.*, para. 556.
[94] *Ibid.*, para. 558.
[95] *Ibid.*, para. 560.
[96] *Ibid.*, para. 573.

Still, it is possible to draw some (very preliminary) lessons from the awards already rendered.

First, economic support mechanisms are especially susceptible to regulatory changes.[97] Incentive schemes promise a certain level of return to investors in exchange for their heavy investments upfront, entailing a certain degree of certainty and predictability.[98] While these incentives provide a much-needed push towards cleaner sources of energy, governments may feel the need to adjust regulatory frameworks to new circumstances.[99] Governments intervene because regulation of energy production, distribution and consumption is a key element of national economic law and policy.[100] Such measures are justified by protection of fundamental public interests and may become particularly frequent in times of budgetary hardship.[101]

Compared with traditional sources of energy, economic incentives for renewable energy are especially susceptible to regulatory changes owing to the high costs of production and the unpredictability of the results of their implementation.[102] While countries have enacted different legal frameworks and introduced diverse reforms, the disputes discussed earlier demonstrate the existence of a tension between the stability of economic support mechanisms and the need to adapt to new circumstances.[103] The design and operation of renewable energy policies may be quite complex in practice, especially in times of economic crisis.[104]

There is a noticeable tension between respect for investment treaty obligations and the need to address the financial crisis.[105] Host states have, *en passant*, alluded to the financial crisis to defend their measures but did not go as far as invoking any sort of *force majeure*. In *Charanne*, Spain argued that legislative reform was aimed at adapting to changing economic circumstances and solving the problem

[97] Tomás Restrepo, 'Modification of Renewable Energy Support Schemes Under the Energy Charter Treaty: Eiser and Charanne in the Context of Climate Change' (2017) 8(1) *Goettingen Journal of International Law* 101, 102.

[98] Avidan Kent, 'Renewable Energy Disputes Before International Economic Tribunals: A Case for Institutional "Greening"?' (2015) 12 *Transnational Dispute Management* 1, 9.

[99] Ana Daza-Clark, *International Investment Law and Water Resources Management: An Appraisal of Indirect Expropriation* (Brill Nijhoff 2017) 48.

[100] Markus Krajewski, 'The Impact of International Investment Agreements on Energy Regulation' in Christoph Herrmann and Jörg Terhechte (eds), *European Yearbook of International Economic Law* (Springer 2012) 343, 345.

[101] Valentina Vadi, 'Beyond Known Worlds: Climate Change Governance by Arbitral Tribunals?' (2015) 48 *Vanderbilt Journal of Transnational Law* 1285, 1318.

[102] Restrepo, *supra* note 97, at 102–3; Risteard de Paor, 'Climate Change and Arbitration: Annex Time Before There Won't be A Next Time' (2017) 8(1) *Journal of International Dispute Settlement* 179, 191.

[103] Giuseppe Bellantuono, 'The Misguided Quest for Regulatory Stability in the Renewable Energy Sector' (2017) 10 *Journal of World Energy Law and Business* 274, 276.

[104] Jorge Viñuales, 'Green Investment after Rio 2012' (2014) 16(2) *International Community Law Review* 153, 164.

[105] Anastasios Gourgourinis, 'Financial Crisis as *Force Majeure* Under International Law and EU Law: Defending Emergency Measures, à l'européenne' in Christian Tams, Stephan Schill, and Rainer Hofmann (eds) *Investment Arbitration Under Intra-EU BITs, International Investment Law and the Global Financial Architecture* (Edward Elgar 2017) 281, 306.

of tariff deficit.[106] The investors contended that the tariff deficit or the fact that the country was going through a difficult economic situation did not exempt the government from complying with investment treaty obligations.[107] In *Isolux*, Spain also argued that the crisis and governmental announcements were explicit and that investors knew about the crisis.[108] The investors rejected that argument, stating that the Government should have alerted investors about the need to undertake reforms and that Spain had numerous possible measures at its disposal but did not adopt any of them.[109] Similarly, in the *Eiser* case the host state argued that, like any state, Spain is entitled to change its regulatory regime to meet compelling economic challenges, such as a tariff deficit, in order to serve public welfare.[110] In *JSW Solar*, the Czech Republic argued that the country was suffering from the effects of the global financial crisis and had a serious budget deficit.[111] Taking into account the government's efforts to deal with 'the solar boom as quickly as possible', investors 'could not have had any legitimate expectations of legislative stasis'.[112] The Czech Republic added that one of the reasons for legislative reform was the need to respond to increasing energy prices in circumstances of 'economic turmoil'.[113] The tribunal acknowledged that the country 'was not only struggling with the effects of the global financial crisis, but also suffering from a political crisis'.[114] The contested measures were a response to developments in the solar sector at a time of economic and political uncertainty.[115] In the words of the tribunal, 'the Czech Republic introduced the measures in pursuit of legitimate objectives including restoring equilibrium in the solar sector, protecting consumers from substantial electricity bill increases and augmenting budgetary resources in a time of global financial crisis'.[116] In the *Antin* case, Spain also argued that the challenged measures were adopted to address the tariff deficit and preserve the sustainability of the electric system.[117] While acknowledging that the tariff deficit posed 'a legitimate public policy problem for Spain', the tribunal held that it emerged before Spain had any significant renewable energy capacity and was not caused by incentives.[118] The existence of such a deficit did not justify eliminating the key features of the legal regime and its replacement by a wholly new regime, not based on any identifiable criteria.[119]

106 *Charanne v Spain, supra* note 12, para. 356.
107 *Ibid.*, para. 304.
108 *Isolux v Spain, supra* note 13, paras 426 and 535.
109 *Ibid.*, para. 380.
110 *Eiser v Spain, supra* note 15, para. 351.
111 *JSW Solar v The Czech Republic, supra* note 16, para. 346.
112 *Ibid.*
113 *Ibid.*, para. 350.
114 *Ibid.*, para. 389.
115 *Ibid.*, para. 406.
116 *Ibid.*, para. 442.
117 *Antin v Spain, supra* note 20, para. 569.
118 *Ibid.*, paras 570 and 571.
119 *Ibid.*, para. 572.

In all these cases, the respondent states realized that the economic support regime they had put in place was overly generous.[120] Governments over-incentivized their original economic support schemes and had to take back much of that support later on.[121] According to Behn, Fauchald, and Létourneau-Tremblay,[122] governments failed to anticipate two external conditions: the dawn of the global financial crisis of 2008 and the evolution in the cost of solar panels. Combined, these two elements made the conditions offered to investors in renewable energies appear to governments as 'an obsolete bargain', with investors collecting disproportionate profits.[123] There was, however, an internal condition that governments could have anticipated: the need for a more flexible regulatory structure which could adjust to changing market conditions.[124] Once they realized the dramatic changes in market conditions, it was too late and governments had to adopt drastic measures.[125]

Second, the precise application of investment protection standards to these cases is far from well-established. While on occasion other standards of protection are also raised cumulatively, investor claims never forget to invoke an alleged breach of fair and equitable treatment.[126] However, the exact content of this standard depends on the language used in investment treaties.[127] Still, arbitral tribunals and scholars generally agree that transparency, stability, non-discrimination, due process, and investors' legitimate expectations are all key ingredients in defining the fair and equitable standard.[128] In pending cases, respondent states will most likely invoke the higher threshold for breaches of the fair and equitable treatment standard, as set in the *Charanne, Isolux, Blusun, JSW Solar*, and *Antaris* awards. Inversely, investors will probably try to demonstrate that host states have crossed the red line drawn in the *Eiser, Novenergia, Masdar*, and *Antin* awards. All nine decisions already available offer a sort of preliminary roadmap for arbitral panels

[120] Masia, *supra* note 30, at 667; Volker Roeben, *Towards a European Energy Union: European Energy Strategy in International Law* (CUP 2018) 59; Institute for Energy Resources, Europe Slashing Renewable Subsidies, 9 April 2014 <https://instituteforenergyresearch.org/analysis/europe-slashing-renewable-subsidies-2/> accessed 24 April 2019; Pablo del Río, Anxo Calvo-Silvosa, and Guillermo Iglesias, 'The New Renewable Electricity Support Scheme in Spain: A Comment' (2015) 6(1) *Renewable Energy Law and Policy Review* 17, 19.

[121] Daniel Behn, Ole Fauchald, and Laura Létourneau-Tremblay, 'Promoting Renewable Energy in the EU: Shifting Trends in Member State Policy Space' (2017) 28(2) *European Business Law Review* 217, 222.

[122] *Ibid.*, 231–2.

[123] Restrepo, *supra* note 97, at 104.

[124] Behn, Fauchald, and Létourneau-Tremblay, *supra* note 121, at 232.

[125] *Ibid.*

[126] Arbitral tribunals in *Eiser v Spain* (*supra* note 15, paras 354 and 355); *Novenergia v Spain* (*supra* note 17, para. 698);and *Masdar v Spain* (*supra* note 19, paras 666–668) invoked considerations of procedural economy to focus exclusively on the breach of the fair and equitable treatment standard.

[127] See Christoph Schreuer, 'Fair and Equitable Treatment (FET): Interactions with Other Standards' in Graham Coop and Clarisse Ribeiro (eds), *Investment Arbitration and the Energy Charter Treaty* (JurisNet 2008) 63, 65ff.

[128] See Dolzer and Schreuer, *supra* note 11, at 119ff.

faced with regulatory changes in renewable energy markets. They all converge in confirming that host states' regulatory powers are not absolute and that drastic legislative changes may breach investment protection standards. Albeit at first glance these decisions seem to reach diametrically opposed conclusions, this is but a reminder that the outcome of each dispute is deeply dependent on the specific regulatory framework under analysis and on how abruptly it evolves through time. Because the body of case law on the interaction between renewable energy incentives and standards of investment protection is still quite limited, arbitral panels are likely to pay careful attention to decisions already made public. While there is no doctrine of binding jurisprudence in international investment arbitration, a strong, persuasive system of precedent has developed over recent decades.[129] More awards can be expected in the coming months, hopefully contributing to defining more consistently and clearly the parameters that delimit host states' regulatory freedom in the renewable energy sector.

Third, the legal and factual context of each claim is of the essence for the outcome of the dispute. While available awards may provide guidance in examining the application of investment standards to the specificities of the renewable energy market, one should not forget that each state enacted a different legal framework to attract investments that later was amended to different degrees. This explains, to a large extent, why different tribunals reached different conclusions in different cases.[130] The outcome of each case will depend on how drastic were the different legislative reforms.[131] Arbitral tribunals will assess the compatibility of those legislative measures against the standards of protection on a case-by-case basis.[132]

Changes to regulatory frameworks might have a significant impact on what until recently seemed like an unstoppable move towards a low-carbon model of development, jeopardizing the credibility of renewable energy policies and generating high investment uncertainty. These measures may affect support for renewable energy in both the present and future. The existence of contrasting decisions in the cases decided thus far underlines the importance of monitoring the gradual evolution of this sprouting segment of jurisprudence. The takeaways from available awards cannot be applied automatically and fully to other pending disputes. While each award is closely connected to its specific legal and factual context, this stream

[129] Stephan Schill, 'International Investment Law and Comparative Public Law—An Introduction' in Stephan Schill (ed.), *International Investment Law and Comparative Public Law* (OUP 2010) 3, 18.

[130] Restrepo, *supra* note 97, at 136.

[131] Daniel Behn, 'Spain Wins First PV Solar Arbitration: A Word of Caution in Using this Case to Predict Outcome in the more than Three Dozen Cases to Come', 27 January 2016 <http://www.jus.uio.no/pluricourts/english/blog/daniel-friedrich-behn/2016-01-26-arbitration-spain.html> accessed 24 April 2019.

[132] Martin Švec, 'The Energy Charter Treaty: Renewable Energy Disputes in Light of the Charanne Case' in Klára Drličková and Tereza Kyselovská (eds) *Cofola International 2016: Resolution of International Disputes Public Law in the Context of Immigration Crisis: Conference Proceedings* (Masaryk University 2016) 237, 246.

of rulings contributes to clarifying the limits to host states' regulatory freedom in the renewable energy sector. This growing case law may also help to delineate more clearly the line between the legitimate expectations of investors and the right of host states to adjust to changing circumstances, namely in face of unexpected economic conditions.

PART IV
PHILOSOPHICAL PERSPECTIVES

Probing Key Concepts and Premises in International Law

Playing Hide and Seek with '*Vergangenheit, die nicht vergehen will*' ('*a Past that Will Not Pass*') in the History of International Law

Ignacio de la Rasilla

'Education is a powerful tool for non-recurrence.
In particular, the teaching of history if approached as a system of investigation'
Report of the UN Special Rapporteur on the Promotion of Truth, Justice, Reparation and Guarantee of Non-Recurrence.
Mission to Spain. Para. 34. 24 July 2014

1 Introduction

As Joseph Kunz remarked in assessing the 'judicial cosmopolitan'[1] ambitions of Hans Kelsen's *Peace through Law*[2] in 1944, it might well be 'an illusion to believe that it will ever be possible to transform world history into nothing but a court procedure'.[3] Arguably, international courts can only have a limited role in dealing with controversial historical questions because of the tensions they face as they 'seek to address diverging aims'.[4] On the one hand, to 'tell the whole truth and to create an historical record'[5] and, on the other, to adhere to 'jurisdictional and evidentiary rules' to be able to 'render justice' to the parties in the case whilst safeguarding the 'fairness' of the judicial process.

The procedural and substantive limitations that international courts must confront when seeking to create a complete 'historical record' are manifold.

[1] Danilo Zolo, 'Hans Kelsen: International Peace through International Law' (1998) 9 *European Journal of International Law* 306.
[2] Hans Kelsen, *Peace through Law* (University of North Carolina Press 1944).
[3] Joseph L. Kunz, 'Compulsory International Adjudication and Maintenance of Peace' (1944) 38 *American Journal of International Law* 673.
[4] Fergal Gaynor, 'Uneasy Partners—Evidence, Truth and History in International Trials' (2012) 10 *Journal of International Criminal* Justice 1257, 1258.
[5] *Ibid.*

Ignacio de la Rasilla, *Playing Hide and Seek with* 'Vergangenheit, die nicht vergehen will' ('a Past that Will Not Pass') *in the History of International Law* In: *How International Law Works in Times of Crisis.* Edited by: George Ulrich and Ineta Ziemele, Oxford University Press (2019).
DOI: 10.1093/oso/9780198849667.003.0014

In international criminal procedure, where the jurisdictional and evidentiary rules are commonly regarded as being originally tilted in favour of the 'adversarial model',[6] these limitations include—as highlighted by Fergal Gaynor—those constraints that such courts face as determined by the scope of their jurisdiction, whether it be *ratione materiae, ratione temporis*, or *ratione loci*.[7] These limitations also extend to the 'temporal, territorial and substantive extent of the indictment'[8] which, furthermore, can be affected by the 'workings' of a 'plea agreement'.[9] Other procedural constraints affecting the creation of a 'complete historical record' by international criminal courts flow from the effects of prosecutorial discretion,[10] confidentiality restrictions, and a range of reasons for excluding evidence given by a party.[11] Moreover, the 'historical objectives' pursued through international criminal adjudication can be affected by implementation of a higher burden of proof, the 'beyond reasonable doubt test', and, no less decisively, by the fact that 'what may be historically relevant may be legally irrelevant'.[12]

Against this background, academic work on the relationship between international criminal trials and history has, understandably, raised doubts as to the extent that 'courts are well equipped to make authoritative findings regarding representation of the past'.[13] However, an indirect—and often overlooked—legacy of judicial proceedings, both international and domestic alike, is their impact on the expansion of historical research. In this sense, judicial treatment of the Spanish Historical Memory Act 2007 illustrates how the judicial unearthing of historical knowledge about the past can be beneficial for the history of international law itself. The Spanish Historical Memory Act 2007 stands as a clear, recent example of how judicial proceedings, even those deemed to have failed, can contribute *inter alia* to reviving interest in historical research of past atrocities and, in doing so, 'defrost' the study of long neglected histories of international law.

It barely needs stressing that unsettled historical scores have been a breeding ground for both national and international crises. Besides their role in crisis

[6] Antonio Cassese and Paola Gaeta, *Cassese's International Criminal Law, 3rd edn* (OUP 2013). Although later 'developments have strengthened the civil law elements in international criminal procedure' at the ICC and the ICTY, thus approaching it as a 'mixed one', Kai Ambos, 'International Criminal Procedure: "Adversarial", "Inquisitorial" Or Mixed?' (2003) 5 *International Criminal Law Review* 1, 5.

[7] Gaynor 'Uneasy Partners', *supra* note 5, 1263.

[8] *Ibid.*, 1266.

[9] *Ibid.*, 1268–9.

[10] *Ibid.*, 1264–5.

[11] *Ibid.*, 1269–71.

[12] Under international criminal law rules, it would not be 'a defence to argue that the other side in the conflict was committing large-scale crimes against one's own side' *Ibid.*, 1264.

[13] Carsten Stahn 'Re-Constructing History through Courts? Legacy in International Criminal Justice'(2015) 1, 6 available at SSRN: <https://ssrn.com/abstract=2616491>.

incubation, they may be essentially constitutive factors of a silent, yet deeply corrosive, crisis of conscience spanning all layers of society. The effects of this type of occasionally self-repressed crisis of conscience can be particularly acute in the twilight area, between the national and the international realms, where most international law scholars perform their social and intellectual roles.

To analyse these two dimensions of the role of historical memory in international law after a long period of dictatorial rule in the light of the Spanish experience since its latest transition to democracy, the chapter proceeds in two parts. The first part of the chapter reviews the enactment of the Spanish Historical Memory Act (HMA) and examines three of its most polemical areas of implementation in the light of the concerns raised by several United Nations human rights bodies charged with overseeing the conflictual politics of historical memory in Spain. These areas are, first, the tracing, identification, and eventual exhumation of victims of the Francoist repression; second, the removal of Francoist symbols from public spaces; and third, Judge B Garzón's failed attempt to start criminal proceedings to investigate Franco's crimes as 'crimes against humanity' against the letter of the Spanish Amnesty law of 1977.

The second part of the chapter builds on Spanish experience in examining some of the most common hurdles—including methodological ones—that an incoming democratic generation of international lawyers may face when attempting a balanced exploration of the history of international law after a long period of authoritarian rule in their home country. For international lawyers in those societies confronted with the dilemma of '*Vergangengeitsbewältigung*' ('*coping with the past*'), such factors may include first, the traditional neglect of the study of the history of international law in a discipline traditionally dominated by a normative rule-based methodological approach to international law; second, the only recent surge of interest among international law scholars in the 'darker legacies' of international law;[14] third, the underlying influence of a national 'pact of forgetfulness' in an elite professionally driven technical discipline with a particular authority and expertise that makes it less susceptible to interdisciplinary engagement by historians; and finally, the adaptability and rejuvenation of national identity myths in a field that tends to cast aside its failures, its pathologies, and its uncomfortable memories in order to embrace a 'narrative of normative progress'.[15]

The 'bad example' set by the short memory span of Spanish international lawyers regarding the intellectual legacy of the handmaidens of the foreign policy of a Spanish dictatorial regime for almost four decades may be of illustrative value to international lawyers in other younger democracies and transitioning countries.

[14] See, e.g., Christian Joerges, Navraj Singh Ghaleigh, and Michael Stolleis (eds), *Darker Legacies of Law in Europe: The Shadow of National Socialism and Fascism Over Europe and Its Legal Traditions* (Hart 2003).

[15] See, e.g., Tilmann Altwicker and Oliver Diggelmann, 'How is Progress Constructed in International Legal Scholarship?' (2014) 25 *European Journal of International Law* 425.

The international legal literature is still ill-equipped to cope with the type of internal crisis of conscience suffered by successive generations of Spanish international lawyers. This should be tackled in a straightforward, contextualized, and educational manner. Unless this happens, a normalization of attitudes that on nationalist grounds excuse past complicit allegiances or, even worse, contribute to the silent glorification of a past of ethical impunity, may be expected. Thus conceived, the potential contribution of the history of international law to unearthing the blind spots of the 'historical memory' of the discipline in national settings is also a long-term investment in international crisis prevention.

2 Controversies Surrounding the Spanish Historical Memory Act

It is estimated that the humanitarian carnage of the Spanish Civil War (1936–1939)[16] left between 500,000 and 600,000 people dead; 300,000 to 500,000 more in exile; hundreds of thousands suffering repression in jails and forced labour;[17] and over 100,000 people unaccounted for. Undeniably, this has left Spanish society affected, with profound scars going back over many decades.[18] In late 2007, the Historical Memory Act, 52/2007[19] (hereinafter HMA) was enacted 'to recognise and broaden rights and to establish measures in favour of those who suffered persecution or violence during the Civil War and the Dictatorship'. It extended the provision of aid to the victims of both the Civil War and of the Francoist regime, and to their descendants contained in a series of earlier, lukewarm laws and decrees.[20] Amidst difficult negotiations between the Spanish political parties,[21] the government of President Zapatero's Socialist Party heralded the HMA as containing 'the

[16] From an international legal perspective, see recently, e.g., Ignacio de la Rasilla, '"*In the General Interests of Peace*"? British International Lawyers and the Spanish Civil War' (2016) *Journal of the History of International Law* 197.

[17] See, e.g., Paul Preston, *The Spanish Holocaust. Inquisition and Extermination in Twentieth Century Spain* (Harper Press 2013).

[18] See, e.g., Michael Richards, *After the Civil War. Making Memory and Re-Making Spain since 1936* (CUP 2013).

[19] Ley de la Memoria Histórica, Ley 52/2007, de 26 de diciembre, por la que se reconocen y amplían derechos y se establecen medidas en favor de quienes padecieron persecución o violencia durante la guerra civil y la dictadura, 26 Diciembre 2007. Available at: <http://leymemoria.mjusticia.gob.es/cs/Satellite/LeyMemoria/es/memoria-historica-522007> accessed 28 April 2019. English version used by the author, available at Equipo Nizkor: <http://www.derechos.org/nizkor/espana/doc/lmheng.html> accessed 28 April 2019.

[20] Since the 1980s, these had recognized rights and benefits in favour of the victims of the Spanish Civil War and General Franco's single-party regime, see Sections 4.2 and 4.3. of the General Report of the Inter-Departmental Commission for the Study of the Situation of the Victims of the Civil War and Francoism (Informe General de la Comision Interministerial para el estudio de la situación de las victimas de la guerra y del Franquismo), 36.

[21] On the difficult parliamentary passing of Act 52/2007 see, e.g., Jean-François Macé, 'Los conflictos de memoria en la España postfranquista (1976–2010) entre políticas de la memoria y memorias de la política' (2012) 114 *Bulletin Hispanique* 749, 768–73.

first explicit legal condemnation of the Francoist regime'[22] since the new onset of democratic rule in Spain.

The purpose of the HMA is the 'recognition and extension of rights in favour of those who suffered persecution or violence, for reasons of politics, ideology or for religious beliefs, during the Civil War or the Dictatorship, to promote their moral redress and the recovery of their personal and family memory'.[23] In pursuit of those objectives, the HMA established that 'all convictions, punishments or other forms of personal violence which took place for reasons of politics, ideology or religious belief' during that period 'are recognised and declared completely unjust in nature'.[24] The HMA also ordered the 'Creation of a Documentary Centre of Historical Memory and General Archive of the Civil War',[25] and the removal from public spaces of commemorative symbols 'which extol, individually or collectively, the military uprising, the Civil War and the repression of the Dictatorship'.[26] The HMA also became known as the 'law of the grandchildren' because one of its provisions, which remained in force until December 2011, resulted in almost a quarter of a million descendants of Spanish citizens being granted Spanish nationality.[27]

As indicated earlier, three areas of implementation of the HMA have been particularly polemical: that is, the tracing, identification, and eventual exhumation of victims; the removal of Francoist symbols from public spaces; and investigation of the crimes of the Franco era by Judge Garzón. These will now be briefly considered in turn.

First, whilst the HMA did 'not codify a right to exhume victims' bodies',[28] it did include provision of 'state help' in tracing, identifying, and the eventual exhumation of victims of Francoist repression, whose corpses are still missing.[29] It has been estimated that this affected approximately 110,000 victims of the Spanish Civil War, who were reported missing and believed to be buried in mass graves. According to Amnesty International, only Cambodia has exceeded this figure.[30] In the years immediately after enactment of the HMA, the Spanish authorities, acting under the socialist government (PSOE), allocated more than 25 million euros to the process of accounting for those who were missing. However, in 2012,

[22] Rafael Escudero, 'Road to Impunity: The Absence of Transitional Justice Programs in Spain' (2014) 36 *Human Rights Quarterly* 123, 142.

[23] Art. 1, Historical Memory Act, 52/2007.

[24] Art. 2, Historical Memory Act, 52/2007.

[25] See Art. 20, Historical Memory Act, 52/2007.

[26] Although the HMA notes that 'exceptions may be provided for artistic or architectural reasons, or in the case of religious spaces', Art. 15, Historical Memory Act, 52/2007.

[27] Seventh Additional Provision. Historical Memory Act, 52/2007 El Pais, 'España suma casi 250.000 nuevos nacionales gracias a la 'ley de nietos' 30/3/2012: available at: <http://politica.elpais.com/politica/2012/03/30/actualidad/1333132776_885506.html> accessed 28 April 2019.

[28] Escudero, *supra* note 23.

[29] See Art. 12, Historical Memory Act, 52/2007.

[30] Amnesty International, 'Why Spain Must Investigate Franco-era Crimes'; available at: <https://www.amnesty.org.uk/blogs/press-release-me-let-me-go/why-spain-must-investigate-franco-era-crimes> 18 June 2013; accessed 28 April 2019.

coinciding with the rise to power of the centre-right party (PP), a party which had criticized the HMA as a 'political attempt to undermine the Transition and reopen old wounds',[31] funding for social entities participating in these exhumation works plummeted.[32]

In late 2013, with an estimated 6,200 people exhumed since the passing of the HMA,[33] the UN Committee on Enforced Disappearances[34] saw fit to remind Spain 'that the search for persons who have been the victims of enforced disappearance and efforts to clarify their fate are obligations of the State even if no formal complaint has been laid'.[35] The Committee further recommended that Spain should 'adopt all the necessary measures, including the allocation of sufficient human, technical and financial resources, to search for and clarify the fate of disappeared persons'[36] and set up a Truth Commission 'of independent experts charged with establishing the truth about past human rights violations, in particular enforced disappearances'[37] during the Civil War and the Dictatorship. Since then, these points have been reiterated by the UN Working Group on Enforced or Involuntary Disappearances and the UN Special Rapporteur on the Promotion of Truth, Justice, Reparation and Guarantee of Non-Recurrence. The latter 'urged' Spain to consider the establishment of an 'independent, but official, mechanism or body, whose aim would consist in achieving an exhaustive understanding of the human rights and humanitarian law violations that occurred during the Civil War and the Franco era'.[38]

The second area of implementation of the HMA referred to earlier, which has possibly attracted the most media and public attention, is the order for removal from public spaces of Francoist symbols. In 2014, the UN Special Rapporteur on the Promotion of Truth, Justice, Reparation and Guarantee of Non-Recurrence congratulated the Spanish Government, acknowledging that the 'majority of inventoried symbols and monuments had been removed'.[39] Nonetheless, Pablo de Greiff's report also stressed that 'names of streets and buildings, commemorative plaques and emblems, which apparently commemorated the senior posts and officials of the Franco regime in different parts of the country'[40] had been preserved.

[31] Escudero, 'Road to Impunity', *supra* note 23, 145.

[32] Amidst a severe economic crisis, the new government reduced 60% of the funds allocated to implementation of the Historical Memory Act and suppressed the Office of Victims of the Civil War and the Dictatorship in charge of coordinating the exhumation of those who disappeared.

[33] Macé, *supra* note 21.

[34] The UN Committee on Enforced Disappearances 'Concluding observations on the report submitted by Spain under Art. 29, para.1, of the Convention', UN Document, CED/C/ESP/CO/1, 12 December 2013, paras 31–33.

[35] *Ibid.*, para. 32.

[36] *Ibid.*

[37] *Ibid.*, para. 33.

[38] Report of the Special Rapporteur on the promotion of truth, justice, reparation and guarantees of non-recurrence, Pablo de Greiff Mission to Spain, A/HRC/27/56/Add.1 24 July 2014, para. 47.

[39] *Ibid.*, paras 27–33.

[40] *Ibid.*

Moreover, the report highlighted that more work was necessary for the 'Valley of the Fallen' to 'be put to good use' and 'reinterpreted', with suitable techniques and pedagogy, in favour of the promotion of truth and memory, and given an educational and preventive purpose'.[41] In 2016, after numerous student campaigns and protests, the crest of 'Harvard Law School' was removed from the Harvard Law School's shield because it constituted an historical reminder that the first law professorship at Harvard Law School, established in 1815, was funded by a bequest from the estate of a wealthy slave owner.[42] Similarly, in Spain, it has, on occasion, become necessary to involve public pressure, and even judicial proceedings, for local government all over Spanish territory to rename many streets. Nine years after the passage of the HMA, these processes of removal and renaming are still in progress.[43]

The third, and the most polemical, area of implementation of the HMA was prompted in late 2008 when, in response to a class action by a victims' association, Judge Garzón declared himself competent to start criminal proceedings to investigate Franco's crimes under the HMA. Judge Garzón became widely known in 1998 as the judge who issued an international warrant for the arrest of former Chilean President, Augusto Pinochet, on the basis of the principle of universal jurisdiction,[44] designed to enable adjudication of crimes committed by former heads of state despite local amnesty laws.[45] The Spanish crimes Garzón sought to investigate were mass killings and illegal detentions and/or disappearances committed in the context of a systematic attack against civilians between 17 July 1936 and 31 December 1951 in Spain. However, soon afterwards, the Spanish National Court decided to set the proceedings aside on the grounds that the crimes that Garzón has defined as 'crimes against humanity' were under prescription and also amnestied. As a corollary, in 2010, Garzón was suspended from office and formally accused of judicial perversion of the course of justice (*prevaricación*). This is an offence committed when 'a judge wilfully or negligently delivers an unfair judgment or when he or she takes a decision knowing that it violates the law'.

Two years later, in February 2012, Garzón was acquitted of those charges by the same Spanish Supreme Court.[46] Based on its findings, the court held that although

[41] *Ibid.*

[42] BBC report: https://www.bbc.com/news/education-35726878.

[43] See, recent news published by *El Pais* El Comisionado de Memoria Histórica propone renombrar 27 calles 'franquistas' 22/07/2016; <http://ccaa.elpais.com/ccaa/2016/07/21/madrid/1469123591_616263.html> accessed 28 April 2019.

[44] See, e.g., Ignacio de la Rasilla 'The Swan Song of Universal Jurisdiction in Spain' (2009) *International Criminal Law Review* 777.

[45] See, e.g., Asier Garrido Muñoz, 'No dédoublement fonctionnel? Eluding avant-garde international human Rights law in Spain: Strategies and judicial parallelisms' (2013) 23 *International Law, Revista colombiana de Derecho internacional*, 153, 161.

[46] This case was one of the three parallel criminal procedures instructed by the Supreme Court against Judge Garzón, one of which eventually led to his condemnation for perverting the course of justice and his barring from serving on the bench for eleven years for having committed the crime of prevarication when acting as examining magistrate for an investigation of a case of corruption involving authorized

the magistrate's behaviour had been wrong it did not contain enough elements to be considered 'judicial perversion of justice' because it lacked the additional factor of 'wrongfulness' required to make out all the required elements of the offence.[47] However, in its same judgement 101/2012, the Spanish Supreme Court reaffirmed the arguments on which the claims of infeasibility of prosecuting crimes committed under Francoism from 1936 to 1951 were based, in its opinion. That is, the acts were not crimes against humanity when committed and therefore the principle of non-retroactivity should be applied to them; they were under prescription; and, finally, all were covered by the Spanish Amnesty Law of 1977. In summary, following the letter of the pre-constitutional 1977 Amnesty Law, which sealed off reconciliation between the so-called two Spains from the haunting spectre of a past that still lingered, heavily weighted with both emotional and political baggage after Franco's death, the Spanish Supreme Court foreclosed the possibility of bringing to bear the inapplicability of the statute of limitations to crimes against humanity[48] for the mass killings and illegal detentions and/or disappearances committed in the context of a systematic attack against civilians between 17 July 1936 and 31 December 1951 in Spain. Moreover, according to the Spanish Supreme Court, the Spanish criminal law system does not provide for

> so-called 'truth trials', that is to say, trials intended to give rise to a judicial investigation into what appear to have been criminal acts, but in which it is impossible for such legal proceedings to lead to a person being found guilty because prosecution is precluded by grounds for the extinction of criminal responsibility, death, prescription or amnesty.[49]

This judicial interpretation has been denounced by several mechanisms of the United Nations, and expressly by the UN Working Group on Enforced or Involuntary Disappearances, the Committee on Enforced Disappearances, and the UN Special Rapporteur on the Promotion of Truth, Justice, Reparation and Guarantees of Non-Repetition. Each one of these has put forward recommendations to try and deal with the incompatibility of the effects of the Amnesty Act with the international obligations undertaken by Spain.

In December 2013, in its concluding observations on the report submitted by Spain under Article 29.1, of the Convention, the UN Committee on Enforced

illegal wiretapping of conversations between some prisoners and their lawyers. 'The Gurtel Case' involved the illegal financing of the Spanish centre-right wing ruling party (PP). Judge Garzón is *inter alia* currently the head of the legal defence team of Julian Assange.

---

[47] For a detailed analysis see Josep M. Tamarit Sumalla, *Historical Memory and Criminal Justice in Spain. A Case of Late Transitional Justice* (Intersentia 2013) 119–63.

[48] *Ibid.*

[49] *Ibid.*

Disappearances, 'urged' Spain 'to ensure that the term of limitation actually commences at the moment when the enforced disappearance ends, that is, when the person is found alive, his or her remains are found or their identity restored'.[50] It also encouraged Spain

> to ensure that all disappearances are investigated thoroughly and impartially, regardless of the time that has elapsed since they took place and even if there has been no formal complaint; the necessary legislative or judicial measures are adopted to remove any legal impediments to such investigations in domestic law, notably the interpretation given to the Amnesty Act.[51]

On 28 November 2014, prompted by judicial obstruction of the cases appearing before the Spanish courts and, by association, those appearing before the European Court of Human Rights (ECtHR), Argentine Federal Judge Servini de Cubria extended the warrants, which had been previously issued in a case opened in 2010 for the extradition of persons suspected of acts of torture committed during the final years of the Franco regime, to seventeen former Spanish officials. This list included seven former ministers, judges, and members of the police forces, who stand accused of the torture, killing, and kidnapping of minors and dissidents during the dictatorship. Although Spain has been reminded by UN human rights bodies of its 'international obligation to either extradite or judge and that the extradition of the accused can only be denied if the Spanish courts themselves initiate investigations and judge those responsible',[52] none of those indicted has so far been extradited from Spain. Amnesty International and other bodies have denounced the dilatory tactics and lack of cooperation by Spain in facilitating what now remains the only opportunity, world-wide, to examine human rights abuses committed during the Franco regime.[53]

This brief survey of some of the key difficulties and controversies surrounding the enactment and effective enforcement of the HMA[54] illustrates how the longest

[50] The UN Committee on Enforced Disappearances, 'Concluding observations on the report submitted by Spain under Art. 29, para. 1 of the Convention CED/C/ESP/CO/1, 12 December 2013, paras 11 and 12.

[51] *Ibid.*

[52] *Ibid.*, 84.

[53] See Amnesty International: <https://www.es.amnesty.org/actua/acciones/espana-extradicion-tortura-franquismo/> and Argentinian Press: <https://www.es.amnesty.org/actua/acciones/espana-extradicion-tortura-franquismo/> accessed 28 April 2019.

[54] See the official responses of Spain to the different UN human rights bodies including inter alia questioning the legal competence 'ratione temporis' of those bodies: (i) 'Observaciones de España al informe del Relator Especial de Naciones Unidas sobre la promoción de la verdad, la justicia, la reparación y las garantías de no repetición, Sr. Pablo de Greiff, sobre su visita a España' A/HRC/27/56/Add.3 17 September 2014; (ii) Misión a España: Comentarios de España al informe del Grupo de trabajo sobre las desapariciones forzadas o involuntarias tras su misión a España, A/HRC/27/49/Add.3 23 de diciembre 2014; (iii) Report on follow-up to the observations of the Committee on Enforced Disappearances concerning its consideration of the report of Spain CED/C/ESP/CO/1/Add.1 16 January 2015.

personal dictatorship in the history of the West, and the ninth longest globally, during the twentieth century, has cast a long shadow over the history of twentieth-century Spain. The next section shows how, by association, that same long shadow of the Civil War and the Franco regime has also loomed large over the study of the history of international law in Spain.

3 The Spanish History of International Law that Fell Between the Cracks

Spanish international law scholars, writing in the democratic post-Franco era, have largely avoided engaging international legal discipline in Spain with the Francoist past. For decades after the 'Transition' to democracy it was as if complete oblivion of the history of international law in Spain was preferable to running the risk of its being tainted by '*Vergangenheit, die nicht vergehen will*' ('a past that will not pass'). However, since the HMA and the Garzón case, there are signs that a timid renaissance of the study of the history of international law in Spain in the nineteenth and twentieth centuries has finally begun to take place.[55]

This rather muted and belated interest by Spanish international law scholars in the history of international law in Spain has been conditioned by a cumulative array of causes. The analysis of the resulting 'pattern' may provide a useful reference point for the reconstruction of other national histories of international law in countries faced with a similar dilemma after a period of authoritarian rule and, perhaps, help prevent those histories from also falling through the cracks of comparative international legal research as happened in Spain for decades.

The factors that have played against the healthy development of historical research into the Spanish history of international law include, first, neglect of the study of the history of international law in a discipline traditionally dominated by a rule-based methodological normative orientation which conditions the approach to the study of history among international lawyers. Second, the only recent surge of interest among international law scholars in the so-called darker legacies of international law.[56] Third, the weight of a 'pact of forgetfulness' on a democratic generation in a profession barely susceptible to interdisciplinary engagement by historians. Finally, the remarkable adaptability and rejuvenation of national identity myths in the field of international law. These four causes, which underlie the long silence of Spanish international lawyers regarding investigation of their own disciplinary history, will be briefly considered in turn.

[55] See, e.g., Ignacio de la Rasilla, 'The Fascist Mimesis of Spanish International Law and Its Vitorian Aftermath' (2012) 14 *Journal of the History of International Law* 207. See, e.g., Yolanda Gamarra and Ignacio de la Rasilla (eds), *Historia del Pensamiento Ius-internacionalista Español del Siglo XX* (Thompson Reuters Aranzadi 2013).

[56] Joerges et al., *supra* note 14.

The first factor behind the lack of critical attention of the 'democratic generation' of Spanish international lawyers to the evolution of its own history of international law during the forty years of Franco's rule, and by extension during the earlier nineteenth and the first part of the twentieth century, is related to the fact that historical writing in international law was, until recently, obscured, as Peters and Jouannet have remarked, by 'the methodological primacy of technicism, (doctrinalism) and pragmatism in international legal scholarship'.[57] Since roughly the turn of the twentieth century, this state of affairs has been positively affected by the so-called turn to history in international law.[58] This development has been partly spurred, *inter alia*, by the influence of so-called new approaches to international law[59] that have introduced both new historiographies and methodologies for the study of the discipline's multiple pasts, and furthered nurtured an understanding of international law 'as an intellectual discipline (and not just a "craft")'.[60] This extension of the domain of international legal research has brought about, as Matti Koskenniemi has noted, a transformation of a field hitherto dominated by 'trans-historical methodology that viewed international law as a trans-historical conversation over great principles or indeed as a project of global progress'.[61]

However, despite increasing production of academic history in international law, the history of international law is still at an early stage of professional establishment. It remains neglected or is a barely taught sub-discipline in universities world-wide, and most of its cultivators are legally trained international scholars with only an 'amateur' or self-educated perspective of interdisciplinary and historical research and its methods. Mainly because of their rigorous legal training during both undergraduate and postgraduate study in 'legal positivism', students of international law can often find it disorienting to try and identify suitable theoretical methodologies and understand how to make the best use of interdisciplinary research in pursuit of their projects. Historical writing in international law is, consequently, still rarely the outcome of a methodologically pursued research plan thoroughly designed in the light of a clear theoretical basis[62] which 'in turn

57 Emmanuelle Jouannet and Anne Peters, 'The Journal of the History of International Law: A Forum for New Research' (2014) 16 *Journal of the History of International Law* 1, 2.

58 See e.g. Bardo Fassbender and Anne Peters (eds), *The Oxford Handbook of the History of International Law* (OUP 2012); on the 'historical turn' or 'turn to history' in international law see, e.g., Randall Lesaffer, 'International Law and Its History: The Story of an Unrequited Love' in Matthew Craven, Malgosia Fitzmaurice, and Maria Vogiatzi (eds), *Time, History and International Law* (Martinus Nijhoff 2008) 27. For the influence of critical theory in its development, see, e.g., George R. Bandeira Galindo, 'Force Field: On History and Theory of International Law' (2012) 20 *Zeitschrift des Max-Planck-Instituts fur europaische Rechtsgeschichte* 86.

59 See, e.g., Thomas Skouteris, 'New Approaches to International Law' (2012) *Oxford Bibliographies of International Law* 1.

60 See, e.g., Martti Koskenniemi, 'Expanding Histories of International Law' (2016) 56 (1) *American Journal of Legal History* 104.

61 Martti Koskenniemi, 'Vitoria and Us' (2014) 22 *Rechtsgeschichte—Legal History Rg* 119, 121.

62 Robert Cryer, Tamara Hervey, and Ball Sokhi-Bulley, *Research Methodologies in EU and International Law* (Hart Publishers 2011), 5.

will determine what kinds of research questions are deemed meaningful or useful, what data is examined and how it is analyzed (the method)'.[63]

As is the case with most of their counterparts in other national settings, contemporary Spanish international law scholars have traditionally tended towards a methodologically homogenous and formalistic approach to international law, understood as a technically oriented juridical discipline that is quite distinct from that of international relations. The traditional methods, techniques, themes, *foci*, and *topoi* associated with rule-based approaches to international law are dominant in Spanish international legal academia. These are conditioned by a series of methodological boundaries, including the one drawn between 'law' and 'non- law'.[64] Another boundary that is often drawn by more traditional approaches is, as highlighted by Andrea Bianchi, the 'distinction between legal and "extra- legal" considerations, the latter being immaterial to international law'.[65]

When transposed to the study of the history of international law, these methodological boundaries lead to exclusions regarding the object of historical interest in the teachings of publicists. Normative or ruled-based approaches to the history of international law are often spurred on by a search for legal certainty and juridical authority in the name of norm advancement, institutional reform, or dispute-settlement resolution. In historiographical terms, this determines that the way rule-based/traditional approaches look to history is, ultimately, conditioned by 'formal pedigrees for establishing the validity of rules, or for explaining their normative force'.[66] When applied to historiographical methods, the methodological boundaries associated with normative or rule-based approaches often result in a rule-based perspective being cast over history that would be precisely the opposite to an interdisciplinary one. This intra-disciplinary approach is fostered by the will to reassert the 'autonomy of (international) law' which is associated with the 'idea that the validity and identity of law must be determined within parameters existing in the law itself'.[67] The methodological exclusion of interdisciplinary approaches is also, as a way to reassert the 'normativity'—despite the well-known paradox of infinite regress[68]—derived from implementing a strict legal methodology against extra-legal revisionist questioning.

This methodological self-limitation sets normative rule-based approaches apart from other approaches to the history of international law which are, usually, and more precisely, driven towards interdisciplinarity, understood as the

[63] *Ibid.*

[64] See Andrea Bianchi, *International Law Theories. An Inquiry into Different Ways of Thinking* (OUP 2016) 24.

[65] *Ibid.*, 26.

[66] *Ibid.*, 24.

[67] *Ibid.*, 29.

[68] See, e.g., Jorg Kammerhofer, 'Hans Kelsen in Today's International Legal Scholarship' in Jorg Kammerhofer and Jean d'Aspremont (eds) *International Legal Positivism in a Postmodern World* (CUP 2014) 96.

effort of 'knowledge production that crosses and/or bridges disciplinary boundaries'.[69] Indeed, non-normative approaches to the history of international law bring methods and perspectives from other disciplines, including history, economics, philosophy, sociology, anthropology, linguistics, or literature to help provide different perspectives of a historical event, or a succession of historical events. Such a range of approaches is better positioned to produce 'innovation in knowledge production—making knowledge more relevant, balancing incommensurable claims and perspectives, and raising questions concerning the nature and viability of expertise'.[70] In Spain, the powerful underlying influence of the normative rule-based approach has left contemporary historical writing in international law as a Cinderella of sorts, trapped between the Scylla of the strong attraction of mainstream orthodoxy for research in international law that is relevant now, along 'mainstream lines',[71] and the Charybdis of its own historical methodological insecurity.

The second factor underlying neglect of the history of international law in Spain is that interest from scholars in the 'darker legacies'[72] of international law is only relatively recent among international law scholars. The implications of the reluctance of the democratic generation of international legal scholars to glance in the mirror of their own disciplinary past is particularly acute in an epistemological community which operates as a professionally driven technical discipline with specific authority and expertise that makes it less susceptible to interdisciplinary engagement by professional historians. The discipline's short memory span is partly explained by the fact that critical examination of past experiences may cast a shadow over the professional reputation of Spanish international lawyers who tend to see themselves, as Koskenniemi remarks, 'among the avant-garde of liberal modernity—against conservative nationalism, sovereignty and power politics'.[73] The sharing of these traditional international collegiate peculiarities among Spanish international law scholars in the democratic period has, furthermore, been compounded by what historians often call a 'pact of forgetfulness' in Spanish universities[74] after the Spanish 'transition' to democracy in the mid-1970s.

All Spanish international law professors who remained in Spain after the Civil War swore, under the University Law of 1943, their complete adherence to the principles of the Spanish Phalanx's 'National Movement' and other fundamental

[69] Robert Froedman, 'Introduction' in Robert Froedman (ed.) *The Oxford Handbook of Interdisciplinarity* (OUP 2010) xxix.

[70] *Ibid.*

[71] Bianchi refers to 'mainstream' in international law paraphrasing Louis Henkin's famous quote—how 'international law as it is taught in most law schools in most countries, most of the time'. *Ibid.*, 22.

[72] Joerges et al., *supra* note 14.

[73] Martti Koskenniemi, 'International Law in a Post-Realist Era' (1995) 16 *Australian Yearbook of International Law* 1.

[74] Richards, *supra* note 18.

laws of the Spanish state under '*Generalísimo*' Franco for almost four decades.[75] Moreover, the 'maestros' of international law in Spanish universities during the Franco regime appointed disciples who have made it to the ranks of the Spanish 'democratic' generation of international lawyers and who, in their turn, have appointed others. From a comparative international law perspective,[76] the Spanish tradition of academic mentorship is significant in understanding a reluctance to investigate the history of international law in a country like Spain where the field of international law still remains a close-knit zone of practice.

The technical-legal specialization of Spanish international lawyers is consistent with their civil servant career-oriented aspirations in a Spanish international legal academia dominated by a peer system with a strong tendency to inbreeding through systems of traditional mentoring in local university environments. Although far from being the sole patrimony of Spanish international legal academia, academic inbreeding generates exclusionary dynamics aimed at retaining social and economic control over a particular disciplinary area. It also fosters academic cronyism and 'clientelism' and results in the intellectual blind acceptance of one's predecessors' and benefactors' epistemological past and methods. Thus, it is easy to understand how, despite the existence of some 'progressive' precedents in cultivating the history of international law in Spain in the mid-1960s,[77] study of the history of the international law profession in Spain was identified with an uncomfortable past by the 'democratic' generation and its successors. These preferred, instead, to jump into the lush professional pastures of the new democratic modernity and the European and international life to which Spain definitively opened itself up in the 1980s and 1990s.

Finally, the fourth factor in a pattern that may be extrapolated to other international legal academies struggling to renew themselves after the transition from an authoritarian regime to a democratic form of government is the adaptability and rejuvenation of national identity myths within international legal scholarship. The Spanish case offers, in particular, a textbook example of the adaptability of the 'foundational' mythical role of Francisco de Vitoria and the Salamanca School through different historical periods of the discipline.[78] In Spain, often sidelined as semi-peripheral among the 'Great Powers' of the last two centuries, the figure of the 'founding father' of international law, Francisco de Vitoria, gradually became enshrined as a leading light in the national identity myth, and a reassuring emblem of a glorious past throughout the late nineteenth century, the interwar and early

[75] See Ley de 29 de julio de 1943 Sobre ordenación de la Universidad española. Boletin Oficial del Estado 212 (31 de julio de 1943), 7406–31.

[76] See Anthea Roberts, *Is International Law International?* (OUP 2017).

[77] See Ignacio de la Rasilla, 'Beyond the Spanish Classics—The Ephemeral Awakening of the History of International Law in Pre-Democratic Spain' (2015) 7 *Monde(s) Histoires, Relations* 137.

[78] See Ignacio de la Rasilla, *In the Shadow of Vitoria. A History of International Law in Spain* (1770–1953) (Martinus Nijhoff 2017).

Franco periods, and during the Cold War.[79] After the Spanish transition to democracy, the Spanish 'classics' of the School of Salamanca, over which Francisco de Vitoria presides, were conveniently updated to fit a new modern democratic sensitivity. During this period, the School of Salamanca became known as the *Corpus Hispanorum de Pace* or the 'Spanish school of Peace'[80] in order to become associated once again with the defence of peace and human rights, the driving forces of the modern narrative of progress of international law.

The occasional engagement of Spanish international lawyers with contemporary post-colonial and critical perspectives on Francisco de Vitoria[81] reflects this deeply rooted defensive attitude towards the intellectual legacy of the 'Spanish classics'.[82] However, in their arguing against the '*leyenda negra*' or in downplaying the overtones of the post-colonial reinterpretation of Vitoria, Spanish international lawyers have never questioned the intellectual 'weaponization' and manipulation of Francisco de Vitoria and the Spanish Classics of the School of Salamanca by Spanish international law scholars during the Spanish Civil War and the Franco years. Likewise, their defence of the remarkable intellectual role of Vitoria 'at the origins of modernity'[83] continues to overlook completely the climate of severe intellectual repression and organically nationalist-directed scientific work in which the figure of Vitoria and the School of Salamanca thrived for decades in Spain after the Spanish Civil War.

4 Conclusions

The polemics surrounding the judicial treatment of the Spanish History Memory Act in Spain provide a fair example of how judicial proceedings, even when failed, can *inter alia* contribute to reviving historical research interest in past atrocities and to rejuvenate the study of long neglected histories of international law. The Spanish History Memory Act also shows that playing hide and seek with the past only contributes to prolonging and exacerbating the incubated international crisis of reputation of a country when this finally bursts out.

Indeed, the difficulties surrounding the implementation of certain provisions of the HMA, the criticisms addressing its incompleteness on certain matters, and the polemics surrounding Judge Garzón's case have all contributed to a further

[79] *Ibid.*

[80] Luciano Pereña (ed.), *Corpus Hispanorum de Pace* (Consejo Superior de Investigaciones Cientificas 1981).

[81] For an overview, see, e.g., Ignacio de la Rasilla, 'Francisco de Vitoria's Unexpected Transformations and Reinterpretations for International Law' (2013) 15 *International Community Law Review* 287.

[82] See e.g. Pablo Zapatero, 'Legal Imagination in Vitoria. The Power of Ideas' (2009) 11 *Journal of the History of International Law* 221.

[83] See the otherwise interesting contributions contained in Jose Maria Beneyto and Justo Corti (eds), *At the Origins of Modernity. Francisco de Vitoria and the Discovery of International Law* (Springer 2017).

refashioning of the Spanish case as one of 'late transitional justice'.[84] This has fuelled a reassessment of the Spanish transition in the late 1970s that for years was praised as a role model for other countries, looking for a peaceful transition to democratic forms of government.[85]

The report issued by the UN Special Rapporteur on the Promotion of Truth, Justice, Reparation and Guarantee of Non-Recurrence echoed this impression in noting that 'the consolidation of democracy constitutes one of the outstanding achievements of the Spanish transition […] and that the Spanish reforms have lessons to offer which may be useful to other countries'. However, Pablo de Greiff also highlighted how 'efforts to cope with the legacies of the Civil War and dictatorship in practically all the spheres of the mandate have been mostly fragmented'.[86] In its official response to the Report of the UN Rapporteur, Spain readily admitted:

> The Spanish Transition constitutes a unique case of national reconciliation without criminal justice due to the deliberated and consensual decision of the vast majority of the parliamentarian political forces to avoid transitional justice. The balance among the different interests, peace and democracy, justice and reconciliation, was found in Spain at the price of renouncing criminal justice.[87]

Enormous advances have been made in Spain over the last four decades with regard to establishing a social and democratic state of law after almost forty years of authoritarian rule. However, despite its collaborative constructive engagement with international human rights bodies and mechanisms,[88] Spain continues to struggle to present an internationally edifying role regarding its transition to democratic rule. As we have seen, the history of international law in Spain features among those areas where, almost forty years after the enacting of the 1978 Spanish Constitution, and thirty years since Spain joined the European Union, Spanish efforts to cope with the legacy of the Civil War and dictatorship in Spain have been at best fragmented and at worst inept.

To be able to provide a truly internationally edifying example, the historical memory of Spain should also begin to encompass the role of Spanish international lawyers who actively contributed to legitimation of Franco's *coup d'état* and the maintenance of his regime over time. Regrettably, the long-neglected study of the

[84] Sumalla, *supra* note 47.

[85] See, e.g., Luis Lopez Guerra, 'The Application of the Spanish Model in the Constitutional Transitions in Central and Eastern Europe' (1998) 19 *Cardozo Law Review* 1937.

[86] Report of the Special Rapporteur on the promotion of truth, *supra* note 38, Summary 2.

[87] 'Observaciones de España al informe del Relator Especial de Naciones Unidas sobre la promoción de la verdad, la justicia, la reparación y las garantías de no repetición, Sr. Pablo de Greiff, sobre su visita a España' A/HRC/27/56/Add.3 17 September 2014, 2–3.

[88] See the official responses of Spain to the different UN human rights bodies, *supra* note 54.

history of international law in Spain before, during, and after, the Spanish Civil War and General Franco's regime, comes with a revealing long delay.[89]

However, the Spanish experience can still be useful for new generations of international lawyers in other younger democracies and transitioning countries. Although general implications should not be drawn from the unique particularities of a national historical case, an inquiry into the 'bad example' provided by Spanish international lawyers regarding critical investigation of their own history has shown the existence of various embedded obstacles in the uphill battle that needs to be fought at the interface of historical memory and international law within the international law profession in many societies confronted with the dilemma of '*Vergangengeitsbewältigung*' ('*coping with the past*'). There are no readymade answers or magic formulae to redress past historical traumatic experiences and their social legacy across the 'invisible college' of international lawyers. However, many an invisible chain may be broken, and many a future international crisis may, perhaps, also be avoided by those who understand that virtue starts at home and, thus, be willing to delve into the dark sides of their own history to contribute to a more enlightened European future.

[89] For a starting point, see de la Rasilla, *supra* note 77.

La Démocratie Radicale dans les Discours Légaux Contemporains au Rojava au Cœur de la 'Crise' Syrienne

Une Analyse Genrée

*Zeynep Kıvılcım**

1 Introduction

La guerre civile qui sévit en Syrie est qualifiée de plus grande 'crise' internationale depuis la Seconde Guerre mondiale. Cette guerre se présente aussi comme une grande crise du droit international. Le système de sécurité collective est paralysé, les institutions internationales établies sont incapables de prendre en compte et de juger les violations flagrantes des droits de l'homme et du droit humanitaire. La situation atteste de l'échec manifeste des mécanismes du droit international des réfugiés dans la protection internationale des millions de personnes qui fuient la Syrie. La violence qui sévit dans la région commence à prendre une ampleur internationale. L'État islamique est devenu, selon le Conseil de Sécurité, 'une menace mondiale d'une gravité sans précédent contre la paix et la sécurité internationales'. Pour certains, la crise syrienne nous conduit vers la fin du système juridique instauré sous l'égide de l'ONU.

Tous ces discours sur la crise du droit international en Syrie paraissent incapables de considérer l'espace de démocratie radicale qui est en train de se construire au Nord de la Syrie: Rojava. Rojava est une fédération formée de trois cantons (Kobanê, Efrîn et Cizîrê) où les peuples utilisent leur liberté nouvellement acquise pour créer une autonomie démocratique sans État, concrétisée dans le modèle politique du 'confédéralisme démocratique'. Un des piliers fondateurs du confédéralisme démocratique est l'égalité de genre qui forge également la légitimité des autorités gouvernant les cantons autonomes du Rojava.

* I would like to thank Mustafa Polat for his assistance with the translation of the Kurdish documentation.

Zeynep Kıvılcım, *La Démocratie Radicale dans les Discours Légaux Contemporains au Rojava au Cœur de la 'Crise' Syrienne: Une Analyse Genrée* In: *How International Law Works in Times of Crisis*. Edited by: George Ulrich and Ineta Ziemele, Oxford University Press (2019).
DOI: 10.1093/oso/9780198849667.003.0015

Ratna Kapur indique que reconnaitre, center sur les sujets périphériques de droit international et se concentrer sur les moments de leurs résistances pourraient effectuer le changement théorique et pratique nécessaire pour la politique légale féministe.[1] Ma contribution poursuivra cet objectif. J'essaierai d'examiner dans une perspective genrée les nouvelles conceptions de la souveraineté et les modes de réalisation du principe de l'auto-détermination au Rojava. C'est le site actuel de la résistance et de la révolte de l'Autre sauvage, sujet périphérique du droit international.

2 Cadre Théorique et Méthodologique

Le mouvement des femmes Kurdes s'efforce de construire une théorie féministe originale, adaptée au contexte du Moyen-Orient. Cette théorie est appelée 'Jinéologie' (Jineoloji).[2] La jinéologie est présentée comme une nouvelle théorie visant à appréhender le domaine des sciences sociales. Elle est une sorte de fusion entre le féminisme (avec de nombreuses références aux différentes tendances du féminisme occidental) et les spécificités culturelles et mythologiques du Moyen-Orient.

Le cadre théorique de la jinéologie se développe autour des articles écrits par le leader du Parti des Travailleurs du Kurdistan (PKK),[3] actuellement emprisonné, et les textes, revues et livres produits par les ateliers des femmes dans différentes villes et prisons de la Turquie sous l'égide de 'l'Académie de jinéologie'. Ces textes énoncent que l'objectif de la jinéologie est de converger les expériences des femmes du monde, plutôt que d'accepter la théorie féministe occidentale, et précisent que la jinéologie ne doit pas subir l'influence des centres de recherche 'androcentriques' des universités ou de l'État mais établir ces propres académies.[4] La jinéologie est une intervention théorique à l'intersection de la lutte des peuples de Rojava et de l'engagement du mouvement des femmes de la Turquie sur la question de genre.

Il serait correct et judicieux d'utiliser la jinéologie comme base théorique pour mon analyse genrée de la politique et des pratiques juridiques de Rojava. Cependant, la jinéologie n'est qu'à ces débuts et il n'est pas possible de trouver le cadre théorique et les outils méthodologiques nécessaires pour procéder à son analyse sous l'angle du droit international. Pour cette raison, ma contribution est

[1] Ratna Kapur, 'The Tragedy of Victimization Rhetoric: Resurrecting the "Native" Subject in International/Post-Colonial Feminist Legal Politics' (2002) 15 *Harvard Human Rights Journal* 1, 29.

[2] *Jin* en Kurde veut dire femme.

[3] Le PKK est en opposition armée, sous forme de guérilla, avec la Turquie depuis 1984. Son leader Abdullah Öcalan est emprisonné depuis 1999. Ses écrits sur la jinéologie sont inspirés par l'œuvre de nombreuses écrivains féministes et queer occidentales et de la Turquie.

[4] Özgür Kadın Akademisi, *Jineoloji Tartışmaları* (Aram Yayınları 2015); Jineoloji Akademisi, *Jineolojiye Giriş* (Aram Yayınları 2015).

basée, d'un point de vue théorique, sur la doctrine juridique féministe et adopte notamment une approche tiers-mondiste.

Selon Charlesworth, l'analyse féministe a deux rôles: un rôle déconstructif et un rôle reconstructif.[5] Ma contribution est plutôt centrée sur la reconstruction. J'analyse les politiques et pratiques juridiques de la Fédération de Rojava comme une tentative pour la construction des formes alternatives de gouvernement qui peuvent mieux répondre aux besoins des femmes et servir leurs intérêts. Mon objectif est d'enquêter, dans une perspective genrée, sur les modes d'exercice du pouvoir souverain au Rojava, région où les communautés résistantes du Moyen-Orient élaborent un nouveau système juridique. J'étudie comment le pouvoir genré s'exerce à travers les discours légaux au Rojava, région où les concepts et les principes de la doctrine eurocentrique du droit international sont renégociés.

Il n'est pas facile d'accéder à la documentation de base pour procéder à une analyse juridique de la révolution de Rojava, les difficultés étant multiples. Bien que cette révolution soit entrée dans sa septième année, les écrits académiques qui la traitent sont extrêmement rares et les études juridiques sont presqu'inexistantes. Les informations disponibles sont essentiellement électroniques et incluent en grande partie la documentation non-académique produite par divers groupes et organisations pro-Rojava. Il est difficile de se prononcer sur la véracité et l'impartialité de ces informations. La présentation des objectifs idéologiques de la révolution est mélangée avec le récit de ce qui a été réalisé sur le terrain. Pour préparer cet article, j'ai utilisé les informations qui se trouvent sur le site Web de l'agence semi-officielle de Rojava.[6] Ce cite fournit des informations de base à jour en turc et en anglais avec les témoignages du terrain. Une deuxième source a été les reportages réalisés et les articles écrits par les universitaires, journalistes et juristes qui ont visité Rojava et ont examiné la mise en pratique des principes et le fonctionnement des différentes institutions.

3 Interroger les Nouveaux Modes de Souveraineté dans la Démocratie Radicale

La déconstruction et reconstruction genrées du cadre libéral de la souveraineté eurocentrique, qui constitue le centre conceptuel de la théorie du droit international public, est une tâche d'une grande d'ampleur qui ne peut être accomplie dans le cadre de cet article. Je me limiterai à mettre en relief certains éléments constitutifs de la conceptualisation de la souveraineté en droit international public, pour pouvoir ensuite exposer le modèle de Rojava et l'aborder comme

[5] Hilary Charlesworth, 'Feminist Critiques of International Law and their Critics' (1994–1995) *Third World Studies* 1, 3.

[6] Anha News Agency, <https://www.hawarnews.com/en/>.

une reconstruction genrée de la souveraineté au Moyen-Orient opérée par l'Autre sauvage. Chantal Thomas relève que l'analyse critique du droit international ne devrait pas porter sur la question de savoir si la souveraineté est en train de s'affaiblir ou de se renforcer, mais se concentrer sur les divers modes de discours juridiques à travers lesquels cette souveraineté est exercée.[7] Mon analyse sur la souveraineté de Rojava tente de suivre cet objectif.

L'accomplissement de la souveraineté nationale unitaire et hiérarchisée est l'idée centrale du droit international. La mutation de l'Autre sauvage en individu civilisé est également accomplie à travers la construction de l'État-nation. Les auteurs féministes comme par exemple Dianne Otto indiquent qu'avec l'investiture de la personnalité juridique internationale des communautés au sein exclusif de l'État-nation, le droit international circonscrit la démocratie à la 'démocratie nationale' gouvernée par les États et crée une obstruction pour les mouvements qui cherchent à 'approfondir' la démocratie.[8] Le droit international restreint l'idée de la politique aux processus politiques formels de l'État et délimite l'application de la démocratie à des segments étroits.[9] Cette conceptualisation de la souveraineté hiérarchisée et de la politique restrictive renforce le dualisme des sphères publique et privée.

Ma tentative pour présenter les articulations de la souveraineté au sein de la Fédération de Rojava, je suivrai trois axes; la décentralisation de l'État-nation, l'approfondissement de la démocratie avec sa reconstruction par le bas et, enfin, la redéfinition de la politique.

Lors de la guerre civile syrienne, le PYD (Parti de l'union démocratique) s'est imposé comme le principal acteur kurde en Syrie. En affirmant représenter les habitants du Rojava, il a déclaré l'autonomie des trois cantons sous son contrôle vis-à-vis de l'État Syrien. Une Charte du Contrat Social du Rojava a été adoptée le 29 janvier 2014 comme la Constitution provisoire de la région autonome syrienne autoproclamée.

Au Rojava, la souveraineté repose sur le modèle dit d''autonomie démocratique', qui a été avancé par le leader emprisonné du PKK inspiré par le penseur libertaire Murray Bookchin.[10] L'autonomie démocratique est une forme de démocratie radicale et décentralisée qui doit être considérée comme une importante tentative de reconceptualisation de la souveraineté sans État. Le confédéralisme démocratique mis en œuvre au Rojava se présente comme 'un paradigme non

[7] Chantal Thomas 'What Does the Emerging International Law of Migration Mean for Sovereignty?' (2013) 14 *Melbourne Journal of International Law* 392, 436.

[8] Dianne Otto, 'Challenging the New World Order: International Law, Global Democracy and the Possibilities for Women' (1993) 3 *Transnational Law & Contemporary Problems* 371, 410–11.

[9] *Ibid.*, 411.

[10] Voir par exemple Murray Bookchin, 'Libertarian Municipalism: An Overview' (1991) 24 *Green Perspectives* 1, 6. Certains auteurs attirent l'attention sur les divergences entre les éléments anarchistes de la théorie de Bookchin et le fait que le PYD, qui est une organisation strictement hiérarchique, domine tous les niveaux de l'organisation politique à Rojava (Voir Leezenberg Michiel, 'The Ambiguities of Democratic Autonomy: The Kurdish Movement in Turkey and Rojava' (2016) 16(4) *South East European and Black Sea Studies* 672–8).

étatique'. La région autonome s'efforce d'éviter tout conflit avec l'Etat syrien, entretenant avec le gouvernement Assad des relations jugées par les commentateurs comme étant 'pragmatiques' et 'ambiguës'.[11]

Jongerden indique qu'à travers le projet d'autonomie démocratique, le confédéralisme démocratique établit un nouvel modèle d'autodétermination qui s'étend au-delà de l'État-nation et de la démocratie représentative: les citoyens sont eux-mêmes les agents de l'autogouvernement et la citoyenneté active dans la démocratie radicale est la nouvelle définition du droit à l'auto-détermination.[12]

L'objectif des conceptions radicales de la démocratie au-delà de la version libérale est de revitaliser le contenu libérateur de la démocratie, tel qu'il est constitué dans l'idée de la souveraineté populaire, non seulement en élargissant les capacités d'autonomie gouvernementale mais aussi dans son extension au domaine de l'économie. Les commentateurs situent la Fédération de Rojava dans le large éventail des formes radicales de la démocratie et considèrent que la démocratie radicale à Rojava établit un nouveau modèle d'autodétermination tout en dépassant le concept de l'État-nation.[13]

Les évolutions mises en place au Rojava sont de trois ordres: introduction de l'autogouvernement direct par les communes, établissement d'une participation égale pour tous les groupes religieux et ethniques dans tous les domaines de la prise de décision, et renforcement de la position des femmes. Le peuple s'auto-organise au sein des assemblées locales des communes et des conseils populaires du voisinage.

Le Contrat Social garantit les droits des femmes dans tous les secteurs de la vie politique, sociale, économique et culturelle. Il énonce que les femmes ont le droit à l'auto-défense et le droit de refuser et d'éliminer toute forme de discrimination basée sur le genre. Il y a le principe de co-présidence, de la commune jusqu'au conseil de ville. Seules les femmes ont le droit d'élire la co-présidente tandis que le co-président masculin est élu par les femmes et les hommes. La démocratie est ainsi construite par le bas et par l'intervention effective des femmes.

La Loi sur les Femmes adoptée en 2015 dispose que la lutte contre la logique patriarcale est la responsabilité de tous au Rojava. Elle dispose que les lois qui concernent les femmes doivent être élaborées en tenant compte de leur volonté. Le sexisme y est érigé en infraction criminelle et la polygamie y est prohibée.[14]

[11] V. Sary Ghadi, 'Kurdish Self-governance in Syria: Survival and Ambition' (2016) *Chatham House for the Royal Institute of International Affairs* 15–19.

[12] Joost Jongerden, 'Radikal Demokrasi ve Ulus Devletin Ötesinde Kendi Kaderini Tayin Hakkı' in Joost Jongerden, Ahmet Hamdi Akkaya, and Bahar Şimşek (eds), *İsyandan İnşaya: Kürdistan Özgürlük Hareketi*, (Dipnot Yayınları 2015) 175–6.

[13] Ahmet Hamdi Akkaya and Joost Jongerden, 'Reassembling the Political: The PKK and the Project of Radical Democracy' (2012) 14 *European Journal of Turkish Studies* 1, 12.

[14] Pour le texte (en langue turque) de la Loi des Femmes, voir: <http://www.yeniozgurpolitika.eu/index.php?rupel=nuce&id=48523> accessed 28 April 2019.

En mars 2016, une conférence s'est tenue à Rmeilan, lors de laquelle a été déclarée 'la Fédération du Nord de la Syrie-Rojava'. En décembre 2016, le projet de Contrat Social a été approuvé par les membres présents à la deuxième conférence de l'Assemblée constituante de la Syrie du Nord. Selon le Contrat Social, le système fédéral démocratique du Nord de la Syrie adopte le système écologique et démocratique et basée sur la liberté des femmes.

La Fédération établit la légitimité de son pouvoir sur la nouvelle conceptualisation de l'administration autogouvernante locale sans État. L'égalité des genres forge la légitimité des autorités gouvernant les cantons autonomes du Rojava. La politique et la démocratie ne sont d'ailleurs pas limitées aux processus de gouvernement, mais étendues à tous les segments de la vie sociale de façon à supprimer la frontière qui sépare la sphère publique et privée. Le contrôle effectif, élément constitutif de la souveraineté, ne signifie plus le contrôle effectif de l'État sur son territoire et sa population, mais le contrôle presque direct de la population, femmes comprises, sur sa propre vie et sur tous les segments de la vie communautaire. Les centres des femmes (*Mala Jin*) et les Asayiş (forces paramilitaires de sécurité composées de femmes) sont importants à cet égard.

Les centres des femmes pour la science et l'éducation (Maison des femmes: *Mala Jin*) ont plusieurs activités. Ils ont pour mission para-juridique de résoudre les conflits qui touchent les femmes. Ils servent de centres d'accueil et d'hébergement pour les femmes en difficulté et ils organisent aussi des formations pour les femmes concernant différents aspects de leur vie, de leurs droits, de leur santé sexuelle et aussi sur la jinéologie.[15] Par leurs activités, ces centres font le lien entre la politique et le droit et la société.

L'utilisation des mesures de droit pénal comme outil pour combattre la violence basée sur le genre est critiquée par les féministes. Ces mesures ont en effet pour conséquence d'entraver l'autonomie et la liberté des femmes.[16] La résolution des conflits par l'intervention directe des femmes au sein des *Mala Jin* est de nature à renforcer le pouvoir des femmes et leur permet de prendre le contrôle de leur vie avec la force qu'elles puisent de leur combat collectif.

Il existe plus de trente centres des femmes dans différentes villes du Rojava. Les cas soumis à ces centres portent sur la violence à l'égard des femmes, le divorce, le mariage précoce ou le mariage forcé. Les cas qui ne peuvent être résolus par le centre sont transmis à des cours populaires.[17] Les statistiques publiées sur les

[15] Arzu Zengin, *Devrimin Rojava Hali* (Ceylan Yayınları 2014) 76–80. 'Beyond Female Soldiers: The Feminism of Rojava' (March 2016) *Alternatives International* <http://www.alterinter.org/spip.php?article4447> accessed 28 April 2019.

[16] Voir, par exemple, Ratna Kapur, 'Gender, Sovereignty and the Rise of Sexual Security Regime in International Law and Postcolonial India' (2013) 14 *Melbourne Journal of International Law* 345, 317.

[17] Jo Magpie, 'Regaining Hope in Rojava', 6 June 2016, *Open Democracy* <https://www.opendemocracy.net/author/jo-magpie> accessed 28 April 2019.

affaires résolues par différentes *Mala Jin* sont présentées comme une preuve de la réussite de la révolution.[18]

Le Contrat Social dispose, à son article 68, que les organisations de femmes et la représentation égale des femmes sont à la base du domaine de la justice et de ses activités institutionnelles. Les décisions relatives aux femmes sont traitées par le système judiciaire des femmes. Selon l'article 69, le système judiciaire comprend un conseil de justice composé des femmes dont les membres sont élus par les conseils populaires. Le conseil traite de toutes les questions et affaires liées aux femmes et à la famille. Il a le droit de surveiller l'action des conseils judiciaires des cantons et assure la coordination avec ceux-ci.

La sécurité intérieure du Rojava est assurée par les brigades d'*Asayiş* (force paramilitaire de sécurité). L'*Asayiş* est basée sur l'égalité des sexes et est co-présidée par un homme et une femme. Les femmes représentent environ 40% des effectifs d'*Asayiş*. Hormis les forces d'*Asayiş* générales, des centres et brigades d'*Asayiş* autonomes composés de femmes sont institués dans chaque ville. Ces brigades sont composées exclusivement de femmes et sont seules compétentes pour toutes les affaires concernant les femmes: violence conjugale, protection des femmes pendant les manifestations ou encore mariages précoces.[19] L'administration des *Asayiş* des femmes a mis en place en 2014 une assistance téléphonique pour venir en aide aux femmes victimes de violences.

4 Une reconceptualisation du Principe d'autodétermination sans État

L 'autodétermination' est né comme un élément 'révolutionnaire et potentiellement explosif'[20] dans la vie internationale, lors de la Première Guerre mondiale. La dynamique de la décolonisation a progressivement accéléré la reconnaissance du droit des communautés à disposer d'elles-mêmes. Les commentateurs indiquent que les nouvelles revendications qui sont apparues après la fin de la Guerre Froide ne sont pas compatibles avec l'autodétermination telle qu'elle a été conceptualisée au moment de la naissance des Nations Unies: les formulations doctrinales de ce droit ne correspondent plus à la pratique.[21]

[18] 'Center of Education and Science for Women settles 9 cases', 26 August 2015, <https://en.hawarnews.org/center-of-education-and-science-for-women-settles-9-cases/>; 'Women's center resolves 16 cases', <https://en.hawarnews.org/womens-center-resolves-16-cases/>.

[19] Florence Bateson et al., *Exploring Women's Role in Peace and Security in the Self-administered Areas of Northern Syria* (Policy Report for Netherlands Organisation for Scientific Research, Utrecht University and the Women's Commission of Rojava) 57–8.

[20] M. Koskenniemi, 'National self-Determination Today: Problems of Legal Theory and Practice' (1994) 43(2) *The International and Comparative Law Quarterly* 241–69.

[21] R. Falk, 'Self-Determination Under International Law: The Coherence of Doctrine Versus the Incoherence of Experience' (2002) *The Self-Determination of Peoples* 33–7.

La doctrine et les tribunaux internationaux se sont davantage intéressés à la relation ambiguë de l'autodétermination avec l'État et ses éléments constitutifs comme base de l'ordre juridique international. Il existe deux tendances principales, qui tirent vers des directions opposées. La première est de contenir le sens sécessionniste de l'autodétermination en limitant son application au contexte particulier de la décolonisation. La deuxième tendance reconnaît et valide la pratique récente et les bouleversements qu'elle a entraînés, dans le cadre d'une approche juridique reformulée.

Afin de réduire l'écart entre la formulation juridique de ce droit et la réalité politique, certains auteurs proposent de mettre l'accent sur la dimension 'interne' de l'autodétermination. Cassese propose que l'autodétermination soit conçue comme base pour le développement de cadres constitutionnels alternatifs, donnant à celles et ceux qui ont un droit à l'autodétermination une autonomie significative: l'autodétermination doit, avant tout, être considérée comme un principe imposant la reconnaissance des droits collectifs à l'autonomie régionale.[22]

Les controverses doctrinales sur la conceptualisation de l'autodétermination interne restent dans le cadre de la démocratie représentative libérale, sans remettre en cause la centralité de l'État dans l'ordre politique. L'autodétermination interne est conceptualisée comme le droit à une forme de gouvernance démocratique lorsque l'État ethno-national est confronté aux revendications des habitants permanents de son territoire qui ne font pas partie de la culture nationale dominante. L'accent est mis sur la question de la présence ou non de procédures de décision étatiques qui permettent aux communautés de participer à la conduite de leurs affaires communes au sein de l'État. Le droit individuel à l'autodétermination est défini comme un droit à la participation au système politique, économique et culturel de l'État.

Le modèle d'autodétermination connu au Rojava dépasse le cadre de la démocratie libérale représentative. Ce n'est pas une pratique d'autodétermination destructrice de l'État en ce sens qu'il n'y a pas d'objectif de sécession et la Confédération démocratique de la Syrie du Nord ne vise pas à se proclamer État indépendant. Cependant, il s'agit d'un exemple révolutionnaire d'autodétermination car, contrairement aux autres pratiques nationales en la matière, il contrecarre l'ordre politique et juridique centré sur l'État et vise à créer une autonomie démocratique sans État.

Karen Knop relève que les groupes revendiquant le droit à l'autodétermination, qui sont par définition marginalisés, n'ont pas pu participer au développement de la norme et qu'ils ont été largement exclus de la participation à l'interprétation et au développement de la formulation juridique au sein des institutions et des tribunaux internationaux.[23]

[22] A. Cassese, *Self-determination of Peoples: A Legal Reappraisal* (CUP 1995) 351–2.
[23] Karin Knop, *Diversity and Self Determination in International Law* (CUP 2002) 374.

Les auteurs féministes avancent que la notion d'autodétermination est masculine dans sa conception, son contenu et son application. Charlesworth et Chinkin soulignent que même si le droit à l'autodétermination permet à 'tous les peuples' de 'déterminer librement leur statut politique et poursuivre librement leur développement économique, social et culturel', l'oppression des femmes au sein de groupes revendiquant le droit à l'autodétermination n'a jamais été prise en compte afin de déterminer la validité de leurs revendications ou la forme que devrait prendre l'autodétermination.[24]

Le principe de l'autodétermination suppose que l'égalité existe entre les groupes de personnes, de sorte que tous ont la possibilité de participer effectivement aux procédures de prise de décision. Il n'existe pas de mécanisme pour s'assurer que les opinions des femmes sont représentées ou pour évaluer si les dirigeants du groupe sont représentatifs des opinions des femmes.[25] Les internationalistes féministes démontrent que le droit à l'autodétermination peut être activé au détriment des femmes et contribuer à leur marginalisation. Elles nous rappellent plusieurs cas où les femmes ont été négligées et où les fruits de la lutte pour l'autodétermination ne leur ont pas nécessairement profité.[26]

Le cadre théorique et la mise en pratique du principe se concentrent sur la composante politique.[27] Si le principe de l'autodétermination est conçu sans accorder une place prioritaire à la subsistance économique, sa mise en œuvre risque de créer des désavantages pour la situation des femmes. Or, il existe une forte interdépendance entre l'autodétermination politique et l'autodétermination économique. Cependant, l'expression politique de l'autodétermination reçoit une attention beaucoup plus grande dans le droit international que son expression économique, sociale ou culturelle.[28]

McDonald suggère que la formulation féministe d'autodétermination devrait insister sur les dimensions internes de ce principe.[29] Il s'agit ainsi de prendre en compte la condition des femmes afin que leur sort s'améliore, en étant davantage associées au processus politique décisionnel, conception sociale du volet interne de l'autodétermination.[30] Il est donc important de voir si les femmes participent à l'interprétation et à la définition des valeurs communes ainsi que des principes directeurs à travers lesquels l'autodétermination est opérée au Rojava.

[24] Hilary Charlesworth and Christine Chinkin, 'The Gender of Jus Cogens' (1993) 15 *Human Rights Quarterly* 73, 63.

[25] Karin Knop, *Diversity and Self Determination in International Law* (CUP 2002) 19.

[26] Mélanie Dubuy, 'La contribution des femmes à la revendication du peuple kurde à l'autodétermination' (2015) 34, *Civitas Europa* 2015/1 104, 93.

[27] Susan MacDonald, 'Kurdish Women and Self-determination: A Feminist Approach to International Law' in S. Mojab (ed.) *Women of a Non-state Nation: The Kurds* (Mazda Publications 2001), 141, 135.

[28] Karin Knop, *supra* note 25, 19.

[29] Susan McDonald, *supra* note 27, 135–57.

[30] Mélanie Dubuy, *supra* note 26, 104.

Le Contrat Social de Rojava réaffirme dans son préambule, le droit des peuples à l'auto-détermination. Selon l'article 7 du Contrat, la Fédération se compose de cantons basés sur des auto-administrations démocratiques, qui dépendent des organisations démocratiques des groupes idéologiques, ethniques, culturels et des femmes de tous les segments sociaux. Le Contrat Social prévoit que le système de coprésidence contribue à l'organisation et à l'établissement du système confédéré démocratique des femmes en tant qu'entité spéciale. La liberté et les droits des femmes et l'égalité des sexes doivent être garantis dans la société et dans la famille. Les femmes ont droit à une participation égale dans tous les domaines (politique, social, culturel, économique, administratif, et autres) et prennent des décisions concernant leurs affaires. Le confédéralisme démocratique est le cadre dans lequel se matérialise l'autodétermination par le bas, à partir des communes. L'autodétermination se transforme en un processus dynamique et continu.

Les féministes nous rappellent que les luttes de libération nationale ou anticoloniale pour l'autodétermination présentent assez souvent leurs priorités au détriment des femmes.[31] Les femmes sont mobilisées pour participer à la lutte, mais les questions des femmes ne sont pas considérées parmi les priorités politiques lors de la définition des objectifs de la révolution. Les femmes prennent activement part au combat pour l'autodétermination mais elles sont repoussées et rejetées une fois que la lutte ou la révolution est réussie. L'exercice de l'autodétermination a priorité sur la liberté et les droits des femmes.

Il ressort des témoignages des différentes délégations qui ont visité Rojava que l'auto-détermination y est genrée, concernant son contenu conceptuel ainsi que les mécanismes de sa réalisation. Les femmes ne sont pas subordonnées à la révolution mais elles mènent cette révolution, dont un des objectifs principaux est de combattre le sexisme. Elles sont non seulement engagées dans le combat armé mais elles œuvrent à une transformation politique, juridique et sociale pour supprimer l'inégalité entre les sexes.[32]

Une Académie des sciences sociales a été ouverte en 2014 à Qamişlo dans le canton de Cizîrê. L'académie compte trois départements: histoire, sociologie et droit. Les cours s'organisent en deux années, une première année où tout le monde suit les mêmes cours, puis une deuxième année où les étudiants choisissent leur matière et ont des cours plus orientés. L'enseignement de droit comprend trois mois d'enseignement théorique, suivis par trois mois de stage. Les personnes qui accomplissent ces six mois de cours travaillent ensuite dans les comités de

[31] Voir, par exemple, Maria Mies, *Patriarchy and Accumulation on a World Scale: Women in International Division of Labor, 5th edn* (Redwood Books 1994), 175–204; Karen Knop, *supra* note 25, 328–49.

[32] Jenna Krajeski, 'What the Kurds Want: Syrian Kurds are Trying to Build a Leftist Revolution in the Midst of a Civil War. Is it a New Middle East, or Just Another Fracture?' (2015) 91, *Virginia Quarterly Review*, 86–105, 86.

réconciliation.[33] Plusieurs dizaines de comités de réconciliation sont établis au Rojava pour remplacer les tribunaux de l'État. Ces comités sont proposés par les conseils ou élus directement par la population, en respectant la répartition par sexe de 40%.

Dans une perspective féministe, l'autodétermination économique est essentielle pour les femmes. Chinkin, Wright et Charlesworth estiment qu'il est important de repenser le contenu de l'autodétermination qui se concentre sur les objectifs masculins de l'agrandissement économique et territorial. Assurer la vie en paix et en sécurité et la subsistance en nourriture devraient être considérés comme les priorités pour l'auto-détermination des individus et des communautés.[34] La mise en place de coopératives indépendantes de femmes au Rojava est une importante démarche en vue de l'accession de ces dernières à l'autonomie économique. Les coopératives jouent un rôle important et doivent devenir, à terme, la forme dominante de l'économie de la Fédération. La première coopérative de femmes a été créée en 2014 et six coopératives de femmes étaient en activité en 2016.[35]

5 Conclusions

Alors que la guerre civile syrienne nous conduit vers une crise du droit international, un espace de démocratie radicale se construit au Rojava. La révolution de Rojava est politiquement et économiquement extrêmement fragile, tout comme l'engagement pris par la Fédération, dans le Contrat Social, de respecter les droits et les libertés fondamentaux.

Les organisations internationales des droits de l'homme sont critiques quant à la conduite envers les dissidents et des dénoncent ses opérations militaires affectant les grandes communautés non kurdes du Nord de la Syrie. Amnesty International et Human Rights Watch (HRW) ont publié des rapports qui accusent le PYD de graves violations des droits humains et du droit humanitaire.[36] Ces rapports mettent en évidence les détentions arbitraires de civils considérés comme des sympathisants ou des membres présumés d'État islamique par le PYD et les procès

[33] 'Nazan Üstündağ İle Rojava Devrimi, Kobane Direnişi ve Türkiye'deki Gelişmeler Üzerine' (2015) 8 Kampflatz <https://www.kampfplatzdergi.com/2015/10/nazan-ustundag-soylesisi.html> accessed 2 July 2019.

[34] Christine Chinkin and Shelley Wright, 'The Hunger Trap: Women, Food and Self-Determination' *Michigan Journal of International Law* (1993) 14 294, 262; Hilary Charlesworth and Christine Chinkin, 'The Gender of Jus Cogens' (1993) 15 *Human Rights Quarterly* 67, 75.

[35] Pour l'information sur les cooperatives au Rojava (en Anglais) voir le page web de *The Co-operative Economy in Rojava and Bakur Project*,<https://cooperativeeconomy.info> accessed 28 April 2019.

[36] Amnesty International, *Syrie. Détentions arbitraires et procès iniques ternissent la lutte du PYD contre le terrorisme*, 7 Septembre 2015. Amnesty International, *Syria: 'We have nowhere to go'—Forced Displacement and Demolitions in Northern Syria*, 13 October 2015, Index number: MDE 24/2503/2015. HRW, *Under Kurdish Rule Abuses in PYD-run Enclaves of Syria*, 19 June 2014. HRW, *Iraqi Kurdish Forces' Destruction of Villages, Homes in Conflict with ISIS*, 13 November 2016. HRW, *Rapport Mondial*, 2017.

iniques qui sont intentés à leur encontre, ainsi que le déplacement délibéré de milliers de civils et la démolition de villages entiers comme sanctions collectives à l'égard de civils dans des villages précédemment aux mains de l'État Islamique, où une minorité était soupçonnée de soutenir ce groupe armé. Amnesty International et HRW pointent aussi le fait que les unités de protection du peuple (YPG) ne respectent toujours pas l'engagement qui a été pris de démobiliser les enfants soldats, en dépit des progrès réalisés.

Cette guerre, théâtre de graves violations des droits humains et du droit humanitaire de la part des différentes parties au conflit, constitue également un foyer très important de résistance où les femmes du Moyen-Orient, sujets périphériques du droit international, réinventent la démocratie, la politique, la souveraineté et le droit à travers leurs pratiques quotidiennes. Les observateurs internationaux signalent que même les dissidents du PYD reconnaissent l'impact de la nouvelle administration sur les femmes.[37] Les commentateurs, y compris ceux qui critiquent certains aspects de la gouvernance au sein de la Fédération, reconnaissent les effets émancipatoires de la démocratie radicale sur la vie des femmes et affirment que l'autonomisation des femmes au Rojava a des effets irréversibles.[38]

Les articulations et modes d'exercice du pouvoir dans les pratiques juridiques du Rojava tendent vers la décentralisation de la souveraineté hiérarchisée et vers l'autogouvernement des citoyens sans État. L'égalité des genres est assurée avec la co-présidence et l'existence de quotas au sein de toutes les autorités gouvernantes. Mais le plus important reste la redéfinition de la politique, de la démocratie et de l'autodétermination en dehors des processus formels de gouvernement par une pratique effective des femmes à travers les comités de réconciliation, les centres des femmes, les *Asayiş* autonomes et les coopératives indépendantes de femmes.

La Fédération de Rojava est actuellement le laboratoire de la déconstruction et de la renégociation progressives de concepts et de principes centraux du droit international qui sont marqués à la fois par l'eurocentrisme et par la domination masculine. La démocratie libérale, la souveraineté ainsi que le principe d'autodétermination sont tous remis en question par la nouvelle législation et la pratique quotidienne. La Fédération constitue un cas d'étude très important pour les internationalistes car elle nous fournit l'exemple d'une forme alternative de gouvernement sans État qui renforce la position des femmes et répond à leurs besoins et sert leurs intérêts mieux que ne le font plusieurs États-nations de la région. La révolution du Rojava mérite aussi l'attention des juristes: elle constitue en effet un exemple de déconstruction genrée du cadre libéral eurocentrique de la

[37] Jenna Krajeski, 'What the Kurds Want' (Fall 2015), *VQR* Online <http://www.vqronline.org/reporting-articles/2015/09/what-kurds-want> accessed 28 April 2019.

[38] Leezenberg Michiel, 'The Ambiguities of Democratic Autonomy: The Kurdish Movement in Turkey and Rojava' (2016) 16(4) *South East European and Black Sea Studies* 685.

démocratie, processus de construction par le bas dépassant les segments étroits gouvernés par l'État-nation et bénéficiant de l'intervention directe des femmes.

Serge Sur indiquait qu'en droit international, le principe d'autodétermination évolue depuis plusieurs décennies: l'approfondissement du principe concerne le libre choix par les peuples de leur mode d'organisation politique et tend à s'introduire dans la structure et le fonctionnement des ordres juridiques internes.[39] Certains auteurs soutiennent avec raison que la perspective kurde pourrait contribuer à cette évolution du principe d'autodétermination lui-même et que cette évolution modifiera les fondements du droit international.[40] La contribution du Rojava au droit international sera particulièrement importante pour la redéfinition du principe d'autodétermination en vue d'en renforcer les dimensions interne et économiques et d'assurer la prise en compte des opinions et des besoins des femmes.

[39] Serge Sur, La créativité du droit international, Cours général de droit international public' (2014) 363 *Recueil des Cours de l'Académie de Droit International* 54–5.

[40] Jean-Denis Mouton, 'La revendication nationale kurde et le principe d'autodétermination' (2015) 1 *Civitas Europa* 164, 155.

PART V

DOMESTIC ENGAGEMENT WITH INTERNATIONAL LAW

The Domestic Judiciary in the Architecture of the Strasbourg System of Human Rights

*David Kosař and Jan Petrov**

1 Introduction

Discussions about the Strasbourg system of human rights protection have followed the prevailing trend in international human rights law debates, a major shift towards domestic implementation and enforcement of international human rights rules.[1] Accordingly, the principle of subsidiarity and the deeper embeddedness of the European Convention on Human Rights (ECHR) in domestic legal practices have become the most prominent topics in recent debates about reforms to the ECHR system. According to the Brussels Declaration, a high-level political declaration by the foreign ministers of forty-seven member states of the Council of Europe (CoE) that addressed the future of the ECHR system: 'the national authorities and, in particular, the courts are the first guardians of human rights ensuring the full, effective and direct application of the Convention—in the light of the Court's case law—in their national legal system, in accordance with the principle of subsidiarity'.[2]

Similarly, scholarly debates have also depicted national authorities, and mainly domestic judiciaries, as the most important interlocutors in ensuring

* We are grateful for the often anonymous feedback of audiences in Berlin, Oslo, Prague, Tartu, and Riga. The research leading to this chapter has received funding from the Czech Science Foundation under grant agreement No. 16-09415S ('Beyond Compliance—Domestic Implementation of International Human Rights Case Law'). A longer version of this chapter, with the expanded part on the role of domestic constitutional courts, appeared in the *Heidelberg Journal of International Law* (2017) 77, 585.

[1] Hellen Keller and Geir Ulfstein, 'Introduction' in Hellen Keller and Geir Ulfstein (eds), *UN Human Rights Treaty Bodies: Law and Legitimacy* (CUP 2012) 5; and, more generally, Anne-Marie Slaughter and William Burke-White, 'The Future of International Law Is Domestic (or, The European Way of Law)' (2006) 47 *Harvard International Law Journal* 328, 350.

[2] High-level Conference on the 'Implementation of the European Convention on Human Rights, our shared responsibility'—Brussels Declaration (2015). For a more recent document on the future of the ECHR system see the Copenhagen Declaration (2018).

David Kosař and Jan Petrov, *The Domestic Judiciary in the Architecture of the Strasbourg System of Human Rights* In: *How International Law Works in Times of Crisis*. Edited by: George Ulrich and Ineta Ziemele, Oxford University Press (2019).
DOI: 10.1093/oso/9780198849667.003.0016

the efficient functioning of the ECHR regime.[3] This is because the European Court of Human Rights (ECtHR), despite being labelled as the most effective international human rights court in the world, is still only an international court with no influence over 'either the sword or the purse'.[4] International courts are empowered to interpret the law in their rulings but they have no power to execute their decisions and have only a few formal instruments detailing how to force states to comply with their rulings.[5] Therefore, domestic actors play an important role in overcoming this gap and in giving effect to the conclusions of the Strasbourg Court.

This chapter concurs that the effectiveness of the ECtHR and of the entire ECHR regime depends to a large extent on cooperation between various judicial and non-judicial domestic actors and their willingness to give effect to the judgments of the Strasbourg Court. In other words, an important part of the Strasbourg human rights regime's current problems can be resolved at the level of domestic implementation of ECHR rights. The novelty of this chapter is that it offers a more nuanced explanation of how the domestic level matters for implementation of ECtHR judgments and for the Convention system as a whole. Its aim is to analyse the significance of domestic actors in the ECHR system's architecture and to provide a framework for studying factors influencing particular domestic actors' treatment of ECHR rights.

More specifically, we show that domestic actors play two crucial roles regarding implementation of ECtHR case law. First, they act as 'diffusers' when they adopt general rules implementing the Strasbourg Court's case law and thus diffuse the ECtHR's conclusions adopted in a single case towards all rights holders at the national level. Second, when such domestic ECtHR-inspired rules are invoked domestically, domestic actors apply and enforce them, thereby acting as 'filters' vis-à-vis the Strasbourg Court because they can prevent or remedy human rights violations at the domestic level. Next, we show that these two roles of the domestic authorities cannot be taken for granted as they ultimately depend on the involvement of various domestic actors in the implementation processes, the attitudes of these domestic actors towards ECtHR judgments, their mutual relations, their power within the domestic system, and their ability and readiness to act. Building on these insights, we make a case for studying the roles and significance of *particular* actors within the processes of implementing ECtHR case law.

[3] See, e.g., Laurence Helfer, 'Redesigning the European Court of Human Rights: Embeddedness as a Deep Structural Principle of the European Human Rights Regime' (2008) 19 *European Journal of International Law* 125; Courtney Hillebrecht, 'Implementing International Human Rights Law at Home: Domestic Politics and the European Court of Human Rights' (2012) 13 *Human Rights Review* 279.

[4] Alexander Hamilton, 'Federalist no. 78' in Clinton Rossiter (ed.), *The Federalist Papers* (Signet 2003) 464.

[5] Harold H. Koh, 'How Is International Human Rights Law Enforced?' (1999) 74 *Indiana Law Journal* 1397; Oona Hathaway and Scott Shapiro, 'Outcasting: Enforcement in Domestic and International Law' (2011) 121 *Yale Law Journal* 252.

Subsequently, we concentrate on the domestic judiciary, which has great potential to contribute to the embeddedness of the Strasbourg Court's case law at the national level and which has often been portrayed as the driving force behind implementing Strasbourg case law. We problematize this relationship between domestic courts and the Strasbourg Court and show that domestic courts can play a variety of roles in implementation processes. First, it is necessary to keep in mind that domestic implementation mechanisms are far more complex than they seem at first glance, and usually no actor, however powerful, can act alone. As a result, the judiciary enters into multiple interactions with other domestic actors and is not necessarily always victorious. Second, there are several actors *within* the judiciary who may have different attitudes to the ECtHR such as the constitutional court, apex courts, lower courts, court presidents, and judicial associations. All these actors, each in its own way, may significantly affect the domestic judicial treatment of the ECHR and ECtHR case law. Third, not all domestic judges unequivocally support implementation of Strasbourg case law, and some of them have shown considerable resistance to the ECtHR. Under what circumstances they do so and to what extent such judicial disobedience is successful remains to be researched in the future.

This chapter proceeds as follows. The second section briefly explains the domestic effects of Strasbourg case law for the parties to a dispute before the ECtHR (*inter partes* effect) as well as for other parties to the ECHR (*res interpretata* effect). The third emphasizes the dual role of domestic authorities in implementing ECtHR case law: the 'diffusing' and the 'filtering' role. The fourth section shows that domestic implementation processes engage a plurality of actors, who may have different attitudes to Strasbourg judgments, who are entangled in a web of mutual interrelations and interactions, and who may have different powers and willingness to employ them. The fifth section, which is the core of this chapter, challenges the traditional perception of domestic courts as the driving force of implementation of ECtHR case law. The sixth section concludes.

2 The Domestic Effects of Strasbourg Case Law

ECtHR case law has had a major influence on the domestic law of most of the Council of Europe (CoE) member states in various areas.[6] ECtHR judgments regularly not only influence the legal order of a respondent state, the direct addressee of an ECtHR ruling, but also stimulate reforms in states which were not

[6] See, e.g., Elizabeth Lambert-Abdelgawad, *The Execution of Judgments of the European Court of Human Rights* (CoE Publishing 2008); Laurence Helfer and Erik Voeten, 'International Courts as Agents of Legal Change: Evidence from LGBT Rights in Europe' (2014) 68 *International Organisation* 77; and David Kosař and Lucas Lixinski, 'Domestic Judicial Design by International Human Rights Courts' (2015) 105 *American Journal of International Law* 713.

parties to the proceedings. This section of the chapter briefly explains the legal grounding of the ECtHR's domestic impact. First, it discusses the *inter partes* binding force of ECtHR judgments and the recent shift from the ECtHR's classic remedial strategy to a more proactive specification of individual and general measures required from 'convicted' treaty parties. Subsequently, it deals with the doctrine of the *res interpretata* effect, which explains what normative implications Strasbourg case law has for states which were not parties to the original dispute.

2.1 *Inter partes* Binding Force of ECtHR Judgments

According to Article 46(1) ECHR the treaty parties are obliged to abide by the final judgment of the ECtHR in any case to which they are parties. The effect of this provision reaches beyond the situation of a particular applicant who was successful at the Strasbourg Court. The Convention's purpose was not only to redress concrete wrongs committed by states but also to secure certain minimal standards of human rights protection within the territory of the parties to the Convention.[7]

As a result, Article 46(1) ECHR urges states to respond to a judgment of the ECtHR in the case of an individual applicant and on the general level, if necessary, in order to prevent future human rights violations of the same kind. This means that the respondent state faces three levels of obligations resulting from a finding by the Strasbourg Court that it violated its ECHR obligations: (i) the duty to pay just satisfaction to the injured individual, if awarded by the ECtHR (Article 41 ECHR); (ii) the duty to adopt individual measures vis-à-vis the specific wrong towards the claimant; and (iii) the duty to adopt general measures to avoid repetition of the violation. As the duty to pay just satisfaction does not require changes in domestic law, we put it to one side. Although individual measures may have wider implications for domestic law (they might require and thus trigger systemic changes in domestic law),[8] this chapter focuses on the duty to adopt general measures because it regularly implies amending domestic legislation, revisiting domestic case law, and changing administrative practice. Pursuant to the law of treaties and, more specifically, the case law of the ECtHR, the ECHR parties are obliged to adjust their legal orders in order to comply with the Convention.[9]

[7] Janneke Gerards, 'The European Court of Human Rights and National Courts: Giving Shape to the Notion of "Shared Responsibility"' in Janneke Gerards and Joseph Fleuren (eds), *Implementation of the European Convention on Human Rights and of the Judgments of the ECtHR in National Case Law* (Intersentia 2014) 19.

[8] For further details see Jannika Jahn, 'Ruling (In)directly through Individual Measures? Effect and Legitimacy of the ECtHR's New Remedial Power' (2014) 74 *Heidelberg Journal of International Law* 26.

[9] See e.g., *Maestri v Italy* App No 39748/98 (ECtHR Grand Chamber, para. 47, 17 February 2004); *Apicella v Italy* App No 64890/01 (ECtHR GC, para. 123, 29 March 2006); *Yordanova and others v Bulgaria*

A related question is whether the ECtHR can indicate as a 'remedy' wider legislative measures as part of its competence in relation to a particular individual complaint.

The ECtHR often declares it cannot engage in the abstract or concrete review of legislation and that it does not have the power to quash the piece of legislation in question. The ECtHR therefore limits its review to the result of the law's application and to declaring whether there was a violation of the Convention or not.[10] This self-perception led to the ECtHR's restrained approach towards remedies[11] in which the Strasbourg Court has concentrated solely on finding a violation of the Convention and left the rest to the states. Under this traditional model of remedies, the ECtHR would not specify what measures should be taken to comply with its judgment as the states would be seen as better placed to decide the appropriate way to prevent repetition of a human rights violation.[12] However, this practice has changed in recent years. The Court started indicating more specific individual and also general measures.[13]. Furthermore, an indication by the ECtHR of general measures is an essential element of the pilot judgment procedure,[14] which aims at reducing the ECtHR's backlog of pending cases that would be addressed by a change of domestic legislation.

Nevertheless, the pilot procedure focuses only on cases relating to the same treaty party. This is an important tool for increasing the effectiveness of the Strasbourg system, but it would hardly be sufficient to reduce the backlog of ECtHR cases in itself. In order to ensure the effectiveness of the Strasbourg system, ECtHR case law needs to be taken into account even by treaty parties that were not party to a case adjudicated by the ECtHR. This brings us to the doctrine of the *res interpretata* effect.

App No 25446/06 (ECHR, para. 163, 24 April 2012); *Paksas v Lithuania* App No 34932/04 (ECtHR GC, para. 119, 6 January 2011).

[10] See Art. 34 ECHR; and, e.g., *F. v Switzerland* App No 11329/85 (ECHR GC, para. 43, 18 December 1987); *Marckx v Belgium* App No 6833/74 (ECtHR Plenary, para. 58, 13 June 1979).

[11] By 'remedy' we mean an indication by the ECtHR of individual and general measures to be taken at the domestic level in order to implement the judgment.

[12] Darren Hawkins and Wade Jacoby, 'Partial Compliance: A Comparison of the European and Inter-American Courts of Human Rights' (2010) 6 *Journal of International Law and International Relations* 35, 40. In the case law of the Strasbourg Court see, e.g., *Marckx v Belgium* App No 6833/74 (ECHR Plenary, para. 58, 13 June 1979), ECtHR (Plenary); *Belilos v Switzerland* App No 10328/83 (ECHR Plenary, para. 78, 29 April 1988); *Scozzari and Giunta v Italy* App Nos 39221/98 and 41963/98 (ECtHR Grand Chamber, para. 249, 13 July 2000).

[13] See, e.g., Helen Keller and Cedric Marti, 'Reconceptualizing Implementation: The Judicialization of the Execution of the European Court of Human Rights' Jurisprudence' (2015) 26 *European Journal of International Law* 829.

[14] For a description of the pilot judgments procedure see, e.g., Antoine Buyse, 'The Pilot Judgment Procedure at the European Court of Human Rights: Possibilities and Challenges' (2009) 57 *Greek Law Journal* 1890; Markus Fyrnys, 'Expanding Competences by Judicial Lawmaking: The Pilot Judgment Procedure of the European Court of Human Rights' (2011) 12 *German Law Journal* 1231.

2.2 *Res Interpretata* Effect

A decision of the ECtHR is binding on the parties to a particular dispute: the judgment gains the status of *res iudicata*. However, the impact of pronouncements by the Court is broader. ECtHR judgments often influence the legal orders of states which were not respondents in particular cases, and thus de facto gain *erga omnes partes* effect. For instance, Ireland, Latvia, and Cyprus changed their regulation of prisoners' voting rights in response to the *Hirst (No. 2)* judgment.[15] The Grand Chamber judgment in *Salduz v Turkey*[16] had already led to reforms of custodial legal assistance in France, Belgium, Ireland, Scotland, and the Netherlands.[17] In response to the pilot judgment in *Hutten-Czapska v Poland*,[18] the Czech Republic adopted a new statute on unilateral rent increases.[19] These are just a few examples. Other states also regularly monitor developments in the case law of the ECtHR beyond the cases against their own governments and adjust their domestic legislation accordingly.[20]

The Court has a general interpretative authority over the Convention (Article 32); its case law acquires a so-called *res interpretata* effect. Via its rulings, the ECtHR interprets the Convention, and this interpretation is to be taken into account by all the treaty parties if relevant for their domestic legal orders. Even though the *res interpretata* effect is not explicitly stated in the Convention, it has been inferred from the very construction of the European system of human rights protection[21] and mentioned in the case law of the ECtHR[22] as well as in political declarations[23] and various CoE documents.[24]

Having sketched the legal basis for the effects of ECtHR case law on the CoE member states, the following section unpacks the Member State into multiple domestic actors and shows how these actors influence implementation.

[15] *Hirst (no. 2) v UK* App No 74025/01 (ECtHR GC, 6 October 2005).

[16] *Salduz v Turkey* App No 36391/02 (ECtHR Grand Chamber 27 November 2008).

[17] See Dimitrios Giannoulopoulos, 'Strasbourg Jurisprudence, Law Reform and Comparative Law: A Tale of the Right to Custodial Legal Assistance in Five Countries' (2016) 16 *Human Rights Law Review* 103.

[18] *Hutten-Czapska v Poland* App No 35014/97 (ECtHR GC, 19 June 2006).

[19] Act No. 107/2006 Coll. Another impulse for adopting this new statute was the case law of the Czech Constitutional Court.

[20] For other examples see the texts referred to in note 24 *infra*.

[21] *Res interpretata* effect is inferred from the joint reading of Arts 1 and 19 ECHR. See Andrew Drzemczewski, 'Quelques réflexions sur l'autorité de la chose interprétée par la Cour de Strasbourg' in Jean Barthelemy et al. (eds), *La conscience des droits: mélanges en l'honneur de Jean-Paul Costa* (Dalloz 2011).

[22] See, e.g., *Opuz v Turkey* App No 33401/02 (ECtHR, para. 163, 9 June 2009); *Rantsev v Cyprus* App No 25965/04 (ECtHR, para. 197, 7 January 2010) and the case law cited therein.

[23] E.g., the Interlaken Declaration (2010).

[24] For further details on the *res interpretata* effect, see Adam Bodnar, 'Res Interpretata: Legal Effect of the European Court of Human Rights' Judgments for other States Than Those Which Were Party to the Proceedings' in Yves Haeck and Eva Brems (eds), *Human Rights and Civil Liberties in the 21st Century* (Springer 2014) 223.

3 The 'Diffusing' and 'Filtering' Role of the Domestic Authorities

The ECtHR is only empowered to interpret the Convention in its rulings, but on its own has little formal power to trigger domestic reform and to change domestic laws and case law in order to put national legal orders into compliance with its rulings. In this regard, the ECtHR, to a large extent, has to rely on national legal and political authorities. As Courtney Hillebrecht put it, 'domestic political institutions, particularly domestic democratic institutions, play an important role in facilitating compliance with international human rights law'.[25]

The following analysis explains how domestic actors facilitate implementation of ECtHR judgments and how they contribute to the functioning of the ECHR system as a whole. They fulfil two main roles in the ECHR system: they are 'diffusers' of ECtHR case law and 'filters' of the ECtHR.

Within the function of diffusing the ECtHR's pronouncements, the domestic authorities are expected to reflect the Strasbourg Court's rulings and adopt domestic rules—via a statutory amendment or a change of domestic case law or administrative practice—which respect the conclusions of the ECtHR. These domestic rules are general and apply to all the rights holders at the national level. The domestic authorities act as 'diffusers' as they spread the effects of an ECtHR ruling. They translate the ECtHR's conclusions from the case of one particular applicant to a general domestic rule applicable to all similar situations. Other treaty parties are obliged to respect the *res interpretata* effect[26] and comply fully with ECtHR judgments.

Once the ECtHR's pronouncements are diffused domestically, domestic actors, especially administrative bodies and national courts, operate as 'filters' vis-à-vis the ECtHR. By respecting and applying the general rules adopted in response to ECtHR case law, the national authorities prevent violations of Convention rights or provide a domestic remedy. The Convention thus becomes embedded[27] at national level, which implies granting protection of Convention rights—as interpreted by the ECtHR—at the national level and preventing applications from being filed at the Strasbourg Court, or at least significantly reducing their total number.

Among other implications, the described model shows that not only establishing a domestic general rule (new legislation) compliant with the ECHR but also the subsequent practice of the law enforcement authorities when applying the rule is crucial from the point of view of the overall effectiveness of the Convention system.

[25] Courtney Hillebrecht, *supra* note 3, at 284. See also Courtney Hillebrecht, 'The Domestic Mechanisms of Compliance with International Human Rights Law: Case Studies from the Inter-American Human Rights System' (2012) 34 *Human Rights Quarterly* 959, 964–72 and 984–5 (regarding the IACtHR).

[26] See Oddný Mjöll Arnardóttir, 'Res Interpretata, Erga Omnes Effect and the Role of the Margin of Appreciation in Giving Domestic Effect to the Judgments of the European Court of Human Rights' (2017) 28 *European Journal of International Law* 819.

[27] Helfer, *supra* note 3.

From a more general perspective, it also shows why the attitude of domestic authorities is crucial for addressing the 'double-faced crisis'[28] of the ECtHR. Effective functioning of the 'diffusing' and 'filtering' role of domestic actors can positively affect both the caseload crisis of the ECtHR (by preventing clone cases) and the legitimacy crisis (not only by increasing compliance, but also by the domestic authorities' greater engagement with ECHR rights).

4 Implementation Processes of the Strasbourg Case Law: Particular Actors *within* the Domestic Arena Matter

The model developed in the third section structures the basic features of implementing ECtHR judgments and illustrates the ties between the ECtHR and domestic actors within the framework of the ECHR system. However, it is notable that these links between the ECtHR and domestic layers of the ECHR regime are more diverse and heterogeneous. In practice, the system is not strictly built along hierarchical lines.[29] Moreover, recent instances of backlash against the ECtHR[30] demonstrate that implementation of ECtHR case law may become a sensitive political issue. Ultimately, domestic responses depend primarily on the ability and willingness of domestic actors to make such a change.

Domestic implementation processes are characterized by four distinctive features: (i) the plurality of actors, (ii) who may have different attitudes towards Strasbourg judgments, (iii) who are entangled in a web of mutual relations and interactions among each other, and (iv) who may have different powers and willingness to employ them. These are further explained in the following paragraphs.

[28] Janneke Gerards and Ashley Terlouw, 'Solutions for the European Court of Human Rights' in Spyridon Flogaitis, Tom Zwart, and Julie Fraser (eds), *The European Court of Human Rights and its Discontents* (Edward Elgar 2013) 165.

[29] See Nico Krisch, 'The Open Architecture of European Human Rights Law' (2008) 71 *Modern Law Review* 183; and Colm O'Cinneide, 'Human Rights within Multi-Layered Systems of Constitutional Governance: Rights Cosmopolitanism and Domestic Particularism in Tension' (2010) *Irish Yearbook of International Law* 19.

[30] The 'backlash techniques' include challenges to the reputation and legitimacy of the ECtHR, principled non-compliance or large-scale non-compliance. See, e.g., Mikael Rask Madsen, 'The Challenging Authority of the European Court of Human Rights: From Cold War Legal Diplomacy to the Brighton Declaration and Backlash' (2016) *Law and Contemporary Problems* 141; Barbara Oomen, 'A Serious Case of Strasbourg-bashing? An Evaluation of the Debates on the Legitimacy of the European Court of Human Rights in the Netherlands' (2016) *International Journal of Human Rights* 407. The most recent examples include Russia's delayed contribution to the Council of Europe's budget and its threats to leave the Convention system as such, and also the draft Copenhagen Declaration prepared by the Danish Presidency of the Council of Europe in spring 2018. For theorizing about determinants of compliance difficulties more generally, see David Kosař and Jan Petrov, 'Determinants of Compliance Difficulties among 'Good Compliers': Implementation of International Human Rights Rulings in the Czech Republic' (2018) 29(2) *European Journal of International Law* 397.

First, a number of national and international actors may take part in domestic implementation processes. At the international level they include, among other actors, third states, governmental, and non-governmental international organizations (NGOs) criticizing non-compliance by the respondent state.[31] International actors, such as the Venice Commission, may provide expertise: through opinions on draft legislation, reports on topical issues, or even *amicus curiae* to domestic constitutional courts.[32] At the domestic level, especially the executive, the legislature, domestic courts, the Ombudsman, and the government agent before the ECtHR, may engage in implementing ECHR rights. Furthermore, civil society, especially domestic NGOs, influences implementation processes. Even though NGOs do not possess sufficient formal powers to change the status quo, they can mobilize around an ECtHR judgment, provide expertise, and generate pressure on the state's authorities to act.[33]

Usually, at least in relation to high-profile cases, multiple actors are involved. As Courtney Hillebrecht states, '[n]o single domestic actor, not even the strongest executive, can satisfy all of the tribunals' mandates, legally or logistically'.[34] Different authors then emphasize the roles of different institutions. Some rely on the power of civil society and NGOs[35] and pressure groups,[36] while others focus on the power of the judiciary,[37] legislature,[38] or the executive[39] to push through policy change. Yet domestic implementation is a complex endeavour that typically comprises a number of actors. It is a complicated system consisting of an ever-changing set of actors whose steps may be important for implementation of an ECtHR judgment.[40]

[31] See, e.g., *D. H. and others v the Czech Republic* App No 57325/00 (ECtHR GC, 13 November 2007); and Hubert Smekal and Katarína Šipulová, 'DH v Czech Republic Six Years Later: On the Power of an International Human Rights Court to Push through Systemic Change' (2014) 32 *Netherlands Quarterly of Human Rights* 288 (which discuss the subsequent implementation process in the Czech Republic).

[32] See, e.g., Maartje De Visser, 'A Critical Assessment of the Role of the Venice Commission in Processes of Domestic Constitutional Reform' (2015) 63 *American Journal of Comparative Law* 701; and Valentina Volpe, 'Drafting Counter-Majoritarian Democracy the Venice Commission's Constitutional Assistance' (2016) 76 *Heidelberg Journal of International Law* 811.

[33] For the role of civil society in implementing ECtHR case law, see Lucja Miara and Victoria Prais, 'The Role of Civil Society in the Execution of Judgments of the European Court of Human Rights' (2012) *European Human Rights Law Review* 528.

[34] Courtney Hillebrecht, *Domestic Politics and International Human Rights Tribunals: The Problem of Compliance* (CUP 2014) 25.

[35] *Supra* note 33.

[36] See Joel P. Trachtman, 'International Law and Domestic Political Coalitions: The Grand Theory of Compliance with International Law' (2010) 11 *Chicago Journal of International Law* 127.

[37] See A. Nollkaemper, 'The Role of National Courts in Inducing Compliance with International and European Law: A Comparison', in M. Cremona (ed.), *Compliance and the Enforcement of EU Law* (2012) 158; Janneke Gerards and Joseph Fleuren (eds), *Implementation of the European Convention on Human Rights and of the Judgments of the ECtHR in National Case Law* (Intersentia 2014).

[38] See Alice Donald and Philip Leach, *Parliaments and the European Court of Human Rights* (OUP 2016), 99–108.

[39] See Harold H. Koh, 'Why Do Nations Obey International Law?' (1997) 106 *Yale Law Journal* 2599, 2657.

[40] See also Karen Alter, *New Terrain of International Law* (Princeton University Press 2014) 19.

Second, the actors involved in implementation processes may have different interests, preferences, and attitudes towards human rights in general or towards a particular issue. Not all of these actors are necessarily in favour of ECtHR rulings in all of the cases. If the actors involved have different preferences, implementation of ECtHR rulings can be described as a political battle,[41] or more generally as a competition between pro-compliance forces and the compliance-opposing camp. In practice, however, the positions of particular actors will hardly be 'black or white', which makes the trajectory of implementation complicated.

Furthermore, the ECHR system consists of forty-seven treaty parties and includes, broadly speaking, three types of states (according to their human rights situation): established democracies, (post-)transition democracies, and hybrid regimes in which the basic norms of democratic governance and the rule of law have not been fully accepted.[42] Smooth functioning of the model presented in the third section of this chapter in practical terms also presupposes a high level of expertise by state officials in human rights law, including knowledge of ECtHR case law in relation to other countries (so that the *res interpretata* effect is effectively guaranteed), as well as the respective language skills.[43]. These assumptions cannot be taken for granted in all forty-seven parties to the ECHR. As a result, especially in (post-) transition democracies and hybrid regimes, effective implementation may be impeded not only owing to political reasons but also owing to ignorance of ECtHR case law, as well as lack of enforcement capacity or willingness in the 'filtering' phase.

Third, domestic actors interact with each other. The proverbial 'implementation ball' may move from one domestic institution to another as a result of their actions. For instance, if the constitutional court strikes down a statute for violating the ECHR, the ball moves to the parliament which can no longer be inactive as it must fill the gap in the law. This may nudge or force the parliament to leave the compliance-opposing camp and implement the relevant ECtHR judgment. Due to the divergent preferences and priorities of domestic institutions regarding human rights, ECtHR judgments may also 'ignite domestic battles over human rights, state sovereignty and the role of international law in domestic politics'.[44] Such Strasbourg judgments may sometimes even result in reshuffling the power of domestic actors, for instance by introducing judicial review in a certain area,[45]

[41] Marinella Marmo, 'The Execution of Judgments of the European Court of Human Rights—a Political Battle' (2008) 15 *Masstricht Journal of European & Comparative Law* 235.

[42] Robert Harmsen, 'The Reform of the Convention System: Institutional Restructuring and the (Geo)Politics of Human Rights' in Jonas Christoffersen and Mikael Rask Madsen (eds), *The European Court of Human Rights between Law and Politics* (OUP 2013) 141–2.

[43] Even though the ECtHR has recently significantly improved access to its case law in other than the two original languages and started to publish translations of its judgments in various languages on its website—the so-called HUDOC (see <http://hudoc.echr.coe.int>). As of 11 July 2016, the number of translated judgments varied from 14 (Dutch) to 2,622 (Turkish).

[44] Hillebrecht, *supra* note 3, at 293.

[45] The ECtHR has, among other things, required the Netherlands to allow full judicial review of the Crown's administrative decisions, *Benthem v Netherlands* App No 8848/80 (ECtHR Plenary,

by reducing the autonomy of one branch of government,[46] by changing the composition of a constitutional organ,[47] or by introducing a new independent body to review police misconduct.[48] Such transfers of powers require lengthy discussion, careful deliberation, and sometimes even *quid pro quo* solutions among the domestic actors involved.

Fourth, the capacities and powers of the actors involved in implementation may differ. As Sonia Cardenas put it, the domestic battle over compliance may rather be affected by the distribution of institutional power than by the greatest commitment to international human rights law.[49] In the same vein, Courtney Hillebrecht concurs and argues, '[i]nternational law, and particularly the tribunals' rulings, can provide an impetus for action for individual actors or coalitions of actors, but their ability to act on that impetus will be limited—or enhanced—by their domestic political power'.[50] For instance, when domestic constraints on the executive, such as independent judiciaries, political competition, free media, and civil society, are weak, as in Russia, a single actor—the executive—can dominate implementation.[51] In contrast, when several strong institutions take part in the implementation process, as in the United Kingdom, the eventual result of this process very much depends on the ability to reach consensus.[52]

Overall, implementation as both process and outcome depends (i) on the number of (domestic) actors taking part in implementation, (ii) on their stances towards the ECtHR judgment to be implemented, (iii) on mutual relations and interactions among these actors, and (iv) on their respective power within the system and their ability and readiness to act.

The actors involved may play different roles in the implementation process. Every actor possesses a certain spectrum of de facto possible options concerning

paras 32–44, 23 October 1985); see also Pieter van Dijk, 'The Benthem Case and Its Aftermath in the Netherlands' (1987) 34 *Netherlands International Law Review* 5.

[46] For instance, the ECtHR has significantly narrowed the scope of parliamentary immunity (see *Karácsony and Others v Hungary* App Nos 42461/13 and 44357/13 (ECtHR GC, 17 May 2016); and earlier case law discussed in David Kosař, 'Policing Separation of Powers: A New Role for the European Court of Human Rights?' (2012) 8 *EuConst* 33, 46–55.

[47] For instance, the ECtHR has de facto forced Ukraine to change the composition of the Ukrainian High Council of Justice (see *Oleksandr Volkov v Ukraine* App No 21722/11 (ECtHR, paras 91, 109–117, and 200, 9 January 2013); for further details see Kosař and Lixinski, *supra* note 6, 737–8 and 756.

[48] See, e.g., *Güleç v Turkey* App No 21593/93 (ECtHR, paras 76 and 80, 27 July 1998); *Hugh Jordan v UK* App No 24746/94 (ECtHR, para. 120, 4 May 2001); *Eremiášová and Pechová v the* Czech *Republic* App No 23944/04 (ECHR, paras 137 and 151–160, 16 February 2012).

[49] Sonia Cardenas, *Conflict and Compliance: State Responses to International Human Rights Pressure* (University of Pennsylvania Press 2007) 13.

[50] Courtney Hillebrecht, *Domestic Politics and International Human Rights Tribunals: The Problem of Compliance* (CUP 2014) 25.

[51] Hillebrecht, *supra* note 3, 288–9.

[52] *Ibid.*, 293–7.

how to react to an ECtHR judgment.[53] According to its preferences, powers, and possible interactions with other actors, a particular actor may essentially influence the dynamics of implementation as a process and, therefore, affect its outcome: the level of compliance with the ECtHR ruling.

However, all these actors operate within a broader system: the state. Fundamental state-level features of the polity and their implications for the implementation of international commitments have been widely studied.[54] Socio-political factors such as regime type,[55] length of democracy,[56] legal infrastructure and domestic institutional capacity,[57] states' reputational concerns,[58] or generally spread human rights expertise and awareness[59] have been reported as influencing compliance with international human rights law. At the same time, legal factors, such as the status of international law in domestic law, and particularly the de facto domestic status of the ECHR and ECtHR case law,[60] the separation of powers doctrine and configuration of constitutional review,[61] or prevailing perceptions of legal and political culture and the concept of democracy among judges in a given country[62] should be taken into account. State-level factors can contribute to explaining variations in the implementation of international human rights law over time and across countries.[63] Moreover, they also co-determine the competences and authority of particular actors, thereby shaping their starting position in the implementation processes at the level of domestic politics.

[53] Alec Stone Sweet and Helen Keller, 'The Reception of the ECHR National Legal Orders' in Alec Stone Sweet and Helen Keller (eds), *A Europe of Rights: The Impact of the ECHR on National Legal Systems* (OUP 2008) 14.

[54] The following list of macro-level factors does not aspire to completeness. We rather mention the factors most relevant for the focus of our article.

[55] Anne-Marie Slaughter, 'International Law in a World of Liberal States' (1995) 6 *European Journal of International Law* 503.

[56] See the discussion in Sharanbir Grewal and Erik Voeten, 'Are New Democracies Better Human Rights Compliers?' (2015) 69 *International Organisation* 497.

[57] Dia Anagnostou and Alina Mungiu-Pippidi, 'Domestic Implementation of Human Rights Judgments in Europe: Legal Infrastructure and Government Effectiveness Matter' (2014) 25 *European Journal of International Law* 205; Courtney Hillebrecht, 'The Power of Human Rights Tribunals: Compliance with the European Court of Human Rights and Domestic Policy Change' (2014) 20 *European Journal of International Rights* 1100, 1117.

[58] Andrew T. Guzman, 'A Compliance-Based Theory of International Law' (2002) 90 *California Law Review* 1823.

[59] Anagnostou and Mungiu-Pippidi, *supra* note 57, at 221; Hillebrecht, *supra* note 3.

[60] Helen Keller and Alec Stone Sweet, 'Assessing the Impact of the ECHR on National Legal Systems' in Stone Sweet and Keller, *supra* note 53, at 683.

[61] Gerards and Fleuren, *supra* note 37, at 363.

[62] See, *mutatis mutandis*, Marlene Wind, 'The Nordics, the EU and the Reluctance Towards Supranational Judicial Review' (2010) 48 *Journal of Common Market Studies* 1039, or Juan A. Mayoral and Urszula Jaremba, 'Perspectives on Europeanization of National Judiciaries: Old and New Questions' (2016) *iCourts Working Paper Series*, No. 59, 10–11.

[63] Courtney Hillebrecht, 'The Domestic Mechanisms of Compliance with International Human Rights Law: Case Studies from the Inter-American Human Rights System' (2012) 34 *Human Rights Quarterly* 959, 963.

Having provided the general framework, in the fifth section of this chapter we explain the role of an allegedly natural ally of the ECtHR—the domestic judiciary—in implementing ECtHR case law. We problematize this one-sided view of the domestic judiciary and show the relationship between domestic courts and the ECtHR is far more complicated.

5 Domestic Judiciaries: The Driving Force of Implementation?

Domestic courts are the most natural allies of the ECtHR that may help to secure implementation of ECtHR judgments and to enhance the legitimacy of ECtHR case law.[64] Domestic courts in general, and constitutional courts in particular, help monitor enforcement of ECtHR judgments in their own states and, by issuing similar decisions, increase support within their own states for those judgments.[65] That also explains why the ECtHR has forged a compliance partnership with domestic judges[66] and empowered them vis-à-vis other branches of government.[67]

However, the domestic judiciary is not a monolithic block either. Hence, it is necessary to unpack it and to understand compliance pushes and pulls *within* the judiciary. At least five actors operate within domestic judiciaries affecting domestic judicial treatment of the ECHR as interpreted by the ECtHR. These actors are the constitutional court (if it exists in a given country), top ordinary courts (the Supreme Court, the Supreme Administrative Court, the Council of State, and other courts of the same stature), lower courts, court presidents, and judicial associations. These actors, each in their own way, play the role of 'judicial gatekeepers' in implementing ECtHR case law into domestic case law. They may have—like domestic actors within the other two branches of government—different interests, preferences, and attitudes towards Strasbourg case law in general as well as towards particular judgments. The position of each of these actors depends, for example, on their openness to supranational sources, values, and beliefs that may or may not carry a special premium, on the legal certainty and stability of the legal system, knowledge of foreign languages, promotion incentives, expectations of its

[64] See Wojciech Sadurski, 'Partnering with Strasbourg: Constitutionalization of the European Court of Human Rights, the Accession of Central and East European States to the Council of Europe, and the Idea of Pilot Judgments' (2009) 9(397) *Human Rights Law Review* 414–20 [who describes the cooperation between the ECtHR and the Polish Constitutional Court that led to *Hutten-Czapska v Poland* App No. 35014/97 (ECHR GC, 19 June 2006)]; Shai Dothan, *Reputation and Judicial Tactics: A Theory of National and International Courts* (CUP 2014) 111–12 (showing other examples).

[65] Dothan, *supra* note 64, at 111.

[66] See Helfer, *supra* note 3, at 158. On the importance of national courts in ensuring compliance with international human rights rulings more generally, see Nollkaemper, *supra* note 37; Koh, *supra* note 39, at 1401, 1413; and James Hathaway, 'Between Power and Principle: An Integrated Theory of International Law' (2005) 71 *University of Chicago Law Review* 469, 506, 520–5.

[67] See Kosař and Lixinski, *supra* note 6, 747–9.

key audience, and on power considerations. Moreover, the position of each actor within the judiciary may change over time.

The significance of the role of constitutional courts and top ordinary courts is clear. Constitutional courts can reinterpret statutes using Convention-conforming interpretation or strike down laws that fail to meet domestic fundamental rights standards, which are often heavily influenced by Strasbourg case law. Some constitutional courts went even further. They de facto constitutionalized the ECHR[68] and started using it as a benchmark, separately from domestic constitutional norms, for judging domestic laws.[69] Top ordinary courts are also powerful players as they may employ ECHR-conforming interpretations and prioritize positions that engage more with ECtHR case law.[70] In doing so, they are also de facto imposing their Strasbourg-friendly positions on the lower courts. Hence, constitutional courts and top ordinary courts may operate as great 'diffusers' and 'filters' in the ECHR system.[71] On the other hand, they also wield significant 'negative power' that can be unleashed. They can impose a narrow reading of Strasbourg case law on the lower courts that may lead to minimalist compliance.[72] In some countries, they may even block an implementation process by finding the Strasbourg position incompatible with the domestic constitution,[73] as in that scenario other political actors will very likely not openly defy the position of their own apex court.[74]

The role of lower courts, court presidents, and judicial associations is less visible and often underestimated. Lower courts do not necessarily have to share the top courts' views of the ECtHR.[75] For instance, in Poland they seem to be more

[68] See, e.g., Keller and Stone Sweet, *supra* note 60, at 686; and Giuseppe Martinico, 'National Judges and Supranational Laws: Goals and Structure of the Research' in Giuseppe Martinico and Oreste Pollicino (eds), *The National Judicial Treatment of the ECHR and EU Laws: A Comparative Constitutional Perspective* (Europa Law 2010) 12–14.

[69] See, e.g., Catherine van de Heyning, 'Constitutional Courts as Guardians of Fundamental Rights: The Constitutionalization of the Convention through Domestic Constitutional Adjudication' in Patricia Popelier, Armen Mazmanyan, and Werner Vandenbruwaene (eds), *The Role of Constitutional Courts in Multilevel Governance* (Intersentia 2013) 21–48.

[70] See e.g. Gerards and Fleuren, *supra* note 37.

[71] See section 3.

[72] For instance, see the unwillingness of the UK and Swiss courts to accept the ECtHR's rulings on the issue of confrontation (see John Jackson and Sarah Summers, 'Confrontation with Strasbourg: UK and Swiss Approaches to Criminal Evidence' (2013) 2 *Criminal Law Review* 114), the narrow reading of the ECtHR's case law on the role of advocates general by the French *Conseil d'État* (see Krisch, *supra* note 29, 194–6, and John Bell, 'Interpretative Resistance' Faced with the Case-law of the Strasbourg Court' (2008) 14 *European Public Law* 134.

[73] See Philip Leach and Alice Donald, 'Russia Defies Strasbourg: Is Contagion Spreading?' (*EJIL:Talk!* 19 December 2015) <https://www.ejiltalk.org/russia-defies-strasbourg-is-contagion-spreading> accessed 10 April 2017; Maria Smirnova, 'Russian Constitutional Court Affirms Russian Constitution's Supremacy over ECtHR Decisions' (*EJIL:Talk!* 15 July 2015) <https://www.ejiltalk.org/russian-constitutional-court-affirms-russian-constitutions-supremacy-over-ecthr-decisions> accessed 10 April 2017; and the discussion on implementation of the 2013 *Anchugov & Gladkov v Russia* judgment in note 85 *infra*.

[74] For a rare exception see *A. and others v UK* App No, 3455/05 (ECtHR GC, para. 157, 19 February 2009).

[75] Rafał Mańko, 'War of Courts' as a Clash of Legal Cultures: Rethinking the Conflict between the Polish Constitutional Tribunal and the Supreme Court Over 'Interpretive Judgments' in Michael Hein,

resistant to the influence of the ECtHR than the Polish Constitutional Tribunal and the Supreme Court.[76] In the Czech Republic, one might witness an even more complex situation—the so-called sandwich scenario: judges appointed after the fall of communism, often fluent in English and French and more keen to implement ECtHR case law, sit in the lowest courts and in the constitutional court, whereas judges who were appointed in the communist era, not well versed in foreign languages and often sceptical of the purposive and value-oriented ECtHR reasoning, occupy seats in appellate courts and the Supreme Court.[77] In other words, the Strasbourg sceptics on the bench are 'sandwiched' by pro-Strasbourg judges.[78]

Court presidents are less visible yet important actors. They are the key players within the Central and Eastern European judiciaries[79] who influence judicial appointments and decide on promotion, case assignment, and other perks,[80] and hence their stance towards the ECtHR also matters. For instance, a court president who is sceptical about international human rights courts might prioritize the appointment of less ECtHR-enthusiastic judges to his court or informally tone down current judges' engagement with Strasbourg case law. Finally, judicial associations, although rarely built on the pro-ECtHR and anti-ECtHR axis, may also induce judges to restraint or openness towards the ECtHR, as they influence promotion in several countries such as France[81] and Italy.[82]

The answer to the question whether the domestic courts are indeed the driving force behind implementation of ECtHR case law thus very much depends on which actors *within* the judiciary adopt an ECtHR-friendly stance and whether they are willing to forge a pro-ECtHR alliance with other key actors. The above-mentioned

Antonia Geisler, and Siri Hummel (eds), *Law, Politics, and the Constitution: New Perspectives from Legal and Political Theory* (Peter Lang 2014) 79–94.

[76] See, e.g., Tomasz Tadeusz Koncewicz, 'Of Institutions, Democracy, Constitutional Self-Defence and the Rule of Law: The Judgments of the Polish Constitutional Tribunal in Cases K 34/15, K 35/15 and Beyond' (2016) 53 *Common Market Law Review* 1753, 1778–80.

[77] See David Kosař, *Perils of Judicial Self-Government* (CUP 2016), 107–8. Note that the composition of the Czech Supreme Administrative Court differs from that of the Czech Supreme Court, as the former was established only in 2003 and lured several young judges who had studied abroad.

[78] *Ibid.*

[79] While court presidents in Western Europe have undergone a profound transformation since the Second World War and exercise less influence than their counterparts in post-communist Europe, they still have their say in some established democracies (see, e.g., Peter H. Solomon, 'The Accountability of Judges in Post Communist States: From Bureaucratic to Professional Accountability', in Anja Seibert-Fohr (ed.), *Judicial Independence in Transition* (Springer 2012) 918–21; and Kosař, *supra* note 77, 390–8.

[80] See *ibid.*; Peter H. Solomon, 'Authoritarian Legality and Informal Practices: Judges, Lawyers and the State in Russia and China' (2010) 43 *Communist and Post-Communist Studies* 351, 354; and Lydia F. Müller, 'Judicial Administration in Transitional Eastern Countries' in Anja Seibert-Fohr (ed.), *Judicial Independence in Transition* (Springer 2012) 965.

[81] In France professional organizations control the *commissions d'avancément* (promotion commissions). For further details regarding the *commissions d'avancément* see Antoine Garapon and Harold Epineuse, 'Judicial Independence in France' in Seibert-Fohr, *supra* note 79, 285–6.

[82] See Carlo Guarnieri and Patrizia Pederzoli, *The Power of Judges: A Comparative Study of Courts and Democracy* (OUP 2002) 54; and Carlo Guarnieri, 'Judicial Independence in Europe: Threat or Resource for Democracy?' (2013) 49 *Representation* 347, 348.

examples make clear that the wholesale support of the domestic courts cannot be taken for granted. The standard scenario in post-communist countries was that the newly established constitutional courts, taking an openly pro-ECtHR position, 'waged war' with the traditional supreme courts, which were far more reluctant to accept Convention standards.[83]

However, recent developments show that even constitutional tribunals, which have been traditionally portrayed as the most effective 'diffusers' of ECtHR case law on the domestic level, have started to resist the intrusion of ECtHR case law into domestic constitutional law. For instance, the Italian *Corte Constituzionale*[84] held in 2015 that only the 'settled case law' of the ECtHR is binding upon Italian ordinary courts, and thus effectively asked the ordinary courts to think twice about what to implement and how to implement it. The Russian Constitutional Court went even further, and in a series of judgments from 2015 and 2016 openly defied the ECtHR Court and found the 2013 *Anchugov & Gladkov v Russia* judgment impossible to implement.[85] Such constitutional court judgments resonate among ordinary courts whose judges may become reluctant to take a pro-ECtHR position as it could be perceived as defiance towards their own constitutional court. In the worst case scenario, ordinary courts then cease to act as 'filters' vis-à-vis the ECtHR Court. In a slightly brighter scenario, ordinary courts will try to substitute for the constitutional court in implementing ECtHR case law, but this comes at a price too; it creates dissonance within the domestic judiciary and sooner or later degenerates into a war between constitutional and supreme courts. In Poland, an inverse scenario may be expected, when a pro-ECtHR Supreme Court faces an anti-ECtHR Constitutional Tribunal.[86] If the Polish conservative government staffs the lower courts with conservative judges,[87] the pro-ECtHR Supreme Court

[83] See, e.g., Wojciech Sadurski, *Rights before Courts: A Study of Constitutional Courts in Postcommunist States of Central and Eastern Europe, 2nd edn* (Springer 2014) 35–43 (mentioning 'wars of courts' in Russia, the Czech Republic and Poland).

[84] See Judgment of the Italian Constitutional Court No. 49/2015 of 26 March 2015.

[85] See Judgment of the Russian Constitutional Court of 14 July 2015 No. 21–П/2015; and in particular Judgment of the Russian Constitutional Court of 19 April 2016 No. 12-П/2016 (in which the Russian Constitutional Court ruled that enforcement of the 2013 *Anchugov & Gladkov v Russia* judgment is 'impossible', because it is contrary to the Russian Constitution). At the same time, however, the Russian Constitutional Court added that the ECtHR judgment could be executable through a possibility of other state authorities to optimize the system of criminal penalties, which would have implications for the voting rights of a convicted person (see provision No. 2 of the judgment). See also Lauri Mälksoo, 'Russia's Constitutional Court Defies the European Court of Human Rights: Constitutional Court of the Russian Federation Judgment of 14 July 2015, No 21-П/2015' (2016) 12 *European Constitutional Law Review* (2016) 377; and *supra* note 73. In 2017, the Russian Constitutional Court declared non-executable also te ECtHR's judgment in *OAO Neftyanaya Kompaniya Yukos v. Russia*. See Judgment of the Russian Constitutional Court of 19 January 2017 No.1-П/2017.

[86] See *supra* notes 75–76 and 83.

[87] See, e.g., Waldemar Żurek, 'The National Council of the Judiciary is under attack in different ways' (VerfBlog, 11 October 2016) <http://verfassungsblog.de/the-national-council-of-the-judiciary-is-under-attack-in-different-ways> accessed 10 April 2017.

might be 'sandwiched' by ECtHR-unfriendly judges sitting in the Constitutional Tribunal and the lower courts.[88]

Other courts have also shown considerable reluctance to adhere to ECtHR case law. For instance, the Portuguese Supreme Court rejected a request for revision following a judgment delivered by the ECtHR[89] and the Swiss and British courts have been unwilling to accept ECtHR rulings on the issue of confrontation in criminal law.[90] Judicial disobedience to the ECtHR is not limited to new post-communist democracies[91] and many judiciaries across CoE members have both pro-ECtHR and anti-ECtHR camps.[92] Whether this disobedience falters and ECtHR case law finds a way into national legal orders depends on the distribution of power within each judiciary and alliances of the pro-ECtHR and anti-ECtHR judicial camps with other actors.[93]

However, the attitudes of domestic courts towards ECtHR case law are still crucial. They may deepen or mitigate the 'double-faced crisis'[94] of the ECtHR. As regards the caseload crisis, the courts are important actors both in diffusing ECHR standards domestically and in preventing eventual ECHR violations by filtering the cases that eventually bubble up to the ECtHR. Domestic courts can introduce and enforce ECHR standards domestically, thereby significantly reducing the number of ECHR violations. At the same time, the engagement of domestic courts with ECHR standards can be seen as an additional input for the ECtHR's legitimacy as domestic judiciaries can contribute to domestic internalization of the ECHR and ECtHR case law. Yet, a number of other actors and factors affect these attitudes, and a positive attitude by domestic courts in all cases cannot be taken for granted.

6 Conclusion

This chapter provides a general framework of the role of domestic actors in implementing ECtHR judgments and argues that implementation of the ECtHR case law is a multifaceted process involving various actors with different interests.

[88] On the 'sandwich' metaphor, see note 77 *supra*.

[89] *Moreira Ferreira v Portugal (no. 2)*, the case is currently pending before the ECtHR's Grand Chamber.

[90] See Jackson and Summers, *supra* note 72.

[91] For a similar conclusion, see Mälksoo, *supra* note 85, at 392.

[92] For further examples see Giuseppe Martinico, 'National Courts and Judicial Disobedience to the ECHR: A Comparative Overview' in Oddný Mjöll Arnardóttir and Antoine Buyse (eds), *Shifting Centres of Gravity in Human Rights Protection* (Routledge 2016).

[93] For instance, it is clear that the Russian Constitutional Court has full backing from the Russian Government and the Russian Parliament for its new position towards the ECtHR. The latter actually made the necessary amendments to the Federal Constitutional Law 'On the Constitutional Court of the Russian Federation' which gave a legislative foundation to the new approach taken by the Russian Constitutional Court in the 2015 and 2016 judgments referred to *supra* in note 85 (for further details see Mälksoo, *supra* note 85, 377–80).

[94] See *supra* note 28.

In order to understand this complex process, it is necessary to unpack domestic implementation dynamics and take into account factors affecting the course and the outcome of compliance processes: the number of actors involved in implementation, the attitude of those actors towards ECtHR judgments, their mutual relations, the relative strength of the domestic actors engaged in compliance mechanisms, and their readiness to act. Such an approach allows us to see more clearly the dual role[95] of the domestic courts in implementing ECHR rights. On the one hand, they are domestic actors embedded in the national setting within a network of relations with other domestic actors. At the same time, however, they play important functions with respect to application of international law[96] and are important actors co-responsible for the functioning of the ECHR system.

Acknowledging these aspects of the ECHR system, it is possible to analyse the role of domestic judiciaries in the implementation process in a more nuanced way. Contrary to existing literature, which has portrayed domestic courts as the driving force behind implementation of ECtHR case law, this contribution has shown that domestic courts can actually play a wide array of roles in the implementation process. First, the domestic courts interact with other domestic actors and are not always victorious. Second, the domestic judiciary embraces multiple actors, such as the constitutional court, apex courts, lower courts, court presidents, and judicial associations. Each of these judicial actors may have a different attitude towards the ECtHR. Third, not all domestic judges support implementation of ECtHR case law, and some of them have shown considerable resistance to the ECtHR.

[95] Geir Ulfstein, 'The European Court of Human Rights and National Courts: A Constitutional Relationship?' in Arnardóttir and Buyse, *supra* note 92, at 57.

[96] More generally, see André Nollkaemper, *National Courts and the International Rule of Law* (OUP 2011).

The Chilcot Report

International Law and Decision-Making in Times of Crisis

*Stephen Bouwhuis**

1 Introduction

The inquiry by the United Kingdom into its decision to intervene in Iraq is one of the longest running and most comprehensive examinations of government decision-making. The inquiry is commonly referred to as the 'Chilcot Report', after its chairperson, Sir John Chilcot.

The Chilcot Report runs to 2.6 million words, took 7 years to complete, considered evidence from 150 witnesses, and considered over 150,000 documents.[1] In particular, the Report examined in detail the processes through which legal advice was provided to, and formed a part of, the decision by the government of the United Kingdom to intervene in Iraq.

The Report provides a vehicle through which to examine the general relevance of international law to the decision to intervene in Iraq and more broadly the role of international law in decision-making; in particular, the practical and ethical aspects of providing international legal advice to government as well as the nature of government legal practice.

Conversely, this chapter does not canvass the legal merit of legal advice ultimately put forward by the UK Attorney General, the Right Honourable Lord Goldsmith QC. That has been extensively covered in the literature. For the purposes of this chapter, it suffices to recall that whilst the Attorney General was originally of the view that a further resolution of the Security Council would be required to revive the authorization to use force contained in Security Council Resolution 678,[2] his advice of 7 March 2003 was that a 'reasonable case' could

* Any views expressed are those of the author and do not necessarily reflect those of present or past employers.

[1] The Right Honourable David Cameron MP, 'PM Statement on the Iraq Inquiry' (6 July 2016) <https://www.gov.uk/government/speeches/pm-statement-on-the-iraq-inquiry-6-july-2016> accessed 6 May 2017.

[2] 'The Report of the Iraq Inquiry: Report of a Committee of Privy Counsellors' ('Chilcot Report') July 2016, ch. 5, para. 184.

Stephen Bouwhuis, *The Chilcot Report: International Law and Decision-Making in Times of Crisis* In: *How International Law Works in Times of Crisis*. Edited by: George Ulrich and Ineta Ziemele, Oxford University Press (2019).
DOI: 10.1093/oso/9780198849667.003.0017

be made that intervention was permitted without such a further resolution of the Security Council.[3] The changed view was due to his new understanding of the negotiating history underpinning Security Council Resolution 1441.[4] Asked for a clearer answer by the Ministry of Defence, and by the Treasury Solicitor on behalf of the public service,[5] he subsequently reached the view that his 'preferred view' was that intervention would be lawful without a further resolution by the Security Council. Neither qualification, 'reasonable case' nor 'preferred view', was contained in the answer provided to Parliament[6] or to his Cabinet colleagues.

That advice was crucial because within the structure for the provision of legal advice within the United Kingdom, the Attorney General represents the highest authority for the provision of such advice. Indeed, the Attorney General represents 'the ultimate and authoritative source of legal advice on international law'[7] within the UK Government.

2 Chilcot Report, International Legal Advice, and Decision-Making in Times of Crisis

The Chilcot Report makes clear that legal advice affirming that the intervention would be lawful was a necessary step in order for the intervention to proceed. As the Prime Minister, Tony Blair, is reported as stating: 'let me make it absolutely clear, if Peter [Goldsmith] in the end had said, "This cannot be justified lawfully" we would have been unable to take action'.[8] Moreover, there are a number of more structural reasons for thinking that the United Kingdom would not have intervened in Iraq without legal advice affirming that the intervention would be lawful.

First, the Chilcot Report provides the strong impression that the military forces of the United Kingdom would not have been prepared to intervene in Iraq without it. For example, the Chilcot Report notes the correspondence between the Permanent Under Secretary at the Ministry of Defence, Sir Kevin Tebbit, and the head of the Civil Service in the United Kingdom, Sir Andrew Turnbull, where Sir Kevin Tebbit states that before intervening in Iraq the Chief of the Defence Staff 'will need to be assured that he will be acting on the basis of a lawful instruction

[3] Lord Goldsmith, 'Legal advice of 7 March 2003, "Iraq: resolution 1441"' para. 28.

[4] Chilcot Report, *supra* note 2, ch. 5, paras 469–476.

[5] Transcript of the Rt Hon. Lord Goldsmith QC, 27 January 2010, 171, lines 11–22; 183, line 12; 85, line 16.

[6] Parliament of the United Kingdom, Written Answers, 17 March 2003, column WA2-WA3 <http://www.publications.parliament.uk/pa/ld200203/ldhansrd/vo030317/text/30317w01.htm#30317w01_sbhd3> accessed 6 May 2017.

[7] Arthur Watts, 'International Law and International Relations: United Kingdom Practice' (1991) 2 *European Journal of International Law* 157, 159.

[8] Chilcot Report, *supra* note 2, ch. 5, para. 140.

from the Prime Minister and the Defence Secretary'.[9] Indeed, the Chief of the Defence Staff, Admiral Boyce, and the Chief of the General Staff, General Sir Mike Jackson, are cited in the Report as saying that they would need 'explicit legal authorisation' for the intervention.[10]

The matter was discussed on 11 March 2003 at a meeting at Number 10 between the Prime Minister; the Deputy Prime Minister, Mr Prescott; the Secretary of State for Defence, Mr Hoon; the Attorney General; Admiral Boyce; and the Foreign Minister, Mr Straw.[11] At least from the notes prepared by the Legal Advisers in the Ministry of Defence, a key concern for the Secretary of State for Defence appears to have been to assure himself of the legality of the action, for as the notes state: 'anybody subject to military law commits an offence if [they] disobey any lawful command'.[12]

Second, whilst not really a focus of the Chilcot Report, Ministers in the United Kingdom at the time[13] would have been expressly required by the Ministerial Code to comply with the law. This requirement specifically included a reference to 'the law, including international law and treaty obligations'.[14] Whilst not legally enforceable, this was at least a public statement of principle against which they could have been publicly held to account.

In summary, having legal advice to the effect that intervention was lawful was a necessary step in the decision-making process in order for the intervention to proceed.

3 Chilcot Report and Broader Legal Culture

Aside from being a necessary step in the process, what then does the process itself tell us about how international law factors more generally within the decision-making processes of the United Kingdom? This is important as the greater degree of institutional entrenchment, the more certain it would be that international law is likely to be taken into account in decision-making by the UK Government and moreover more likely it will be followed.[15]

Perhaps unsurprisingly, there is not a great deal of academic literature which analyses the degree of institutional entrenchment of international law into

[9] *Ibid.*, ch. 5, para. 506.
[10] *Ibid.*, ch. 5, para. 508.
[11] *Ibid.*, ch. 5, para. 605.
[12] *Ibid.*, ch. 5, para. 611.
[13] Although see subsequent clarifications regarding the current code, which is not as express: United Kingdom, Ministerial Code (2015), para. 1; HC Deb 3 November 2015, 870; HC Deb 24 November 2015, 870, column 1188.
[14] United Kingdom, Ministerial Code (1997), para. 1 (Ministers of the Crown).
[15] See generally Fernando G. Nuñez-Mietz, 'Lawyering Compliance with International Law: Legal Advisers in the "War on Terror"' (2016) 1 *European Journal of International Security*, 215.

government decision-making. Of what exists, perhaps the most useful analysis is the framework employed by the academic, Fernando Nuñez-Mietz, who employs six criteria in assessing the degree of institutional entrenchment of international law into government decision-making:[16]

1. Centralization, which is the degree to which there is a single chain of legal communication through which advice must proceed or whether it can come to decision-makers through diverse channels;
2. Inclusiveness, which is the degree to which relevant actors are involved in the process;
3. Transparency, which is the degree to which the inputs to the legal advice and its construction are openly composed;
4. Decisional function, which is the degree to which lawyers are involved in the decision-making process; are they 'in the room', so to speak, or kept at a distance;
5. Timing, whether the lawyers are involved at the outset or function as a final check, and
6. Advising initiative, which is whether the legal advisers feel empowered to advise where they see a matter as inconsistent with international law.

These criteria appear particularly useful in canvassing the key questions to be addressed in assessing the degree of institutional entrenchment of international law into government decision-making. In particular, whether the key legal advisers are involved early, feel empowered to advise and whether relevant actors are involved in a transparent way.

One element which could be considered missing, however, is the extent to which issues of international law are canvassed in public debates and what Nuñez-Mietz refers to as the 'interpretative community'.[17] Such debates reflect the importance of international legal issues more generally in a society and such a broader discussion is likely to lift the quality of discussion within government by informing it and demanding a level of rigour to legal advice. Such debates act as an external check on the internal advice provided within government as where the actions taken by a government are questionable in terms of international law, the subsequent public questioning of the legality of the action will be likely to require the government to justify its actions further.

Accordingly, this chapter employs this further criterion concerning the extent to which issues of international law are canvassed in public debates and the interpretative community as a further criterion in assessing the degree of institutional entrenchment of international law into government decision-making.

[16] *Ibid.*, at 222–3.
[17] *Ibid.*, at 225.

3.1 Centralization

Nuñez-Mietz's first criterion concerns the degree of centralization in the provision of international legal advice; that is, the degree to which there is a single chain of legal communication through which advice must proceed or whether it can come to decision-makers through diverse channels.

On this first criterion, the United Kingdom would appear to score well. Indeed, within the UK bureaucracy, the role of the Office of the Legal Adviser in the Foreign Commonwealth Office of the United Kingdom is one that is institutionally entrenched.[18] This ranges from generally being consulted on matters of international law to a practice whereby the authors of the relevant legal advice are generally consulted as part of decisions taken regarding that advice.

Moreover, the role of the Law Officers, which includes the Attorney General and Ministerial colleagues,[19] is itself entrenched in the Ministerial Code of the United Kingdom, the most recent version of which provides that '[t]he Law Officers must be consulted in good time before the Government is committed to official decisions involving legal considerations'.[20]

In summary, on this criterion the United Kingdom would appear to score well; the Chilcot Report is consistent with there being a well-established chain through which international legal advice is provided. This chain remained intact despite the pressures associated with a decision to intervene militarily in another state. This is particularly notably as a sense of crisis within a government can lead decisions-makers to try to bypass or otherwise restructure decision-making to avoid the usual checks and balances. For example, in the United States the legal advisory memoranda authorizing the use of waterboarding—known as the 'torture memos'—were developed and considered in a manner which avoided the usual checks and balances in the system.[21]

3.2 Inclusiveness

Nuñez-Mietz's second criterion concerns inclusiveness, which is the degree to which relevant actors are involved in the process.

[18] See, e.g., Committee of Legal Advisers on Public International Law, 'The Office of the Legal Adviser to the Ministry of Foreign Affairs: United Kingdom', 3 <https://rm.coe.int/CoERMPublicCommonSearchServices/DisplayDCTMContent?documentId=090000168045d6b9> accessed 6 May 2017.

[19] Watts, *supra* note 7, 159.

[20] United Kingdom, Ministerial Code (2015), para. 2:10.

[21] See, e.g., Jack Goldsmith, *The Terror presidency: Law and Judgment Inside the Bush Administration* (Norton 2009); Philippe Sands, *Torture Team: Uncovering War Crimes in the Land of the Free* (Penguin 2009); Michael Scharf, 'The Torture Lawyers' (2010) 20 *Duke Journal of Comparative & International Law* 389.

In this regard, one has the impression from reading the Chilcot Report that lawyers from the Foreign and Commonwealth Office (FCO) were reasonably well integrated into the planning process.[22] Particularly notable was the Cabinet Options paper of March 2002,[23] which attached a copy of the legal advice produced by the Office of the Legal Adviser in the FCO. This legal advice noted that the revival argument would be unlikely to find general support.[24]

However, in this particular instance, when the legal issues rose up to the level of consideration by the Attorney General, there appears to be a more limited set of individuals who were included in the discussions regarding the advice.

The Attorney General did indeed consult in developing his advice. In particular, he consulted the Permanent Representative of the United Kingdom to the United Nations, Sir Jeremy Greenstock, the Foreign Minister, and the Prime Minister. He also consulted lawyers in the United States, and in particular the legal adviser to the State Department, William Taft IV, the President's counsel, Judge Gonzales, and Secretary of State Condoleezza Rice.[25] However, it appears that only a relatively narrow set of individuals was involved in these consultations. Moreover, as discussed further in relation to the next criterion, those involved were not always given the complete picture. Principally, the full advice of 7 March 2003 was not circulated at the Cabinet meeting at which the decision to intervene in Iraq was made.

On this criterion, at least in this instance, there does not appear to have been a large degree of inclusiveness, particularly as to the content of the more detailed legal advice of 7 March 2003. To some extent, though, a narrowing of the actors involved is typical of decisions involving a high degree of secrecy, such as a decision to intervene militarily in another state. However, in this case what was not shared was the more detailed legal advice, rather than the fact that an intervention was being contemplated. This does show that on this criterion the process fell short of what might have normally been expected.

3.3 Transparency

Nuñez-Mietz's third criterion concerns transparency, which is the degree to which the inputs to legal advice and its construction are openly composed.

It seems clear that at least the Prime Minister was aware of the earlier draft advice of 14 January 2003, where the Attorney General set out his view that a second

[22] See especially Transcript of Sir Michael Wood, 15 January 2010 (Transcript Wood), paras 6 and 32.

[23] Memo from Overseas and Defence Secretariat, 'Iraq Options Paper, March 2002' <http://www.iraqinquiry.org.uk/media/211103/2002-03-08-paper-cabinet-office-iraq-options-paper.pdf#search=iraq%20options%20paper> accessed 6 May 2017.

[24] Iraq: Legal Background <http://www.iraqinquiry.org.uk/media/211107/2002-03-08-paper-fco-iraq-legal-background.pdf#search=Iraq%20Legal%20Background> accessed 6 May 2017.

[25] Transcript of the RT Hon. Lord Goldsmith QC, 27 January 2010 (Transcript Goldsmith), 109, line 19; 112, line 6.

resolution would be required. It also seems clear that the Foreign Minister was also at least aware of the initial doubts that the Attorney General had regarding the argument concerning revival of the authorization to use force in Security Council Resolution 1441.[26] The Foreign Minister had also been advised by his department, the FCO, that it would not be lawful to use force against Iraq without a second resolution of the UN Security Council.[27]

One of the key findings of the Chilcot inquiry, however, was that written advice setting out the conflicting arguments regarding the legal effect of Resolution 1441 and whether, in particular, it authorized military action without a further resolution of the Security Council, should have been provided more widely to Ministers, to the Cabinet, and to the senior officials whose responsibilities were directly engaged. In particular, the Chilcot Report notes that the Secretary of State for Defence had not been advised of these concerns,[28] although he had at least seen the full advice of 7 March 2003, as had the Chiefs of Staff.[29] The Chilcot Report also notes that the Chancellor of the Exchequer, Mr Gordon Brown, and the International Development Secretary, Ms Clare Short, had not seen the full advice of 7 March 2003.[30]

Conversely though, one also gets the sense from reading the Chilcot Report that equally no-one, at least in the Cabinet discussion, really sought it. That might have been because it was presented to the Cabinet in too straightforward a manner or it may have been a reluctance to dig too deeply into the legal advice. In this regard the Chilcot Report quotes the Attorney General as saying:[31]

> What actually happened was that I started to go through the PQ [Parliamentary Question], which had been handed out as this framework. Somebody, I can't remember who it was, said 'You don't need to do that. We can read it.' I was actually trying to use it as a sort of framework for explaining the position, and there was a question that was then put. I do recall telling Cabinet, 'Well there is another point of view, but this is the conclusion that I have reached', and then the discussion on the legality simply stopped, and Cabinet then went on to discuss all the other issues, the effect on international relations, domestic policy, and all the rest of it.
>
> So the way it took place was that I was ready to answer questions and to deal with them and in the event that debate did not take place.

[26] Chilcot Report, *supra* note 2, ch. 5, paras 232 and 234. See also, Transcript Goldsmith, *supra* note 25, at 100, lines 10–17.
[27] Chilcot Report, *supra* note 2, ch. 5, paras 344–348.
[28] *Ibid.*, ch. 5, para. 238.
[29] *Ibid.*, ch. 5, para. 587.
[30] *Ibid.*, ch. 5, para. 588.
[31] *Ibid.*, ch. 5, para. 840.

Indeed, the Chilcot Report itself notes that '[t]here was little appetite to question Lord Goldsmith about his advice, and no substantive discussion of the legal issues [at the Cabinet meeting] was recorded'.[32]

Moreover, one would also think that at least some ministers would have been aware that the issue was controversial. Certainly, there was no shortage of academics willing to offer a view on the issue and it was also of intense media interest. Indeed, the Chilcot Report quotes the Attorney General as saying: '[t]he Cabinet, I'm sure knew that there were two points of view because that had been well-travelled in the press'.[33]

There is a further issue raised in the Chilcot Report, however, as to whether the draft advice of 14 January 2003 should have been more widely shared.[34] On this, however, I do not share the Report's view. In formulating legal advice, particularly where it is finely balanced, it is not unusual to go back and forth in developing one's reasoning. Whilst it is useful to indicate the level of uncertainty surrounding a particular view in the advice it does not seem to be of great use to the client to also have to wade through the various drafts of the advice.

In summary, a level of transparency in the construction of the advice appears wanting in this particular instance and more could have been done to ensure that key decision-makers were aware of the conflicting arguments concerning the interpretation of Security Council Resolution 1441.

3.4 Decisional Function

Nuñez-Mietz's fourth criterion concerns the decisional function, which is the degree to which lawyers are involved in the decision-making process; are they 'in the room', so to speak, or kept at a distance. Early involvement of the lawyers is consistent with a well-functioning office of the legal adviser.[35] Conversely, the understandings of legal frameworks and language in which lawyers are trained can be useful in bridging differences between conflicting states or generating deal breaking alternatives.[36] Indeed, previous interventions where lawyers were excluded from decision-making have tended not to fare very well for the United Kingdom.[37]

In this instance, the lawyers from the FCO do indeed seem to have been involved in the early stages of planning the intervention.[38] However, in terms of the

[32] *Ibid.*, Executive Summary, para. 490.

[33] *Ibid.*, ch. 5, para. 858, a point also made by the Foreign Minister (*ibid.*, ch. 5, para. 865).

[34] *Ibid.*, ch. 5, para. 913.

[35] Stephen Bouwhuis 'The Role of an International Legal Adviser to Government' (2012) 61(4) *International Comparative Law Quarterly* at 939, 950.

[36] See, e.g., Graham Allison and Philip Zelikow, *Essence of Decision: Explaining the Cuban Missile Crisis, 2nd edn* (Pearson 1999).

[37] *Ibid.*, 942.

[38] See especially Transcript Wood, *supra* note 22, paras 6 and 32.

level of influence of the legal adviser upon decision-making, one gets the sense that, although involved, the lawyers in the FCO, and indeed the Attorney General himself, were kept at somewhat of a distance from the key decision-making processes. Admittedly, the Attorney General, who provided the definitive legal advice on the question of intervention, spoke at the relevant Cabinet meeting where the decision was taken. However, as discussed in the previous section, that appeared to have been largely a perfunctory discussion.

Moreover, although the Attorney General himself was also at least following developments,[39] one gets a sense of a bystander to the key decisions being taken throughout this period. The Attorney General himself notes that he would have liked to have been involved earlier, for example, in the development of resolution 1441, although he also notes how impractical that would be, particularly as his role is one of deciding difficult legal issues across the spectrum of legal issues facing the entirety of government.

In part this seems structural. First, in the sense that the Attorney General had a limited role within the decision-making process more generally, the Cabinet meeting at which he attended being only his second during the term of this government.[40] This contrasts with other 'Western' governments, where the Attorney General is a standing Cabinet member.[41] Second, the lesser role also appears structural in that the Attorney General is required to advise across the spectrum of legal issues facing the entirety of the government and so would be unlikely to have the time to be engaged in the issue on an ongoing basis.

3.5 Timing

Nuñez-Mietz's fifth criterion concerns timing, namely whether the lawyers are involved at the outset or function as a final check on decision-making. In the present instance, the timing for the delivery of the formal advice on the legality of action in Iraq was late. Indeed, its provision on 7 March 2003 was less than two weeks before the invasion of Iraq and at a time when British armed forces were already massed for intervention.

Moreover, this late timing appears deliberate. Although a formal request for advice was issued on 9 December 2002, at the time the Foreign Minister also made clear that the advice was 'not needed "now"'.[42] The rationale was that until it had become clear that a further resolution could not be obtained, there was no formal need to rely on such advice.

39 Transcript Goldsmith, *supra* note 25, at 26, lines 14–26, line 24.
40 *Ibid.*, 199, lines 12–20.
41 See, e.g., the Cabinet <https://www.whitehouse.gov/administration/cabinet> accessed 6 May 2017.
42 Chilcot Report, *supra* note 2, ch. 5, para. 99.

As the Attorney General stated:

> Well, in a sense, it wasn't necessary for me to give advice until it mattered, and it wouldn't really matter until we were at the point, if we ever came to the point—I very much hoped we wouldn't, but we did—we came to the point that a decision had to be made whether it was lawful to go to use force, and it is not uncommon in government that the Attorney General's advice is not asked for until it matters.[43]

This was of course at odds with the view of Sir Michael Wood, who stated that having the advice back in early December 2002 would have been 'highly desirable' as legal advisers within the FCO 'were having to advise on whether SCR 1441 authorised the use of force without a further decision of the Security Council without the benefit of the Attorney's advice'.[44]

Conversely, the Chilcot Report makes clear that on a number of occasions prior to this, the Attorney General went to lengths to ensure that his views were well known to key decision-makers in the lead up to the decision to intervene in Iraq. In particular, the Attorney General:

- wrote to the Secretary of State for Defence regarding remarks that he made regarding the use of self-defence as a basis for intervention;[45]
- met with the Prime Minister in July 2002 and expressed the view that self-defence and humanitarian intervention would not provide a sufficient basis for intervention;[46]
- telephoned the Foreign Minister during October 2002 to express concerns regarding the drafting of Security Council Resolution 1441;[47]
- met with the Foreign Minister in November 2002 to express concerns regarding the legality of intervention;[48]
- clarified perceptions of his views with the Foreign Minister and the Prime Minister's Chief of Staff, Jonathan Powell, following the adoption of Security Council Resolution 1441;[49] and
- sent a note to the Prime Minister in January 2003 noting his provisional view that a second resolution was still required.[50]

The Chilcot Report also reflects an understanding of key decision-makers as to what these views were. For example, the Report recounts a conversation between

[43] Transcript Goldsmith, *supra* note 25, at 56, lines 21–57, line 4.
[44] Chilcot Report, *supra* note 2, ch. 5, para. 131.
[45] Transcript Goldsmith, *supra* note 25, at 17, line 19; at 19, line 23.
[46] *Ibid.*, 21, lines 12–24, line 8.
[47] *Ibid.*, 26, lines 11–29, line 16.
[48] *Ibid.*, 32, lines 6–33, line 1.
[49] *Ibid.*, 53, lines 6–54, line 11.
[50] *Ibid.*, 89, lines 20–91, line 18.

the Prime Minister's Chief of Staff and the Attorney General on 11 November 2002, where the Chief of Staff is reported as being 'at pains' to ensure the Attorney General that 'No.10 were under no illusion as to the Attorney's views'.[51]

Indeed, on this occasion that conversation was followed by a telephone call on 12 November 2002 between the Attorney General and the Foreign Minister at which the Attorney General stated that it 'seemed implicit' in Security Council Resolution 1441 that, in the event of non-compliance, 'it would be for the Security Council to decide whether Iraq' was in "material breach"'.[52]

When asked directly 'do you think the fact that you came in late in the day, the advice you gave late in the day and in draft form, had a material impact on how things developed?' the Attorney General responded:[53]

> I don't think so. Because I had been at pains, as you have seen, to try to make sure that those who were moulding the policy didn't have a misunderstanding about, at least, what my view might be, and I had been involved. I think—I'm not sure to what extent the Foreign Office legal advisers appreciated this.

On this criterion, then, the record appears mixed. Although formal advice was provided late, the Attorney General went to some considerable lengths to ensure that the key decision-makers were aware of his view in the lead-up to the decision to intervene in Iraq.

3.6 Advising Initiative

Nuñez-Mietz's sixth criterion concerns the advising initiative, namely whether legal advisers feel empowered to advise where they see a matter as being inconsistent with international law. On this criterion the Chilcot Report paints a positive picture.

As noted in discussing criterion five, the Attorney General himself was found to have put his advice to the Prime Minister three times without having been asked to do so and at least on one occasion after explicitly having been informed that it was not required.[54] Moreover, the Legal Adviser within the FCO, Sir Michael Wood, also went to some considerable lengths to ensure that his views were known. This shows good respect for the advising initiative within the decision-making process of the UK Government[55]

[51] Chilcot Report, *supra* note 2, ch. 5, para. 10.
[52] Chilcot Report, *supra* note 2, ch. 5, para. 27.
[53] Transcript Goldsmith, *supra* note 25, at 100, lines 23, 101, line 8.
[54] Chilcot Report, *supra* note 2, ch. 5, para. 290.
[55] Nuñez-Mietz, *supra* note 15, at 223.

Particularly notable in the Chilcot Report was the exchange between Sir Michael Wood and the Foreign Minister and the subsequent intervention by the Attorney General to reaffirm the right of government legal advisers to provide unsolicited advice when they believe that a course of action would be unlawful.

The circumstance arose when Sir Michael Wood informed the Foreign Minister of his view that 'absent extraordinary circumstances', a second Security Council Resolution would be required.[56] This prompted the Foreign Minister to respond in writing, noting that he did not accept the advice and that in his view there 'is a strong case to be made that UNSCR 678' and subsequent events provided 'a sufficient basis in international law to justify military action'.[57] The letter was copied to the Attorney General, and the Prime Minister's Foreign Policy Adviser, Sir David Manning, and senior officials in the FCO.[58]

This in turn prompted the Attorney General to write:[59]

> It is important for the Government that its lawyers give advice which they honestly consider to be correct ... they should give the advice they believe in, not the advice which they think others want to hear... But if a Government legal adviser genuinely believes that a course of action would be unlawful, then it is his or her right and duty to say so. I support this right regardless of whether I agree with the substance of the advice which has been given.

On this criterion then the United Kingdom would appear well served and indeed this confidence to advise was not diminished by the nature of the action being contemplated. Moreover, that Elizabeth Wilmshurst, Deputy Legal Adviser in the FCO at the time, resigned over the matter shows a high regard more generally for principles within the FCO. The Deputy Legal Adviser clearly felt that continuing in her role would be inconsistent with her values.[60]

3.7 Interpretative Community

Aside from the six factors relevant to the institutional entrenchment of international law into government decision-making proposed by Nuñez-Mietz, he also discusses the interpretative community.[61] This is essentially the academics, judges, government officials, and other experts that constitute the international

[56] Chilcot Report, *supra* note 2, ch. 5, para. 344.
[57] *Ibid.*, ch. 5, para. 353.
[58] *Ibid.*, ch. 5, para. 354.
[59] *Ibid.*, ch. 5, para. 357.
[60] Elizabeth Wilmshurst, Letter dated 18 March 2003, <http://www.iraqinquiry.org.uk/media/242786/2003-03-18-minute-wilmshurst-to-wood-untitled.pdf#search=wilmshurst%20letter> accessed 6 May 2017.
[61] Nuñez-Mietz, *supra* note 15, at 225–6.

legal community. Such a community constrains interpretation in that states generally seek to operate within the expectations and conventions of the community.[62] More specifically, these expectations and conventions constrain legal advisers in that they will generally seek to develop their advice in a manner consistent with these expectations and conventions.[63]

The strength of the interpretative community in the United Kingdom was felt in the present instance through the legal opinions offered on the question of the legality of intervention by those in academia and at the bar. It was also reflected in the level of press coverage of the legal question as part of the general media coverage in the lead up to the intervention. Situations of crisis tend to exacerbate this factor and the decision taken by the United Kingdom to intervene in Iraq was no exception. Indeed, the long lead time and gradual military build-up to the intervention amplified the opportunities for the press and members of the interpretative community to express themselves.

The debate within the academic community and media then fed back into the decision-making process within the Government, placing pressure on the Attorney General to consider his advice carefully. In particular, he seems to be aware that the revival argument was not generally supported within the academic community; indeed, his advice of 7 March 2003 refers to the view that he finally reached being 'not widely accepted among academic commentators'.[64]

The extent of the debate and its ability to feed back into the decision-making process shows the strength of the interpretative community in the United Kingdom. This was amplified, rather than diminished, by the nature of the action being contemplated.

4. Conclusions

Whatever you think of the view finally reached by the Attorney General, the picture that emerges of the level of entrenchment of international law within the government of the United Kingdom is positive in terms of the general role of international law within government decision-making. The Chilcot Report supports the view that the military forces of the United Kingdom would not have intervened without advice to the effect that the intervention was legal, making the legal advice a necessary part of the decision-making process. The general structure and processes for the provision of such legal advice within the UK Government is well entrenched and centralized. Moreover, legal advisers appear empowered to express their views,

[62] Ian Johnstone, 'Treaty Interpretation: The Authority of Interpretive Communities' (1990–1991) 12 *Michigan Journal of International Law* 371, 390.

[63] *Ibid.*, 390–1 and 392–3.

[64] Lord Goldsmith, 'Legal advice of 7 March 2003, "Iraq: resolution 1441"', para. 10.

even when not wanted. These structures and processes remain in place despite the pressures placed upon the individuals by the nature of the action being contemplated. The academic community and media were also well engaged in the legal debate.

There are, however, other aspects that were less than ideal in the process through which the advice was formulated with regard to the question of whether the United Kingdom should intervene in Iraq. In particular, it appears that more could have been done to alert key decision-makers to the more finely balanced nature of the legal advice and there could perhaps have been more involvement of either the Attorney General or the Legal Adviser of the FCO in the key decision-making processes. If that seems too positive then it can be contrasted with the circumstances in the United States under which the legal advices that formed the basis for the decision to employ interrogation techniques, including torture, were developed. As noted in this article, those legal advices, later overturned by the Obama Administration,[65] appear to have been produced in a manner which avoided the usual checks and balances in the system.

To quote Nuñez-Mietz:[66]

> the War Council became a self-insulated group of legal advisers with privileged access to top policymakers. This privileged access implied a de facto centralization of legal advising on matters related to the War on Terror, subverting the well-established decentralised structure of legal advising within the Executive.

In the United Kingdom, by contrast, the legal advice concerning the legality of intervention in Iraq was developed through well-established government channels. That is not to say that the process could not have been better. It is to say, however, that the picture that emerges from the Chilcot Report is of decision-making processes in which international legal considerations are well entrenched. In particular, it appears to have been a necessary step to obtain the legal advice as otherwise the military forces of the United Kingdom would have been unwilling to intervene in Iraq. This tells us that international legal advice played a key part in the decision-making process leading to the decision to intervene and that favourable legal advice was seen as a requirement for the intervention to proceed. This parallels similar (though different processes) in other 'coalition' governments at the time, whereby favourable legal advice was obtained prior to the forces of that government taking place in the intervention.

One further gets the sense from the Chilcot Report, and the statements made by the UK Prime Minister cited in this chapter, that the United Kingdom would

[65] Executive Order 13491—Ensuring Lawful Interrogations, section 3(c) <https://www.gpo.gov/fdsys/pkg/CFR-2010-title3-vol1/pdf/CFR-2010-title3-vol1-eo13491.pdf> accessed 6 May 2017.

[66] Nuñez-Mietz, *supra* note 15, at 226.

not have intervened without favourable legal advice. This sense was reinforced by the decision by the UK Government in August 2013 not to undertake air strikes against the Syrian government of President Bashar al-Assad in response to the use of chemical weapons in Syria. Whilst initially supportive of such an intervention, the UK Government decided against taking military action in Syria following a vote by the House of Commons against these air strikes. Such a reversal of position, following a vote by the House of Commons, reflects a respect for proper process consistent with wanting to ensure that any such intervention is legal and has general support, at least as reflected in a Parliamentary vote.

An interesting counterfactual would have been if any of the other governments which intervened in Iraq did receive internal legal advice from their government lawyers stating that the intervention was not lawful. However, that does not appear to have been the case, and indeed it is rare for a government to set out plainly its processes for decision-making in the case of an intervention, let alone a clear counterfactual, where a government publishes its legal advice stating that something would be unlawful, but it is doing it anyhow. This is in part why the Chilcot Report is so useful: it is a rare example where the processes involved, the conversations between the key actors, and the changes in their thinking over the period leading up to the decision to intervene are set out in such detail.

PART VI
EPILOGUE

Reflections

How International Law Functions in Times of Crisis

*Jean-Marc Sauvé**

1 Introduction

The European continent is today facing a multifaceted crisis that extends over several levels, forming a complex tangle that must be unpicked in spite of its uncertain and tentacular appearance.

To help us in this task, let us refer to the work of philosopher Paul Ricoeur who, in a lecture in 1986,[1] noted the originality and diversity of the crises experienced by modern societies. Traditionally, in the medical, economic, and political fields, there is nothing unexpected or disorderly about crises. They are a necessary, sometimes extreme, stage in a course of events that is coming to an end. They are indicative of a person's state of health, the degree of maturity of an economy, or the extent to which a political regime is supported. Crises are well-ordered intelligible processes that determine the future. They are 'the critical moment when choices must be made and decisions taken with discernment'.[2] They are not just destructive, they can also have purgative, soothing virtues when they pave the way for a new phase of growth or progress. Economic crises thus form the join between Kondratiev or Juglar cycles of expansion; political crises, in a sense conveyed by the philosophers of the Enlightenment,[3] go hand in hand with profound changes in societies and can contribute, through the breakdowns they bring about, to establishing a fairer political order.

Seen in the light of these traditional models, the present appears to denote a double fracture: the crisis is no longer periodic or short term; it has become

* Written in collaboration with Stéphane Eustache, administrative judge.

[1] P. Ricoeur, 'La crise: un phénomène spécifiquement moderne?' (1988) 120 *Revue de théologie et de philosophie*, 1–19.

[2] M. Revault d'Allonnes, 'Crise et modernité' (2013) 7 *Journal for Political Thinking*, 1.

[3] 'You trust in the present order of society without thinking that this order is subject to inevitable revolutions and it is impossible for you to foresee or prevent the one which may affect your children. The noble become commoners, the rich become poor, the monarch becomes subject. Are the blows of fate so rare that you can count on being exempted from them? We are approaching a state of crisis and the age of revolutions. Who can answer for what will become of you then?' Jean-Jacques Rousseau, *Emile, or on Education*, Book III, 1762 (Basic Books 1979) 158.

Jean-Marc Sauvé, *Reflections: How International Law Functions in Times of Crisis* In: *How International Law Works in Times of Crisis*. Edited by: George Ulrich and Ineta Ziemele, Oxford University Press (2019).
DOI: 10.1093/oso/9780198849667.003.0018

permanent. It does not enlighten us about the direction of change. It has become a source of indecision, disorders, and uncertainties as to its causes and its effects, its diagnosis, and remedies. Crises no longer point as clearly as they once did to the post-crisis horizon. This dual breakdown undoubtedly stems from the deep-seated undermining of our conception of progress and of individual and collective identities. Today we are confronted with the dizzying prospect of an endless crisis, without order or limit.

First I would like to explore, on what might be called a homeopathic basis, the full economic, social, political, and environmental dimensions of this dizziness. I will then concentrate on the specifically legal dimension of contemporary crises: I will attempt to show how international law is at one and the same time a traditional tool for solving crises, and one that can also contribute to intensifying and prolonging their effects. Finally, I will humbly attempt to identify some tools for if not solving, then at least regulating and managing current crises, based on my own experiences as a former government official and current head of a national Supreme Court.

2 The Current Succession of Sectoral and Regional Crises Bordering to a Systemic and Global Crisis

Let me begin by outlining the diversity of these crises depending on whether their cause is an exogenous shock (section 2.1) or on the contrary shocks that are endogenous to Europe (section 2.2).

2.1 Exogenous Shocks Affecting European Societies

2.1.1 The global financial crisis

This started in the United States in July 2007 before suddenly and brutally deteriorating in September 2008 when a major American bank went bankrupt. It then spread to the global economy within just a few days, in particular to the European financial and banking systems. Without venturing into an analysis of the complex causes of that crisis, it is clear that it originated in internal imbalances on the US markets, in particular insufficient restrictions on access to mortgages, ineffective regulation of banking activities, against the backdrop of a highly accommodating monetary policy, which—incidentally—central banks continue to avail themselves of today. This crisis that originated in the banking and financial sectors caused the leading world economies to enter into recession. According to the economist Thomas Piketty, the 'Great Recession'[4] of 2007–2009 led to an

[4] <http://piketty.blog.lemonde.fr/2016/01/08/2007-2015-une-si-longue-recession/>

approximately 5% drop in economic activity in less than two years, making this the most serious world recession since the crisis in the 1930s. Between the first quarter of 2008 and the second quarter of 2010, unemployment in the (EU) of 28 States increased to just over 7 million people; that is, a European unemployment rate of 9.7%, which at that time was the highest rate recorded since the beginning of the 2000s.

2.1.2 The trans-mediterranean migratory crisis

This came in the form of a considerable influx to Europe of migrants coming from North Africa, and then the Near East and sub-Saharan Africa in the wake of what was referred to as 'the Arab Spring'. With the toppling of the political regimes in Tunisia, Egypt, and Libya, followed by the Syrian crisis as of autumn 2011, south–north migrant flows increased sharply, either directly from the regions concerned, or indirectly by prompting migrants from more remote regions to come to Europe. In 2013, 1.7 million nationals from third countries immigrated to the EU. In 2014 1.9 million arrived; in 2015 1.8 million. Some of these migrants are asylum seekers in the context of the civil war in Syria: their numbers in the EU more than doubled between 2011 and 2014, reaching nearly 1.26 million people in 2015, double the previous peak reached in 1992 for a smaller EU of 15 Member States.[5] This figure continued to grow in 2016: 665,000 for the first 7 months as compared to 434,000 for the same period the previous year. These lasting, large-scale migrant flows are not uniformly distributed. They are concentrated in the states that lie on the outer borders of the EU, in particular the Mediterranean area and Central Europe. They then extend onwards to other EU Member States, which are the desired final destinations, in particular Germany, the United Kingdom, and France. For instance, in 2014, the number of migrants from third countries that reached Germany was well above 500,000. For the United Kingdom and France these figures were respectively 345,000 and 207,000. That year, 90% of asylum seekers were concentrated in 9 Member States, with nearly one-third in Germany, which in 2015 hosted 442,000 asylum seekers.[6] Confronted with this situation, the mechanism for transferring asylum seekers between Member States set out by the Dublin Convention and Dublin Regulations proved to be totally inadequate for dealing with this new refugee and migrant situation.

2.1.3 The third exogenous shock affects our security and is rooted in the emergence of new threats to the peace and stability of Europe

These threats lie in three concentric circles whose centre is the territory of the EU around which several areas of instability revolve. First of all, in the largest circle, there are the armed conflicts that have taken place or that continue in the Sahel,

[5] <http://ec.europa.eu/eurostat/statistics-explained/index.php/Asylum_statistics>
[6] <http://ec.europa.eu/eurostat/statistics-explained/index.php/Asylum_statistics>

the Middle East, and the north of the Arabian Peninsula, where the Syrian conflict erupted in 2011 and violence resumed in Iraq. In the second circle, which includes the neighbouring states that border directly on to Europe, conflicts have also broken out destabilizing all the peripheral regions: in Ukraine, where the country's territorial integrity was attacked and where some territories are occupied; in Turkey, which as a result of the Syrian crisis is experiencing a massive influx of refugees—more than 1 million since 2011 according to the UN High Commissioner for refugees (HCR)—and is furthermore affected by major tensions connected with the Kurdish crisis and the worrying developments in its political situation particularly since the attempted coup on 15 July 2016 and the engagement of armed troops on Syrian territory. Finally, the last circle of violence and threats covers the EU itself and more specifically the western states of the Union, which were struck by Islamist terrorism beginning in March 2004 in Madrid and London in July 2005. These events, sparked from the outside, increased in number in recent months, particularly in France but also in Belgium and Germany. What these attacks express is a denial of the founding principles of the rule of law and of democratic values. This is no doubt the most painful and deeply felt shock that we have collectively suffered because it touches the heart of national identities and of the European project.

Over a period of ten to fifteen years, Europe has faced a triple exogenous shock: in the areas of the financial markets, migration, and security, the harmful effects of which were compounded and which mutually reinforced one another. However, it would be far too simplistic to attribute the current state of crisis to external upheavals alone, as if this state of affairs was the outcome of contingencies and could be exonerated from a critical examination of how our institutions and societies function.

2.2 Endogenous Shocks that Weaken Europe from the Inside

2.2.1 Economic shocks

Starting in 2010. even more so in 2012, the risk premiums required for bonds issued by some Member States in the Eurozone rose to an excessive and unsustainable level that did not faithfully reflect their macro-economic situation but instead were designed to cover the risk of a breakdown of the Eurozone. Undoubtedly the sequence of events that transformed a financial crisis into an economic one and then into a crisis of European public debt was amplified by intense financial speculation. But this sequence is rooted in the deep-seated vulnerabilities internal to the Eurozone, which is by no means an optimum currency area.[7] Hindrances to the mobility of factors of production continue to exist while the economic structures

[7] R. Mundell, 'A Theory of Optimum Currency Areas' (1961) 51 *American Economic Review* 715–25.

of its members are increasingly diverse. Disparate shocks that inevitably occur are first dealt with at the level of individual states rather than through a common fiscal policy. Furthermore, the management and conduct of a single monetary policy are burdened, even shackled, by divergences in rates of inflation and growth and the diversity of funding structures within the zone. In short, the European policy mix since 1999 can be described as 'sub-optimal', 'too restrictive',[8] and insufficiently effective, particularly since the economies of the Eurozone states have diverged in the meantime and structural differences between them are even greater.

2.2.2 Environmental shocks

Climate change is a transnational phenomenon and represents an immediate and potentially irreversible threat to human societies and natural ecosystems throughout the world. In December 2015 at the Paris climate conference, COP 21, states expressed deep concern as to the urgency of closing the significant gap between the results obtained in the area of greenhouse gas emission reduction and the global and very rapid development in the level of those emissions. While some progress is reported, it is clearly insufficient and incommensurate with what is at stake. In October 2014, EU member states set a binding target for reduction in greenhouse gas emissions. In line with those ambitions, the Paris Agreement is designed to strengthen the global response to the threat of climate change by containing the increase in the average temperature of the planet well below 2°C as compared with pre-industrial levels and by pursuing action initiated to limit this temperature increase to 1.5°C.[9] Although 177 states signed the Paris Agreement in New York on 22 April 2016, it will not enter into force until it is ratified by at least 55 states representing a total of 55% of the world's greenhouse gas emissions.

2.2.3 Societal and political shocks

European societies appear to be struggling with a loss of bearings and a preoccupying inclination to turn inward and withdraw in the context of major economic and social transformations connected with globalization and the information society, which in France is referred to as the 'uberization' of the economy. While these changes generate opportunities and the promise of new activities, they also destabilize entire swathes of the traditional economy and undermine the standard of living, hopes, and faith in progress of some portions of the middle class. A form of exhaustion of liberal policies implemented some thirty years ago and the growing inequalities that they generate also feed this development. As a result, anxiety relating to identity in connection with the opening of borders and

[8] J.-P. Matière, 'Fondements et enseignements de la crise de la zone euro' (2015) 591 *Revue de l'Union européenne*, 489; M. Lelart, 'La zone euro et la crise financière international' (2014) 581 *Revue de l'Union européenne* 471.

[9] Art. 2 of the Paris Agreement of 12 December 2015.

migration has developed with attitudes ranging from increasing doubts about the feasibility of integrating foreigners to outright xenophobia. Added to this is the fear of downward social mobility within the regions and social groups threatened by current changes. The political consequences of the situation are highly visible and damaging. They can be seen in the rise in influence, and sometimes accession to power, of new political forces that challenge traditional elites and political parties. It is a situation associated with powerful centrifugal forces that threaten the cohesion and unity of states but moreover undermine the very principle of the European project. In this respect, the results of the Dutch referendum on 6 April 2016 relating to the Ukraine–EU Association Agreement and those of the British referendum on 23 June 2016 on its membership of the EU brought out into the open the degree to which the ideal of the European enterprise has crumbled, no doubt hitherto underestimated. For a majority of the people of this great democratic nation profoundly rooted in European history to opt in favour of its withdrawal from the Union is no doubt the most alarming sign of loss of confidence in our common capacity to act. This is no longer attributable solely to tiny extremist groups that have always prospered from situations of economic turmoil. Now an entire nation is reversing the course of the history of European integration. One can anticipate that Brexit will lead to disappointment and an aftershock in the United Kingdom and in Europe because the Union is all too often an outlet for venting frustration for those who have been excluded by globalization, and a scapegoat, so to speak, in the face of economic and social difficulties. Of course the Union may have contributed but these difficulties will not cease to exist without the Union or outside it.

So a triple endogenous shock—economic, environmental, and political—is compounded by and intermingled with a triple exogenous shock arising from the financial, migrant, and security crises. These factors are so tightly intertwined that the line between internal and external causes is very faint, yielding a confused impression of general ongoing crisis. This impression is confirmed by the limitations and loss in efficiency of the traditional means for understanding and managing crises and, in the first place, of legal instruments.

3 The Ambivalent Ties of International Law with European Crises

Clearly, international law is not neutral or purely operational: although more often than not external to European crises, it can also cause, worsen, accompany, and contribute to resolving them or otherwise. It is therefore important to identify clearly the properly legal dimension of these crises, show how law can or cannot be an underlying factor for some of these and may be used as a tool for resolving or aggravating matters (section 3.1). Additionally, the emergence of crisis-management international law is not a temporary or contingent phenomenon; it is one of the far-reaching changes that affect the sources and principles of traditional international law (section 3.2).

3.1 The Translation of Sectoral Crises into the Legal Realm

Because it is a tool for regulating social relations and a technique for implementing public policy on the domestic and international levels as well as an instrument for guaranteeing fundamental rights, the law in general, and international law in particular are central components in the mechanics of every sectoral crisis. However, they are by no means unidirectional: they allow for a better understanding, handling, and resolution of these crises but they can also distort, amplify, and prolong them. Without claiming to be complete, let me highlight the legal origins and manifestations of contemporary crises in some areas.

3.1.1 The increasing role of legal questions in economic and financial affairs

During the Eurozone crisis, the design and conduct of economic and monetary policy on several occasions hinged on legal questions and the answers provided thereto by national supreme or European courts. As is apparent in the *Pringle*[10] and *Gauweiler*[11] cases, these answers in the end contributed to resolving the crisis, but that was by no means a foregone conclusion. Never before had the role of law and of legal experts been so important for steering economic policy precisely because of the European dimension. These questions would never have arisen within a national framework.

3.1.2 The role of law in migratory and security crises

Law is not the cause of these crises but, increasingly often, it is suspected or accused of intensifying them, making their solution excessively complex, and contributing to inefficiency. However, as is apparent from the migrant crisis, confusion often arises about the primary and secondary causes: serious inadequacies in the

[10] C-371/12 *Thomas Pringle v Government of Ireland and Others* ECLI:EU:C:2012:756. This case was referred by a member of the Irish Parliament against the European stability mechanism which was instituted pursuant a decision of the European Council providing for the addition to the Treaty on the Functioning of the European Union of a new provision whereby Member States whose currency is the euro may establish a stability mechanism to be activated if indispensable to safeguard the stability of the euro area as a whole. The applicant argued that this decision entailed an alteration of the competences of the EU. The Court of Justice of the European Union found that the stability mechanism did not infringe on state competence since it aimed at guaranteeing the stability of the Eurozone and that monetary policy is an exclusive competence held by the European Union.

[11] CJEU, Grand Chamber, 16 June 2015, *Peter Gauweiler*, C-62/14. This case was referred by the German Constitutional Court against the 'OMT programme' by which the European Central Bank aimed at purchasing on secondary markets government bonds of Member States of the euro area. The Court of Justice found that this programme falls within the scope of competence of the European Union and does not violate EU law.

management of applications for asylum undoubtedly derive from the imperfections of the 'Dublin' system but they are mainly the expression of an unfinished political process that has failed to lead to a truly common policy of asylum. Rather than criticizing the political causes, there are those who prefer to denounce a given legal transposition and who oversimplify the complex balance between competing interests and requirements that must be met and stabilized by law. Law highlights and develops all the dimensions of the complexity of the migrant crisis, rather than creating or amplifying it. Law is liable to come under scrutiny at the state and EU levels. One of the noblest functions of law—–protecting fundamental rights—runs the risk of being called into question in the name of efficient management of migrant flows. Law can also be presented, depending on the case, either as infringing freedoms or as hindering the fight against terrorism inasmuch as it constantly seeks out a balance between law enforcement and repression of crime on the one hand and guaranteeing freedoms on the other. Clearly, this difficult reconciliation between freedom and security lies at the heart of controversial political debates that alternately denounce the attack on the rule of law and the decline of freedoms.

3.1.3 The intrication of legal questions and the populist crisis

With the juridification of social relations, law deals increasingly with sensitive social issues relating to bioethics, standards of behaviour, the family, and minorities—questions on which it is difficult to reach a consensus at the national level, let alone at the European level. The dynamics of fundamental rights has accelerated and it encounters support and enthusiasm on its way as well as opposition and resistance, each with its own share of legitimacy. More than ever before, law is the language of social debates and protests: far from delimiting and settling them, it opens and develops them, providing fresh impetus, to the extent that there is no longer any obvious consensus about the consequences to draw from words like liberty, equality, dignity. In these circumstances, the legal community must be careful to avoid a double pitfall: on the one hand, the headlong rush towards guaranteeing rights that runs the risk of erasing some legitimate restrictions and national specificities and, on the other, the threat of clinging to identity and exacerbated conservatism. The difficulty is heightened by the fact that this narrow path between two extreme tendencies does not travel only inside national frontiers: it continues on into the neighbouring states that are facing the same challenges and provide precedents or serve as examples or else, on the contrary, as antithesis. It also extends into the court rooms of the European courts at Strasbourg and in Luxembourg.

In the fields of the economy, security, and society, law does not only reveal a crisis. It directly influences how the crisis develops, often when it has reached a climax. Through its symbolic reach, law accompanies the dramatization of the crisis, in principle to take it to its denouement. But when final court decisions, whether national or European, are vigorously contested, clearly the pacifying function of law withers and dissension may win the day. While legal experts are given a voice increasingly often, their discussions are instrumentalized and heard on the basis of personal preference. In any case, they are not given the last word.

3.2 The Transformation of International Law

The term 'crisis' might appear excessive at a time when international law has never been so vigorous. I use the term in an epistemological sense derived from the history of science[12] to designate a series of fundamental changes and a form of paradigm crisis for conventional international law.

3.2.1 States no longer hold the main role

While traditionally most international law originated from states, today it comes more from other actors. Infra- and supra-state actors now compete with, avert, or even neutralize the centrality of state normative power.

3.2.1.1 The rise of infra-state actors

The growing disproportion between the power held by major multinational corporations or their associations and that of states, in spite of the fact that the latter represent huge consumer markets, has become a topic of concern when this discrepancy undermines the capacity of states to fulfil their sovereign powers. That remit includes safeguarding fundamental rights and freedoms that requires public authorities to bring about a fair reconciliation between public and private interests. In the area of digital technology, for instance, it is clear that such reconciliation—which puts transparency and protection of privacy, safeguarding law and order, and the defence of freedoms in the balance—cannot be spontaneously achieved simply by the free play of market forces or on the sole basis of soft law rules drafted or inspired by large corporations. Beyond the question of regulating new markets, however, states must preserve the foundations of their social compact and, in particular, their tax sovereignty. In this area, they are confronted with strategies of avoidance and evasion that are increasingly sophisticated, carried out by specialized firms with the help of certain countries that adopt permissive taxation rules and enter into advance tax rulings that encourage certain forms of fiscal dumping, sometimes opening the door to fraudulent practices. In this field, the weakness of international coordination and absence of common rules on transparency and regulation have undermined the sovereignty and normative power of all states and has impoverished their populations, in a ruthless form of globalization.

[12] See the seminal works of A. Koyré, *From the Closed World to the Infinite Universe* (Johns Hopkins Press, 1957); *Du monde clos l'univers infini* (Gallimard coll Tel 2003), and the works of T. Kuhn, *The structure of Scientific Revolutions* (University of Chicago Press 1962); *La structure des révolutions scientifiques* (éd. Flammarion, coll. Champs 2008).

3.2.1.2 The resilience of states even as sources of international law evolve

Indeed, states increase their influence and contribution by sitting on international organizations and sharing a number of sovereign attributes within integrated institutions. Seen from this angle, the expansion of supra-state sources is the expression of their sovereignty and a means to defend it. One of these sources, EU law, has three specificities.

The first pertains to the magnitude of the field of application of EU law and the extent to which Member States transfer their authority to its advantage. The EU's area of competence has been extended to many fields beyond the economy and the principal freedoms of movement (e.g., environment, internal affairs, justice, monetary policy).[13] While competition was the first matrix for EU law, it is no longer truly its backbone. With the recognition of the general principles of law and the entry into force of the Charter of Fundamental Rights (the Charter), the EU has come of age as a union of law. The institutions and bodies of the EU must comply with the Charter and so must national acts that set out the detailed rules for applying regulations, transposing directives, or protecting, even indirectly, the interests of the EU. This is how Article 51 is construed by the Court of Justice of the European Union (CJEU) in its Grand Chamber judgment (*Åkerberg Fransson*) of 26 February 2013: 'the fundamental rights guaranteed by the Charter must ... be complied with where national legislation falls within the scope of European Union law'.[14] In French, the lexical shift performed by the CJEU from '*mise en oeuvre*' [implementation] to '*champ d'application*' [scope] of the Charter highlights the broad interpretation of its significance.[15] Thanks to this interpretation, its field of

[13] Since the Rome Treaty (25 March 1957) that instituted the European Atomic Energy Community (EAEC) and the European Economic Community (EEC), and provided for a customs union—which was instituted on 1 July 1968—and the implementation of common policies, e.g., in agriculture; the Single European Act (17 and 28 February 1986) that sets the date for completion of the internal market at 1 January 1993, provides for the establishment of a single market and consequently the abolition of any regulatory or tax restriction to freedoms of movement; the Maastricht Treaty (7 February 1992) that maintained the European Community as a legal entity but removed its 'economic' epithet (the EC disappeared in legal terms with the Lisbon Treaty), erected the European Union on three 'pillars'—the Community pillar (former EC, ECSC, EAEC), the CFSP pillar and the 'justice and internal affairs' pillar, which establishes European citizenship and provides for the creation of a single currency on 1 January 1999; the Treaty of Amsterdam (2 October 1997) that incorporates new matters within the scope of the community in the areas of police, migration, justice, and employment and creates an 'area of freedom, security and justice' by integrating the Schengen agreement into EU law; the Nice Treaty (26 February 2001) which modifies the decision-making and institutional system of the EU and adopts the EU Charter of Fundamental Rights; finally, the Lisbon Treaty (13 December 2007) and, more recently, the treaty establishing the European Stability Mechanism (16 and 17 December 2010) and the Treaty on stability, coordination and governance in the EU (1 and 2 March 2012).

[14] OJ 26 February 2013, *Åkerberg Fransson*, C-617/10, § 21.

[15] In French, Art. 51, titled 'champ d'application', indeed sets out that '*Les dispositions de la présente Charte s'adressent* [...] *aux Etats membres uniquement lorsqu'ils mettent en œuvre le droit de l'Union.*' In English too, there is a shift: Article 51, titled 'Field of Application' sets out that 'The provisions of this Charter are addressed to the Member States [...] only when they are implementing Union law' and the CJEU underlines that the Charter is to be applied 'within the scope of European Law' (§ 21). In German, Art. 51, titled '*Anwendungs bereich*', sets out that '*Diese Charta gilt* [...] *für die Mitgliedstaaten ausschließlich bei der Durchführung des Rechts der Union*' and the CJEU stresses that the Charter must be applied '*in den Geltungsbereich des Unionsrechts*' (§ 21).

application coincides, apart from some exceptions,[16] with that of the general principles of law and can now be summarized in a simple sentence: 'The applicability of European Union law entails applicability of the fundamental rights guaranteed by the Charter.'[17]

The second specificity of EU law pertains to conditions relating to justiciability and to the consequent duties of national courts. EU law is distinctive due to the very large share of standards with direct effect; that is, those whose sole purpose is not to regulate relations between states and which require no additional act to produce effects on subjects of law. These direct effect standards naturally include European regulations,[18] but also, according to CJEU case law,[19] the clear, specific, and unconditional provisions of European directives that have not been regularly transposed into domestic law within the allowable time frame. As a result, the scope of direct effect European norms has broadened. Simultaneously, the range of categories of national legislation against which this direct effect is called into play has widened. Indeed, direct effect overrules any domestic legal standard, be it a law, a regulatory act, or even an individual decision. Interpreted in this way, direct effect and the principle of primacy have had decidedly concrete consequences on the duties of national courts, which are the primary guardians of the application of EU law. It is they who, of their own motion, must refuse to apply national provisions that are contrary to EU law, even if adopted subsequently, as soon as the European standard becomes applicable; that is, without requesting or waiting for prior, effective 'removal' of these provisions by the competent national authorities.[20] The same applies when national laws require a court to initiate interlocutory proceedings for review of constitutionality. In France, where such a procedure exists, the *Conseil constitutionnel*[21] and the *Conseil d'État*,[22] endorsed by the *Melki and Abdeli* judgment of the CJEU,[23] specified that ensuring the immediate effectiveness of EU law is incumbent upon national courts and, if necessary, it is their duty to refer a

[16] As ruled by the CJEU, the field of application of Art. 41 of the Charter titled 'Right to good administration' stands alone and is more limited than that of the Charter's other articles; Art. 41 is addressed not to the Member States but solely to the institutions, bodies, offices and agencies of the European Union C-166/13 *Sophie Mukarubega v Préfet de police, Préfet de la Seine-Saint-Denis*, ECLI:EU:C:2014:2336, § 44–45.

[17] CJEU 26 February 2013, *Åkerberg Fransson*, C-617/10, § 21. In English: 'The applicability of European Union law entails applicability of the fundamental rights guaranteed by the Charter.' In German: '*Die Anwendbarkeit des Unionsrechts umfasst die Anwendbarkeit der durch die Charta garantierten Grundrechte.*'

[18] European regulations have a vertical and a horizontal direct effect (full direct effect), see: Case 43–71, *Politi s.a.s. v Ministry for Finance of the Italian Republic* ECLI:EU:C:1971:122.

[19] Case 41–74, *Yvonne van Duyn v Home Office* ECLI:EU:C:1974:133 and C-148/78 *Public Prosecutor v Tullio Ratti* ECLI:EU:C:1979:110.

[20] C-106/77 *Amministrazione delle Finanze dello Stato v Simmenthal SPA* ECLI:EU:C:1978:49, § 24 and 26.

[21] CC No. 2010-605 DC dated 12 May 2010, *Loi relative à l'ouverture à la concurrence et à la régulation du secteur des jeux d'argent et de hasard en ligne.* Bill on the opening to competition and regulation of online gambling and games of chance.

[22] CE 14 May 2010, *Rujovic*, No. 312305.

[23] C-188/10 and C-189/10 *Melki and Abdeli* ECLI:EU:C:2010:363.

question for a preliminary ruling to the CJEU without waiting for the outcome of interlocutory proceedings for review of constitutionality. A recent case judged by the *Conseil d'État* showed up the implications of this requirement in cases where interpretation of EU law determines the admissibility of an interlocutory review of constitutionality. In the *Jacob*[24] case, there were serious doubts about the compatibility of domestic law with a European directive. In the event of this incompatibility being ascertained, the disapplication of domestic law would have justified initiating a constitutionality review—on the grounds of the principle of equality—of the applicable rules for the operations under scrutiny, which were transborder or domestic. To clarify these serious doubts, the *Conseil d'État* referred a preliminary question to the CJEU and decided, as things stood, not to initiate proceedings for review of constitutionality.[25] Following the *Melki* and *Abdeli* decision very closely, the *Conseil d'État* hence decided first to enter into dialogue with the judges in Luxembourg before, if needed, entering into dialogue with its immediate neighbour, the French constitutional court. This example shows how direct dialogue between judges, if well ordered, can effectively avoid any conflict of loyalty between EU law and national—especially constitutional—law.

The third specificity of EU law that I would like to discuss involves its completeness and autonomy in relation to international law. When the EU adheres to new international instruments, it cannot do so at the cost of impairing the principle of conferral of powers or the European institutional balance, in particular the CJEU's exclusive competences. In two opinions issued in 1994[26] and 2013,[27] the CJEU has constantly and firmly asserted this when plans to adhere to the European Convention on Human Rights (ECHR) were being examined. Once an international convention has been incorporated into the legal order of the Union, any disputes relating to its application come under a strictly European system of scrutiny, including when the agreement is mixed and falls within the shared jurisdiction of the Member States and of the Union. In this regard, two Member States may not obtain a ruling from an international arbitration court for a dispute relating to the application of a mixed agreement without infringing the exclusive competence of the CJEU and the principle of loyal cooperation.[28] Beyond that, from a material standpoint, the autonomy of EU law can be seen in the observance of fundamental rights. As shown in the *Kadi I* case, Union acts cannot fail to abide by those rights, including when such an act implements resolutions adopted by the Security Council of the United Nations.[29] In this way, the autonomy of the EU legal

[24] CE, Ass. 31 May 2016, *Jacob*, No. 393881.

[25] CE 31 May 2016, *Jacob*, No. 393881.

[26] Opinion 2/94 *Opinion of the Court* ECLI:EU:C:1996:140.

[27] Opinion 2/13, *Opinion of the Full Court* ECLI:EU:C:2014:2454 in particular, parts 155–159.

[28] C-459/03 *Commission v Ireland* ECLI:EU:C:2006:345.

[29] C-402/05 P and C-415/05 P *Kadi and Al Barakaat International Foundation v Council and Commission* ECLI:EU:C:2008:461.

order, which the CJEU described as 'constitutional', is protected. Its contours were subsequently detailed in the *ZZ*[30] and *Kadi II* decisions[31] in terms of rights of defense, onus of proof, and rules of conciliation between freedom and security.

The scope, direct effect, and administrative and material autonomy of EU law are essential characteristics that break away increasingly clearly from conventional international law.

3.2.2 The extraterritorial application of national rights

In contrast to the previous transformation, these characteristically extend the powers and sources of states. Under private international law, states traditionally have considerable leeway in defining the non-exclusive, concurrent prescriptive jurisdiction[32] they exercise.[33] However, state jurisdiction must be exercised in a reasonable manner; that is, referrals cannot be made to state bodies if there is no or very little connection with its legal order.[34]

3.2.2.1 *'Foreign cubed cases'*

In these cases, a foreign plaintiff (i) files a complaint against a foreign defendant (ii) before a national court for deeds committed abroad (iii). Let me quote two concrete examples of the hyper-extraterritoriality of this three-tiered foreign element in the legislation of some countries. In the area of anticorruption of government officials under US legislation, the Foreign Corrupt Practices Act (FCPA) passed in 1977 makes it possible to incriminate foreign entities that bribe civil servants or government officials abroad. In December 2014, under a plea agreement, the French company Alstom agreed to plead guilty and pay a US$772 million fine for violating this law for the purpose of winning a contract in Indonesia. Another example is in the area of economic embargoes. The Trade with the Enemy Act (TWEA) that was adopted during the First World War and the FCPA authorize the President of the United States to order economic sanctions against countries or entities with which the United States is at war or that endanger American national security, foreign policy, or its economy. In June 2014, the bank BNP Paribas agreed to pay a record fine of US$8.9 million for having provided banking services to Cuban, Iranian, and Sudanese entities that were subject to embargo measures. In this case, the territorial connection with the *lex fori* was grounded in the fact that transactions were performed *via* American financial institutions: interbank transfers in dollars went

[30] C-300/11 *ZZ v Secretary of State for the Home Department* ECLI:EU:C:2013:363.

[31] CJEU, Grand Chamber, 18 July 2013, *European Commission et al. v Kadi*, C-584/10.

[32] In this respect prescriptive jurisdiction is unlike enforcement jurisdiction, which is subject to the absolute principle of territoriality.

[33] PCIJ 7 Sept. 1927, publication of PCIJ, Series A, No. 10, *Lotus*.

[34] On this point see: D. Bureau and H. Muir Watt, *Droit international privé*, Vol. I 'partie générale', (PUF, coll. Thémis droit, 2nd ed., 2010) 76 and 80.

through a clearing house located on US territory.[35] These examples undeniably show that there is a strong trend towards extraterritoriality in US law, which has further developed via intergovernmental agreements on taxation since the adoption of the Foreign Account Tax Compliance Act (FATCA) passed in 2010.[36] These agreements, however, whether they are bilateral[37] or multilateral,[38] also include reciprocal obligations for all parties including the United States. This trend has also given rise to some opportune European directives[39] on the matter of automatic, compulsory exchanges of information in the area of taxation.

3.2.2.2 *The limits and ambiguities of extra-territorial expansions*

On the one hand, the extraterritorial element of national legislations has declined somewhat. In its famous *Kiobel* decision of 17 April 2013, the US Supreme Court recognized that it lacked jurisdiction to examine claims presented by Nigerian citizens who, on the basis of the Alien Tort Statute (ATS), accused a Dutch company of aiding and abetting serious violations of human rights. In this decision, the Court argued that there is a principle of presumption against the extraterritoriality of US federal laws, unless there is a clear indication from Congress to the contrary. This opinion is consistent with the US Supreme Court decision of 24 June 2010 in *Morrison versus National Australia Bank Ltd* that set aside the application of the Securities Exchange Act in an action brought by Australian investors relating to purchases of an Australian company's shares conducted on an Australian market.[40] Nonetheless, the mechanism of presumption put forward in 2013 does not preclude the possibility of re-examining the question of 'reasonable limits'[41] in the exercise of prescriptive jurisdiction of states and its corollary, the question of the emergence of international rules of courtesy ('comity').[42] One must be careful not

[35] On this case see: Y. Quintin, 'Aux frontières du droit: les embargos américains et l'affaire BNP Paribas' (Sept 2014) 5 *Revue de droit bancaire et financier* study 21.

[36] On this point see: P. Athanassiou, M. Prokop, and A. Theodosopoulou, 'Effets extraterritoriaux du droit américain sur les institutions financières non-américaines, une vue d'ensemble' (Sept 2014) 5 *Revue de droit bancaire et financier* study 20.

[37] Agreement entered into in Paris on 14 November 2013 between the Government of the French Republic and the Government of the United States of America for the purpose of improving international tax compliance and to implement FATCA, published by decree No. 2015-1 dated 2 January 2015.

[38] Multilateral agreement signed in Berlin on 29 October 2014 between the competent authorities on automatic exchange of information relating to financial accounts.

[39] Directive 2011/16/EU of the Council dated 15 February 2011 on administrative cooperation in the field of taxation, repealing Directive 77/99/EC.

[40] On this point see: M. Dubertret, 'Affaire Morrison v. National Australia Bank Ltd: l'espoir d'un nouvel âge?' (July 2010) 4 *Revue de droit bancaire et financier* study 17.

[41] H. Muir Watt, 'L'Alien Tort Statute devant la Cour suprême des Etats-Unis, territorialité, diplomatie judiciaire ou économie politique?' (2013) 3 *Revue critique de droit international privé* 595.

[42] See on this point: the concurring opinion of Judge Breyer in the *Kiobel* case: although he endorses the same solution as the majority opinion, Judge Breyer bases his position not on the presumption against extraterritoriality of the ATS but on the principles and practices of international relations that tend to restrict the extraterritorial application of the *lex fori* to the most serious crimes or to the most significant infringements of national interests. See for an analysis of this position: N. Maziau,

to minimize the risk of 'forum shopping' whereby, for instance, someone who has committed serious violations of fundamental rights might benefit from complete jurisdictional immunity.

On the other hand, it is noteworthy that the EU itself, although it does not have the political strength and economic power of the United States, also issues norms that are extraterritorial in scope, in particular in the area of competition and, more recently, the area of digital technologies with the *Google Spain*[43] and *Schrems*[44] rulings. Additionally, the EU has also responded to foreign extraterritorial legislation by adopting 'blocking statutes' as permitted by EC Regulation No. 2271/96[45] following adoption of the Helms–Burton and Amato–Kennedy laws. Furthermore, it can impose heavy fines in the event of failure to comply with EU law by non-European corporations established within its territory, as recently demonstrated by the record fine of €13 billion imposed by the Commission on Apple for failing to observe European rules applicable to state aids.[46] The CJEU will shortly be examining this case.

Thus, whether in the case of the sources or the founding principles of international law, both public and private, sweeping changes are currently in process—some of which, in particular within the EU, are drawing the contours of a new model. Without claiming to see into the future, some methodological milestones can arguably be identified, and some climbing ropes prepared and used so as to improve the regulation of the normative interactions between national and European legal orders and thereby avert and anticipate certain risks of the machinery creaking or even jamming.

4 Towards a Better Regulation of Legal Pluralism

4.1 The Need for More Consultation with the Relevant International Actors

The globalization of law destabilizes, without entirely invalidating, the conventional conception of the hierarchy of norms and of relations between legal orders.

L'arrêt Kiobel: reconnaissance différée d'une responsabilité des sociétés multinationales pour les crimes contre les droits de l'Homme, (2013) 189 *Recueil Dalloz* 1316.

[43] C-131/12 *Google Spain SL and Google Inc. v Agencia Española de Protección de Datos (AEPD) and Mario Costeja González* ECLI:EU:C:2014:317.

[44] CJEU, Grand Chamber, 6 October 2015, *Maximillian Schrems v Data Protection Commissioner*, C-362/14.

[45] *Regulation (EC) No. 2271/96 of the Council dated 22 November 1996 protecting against the effects of the extra-territorial application of legislation adopted by a third country, and actions based thereon or resulting therefrom.*

[46] See the European Commission's press release: <http://europa.eu/rapid/press-release_IP-16-2923_fr.htm>.

The strictly pyramid-shaped model has been replaced by a network[47] of norms that, between one system and the other, mirror and respond to one other. At the junction between internal and international orders stands a zone of continuous exchange and perpetual influences. The magnitude of normative interactions between legal orders today calls for more intensive action in three areas: coordination of jurisdiction, standardization of rights, and integration of legal orders.

4.1.1 The importance of the principle of subsidiarity for a better coordination of jurisdiction

4.1.1.1 The recognition of national margins of appreciation in the Convention's system

Indeed, states are left a margin of appreciation 'by reason of their direct and continuous contact with the vital forces of their countries'[48] when attending to the application of rights and freedoms guaranteed by the Convention. The magnitude of these margins is not always identical or unlimited; it varies depending on the nature of the interests involved and the degree of consensus between the legislation of the forty-seven States of the Council of Europe. The more the protected interests involve 'a key aspect of individuals' identity' such as filiation,[49] for instance, or 'a strong interest for a democratic society' such as freedom of expression,[50] the more restricted the margin. In contrast, these margins are broader when what is at stake is a choice of society, 'matters of general policy ... [relating in particular to] the relations between the state and religions'[51] or sensitive issues of morality or bioethics.[52] In such cases, the European Court of Human Rights (ECtHR) has a duty to exercise a degree of restraint in its review of Convention compliance, since such review will lead it to assess a balance that has been struck by means of a democratic process.[53] National margins of appreciation are also broader when there is no 'common ground'[54] or 'consensus within the Member States of the Council of Europe'.[55] For the principle of subsidiarity to

[47] F. Ost and M. Van de Kerchove, *De la pyramide au réseau. Pour une dialectique du droit,* (Presses des facultés universitaires de Saint Louis 2002).

[48] ECtHR, Full court, 7 December 1976, *Handyside v United Kingdom*, App No 5493/72, § 48.

[49] ECtHR 26 June 2014, *Mennesson v France*, App No 65192/11, § 80.

[50] ECtHR, Grand Chamber, 22 April 2013, *Animal Defenders v United Kingdom*, App No 48876/08, § 102.

[51] See on the topic of displaying crucifixes in classrooms of state schools: ECtHR 18 March 2011, Grand Chamber, *Lautsi v Italy*, App No 30814/06; on the topic of wearing the Islamic veil in higher education establishments: ECtHR 10 November 2005, Grand Chamber, *Leyla Sahin v Turkey*, App No 447774/98, § 109–110.

[52] See on the topic of legislation on the right to abortion: ECtHR, Grand Chamber, 16 December 2010, *A., B., C. v Ireland*, App No 25579/05; on the topic of the conditions for resorting to *in vitro* fertilization: ECtHR, Grand Chamber, 3 November 2011, *S.H. v Austria*, App No 57813/00; on the topic of resorting to assisted suicide: ECtHR 20 January 2011, *Haas v Switzerland*, App No 31322/07.

[53] ECtHR, Grand Chamber, 1 July 2014, *SAS v France*, App No 43835/11, § 154.

[54] ECtHR 28 November 1984, *Rasmussen v Denmark*, App No 8777/79, § 40.

[55] ECtHR 26 June 2014, *Mennesson v France*, App No 65192/11, § 77.

exert its regulatory virtues fully, it must lead national authorities to systematically, thoroughly, and if possible preemptively preventively analyse the compatibility of internal law with European guarantees. However, this principle also demands that the ECtHR adopts stable, consistent positions, makes clear what this common ground is—that is, identifies the matters on which there is a consensus in Europe—and conducts a reasonable evaluation of national margins of appreciation, so that the authorities of the states parties can use them confidently without any need for self-restraint.

4.1.1.2 *The principle of subsidiarity as a regulatory principle within the European Union*

The principle of subsidiarity is an autonomous concept.[56] In contrast to federal states, it is not a general principle of state organization and it is not based on a functional hierarchy between the supreme federal authority and the subordinate state subdivisions. Furthermore, unlike the system of the ECHR, the principle of subsidiarity regulates the exercise of supranational decision-making powers within the Union, which has its own legislative and executive institutions and operates in far broader areas than merely fundamental rights. That means in particular that the duties of a CJEU judge in Luxembourg are not strictly analogous to those of a ECtHR judge in Strasbourg. In the first case, the court attends *in abstracto* to the uniform interpretation of the law of the Union through a mechanism of preliminary ruling, a task that accounts for two-thirds of its activity. The second, which is referred to after all internal remedies have been exhausted, rules *in concreto* on particular disputes that call into question the rights protected by the Convention. Naturally, the interpretation by the CJEU of the law of the Union is not abstract and disembodied. It predetermines in part the outcome of the disputes to which it applies. Similarly, the settlement of a topical case by the ECtHR is the opportunity to establish general principles of interpretation and define jurisprudential guidelines. Hence, there is a true kinship between these two Courts but each retains its own identity, which is partly reflected in the specificity of the principle of subsidiarity in the Union. In any case, this principle must effectively be implemented, which implies both reasonably receptive national courts, and also some restraint in the exercise of the competences of the Union. National constitutional powers must be observed and preserved and to that effect a careful and genuine dialogue must be conducted between the CJEU and national supreme courts.

[56] As set out in Art. 5 of the TEU, pursuant to this principle, 'in areas which do not fall within its exclusive competence, the Union shall act only if and in so far as the objectives of the proposed action cannot be sufficiently achieved by the Member States, either at central level or at regional and local level, but can rather [. . .] be better achieved at Union level'.

4.1.2 The standardization of fundamental rights

4.1.2.1 The technique of compliant interpretation

National courts ensure that internal rules are interpreted in compliance with the international commitments undertaken by their country and, in particular, the rules and principles of the law of the EU[57] and the ECHR. In France, to quote an example already mentioned, the *Conseil constitutionnel*[58] and the *Conseil d'État*[59] assessed national legislation relating to implementing interlocutory proceedings for review of constitutionality in accordance with the requirements of EU law, as later reaffirmed in the *Melki and Abdeli*[60] decision of the CJEU.

4.1.2.2 The recognition of the equivalence of protections

National courts commonly uphold rights and rise their level of protection via the principle of the equivalence of protections. Indeed, it is not desirable for them to review compliance with a fundamental right in isolation under their own legal order if this right is recognized and effectively protected under another relevant legal order. Once again, I will speak from my own experience. When the constitutionality of a regulatory act implementing a directive is challenged before a French administrative court, the latter begins by ascertaining whether EU law recognizes the rule or constitutional principle called upon and guarantees its effectiveness. If that is the case, it rules on the question of constitutionality brought before it in the light of EU law, after having, if needed, referred to the CJEU for a preliminary ruling. If not, when the administrative court does not ascertain that protections are equivalent, it directly examines compliance of the transformation act, and therefore of the directive, with the Constitution. As a result, in the area of secondary EU legislation, direct, independent review of constitutionality is only exercised when the protections afforded by the law of the Union and those afforded by national constitutional law are not equivalent.

International judges also resort to these standardization techniques. To uncover general principles of law, the judges in Luxembourg refer to national constitutional traditions and to international instruments that Member States[61] have adhered to, in particular to the ECHR.[62] This is now explicitly provided for in Article 4 §2 of TEU. Furthermore, the Charter and the ECHR both include a 'matching clause' in their respective Article 53, to the benefit of greater protection.[63] Pursuant to this

[57] See, e.g., on the topic of interpretation of legislation consistent with Council Directive 2003/109/EC dated 25 November 2003: CE 16 December 2013, *Nouri-Shakeri*, No. 366722; or with Council Directive 90/435/EEC dated 23 July 1990: CE 15 December 2014, *SA Technicolor*, No. 380942.

[58] CC No. 2010-605 DC dated 12 May 2010, *Loi relative à l'ouverture à la concurrence et à la régulation du secteur des jeux d'argent et de hasard en ligne*. Bill on the opening to competition and regulation of online gambling and games of chance, cons. 14 and 15.

[59] CE 14 May 2010, *Rujovic*, No. 312305.

[60] C-188/10 and C-189/10 *Melki and Abdeli* ECLI:EU:C:2010:363, § 50.

[61] Case 4-73, *Nold, Kohlen- und Baustoffgroßhandlung v Commission of the European Communities* ECLI:EU:C:1974:51, §13.

[62] Case 36-75, *Roland Rutili v Ministre de l'intérieur* ECLI:EU:C:1975:137, § 32.

[63] See Art. 53 of the ECHR: 'Nothing in this Convention shall be construed as limiting or derogating from any of the human rights and fundamental freedoms which may be ensured under the laws of

clause, the CJEU takes into consideration the standards of the ECHR when applying and interpreting the Charter.[64] By way of example, last year, Articles 6,[65] 7,[66] and 49[67] of the Charter were explicitly interpreted with reference to respectively Articles 5, 8, and 7 of the Convention and the relevant Strasbourg case law. The same applies to Article 17 of the Charter in respect of Article 1 of the Convention's first protocol.[68]

The Strasbourg ECtHR judges share this concern for standardization and they have developed their own tools. Thus, they consider that a state that applies the law of the Union is presumed to abide by the requirements of the Convention, unless it has been demonstrated that there is a '*manifest deficiency*'.[69] This mechanism of presumption of equivalence does not, however, operate automatically. The ECtHR indeed readily sets it aside when Member States have some leeway in applying EU law. One instance of this is the transfer measures of asylum seekers taken under the 'Dublin' scheme as a result of the 'sovereignty clause' it contains.[70] When the presumed equivalence is lacking, the judges strive to use similar but not always identical criteria to prevent an asylum seeker from being transferred to a Member State.[71] In addition, when the equivalence of protections is applicable in principle, the ECtHR readily rebuts the presumption of equivalence if the supervisory

any High Contracting Party or under any other agreement to which it is a party'; Art. 53 of the Charter: 'Nothing in this Charter shall be interpreted as restricting or adversely affecting human rights and fundamental freedoms as recognised, in their respective fields of application, by Union law and international law and by international agreements to which the Union, the Community or all the Member States are party, including the European Convention for the Protection of Human Rights and Fundamental Freedoms, and by the Member States' constitutions.' Additionally, see Art. 52 § 3 of the Charter: 'In so far as this Charter contains rights which correspond to rights guaranteed by the Convention for the Protection of Human Rights and Fundamental Freedoms, the meaning and scope of those rights shall be the same as those laid down by the said Convention. This provision shall not prevent Union law providing more extensive protection.'

---

[64] See on this point: R. Tinière, 'Le rôle de la Charte dans la jurisprudence de la Cour de justice de l'Union européenne depuis l'avis 2/13: vers un modus vivendi avec le droit de la Convention?' (2016) 600 *Revue de l'Union européenne* 400.

[65] C-237/15 *Minister for Justice and Equality v Francis Lanigan* ECLI:EU:C:2015:474, para. 57 (in the case of keeping a person who is the subject of a European arrest warrant in detention).

[66] C-419/14 *WebMindLicenses kft v Nemzeti Adó- és Vámhivatal Kiemelt Adó- és Vám Főigazgatóság* ECLI:EU:C:2015:832, paras 70–72 (on the subject of obtaining evidence in the context of criminal proceedings); C-583/13 *Deutsche Bahn and Others v Commission* ECLI:EU:C:2015:404, paras 19–23 (on the topic of the inviolability of the home).

[67] C-105/14 *Tarico and others* ECLI:EU:C:2015:555, para. 57 (on the topic of extension of the limitation period and its immediate application).

[68] C-398/13 *Inuit Tapiriit Kanatami and Others v Commission* ECLI:EU:C:2015:535, paras 60 and 61 (on the topic of the right to property and the functional notion of 'possessions').

[69] ECtHR, Grand Chamber, 30 June 2005, *Bosphorus Hava Yollari Turizm ve Ticaret Anonim Sirketi v Ireland* App No 45036/98, § 156.

[70] See in relation to a decision to transfer to Greece: ECtHR, Grand Chamber, 21 January 2011, *M.S.S. v Belgium and Greece*, App No. 30696/09, § 358; on a decision to transfer to Italy: ECtHR, Grand Chamber, 4 November 2014, *Tarakhel v Suisse* App No 29217/12, § 120–122.

[71] Which is not always the case: according to the Court of Justice, only 'systemic flaws' can justify not proceeding with a 'Dublin' transfer: on this point see C-411/10 *N.S. v Secretary of State for the Home Department* ECLI:EU:C:2011:865, § 85.

mechanisms provided for under EU law have not been fully deployed. In such a case, the ECtHR considers that 'the interest of international cooperation would be outweighed by the Convention's role as a constitutional instrument of European public order in the field of human rights'.[72] As demonstrated by the *Michaud v France* case, such a rebuttal of the presumption of equivalence is not purely hypothetical when a national court refuses to implement the preliminary ruling procedure set out in Article 267 TFUE.[73] In a recent case, *Avotins v Latvia*, the ECtHR, however, stated that the lack of a referral for a preliminary ruling cannot stand in the way of the presumption of equivalence if the national court can directly process the issue pertaining to the interpretation of EU law.[74] Nonetheless, the Court is cautious: taking the opposite course to that of the CJEU's Opinion 2/13, it underlines that '[l]imiting to some exceptional cases' the review by a Member State of compliance with fundamental rights by another Member State when they apply EU law could, in some concrete situations, run counter to the mechanism of equivalent protections.[75]

4.1.2.3 The harmonization of rights through spontaneous practices of convergence

When national courts rule on a new question of principle, even under domestic law alone, they look not only to their own legislation and case law but also to the case law of the European Courts. Allow me once again to share my own experience. When examining a new question, the answer to which will produce case law, the judges of the *Conseil d'État* do not only ask: how do we view this on the basis of our case law? They also ask: how do or how might the other French supreme courts, and specifically the *Conseil constitutionnel*, view this? They apply the same test to the CJEU and the ECtHR. They also gather information on how other supreme courts in European countries and in North America view the issues in dispute. Thus, the analysis of these legal questions by national judges takes into account the viewpoint of international judges and of other national judges. The aim is not to align their own assessment with the majority view mechanically, or the position of any given supreme court, but rather to be enlightened, informed, and as relevant as possible. Confronted with comparable situations as a result of the expansion of world trade and the standardization of living conditions, states have improved, or are trying to improve their legislative and judicial function in the light of solutions devised by their neighbours. Let me give a recent example. In France, the enrichment of

[72] ECtHR 6 March 2013, *Michaud v France*, App No 12323/11, § 103.

[73] ECtHR 6 March 2013, *Michaud v France*, App No 12323/11, § 115.

[74] ECtHR, Grand Chamber, 23 March 2016, *Avotins v Latvia*, App No 17502/07, § 109.

[75] ECtHR, Grand Chamber, 23 May 2016, *Avotins v Latvia*, App No 17502/07, § 114. In this case, the senate of Latvia's Supreme Court ordered the enforcement in Latvia of a decision delivered *in absentia* by a Cypriot court: applying the *Bosphorus* presumption, the Court noted *in concreto* the absence of manifest deficiency in the protection of the fundamental rights that might overturn the presumption. See on this point: C. Picheral, 'Des réponses potentielles de la Cour européenne des droits de l'Homme à l'avis 2/13' (2016) 600 *Revue de l'Union européenne* 426.

the *ne bis in idem* principle was the outcome of a convergence between European and constitutional case law: in the wake of the ECtHR *Zolotouchine*[76] and *Grande Stevens*[77] decisions and the *Åkerberg Fransson*[78] ruling of the CJEU, the *Conseil constitutionnel* redefined the conditions for allowing double penalties—both criminal and administrative—to be imposed in financial,[79] then tax,[80] and accounting[81] areas, making them more restrictive.

4.1.3 The strengthening of European integration through the Charter of Fundamental Rights

The scope of the Charter, as interpreted by the CJEU,[82] coincides, save for some exceptions,[83] with that of the general principles of EU law. In so doing, it is confronted, sometimes brutally, with the rights protected by other treaties, and by the constitutional guarantees of the Member States. In these circumstances, the risks of divergence and 'disharmony' between EU law and the ECHR have escalated, with the CJEU readily adopting an 'autonomous' conception of the principles protected by those treaties. The *Åkerberg Fransson* ruling remarkably illustrates this: while the Courts of Luxembourg and Strasbourg use the same criteria to assess the criminal character of a tax penalty, the first, in contrast with the second,[84] makes applying the principle of *ne bis in idem*, as set out in Article 50 of the Charter, conditional upon the remaining applicable penalties being 'effective, proportionate and dissuasive'.[85] In addition, a stringent framework for the combined application of EU law and of the Member States' constitutional guarantees has been instituted by the CJEU's *Melloni* decision.[86] Thus, when an act in EU law calls for national implementing measures, states remain free to apply their national standards for protection of fundamental rights, provided they comply with two conditions simultaneously: 'the level of protection provided for by the Charter, as interpreted by

[76] ECtHR 10 February 2009, *Zolotoukhine*, App No 14939/03.

[77] ECtHR, Grand Chamber, 4 March 2014, *Grande Stevens*, App No 18640/10.

[78] C-617/10 *Åklagaren v Hans Åkerberg Fransson* ECLI:EU:C:2013:105.

[79] CC No. 2014-453 QPC dated 18 March 2015, *John L.*

[80] CC No. 2016-545 QPC dated 24 June 2016, *Alec W.* and CC No. 2016-546 QPC dated 24 June 2016, *Jérôme C.*

[81] CC No. 2016-550 QPC dated 1 July 2016, *Stéphane R.*

[82] See the broad interpretation adopted by the Court of Justice in its judgment C-617/10 *Åklagaren v Hans Åkerberg Fransson* ECLI:EU:C:2013:105.

[83] See on the topic of the scope of Art. 41 of the Charter: *YS*, C-141/12 *YS v Minister voor Immigratie, Integratie en Asiel and Minister voor Immigratie, Integratie en Asiel v M and S* ECLI:EU:C:2014:2081, § 67; the right to be heard, which is consecrated by this article is nonetheless 'an integral part of the rights of the defence, which is a general principle of EU law': see on this point CJEU 5 November 2014, *Sophie Mukarubega*, C-166/13, § 45; C-249/13 *Khaled Boudjlida v Préfet des Pyrénées-Atlantiques* ECLI:EU:C:2014:2431, § 34.

[84] See on this point V. Skouris, 'Développements récents de la protection des droits fondamentaux dans l'Union européenne: les arrêts Melloni et Åkerberg Fransson' (2013) fasc. 2 *Il diritto dell'Unione Europea* 229.

[85] C-617/10 *Åklagaren v Hans Åkerberg Fransson* ECLI:EU:C:2013:105.

[86] C-399/11 *Stefano Melloni v Ministerio Fiscal* ECLI:EU:C:2013:107. See on this point, the Spanish Constitutional Court's reply: Aida Torres Perez, 'Melloni in Three Acts: From Dialogue to Monologue' (Sept 2014) 10(2) *European Constitutional Law Review* 308–31.

the Court, and the primacy, unity and effectiveness of EU law are not thereby compromised'.[87] If the latter condition is not fulfilled, the national standard, regardless of whether it is more protective or constitutional, must be disapplied. Advocating an *autonomous* European legal order could produce new frictions in Member States and within the Council of Europe at a time when the prospect of the Union adhering to the ECHR is becoming more remote, not to say implausible, following the opinion issued by the CJEU in December 2014.[88]

To improve the regulation of legal pluralism in Europe requires three fundamental operations: first, a working, balanced coordination of powers; second, an ongoing, realistic standardization of fundamental rights; finally, the concerted and flexible integration of legal orders. These operations will contribute to shaping a more robust and resilient framework for dealing with contemporary crises. It is my conviction that the legal community has a major responsibility to shoulder at a time when new tensions are emerging.

4.2 Tensions between Constitutional Identities and National Sovereignties

An angelical, completely irenic conception of the relations between legal orders would be out of place. It is only natural for areas of friction to exist but there is also a significant risk of divergence and disagreement about the rules that should regulate these orders. The current 'crisis' in international law is a crisis that derives from the foundations of international law rooted in the state and more especially the principles of constitutional supremacy and national sovereignty.

4.2.1 In the field of fundamental rights, the risks of conflict between primacies have grown

The law of the Union and national constitutions enshrine a duty of mutual respect. In EU law, this duty arises in particular from Articles 4 and 6 of the TEU and from Article 53 of the Charter. Furthermore, most Member States set aside a special place for EU law in their constitutions. In France, title XV of the Constitution is devoted entirely to the EU. Some very specific and binding requirements have been inferred from Article 88-1 in the area of transposing European directives into national law. Pursuant to Article 88-2, it is the duty of lawmakers to set out the rules

[87] CJEU, Grand Chamber, 26 February 2013, *Stefano Melloni*, C-399/11, § 60; also, the *obiter dictum* in the *Åkerberg Fransson* judgment on the same day: CJEU, Grand Chamber, 26 February 2013, *Åkerberg Fransson*, C-617/10, § 29.

[88] CJEU, Full Court, 18 December 2014, Opinion 2/13; see on this point, H. Labayle and F. Sudre, 'L'avis 2/13 de la Cour de justice sur l'adhésion de l'Union européenne à la Convention européenne des droits de l'Homme: pavane pour une adhésion défunte?' (2015)1 *Revue Française de Droit Administratif* at 3.

pertaining to the European arrest warrant in compliance with acts of the EU on this subject. Nonetheless, cases of direct confrontation between EU law and national constitutions are frequent and liable to remain so in the future, even though to this date they have not led to systemic crises. It is essential today to put the instruments for preserving national constitutional identities to good use. With its pioneering decisions, *Solange I* and *II*,[89] the German Federal Constitutional Court has devised instruments of this type that ensure that the constitutional kernel is preserved, including the principle of the dignity of human beings and other fundamental rights, as well as the founding principles of the German state, which cannot be impaired by EU law nor, for that matter, amended under domestic law pursuant to the '*eternity clause*'.[90] Many states now exercise this control in ways that are inherent to their legal traditions. In France, an act that transposes a European directive into internal law is in principle covered by jurisdictional immunity before the Constitution and this immunity is lifted only if the legislation in question infringes a rule or principle inherent to the 'constitutional identity of France'[91]—according to the broad and malleable expression used by the *Conseil constitutionnel*. A situation of this type has thus far never occurred and could only do so if a strictly national principle or a strictly French conception of a shared principle is disregarded.

The constitutional identity review relates to a hypothetical and 'extreme'[92] situation—to use the words of Advocate-General Villalon in the *Gauweiler* case—when there is a major discrepancy between national constitutional guarantees and European guarantees. In our view, this review has a powerful preventive and deterrent effect. Resorting to it becomes increasingly hypothetical as the equivalence of protections grows and fundamental rights become standardized across the Union. National supreme courts nonetheless remain on guard. In a decision dated 15 December 2015 concerning European arrest warrants, the German Federal Constitutional Court, while reaffirming the principles of openness to international law (*Völkerrechtsfreundlichkeit*) and to EU law (*Europarechtsfreundlichkeit*), emphasized that constitutional identity review may entail—in some 'exceptional cases' and under very 'stringent' conditions—disapplication of Union acts,[93] in this instance a European arrest warrant. The CJEU echoed this position and took it into

[89] *Solange I* judgment of 29 May 1974, BVerfGE, 37, 271—RTD eur. 1975.316—and *Solange II* judgment of 22 October 1986, BVerfGE 73, 339—RTD eur. 1987.537.

[90] Art. 79 sub-§. 3 of the Fundamental Law.

[91] CC No. 2006-540 DC dated 27 July 2006, *Loi relative au droit d'auteur et aux droits voisins dans la société de l'information*, cons. 19 [Law relating to copyright and related rights in the information society].

[92] See P.C. Villalon, re CJEU, C-62/14 *Peter Gauweiler and Others v Deutscher Bundestag* ECLI:EU:C:2015:400.

[93] *European Arrest Warrant* Decision dated 15 December 2015, 2 BvR 2735/14. In the same decision, the German Federal Constitutional Court emphasized the limits imposed by the observance of the Charter of Fundamental Rights to the principle of mutual recognition and to the practical enforcement of a European arrest warrant. See on this point: A. Gaillet, 'Confiance et méfiance autour du mandat d'arrêt européen. La décision de la Cour constitutionnelle fédérale allemande du 15 décembre 2015' (2016) 20 *L'Actualité Juridique Droit Administratif AJDA* 1112.

consideration in a Grand Chamber judgment—*Aranyosi* and *Caldararu*—dated 5 April 2016.[94] Similarly the UK Supreme Court, in the *Pham* decision of 25 March 2015,[95] expressed concern about the excessively broad conception of the powers of the Union in matters relating to granting and withdrawing Member State nationality, which is an area of competence that lies at the heart of 'the identity of the nation State' and pertains to the sovereignty of the UK Parliament. In a previous decision dated 22 January 2014, *HS2*,[96] concerning evaluation of the environmental effects of a plan to build a high-speed railway line, the UK Supreme Court had already stepped back somewhat from a broad interpretation of the secondary legislation of the Union that could lead to interference by national and European judges in the UK Parliament's decision-making powers.

What we see are signs of concern coming from various national supreme courts. In this context, new responsibilities rest on the shoulders of national and European judges. It is the task of national judges to determine both the content and the limits of constitutional kernels. A definition that is too broad or too vague and general would directly threaten the unity of EU law. As for European judges, they must spell out the scope and limits of EU law and the magnitude of Member States' margins of appreciation.[97] Within those margins, the national review of constitutionality should apply in accordance with the *Melloni*[98]criteria, as clarified by the previously mentioned *Aranyosi* and *Caldararu*[99] judgment. This review may lead to a situation where an internal provision that lies within the scope of the national margin of appreciation is abrogated due to its unconstitutionality notwithstanding that it indirectly contributes to the implementation of EU law. Clearly, this type of situation requires a genuine and constructive dialogue between the supreme national courts and the CJEU. This is what happened for instance in the *Jeremy F*[100] case, when for the first time the French *Conseil Constitutionnel* made a referral for

[94] C-404/15 *Aranyosi and Căldăraru v Generalstaatsanwaltschaft Bremen* ECLI:EU:C:2016:198C16: 'where there is objective, reliable, specific and properly updated evidence with respect to detention conditions in the issuing Member State that demonstrates that there are deficiencies, which may be systemic or generalized, or which may affect certain groups of people, or which may affect certain places of detention, the executing judicial authority must determine, specifically and precisely, whether there are substantial grounds to believe that the individual concerned by a European arrest warrant, issued for the purposes of conducting a criminal prosecution or executing a custodial sentence, will be exposed, because of the conditions for his detention in the issuing Member State, to a real risk of inhuman or degrading treatment, within the meaning of Article 4 of the Charter, in the event of his surrender to that Member State' (operative part of judgment).

[95] [2015] UKSC 19, *Pham v Secretary of State for the Home Department*, 25 March 2015.

[96] [2014] UKSC 3, *R (on the application of HS2 Action Alliance Limited) (Appellant) v The Secretary of State for Transport and another (Respondents)*, 22 January 2014.

[97] See, e.g., in the area of taxation, the regime for relations between parent companies and subsidiaries: CC No. 2015-726 DC of 29 December 2015, *Loi de finances rectificative pour 2015*, cons. 7 and 8; CC No. 2015-520 QPC du 3 February 2016, *Société Metro Holding France SA*, cons. 9.

[98] C-399/11 *Stefano Melloni v Ministerio Fiscal* ECLI:EU:C:2013:107.

[99] CJEU, Grand Chamber, 5 April 2016, *Aranyosi* et *Caldararu*, C-404/15 and C-659/15.

[100] CC No. 2013-314 QPC dated 4 April 2013, *Jeremy F.* (referral to the Court of Justice of the European Union); C-168/13 *Jeremy F. v Premier ministre* ECLI:EU:C:2013:358; CC No. 2013-314 QPC dated 14 June 2013, *Jeremy F.* (decision on merits, abrogation).

a preliminary ruling to the CJEU, prior to annulling a number of provisions in the code of criminal procedure implemented to enact European arrest warrants that were subject to a national margin of discretion. More than ever before, the referral for preliminary ruling mechanism is the keystone of the Union's judicial system.

Today, it enables a face-to-face *constitutional* dialogue to be set up between judges. Because this dialogue touches on the fundamental rights of persons, that is, the kernel of national identities and the foundations of the Union, it creates new responsibilities for all judges: a greater need for cooperation, openness, and goodwill as well as more realism and flexibility. These should enable us to accompany current developments in fundamental rights that are yet to be completed, while observing the foundational balances that need to be maintained between national traditions and the unity, autonomy, and effectiveness of EU law. Today, this constitutional dialogue no longer concerns only the fundamental rights of persons; it is beginning to develop in the field of protection of sovereign powers of states and is liable to create new risks of turbulence.

4.2.2 Towards a shared implementation of sovereignty within the European Union

European integration has undoubtedly deepened changes in state sovereignty, which appears less as an absolute and indivisible power than as a purposeful power capable of exerting a self-limiting influence on the state in favour of supra-state entities. While European integration accentuates this phenomenon, it also clearly shows up the advantages deriving from shared sovereignty. A simple fictional scenario in the area of monetary policy for instance easily demonstrates how, in the absence of any transfer to the Union's institutions that are subject to review by the CJEU, the national exercise of this review would be weakened. This does not mean that the state has relinquished all of its sovereign powers. However broad the scope of the Union's duties, it acts within the limits of the framework set up by the Treaties and does not possess the *compétence de sa compétence* [jurisdiction over its jurisdiction]—which is the distinctive mark of state sovereignty. The principle of conferral of powers guarantees control over what transfers are allowed, but it must not be an inhibitive straitjacket that deprives the Union of its legitimate margin for intervention. In the area of monetary policy, the European Central Bank was able to adopt, in compliance with the European treaties and specifically Articles 119 and 123 TFEU, an unprecedented scheme for OMTs (outright monetary transactions) that allows for the purchase of the public debt of some Eurozone Member States on the secondary market, without any predetermined quantitative limitation but under highly specific conditions. As noted by the CJEU in the *Gauweiler* decision[101] in answer to the first preliminary question

[101] CJEU, Grand Chamber, 16 June 2015, *Peter Gauweiler*, C-62/14.

raised by the German Federal Constitutional Court,[102] the OMT scheme does indeed fall within the scope of monetary policy and therefore the competence of the European Central Bank. It cannot be equated with an economic policy measure simply on the basis that it is liable to have indirect effects on the stability of the Eurozone or encourage the states concerned to better accommodate the macroeconomic adjustment programmes of the European Stability Mechanism (ESM). The Court therefore reaffirmed the purposive approach of its *Pringle* decision.[103] It furthermore ruled that the OMT programme was sufficiently delimited *ratione personae, materiae*, and *temporis*, in spite of making no provision for an *ex ante* quantitative limit. The Court underlined in particular that only those Member States that were subject to a macroeconomic adjustment programme and had regained access to the bond market could avail themselves of the OMT scheme and that the latter would focus on government bonds with a maturity of less than three years. Finally, with regard to compliance with Article 123 of the TFEU that prohibits monetary financing of public debt, the guarantees announced by the Governing Council avert, according to the CJEU, a situation whereby implementation of the OMT scheme would in practice have an effect equivalent to the direct acquisition of sovereign bonds from Member States. In its decision dated 21 June 2016,[104] at the cost of some unmistakable efforts and reservations, the German Federal Constitutional Court did not call into question the overall meaning of the CJEU's decision. However, it constrained it by giving a restrictive interpretation of the conditions for implementing the OMT scheme. Furthermore, the German Supreme Court does not relinquish its power to review *ultra vires* acts of the Union. But even if it is constitutional, for a national court to conduct this review seems impractical as the natural and ultimate judge of the observance of European treaties and in particular the exclusive powers of the Union is the CJEU in Luxembourg. An *ultra vires* review conducted in all areas by a national court on the basis of domestic principles such as popular sovereignty, suffrage, and parliament's right to vote the budget, is liable to generate new and serious tensions in the Union's jurisdictional system and, more generally, to create confusion as to the role of national courts vis-à-vis the political authorities of the Member States and of the Union. It should hence be exercised with the greatest care. In any case, in the case of OMTs, constitutional dialogue was able to remain careful, realistic, and, *in fine*, fruitful.

[102] Judgment of 14 January 2014, 2 BvR 2728/13; CJEU, Grand Chamber, 16 June 2015, *Peter Gauweiler*, C-62/14. See on this point: H. Gaudin, 'L'affaire OMT devant son (ses) juge(s). En attendant Karlsruhe, plaidoyer pour un dialogue constitutionnel' (2016) 19 *L'Actualité Juridique Droit Administratif AJDA* 1050.

[103] In the absence of a precise definition of monetary policy in the European treaties, since the *Pringle* judgment (C-370/12 *Thomas Pringle v Government of Ireland and Others* ECLI:EU:C:2012:756 , para. 53), the CJEU delimits its realm with reference to the objectives it pursues.

[104] Judgment of 21 June 2016, 2 BvR 2728/13.

5 Conclusions

The solutions to contemporary crises will be primarily political, but law can make a contribution and the legal community has a role to play in this respect. I would like to conclude by formulating three priorities. First, by recalling the benefits of international cooperation and of European integration, in particular in fighting transnational threats to the security of the Union and its neighbouring states. In a world that will inevitably be more open, the organization of international society must be enhanced and supported by a specially developed didactic approach. States and peoples are the primary victims of discourses and strategies founded on isolation and autarchy. Second, a firm but balanced stance must be taken and defended on the question of fundamental rights. It is worrying to see that some of these are now manifestly shattered at the periphery of Europe, and now within Europe itself. I am deeply concerned about and I condemn this situation. There can be no question of marking a 'pause' in the progress of fundamental rights, even though we must be ever more attentive to the existence of a consensus on sensitive issues. Finally, in the contemporary framework of legal pluralism, national identities and sovereignties must be reconnected with the European enterprise. In the short term, the responsibility of the legal community, in particular of judges, is to bring about convergence between the national and the international without annihilating one or the other, nor merging them. That is no doubt the most urgent and important task to perform if we want law to contribute usefuly to resolving current crises. It is not a matter of reining in national identities and their constitutional component; that would be tantamount to distorting the realities on which the European enterprise is anchored. Instead, the dynamic that must be set in motion cannot dispense with reinforcement of European integration and of guarantees of the rule of law, on penalty of abandoning the ideal pursued by the European enterprise.

Index

Note: *For the benefit of digital users, indexed terms that span two pages (e.g., 52–53) may, on occasion, appear on only one of those pages.*

How International Law Works in Times of Crisis. George Ulrich and Ineta Ziemele, Oxford University Press (2019).
DOI: 10.1093/oso/9780198849667.001.0001

The manufacturer's authorised representative in the EU for product safety is Oxford University Press España S.A. of el Parque Empresarial San Fernando de Henares, Avenida de Castilla, 2 – 28830 Madrid (www.oup.es/en or product.safety@oup.com). OUP España S.A. also acts as importer into Spain of products made by the manufacturer.

www.ingramcontent.com/pod-product-compliance
Lightning Source LLC
LaVergne TN
LVHW020056220926
848484LV00002BB/575
9780198849667